Freedom of the Will

Freedom of the Will

A Wesleyan Response to Jonathan Edwards

BY DANIEL D. WHEDON

JOHN D. WAGNER, EDITOR

WIPF & STOCK · Eugene, Oregon

FREEDOM OF THE WILL
A Wesleyan Response to Jonathan Edwards

Wipf & Stock
Division of Wipf and Stock Publishers
199 W. 8th Ave., Suite 3
Eugene, OR 97401

www.wipfandstock.com

ISBN 13: 978-1-55635-981-1

Manufactured in the U.S.A.

Previously Published by Carlton & Porter, 1864

Contents

Contents

Section III: The Theological Argument

Contents

PART THIRD: The Positive Argument Stated

Preface

A NY SUBSTANTIAL CONTRIBUTION TO reconciliation of the sense of responsibility with our intellectual conclusions on the nature of choice, must be a service to true psychology, consistent theology, and rational piety. It can hardly be expected that any single mind will at the present time so solve this problem, even with all the aids his predecessors in the discussion afford, as to leave nothing to his successors to elucidate. Yet the present writer would not offer this treatise to the public did he not believe that even with so ancient a debate he had furnished some new thoughts, and brought the difficulty nearer to a solution.

Upon such a subject it is a matter of course that, agreeing or disagreeing, a writer would have something to say of Jonathan Edwards, President of College of New Jersey.[1]* Disagreeing with him fundamentally, the present writer has taken an unequivocal but respectful issue with that great thinker. Whether he has not demonstrated forever the existence of a number of undeniable fallacies in Edwards' "Inquiry" on the Will**, fallacies that vitiate its most important conclusions, is for the reader to judge.

The method of Edwards was first to institute a psychological and logical investigation of the operations of the volitional faculty demonstrating its necessity in action, and then to bring the moral intuitions into accordance with the intellectual conclusions. His apparent success in the first part was signal, but not half so signal as his failure in the second. That Edwards should have so failed by that route is a justification of a despair of any possible sources. We have in a measure reversed the method. We have first assumed the prior validity of the intuitions, and then sought by their guidance to ascertain how our psychology and logic may be brought

---

1. * Later renamed Princeton University.
** Jonathan Edwards, *An Inquiry Into the Modern Prevailing Notions Respecting That Freedom of the Will Which is Supposed to be Essential to Moral Agency, Virtue and Vice, Rewards and Punishment, Praise and Blame* (Andover: Gould, Newman and Saxton, 1840) All quotations from Edwards come from this central work unless otherwise noted.

into harmony with their dicta. It is for others to decide how satisfactory the reconciliation.

In acuteness the intellect of Edwards has scarcely been surpassed. No cause, perhaps, ever had a keener advocate. *Advocate*, we say; for the intellect of Edwards was not, we venture to suggest, like that of Bacon, *judicial*, but *forensic*. He was not the Chancellor in the high court of thought, but the Attorney. He was born to his case; he accepted it as of course; his mind was shaped by and to it; and if his philosophy and theology are not triumphant, it is not, we repeat, for the want of about the most acute advocate that ever framed a special plea.

If there is a class of thinkers perfectly satisfied with the Edwardian method of reconciliation, or who see not the discord to be reconciled, or who find a moral advantage in holding both sides of the contradiction, this work can scarcely be considered as written for them. It is rather dedicated to the acceptance of those who feel the discord, and seek a more satisfactory harmony; of those who recognize the discord as absolute, and reject the doctrine of responsibility; but especially of those who, called to the sacred office of explaining and impressing the law of accountability upon the conscience, appreciate the necessity of making it acceptable to the reason.

Daniel D. Whedon

PART FIRST
The Issue Stated

I

Will Isolated and Defined

IN THE FOLLOWING TREATISE we assume as correct the ordinary generic classification of the operations of the human mind into Intellections, Sensibilities, and Volitions. The Intellect is that by which all things, material or immaterial, external or internal, moral or unethical, are cognized by the soul. The Sensibility is the capability of the mind of experiencing the feelings, namely, the emotions by which the mind is excited, or the desires by which it becomes desirous of objects. The Will is the volitional power by which alone the soul consciously becomes the intentional author of external action—external, that is, to the Will itself—whether of mind or body.

All the operations of the first two of these faculties, namely, Intellect and Sensibility, are universally felt, and acknowledged to be necessary and absolutely caused. Present the object before the perceptive power (the power being voluntarily or necessarily fixed), and the object must be perceived as it presents itself. As when we place the object before a fixed mirror, the mirror forthwith presents the correspondent image, so when we place the object before the fixed intelligence, the intelligence forthwith presents the perception. We may withdraw either the object or the mind; but when the two are brought into the proper juxtaposition the perception *necessarily* exists, just as it does exist. The Carthaginian, with his eyelids severed, could not but see the blazing orb of the sun to which his naked eyeballs were forcibly exposed. Neither the sensorium nor the mind can vary or reject the sensation when there is no alternative or contrary power either in the intellective or sensitive nature. No physical causation is more absolute than that which exists between the object and its mental results.

It is when penetrating more deeply we arrive at the Will—the mysterious seat of the volitional and responsible power—that the difficulty and controversy arises. The necessitarian[1*] affirms that between the motive and volition there exists the same absolute causation as between the object and the perception; a causation equivalent, therefore, in absoluteness and necessity, with any instance of physical causation. As when you place an externality before the mind the idea arises, as when you place an object before a mirror the image necessarily arises, so when you present before the Will the motive, the volition as necessarily springs forth. Contrary power, varying power, alternative power, freedom, are wholly non-existent and even inconceivable. Now no causation, however physical or mechanical, can be more absolute than where the power of a diverse result is inconceivable.

FREEDOMISTS MAINTAIN

The freedomist, on the other hand, maintains that in Will—alone of all existences—there is an alternative power. Every species of existence has its own one and singular property. Matter alone has solidity; mind alone has intelligence; cause alone has efficiency; and Will alone of causes has an alternative or pluri-efficient power. It is the existence or non-existence of this power in Will which constitutes the dispute between the necessitarian and the freedomist.

From what has been said above, we might define Will to be that faculty of the mind in whose exercises there is not felt the element of necessity. But this is a definition in which all parties might not agree.

The definition of Edwards, that Will is "the power to choose," is on his own principle manifestly defective. It has the objection Edwards brings against another definition, namely, that it needs definition as much as the term to be defined. *Choose* is a word as obscure as Will. In fact, if the definition is true, then to choose is to will; and the definition is no more than saying that the Will is the power to will, which is about the same as defining a thing by itself.

Nearer to an exact definition, yet not exact, is that of Coleridge[2]: "Will is that which originates action or state of being." It may, however, be truly said that all cause originates action or state of being, and some further limitation seems therefore necessary. We define Will to be that

1.* One who agrees with Edward's position on the Will—Editor.

2. Samuel Taylor Coleridge (1772–1834), a prominent religious philosopher of his era.

power of the soul by which it intentionally originates an act or state of being. Or more precisely, Will is the power of the soul by which it is the conscious author of an intentional act. And this definition furnishes a complete demonstration that the Will is a clearly different faculty from any other in the mind; for it is always distinguished and characterized by the intention, and also, as we shall hereafter note, by motive. Volition, indeed, might be defined as that act of the mind that it performs with intention.

Edwards and the older necessitarians held volition to be the same as desire, or at least to be included generically under it. This assumption would settle the question of necessity, inasmuch as it is by all conceded that desires are in nature necessary; while, on the other hand, modern concession of the difference of the two is no surrender of the necessity of Will.

How indiscriminately the various terms belonging to the different faculties were used by elder necessitarians may appear from the following words of Edwards: "Whatever names we call the act of the Will by—choosing, refusing, approving, disapproving, liking, disliking, embracing, rejecting, determining, directing, commanding, forbidding, inclining, or being averse, a being pleased or displeased with—all may be reduced to this of choosing."(14) Now, of the above terms, in order to a great precision, we may say, 1. Approving, disapproving, coming to a conclusion and deciding, belong more properly to the intellective or moral faculty; 2. Liking, disliking, inclining, being averse, being pleased with or displeased with, to the sensitive nature; 3. Choosing, refusing, rejecting, determining, sometimes deciding, to the Will; 4. Embracing, directing, commanding, and forbidding, to external acts.

Desire, be it ever so intense, never becomes volition, but by a distinct movement known to consciousness; and no action can follow until volition arises. Desire is uneasy and a stimulant; Will is decisive, and brings all the mind to acquiescence. Yet volition, like desire, is appetite and preference; it is a conscious free act of fixing a settlement upon its object, to which it brings the unity of the man.

Will may be distinguished from desire by the following points: 1. Volition is consciously distinct in nature from even the culminating desire. It is felt to be an *act*—a decisive movement—a putting forth of energy. It is a conscious projection, from interior power, of action upon its object. Desire is the flowing forth of appetite for an object; a volition is the putting forth of action upon it. 2. Volition and desire differ in their objects. Desire is an appetite for some perceived agreeable quality or agreeable thing in its object. The object of the volition is the post-volitional voluntary act, which it effectuates. 3. We can conceive a being full of coexisting and contending desires and emotions, but without any power of volition, and so hemmed forever into a circle of passivities. 4. To volition, and not to any other mental operation, belong, as before said, intention and motive. This peculiarity alone would be sufficient to distinguish volition as a unique operation and Will as a special faculty. 5. There is no mental faculty that our unconsciousness so identifies with the self as the Will. When the Will governs the appetites or passions, we naturally say that the Man governs them; when they govern the Will, we say the man is governed by them. 6. The Will is alone that power by which man becomes properly an agent in the world. It is the bridge over which he passes in his active power to produce effects, according to design, on objects around him.

FEELINGS OR FACULTIES

No matter how intense or powerful may be his other feelings or faculties, he could never execute any projects, shape any objects, or make any history which he could call intentionally his own, without the faculty of Will. 7. Upon Will alone primarily rests from above the weight of moral obligation. And surely if, of all possible events, volition alone can be the primary object of obligation, it ceases to be an arrogant or wonderful claim that in volition alone should exist the element of freedom. The necessitarian allows that in one respect at any rate the event volition is absolutely unique; it is sole and singular among things; the freedomist, consequently, only claims for that unique super-structure, responsibility, an equivalently unique basis, freedom. 8. It is a fact that, while among all thinkers there is a perfect unanimity in attributing necessity to all the other mental operations, there is, to say the least, a very extensive and perpetuated denial of necessity in the volition. The necessitarian is bound to account for both this unanimity and this dissent. Here, then, is a distinction permanent and extensive between desire and volition. The desire is a mental operation to which all thinkers with perfect unanimity ascribe necessity; the volitions are a mental operation in which all deniers of necessity affirm with an equal unanimity that freedom resides.

Inclination belongs to the feelings, and not so properly either to the intellect or the Will. From his perception of an object a man feels inclined to choose it. It is the feelings that incline, and the Will remains quiescent until the initiation of the choice. "A mere inclination to a thing," says Dr. South, "is not properly a willing of that thing."

The *dispositions* are the feelings viewed in relation to any particular object or volition. A man is said to be disposed to any object or act when his feelings are favorable to it; indisposed when they are in the reverse.

A *choice* is always a volition, but of a particular kind. It is, namely, a volition by which the agent appropriates to himself one of a class of objects or causes of action on account of some perceived comparative preferability in it. I choose, that is, appropriate to myself, one of a lot of apples, because I see it comparatively most eligible or preferable. I choose one of two roads at a fork because I see it comparably the preferable. I choose from among professions that which seems comparatively most eligible. I choose God, not I will God. I choose virtue, not I will virtue. Choice, then, is an appropriative comparative volition; usually, however, including also the external act. By it I will one of several things to be mine. To say that I will as I choose, is simply to say that one volition is as another volition. Definitions that make a choice not to be a volition are incorrect. In this treatise choice and volition are used interchangeably.

To *please*, as an intransitive, expresses a volition, and usually signifies to will authoritatively. So a deity or an autocrat pleases that a thing be thus or so, or he does as he pleases. That is, he does as he authoritatively wills, chooses, or determines.

To *purpose* is to will, to determine, predetermine, or resolve that something shall be willed or done at a future time. I now will or purpose to go to the city tomorrow. A purpose wills or predetermines now that perhaps an immense number of volitions shall take place. A volition thus comprehensive of many volitions, to which they more or less conform, may be called a Standard Purpose. This comprehensive purpose resolves the mind into a state of permanent determination. A man may act in view of one great life purpose.

The *preference* is a recognition by the intellect that a given object or course is, on some account, or upon the whole, rather to be chosen than, or held in some way superior to, another with which it is compared. When a man on some account intellectually prefers an object he generally has a feeling of inclination to choose it. Nevertheless there may be coexistent with this preference an opposing inclination on some other account, in favor of which the Will may decide. Opposite dispositions and desires may, and often do, coexist in the same mind. Different affections, operations, and forces may exist within the soul, and, at the same instant, fluctuate and struggle for mastery. This agitation might last forever had man, as previously said, no faculty of Will. He would be like the troubled sea that cannot rest. It is by volition that the faculties are brought to unity and settlement.

Nevertheless to the Will also belongs a preferential state. When a volition has resolved the Will into a settled purpose that at the proper time it will give a particular volition, or adopt a certain cause or object, then so long the Will permanently prefers that volitional course or object to an alternate one.

The term *indifference* was often used by the old writers on the freedom of the Will in a technical sense. In ordinary language it now refers to the feelings as being wholly without inclination for or against an object. But as in the feelings there may be no inclination, so in the Will there may be no volition; and until the Will chooses or differentiates, there is an indifference, non-differentiation, or quiescence. Whatever may be the coexisting and struggling or fluctuating inclinations and preferences, the Will does not differentiate or cease to be indifferent until it volitionates, chooses, or wills.

INTERIOR VOLITIONAL ACT

Consequent upon the interior volitional act performed by the Will is the external voluntary act performed by the body, obeying and executing the imperative volition. Yet it is not the body and the limbs alone that obediently execute the determinations of the interior Self through the Will. The mind, also in its operations, intellective and emotional, is more or less under the Will's control. To trace how complete this partial volitional control over body or mind is, is not our present purpose.

The *intention* of an act, volitional or voluntary, objectively, is the result had in view to be produced by the act. This result may be immediate, or more or less remote. Of the same act, the intentions may be stated with a great variety. Thus an archer draws his bow. His intention is the discharge of an arrow. That is, such is the immediate result imaged and intended in his mind. But, more remotely, his purpose is that the arrow pierce the body of a stag. Still further remote, there are other successive intentions; and it is difficult to ascertain, often, the ultimate intention of an act or volition. For the intention, near, remote and ultimate, whether accomplished or not, the agent is responsible. For all the legitimately calculable consequences, the agent is responsible. How far even for any consequences of a deliberately wicked act an agent may be responsible is debatable; since he who breaks law is fairly warned by his own reason that he indorses disorder, and so makes any disastrous consequences legitimate and responsible.

Suppose, however, that, without any culpable want of care, the arrow of the archer, missing its aim, is so deflected by some object as to hit and slay his prince. At once he is seen as not responsible for the result accruing. He is not responsible because this result was not intended; that is, framed in his conception as that which he, as a volitional agent, exerted his power to bring into existence. Though partially an effect by him, that result comes upon him as unconceivedly as a lightning flash darting across his path. For the conception unsanctioned by the volition, and for the result unconceived and unintended, yet accomplished, there is equally no responsibility.

As the intellect, the emotions, and desires conditionally precede the volition, so we may call these the prevolitional conditions. The act of body or mind which follows as a consequence of the volition obeying its power and executing its requirements may therefore be called post-volitional; so that the position of the act of Will is with great precision identified. The willing act is adjectively called volitional; the consequent act of body or mind is called voluntary. When an athlete strikes a blow, his willing the blow is volitional, and the physical motion of the arm that obeys and executes his volition is a voluntary act. So that we have the prevolitional, the volitional, and post-volitional or voluntary operations as the sum total of all human affections and activities.

The occasional confounding of the terms volitional and voluntary, and the transfer of the latter from the post-volitional act to the volition itself, is the source of some error and some unintentional sophisms. Thus Dr. Pond wrote:

> If we originate our own voluntary exercises we must do it voluntarily or involuntarily. If we do it involuntarily, there is nothing gained certainly on the score of freedom. There can be no freedom or voluntariness in an involuntary act of origination more than

there is in the beating of the heart. But if we originate our own voluntary exercises voluntarily, this is the same as saying that we originate one voluntary exercise by another, which runs into the same absurdity as before.[3]

To this we may for the present reply, that as the terms voluntary and involuntary are predicable only of the external actions in reference to the Will, the volitions are neither voluntary nor involuntary, but volitional. They are not intrinsically, as free, the product of a previous volition; nor in that does their freedom consist. What their freedom does imply appears in the proper place by our definition.

Jonathan A. Edwards, in his remark on his father's "Improvements in Theology," has the expression, "such volitions being, by the very significance of the term itself, voluntary."[4] A voluntary volition is impossible. So on the same page he uses the term "spontaneity," not, evidently, as Webster defines it, to signify voluntariness, but as the abstract of volition, volitionality.

When we say that the Will wills, we really mean that the entire soul, or self, wills. It is the man who wills, and his Will is simply his power or being able to will. And the free Will is really the man free in willing. So it is the man, the soul, the self, that perceives, feels, and thinks. The faculties are not so many divisions of the soul itself, but rather so many classes of the soul's operations, and the soul viewed as capable of being the subject of them. And as in volition the whole soul is the Will, and in thinking the whole soul is the intellect, so it follows that the Will is intelligent, and the intelligence is volitional. When, therefore, we speak of Will, we speak not of a separate, blind, unintelligent agent, but of the whole intelligent soul engaged in and capable of volitional actions. It is in no way a separate substance or agent.

---

3. Enoch Pond, "The Works of Jonathan Edwards Reviewed," *The American Biblical Repository* 11 (1844): 387–388.

4. Tryon Edwards, *The Works of Jonathan Edwards D.D.* vol. 1 (Andover: Allen, Morrill & Wardwell, 1842), 483. This is the collected works of Jonathan A. Edwards, son of the famous theologian, and hereinafter referred to as the Younger Edwards.

II

Freedom of the Will Defined

FREEDOM IS EXEMPTION. EITHER it is exemption from some impediment to the performance of some act, which is a freedom to the act; or it is an exemption from a limitation, confinement, or compulsion to perform the act; and this is a freedom in direction from the act.

To non-volitional objects there belong only the first of these two freedoms. All mechanisms are free only to the sole mode of act or state in which they are, or are about to be. The clock that strikes is free not from but only to the stroke. The river that flows is free only to the current, but not from. The lake that stands is free only to that stand, and not, at the same time, from the stand. But to volitional agents we do not with propriety ascribe freedom in the performances or occupancy of an act or state unless the exemptions exist both to and from the act or state. We hardly say of a man bound fast to the floor that he is free in lying there, or free to lie there. If he is unbound, and still voluntarily remains lying, we say then that he does so freely. There is an exemption both from impediment and from limitation; that is, there is freedom both to and from the act. He performs either way freely: freely, because he is exempt from obstacle both ways, and free to or from both.

What is thus true of the freedom of a volitional agent in external action is, by parity, true of the same agent in volitional action. An agent exempt only from impediment, and so free only to the act, has not the proper freedom of a volitional agent, but of a machine. As the clock-hammer in the given case is free only to the stroke, so the agent in the given case is free to the given volition, and not also in direction from it. He has only the freedom of a mechanical object, not the freedom of a volitional agent.

Freedom is not identical with power. The freedom and the power are different, and either may be antecedent condition to the other. Either the freedom is an antecedent and a requisite condition to the existence or possible exertion of the power; or, in the reverse, the power is antecedent condition of which the freedom is the consequence. Thus, when the freedom is an exemption or deliverance from some restriction laid upon the capabilities of body or mind, then there comes, as a consequence, a new power of action or exertion. But when the freedom is exemption from internal or intrinsic restriction, impotence, or want of faculty, then the added power or faculty is antecedent, and the freedom of action or exertion is the consequence. Thus in the former case a removal of a fetter from the arm is a freedom, which gives power for striking; or the removal of an opiate from the mind gives power for thought. In the latter case the bestowment of efficient wings upon the bird gives power and so freedom for or to flight; the bestowment of vigor upon the intellect gives freedom to thought.

FREEDOM NOT IDENTICAL

In the case of Will the freedom is not identical with the power, but is a consequence of its existence. The confinement to a solely possible volition or direction is supposed to be intrinsic in the agent; and the bestowment of a power, or faculty, or removal of incapacity, for contrary volition, so that a volition either to or from the given direction is possible, creates that much a freedom. Hence the freedom is not identical with the additional contrary power, but is based and consequent upon it. I am free to will either way, because I have power or faculty either way. This distinction, though metaphysically accurate and important, seldom needs in our discussion to be noted. As each implies the other, and both are alike in debate, they may be usually treated as identical.

In the case of Will, the whole debate is as to the existence of this freedom *from*. In all their conceptions and definitions of freedom of Will, necessitarians never get beyond that sole freedom to the act or state that belongs to mechanics and to mathematicians. It is a liberty from, as well as to which all freedomism asserts for the responsible agent. The question then arises, Freedom from what?

The question in regard to Will, we may answer, is awakened by the moral sense. When a man is morally obligated or divinely commanded to will otherwise than he does, the question immediately arises, Can he will otherwise than he does will? Is he free from, as well as to, this act? Or is he limited by necessity in the given circumstances to will just this one way. Suppose that one way to be contrary to the command of Almighty God, or to his own best reason, or to the obligations of eternal right, or to his endless well-being. Between that way and his Will, is there a sure tie securing that the disastrous volition shall be put forth? Is there any fate, predestination, antecedent causation, or law of invariable sequence, by which, all other directions being excluded, the Will is like a mechanism, limited to one sole way? The moment these questions are asked the great debate between necessity and freedom commences.

These questions suggest the definition of the freedom the moral sense requires. Bishop Bramhall defines it as "an immunity from inevitability and determination to one." We should define it as the power or immunity to put forth in the same circumstances either for several volitions. Or supposing a given volition to be in the agent's contemplation, it is the unrestricted power of putting forth in the same unchanged circumstances a different volition instead. Hence, it is often at the present day called the power of contrary choice.

Mechanical freedom then to any action is exemption from all impediment or preventive of positive action, and so is freedom solely to the act. Voluntary freedom is exemption from impediment to the being or doing as we will, and is freedom to or from a certain post-volitional set. Volitional freedom, in regard to a given volition, is immunity to put forth it or other volition, and is freedom to or from it. Power solely to a thing being, in the given case, and with the given motives, without alteriety or alternatives, we call a nonalternative power, in opposition to a power which, being at once either to or from, we call alternative power, or alternativity. We extend the term to any number of different alternatives. The alternativity is as extensive as the disjunctive proposition that should enumerate them. Thus, this, or that, or the other, or still another, is the possible object of alternative choice.[1] Against the exceptions and evasions of

1. For the introduction of a few new terms we think it scarcely necessary to apologize. Our reason for such introduction is not certainly a mere fondness for novelty, but a purpose to secure easiness and clearness of expression . Where these ends are to be attained, discussions in mental science ought not to be excluded from the privilege, so plentifully used in physics, of framing convenient additions to its terminology. And no department of mind is so poorly equipped with a nomenclature as the Will. The very ambiguity of that primal word itself is a glaring instance. It is a proof of this eminent poverty and a shame to our English language that such a sentence as the following is possible: *The will will will a will.* For the verb *will* we have in English no word separate in form from the noun *Will*; since the term *choose* varies in meaning from the verb *will*. We must say the

this definition by necessitarians, the phrase "in the same circumstances" is an important limitation. Necessitarians ambiguously grant that the will has a power of choosing a different from a given way, provided the circumstances are changed,[2] just as a compass needle has a power of pointing a different from a given way, namely, provided the circumstances be different from the given way. But the compass needle has not the power in the same given and unchanged conditions of pointing alternatively either one of two or more different ways. It cannot point one of several ways with the full power at the initial instant of pointing another way instead. It has solely the general power or faculty of pointing as attendant circumstances or antecedents shall cause it to point. Logically, however, the phrase is unnecessary; for the act under changed circumstances would not be the same act. No one is so unwise as to deny that the Will can act differently in different cases.

The word "instead" is important in one of the above formulas of definition. The proposition that the Will puts forth one volition with full power to another volition, may either captiously or innocently be understood to imply the power to put forth two opposite volitions at the same time.[3]

This Freedom of volition must be within the Will, and not without the Will. It must be intravolitional and not extravolitional. A freedom of the Will, consisting of unimpeded power of diverse volition, cannot lie out of the Will, namely, in the intellect, nor emotions, nor nervous system, nor corporeal frame.

Will wills, or the Will chooses. And the proper participle of the verb *to will,* namely *willing,* has sunk into an adjective.

2. "That which is contended for is not merely that the will may put forth a choice, the contrary of what actually occurs, supposing such a change to occur in its circumstances as would induce it (which all admit), but that in precisely the case in which it exercises a given choice, it is fully adequate to a contrary election." *Theological Essays Reprinted from the Princeton Review* (New York: Wiley and Putnam, 1846), 254; hereinafter referred to as "Princeton Essays" or "The Princeton Essayist."

3. "The question is not whether the will, in one and the same act of choice, may or may not choose two contrary objects. This is too absurd to be maintained." (Princeton Essays, 251).

"Contrary choice is willing as he does and otherwise—choosing as he does and does not." Edward A. Lawrence, "The Old School in New England Theology" *Bibliotheca Sacra* 20 (April 1863): 323. This misstatement is the more noticeable from its being made in full view of the definition, furnished by the present writer, containing the terms that excluded it.

Our definition, therefore, excludes the favorite distinction made by necessitarians, (which will be fully considered hereafter) between "moral" and "natural" ability; that is, an ability in the Will and an ability outside the Will. Thus to a similar definition of free Will given by Dr. West,[4] namely, that the agent can will otherwise than a given way, the younger Edwards makes the following irrelevant exception: "If by *power* and *can* he means natural power, I agree that in any given case we have a power to act or decline the proposed action. A man possesses liberty when he possesses a natural or physical power to do an action, and is under no natural inability with respect to that action."[5] By this "natural or physical power," Edwards means power outside the Will externally to execute or fulfill its volitions.

MAN POSSESSES LIBERTY

A man possesses liberty indeed in such a case, but not liberty in the Will, or of the Will, but liberty of the muscular power. A physical strength or energy sufficient, within a man's system, even to a given volition, is not in itself adequate power in the existing circumstances in the Will to such a volition. An ox may possess sufficiency of physical strength even in his volitional energies to will a moral volition, but that does not constitute the adequate power.

Of the definitions of Freedom of Will given by necessitarians, we may mention three. The first is that of Edwards, which is indeed a definition of a Freedom, but not of a Freedom in the Will; the second is that of Hobbes, which is truly located in the Will, but is not a Freedom, certainly not a Freedom within the present argument; the third is a blending of the two, or rather a running of the former into the latter, subjecting it to all the objections belonging to the latter. The definition of Freedom by Edwards is: *the power of doing as we please.* That by Hobbes is: *exemption from impediment extrinsic to the nature of the subject.* The blending of the two is: *the power of willing as we will.*

1. The definition of Edwards is in the following words: "The plain and obvious meaning of the words freedom and liberty, in common speech is power, opportunity, or advantage that anyone has to do as he

---

4. Samuel West (1730–1807), was pastor of the Massachusetts Standing Order and theological opponent of Jonathan Edwards.

5. Tryon Edwards, *The Works of Jonathan Edwards*, 1:310.

pleases. Or, in other words, his being free from hindrance or impediment in the way of doing or conducting, in any respect, as he will."(49) Of this definition of liberty he boasts in words of great pomp and defiance, as expressing the only liberty conceivable:

> therefore no Arminian, Pelagian, or Epicurean can rise higher in his conceptions of liberty than the notion of it which I have explained, which notion is apparently perfectly consistent with the whole of that necessity of men's actions which I suppose takes place. And I scruple not to say it is beyond all their wits to invent a higher notion or form a higher imagination of liberty, let them talk of sovereignty of the will, self-determining power, self-motion, self-direction, arbitrary decision, liberty ad utrumvis, power of choosing differently in given cases, etc., etc., as long as they will. It is apparent that these men, in their strenuous affirmation and dispute about these things, aim at they know not what, fighting for something they have no conception of, substituting a number of confused unmeaning words instead of things and instead of thought. They may be challenged clearly to explain what they would have; they never can answer the challenge. (419) [6]

Of this definition we may remark that it is to be excluded from the discussion as being, so far as freedom in the Will is concerned, not a poor definition, but no definition at all. And when Edwards boasts that this is the only conceivable freedom, he emphatically denies all freedom to the Will. It is a freedom not to will, but to do; that is, perform or execute what we have previously willed. It is a freedom belonging to external action, located out of and subsequent to volition; a freedom of the post-volitional operations. It takes not existence until the Will is done and is out of the question. It is corporeal and voluntary freedom, not volitional freedom.

---

6. We may here passingly remark: 1. That "the power of choosing differently in given cases" is just the "power of contrary choice," (and under the term *choice* Edwards includes volition), which is maintained by some at the present day who hold Edwards as a standard. But it is plain that Edwards here repudiates it in his highest strain, denouncing it as the very theory his treatise had demonstrated to be false, unmeaning, contradictory, and unthinkable. 2. Edwards defines for us a freedom which is no freedom, and by his very declaration that this is the highest (in his view) conceivable, he excludes all others, specifically excluding power of contrary choice. There is no freedom but a no-freedom. This is just as if a materialist should define spirit to be matter, declare that no higher notion of spirit is "conceivable," and then claim to be a spiritualist, a believer in the highest possible spirit. So that very passage (which is habitually quoted to prove that Edwards maintains the highest freedom of will) really sweeps all free will from existence.

The Will is not its subject. But a freedom of Will that belongs not to the Will and is no quality of Will, is a contradiction.

This power of "doing as we will," which Edwards proclaims thus magniloquently to be the only conceivable sort of freedom, is also excluded as not meeting the demands of the moral sense. It consists in a subjection absolutely perfect, first, of the external or post-volitional act to the volition. Then the volition is, with as absolute a perfection, subjected to the causative strongest motive. And the strongest motive is brought upon the mind by a chain of antecedent necessary causes. Thus this freedom consists in bringing act, volition, and motive into existence as so many fixed links in the endless chain of fixed necessitations. The freedom at last consists in fixing both the being and action of the agent under necessitative causation as absolutely as the fossil petrifaction is fixed in its solid rock. "What does your free-will consist in," says Voltaire, as quoted by Fletcher,[7] "but a power to do willingly what absolute necessity makes you choose?"

WILL IS DRAWN

The fact that the Will is drawn or secretly attracted so that its volition goes forth eagerly and of itself, as the soul does of itself by its own spontaneous power go after happiness, renders the necessity none the less absolute. Around the faculties of the soul a surrounding line of causation is still thereby nonetheless absolutely drawn because it is delicately drawn and finely shaded. The resisting power at the spring of the Will may be as completely annihilated by a seduction or a fascination as by a rude impulsion. Causation securing effect, which Edwards maintains must rule at every infinitesimal point to secure us from atheism, truly secures this so called free forthgoing of the soul as the steam power secures the movement of the car. No fine word painting will change this necessity to freedom.

II. Mr. Hobbes endeavors to give his definition of liberty a scientific form:

> Liberty is the absence of all impediments to action that are not contained in the nature and intrinsical quality of the agent. As, for example, the water is said to descend freely, or to descend by the channel of the river, because there is no impediment that way;

---

7. John Fletcher (1729–1785) was a contemporary of John Wesley's and was the first prominent systematic theologian of Methodist theology.

but not across, because the banks are impediments. And though the water cannot ascend, yet men never say it wants the liberty to ascend, but the faculty or power, because the impediment is in the nature of the water and intrinsical [8]

From this definition it results that if the impediment or necessitation excluding the contrary volition is simply intrinsic and not extrinsic, the Will is still free. Natural or internal necessity is thereby compatible with freedom.

On the definition we make the following points:

1. Liberty is truly defined by Hobbes to be "an absence of impediment to action," as we have defined it to be an exemption from limitation. But when he confines it to exemption from impediment that is "not contained in the nature and intrinsic quality of the agent," that is, to external impediment, he makes a fictitious qualification. A being may be as truly said to be free from an intrinsic and natural impediment or circumscription or limitation as from an extrinsic. A being is often said to be free from the intrinsic accident of disease; a man pardoned is held free from intrinsic guilt. Our Saviour, even as man, was free from intrinsic depravity. A learned man is free from his own natural ignorance and prejudices. A being may be said also to be free from any supposable disadvantage, real or imaginary, intrinsic or extrinsic. Spirit is free from the pressure of gravitation. Angels are free from original sin. And, what is decisive as to volitional freedom, a being may possess or be free from impediment, impotence, or want of faculty in his own nature that disables him from performing the proper conditions belonging to his responsible position or to his own well being. God's prevenient grace contributes to this. For, in this sense, alternative Will may be truly and properly called free; free from that necessity or unipotence, that limitation to one solely possible effectuation, to which all other cause is limited, and which would disable the agent from performing the probationary conditions belonging to his responsible well-being. The limitation assigned, therefore, by Hobbes's definition of liberty, to an immunity from an extrinsic impediment, falls to the ground, and the word is used within its true limits as an antithesis to real or supposable intrinsic limitation or impediment.

8. Thomas Hobbes, *A Letter About Liberty and Necessity* (London: Printed by J.C. for W. Crook, 1677), 6.

Negatively, also, beings may be truly said to be not free from intrinsic and natural negative impediments or affirmative limitations to particular modes of action. Matter is not free from gravitation or the laws if motion. Mind is not free from finite circumscription. Necessary cause is not free from a unification to a single and solely possible effect. Perception is not free from a conformity to the exact appearance of the object perceived. And so the necessitated Will is not free from an absolute and fixed obedience to the sole strongest motive force. It has no alternative but to obey, and is therefore inalternative.

If action, volitional or otherwise, be required of an agent, he ought to be free to such action; but he cannot be free to it unless he possesses the power for it. He is not free to the exertion of power which he does not possess. He has not the power, which, as already said, is the basis and condition of the freedom. If he is responsibly required, then he is not free from such want of power, impotence, or impediment to the discharge of his requirements as a responsible being.

2. Though an inanimate object, when exempted from supposable impediments would always be called free, not so a living agent. He must possess not only power (and exemption from prevention) to the act, but power reversely from the act. Water may descend the channel freely, or stand in the spring freely; but a man in a prison, however willing and unimpeded his stay, does not stay freely, for he can do no otherwise than stay. A stone cast from the pinnacle of the temple in its descent falls freely; but a man who has leaped from the same point, however willingly he thence tends to the earth, does not tend freely, for he can do no otherwise. A man may be impelled to walk through the narrow paths of a labyrinth walled on either side; he may be pleased with the operation; in so walking he may do as he is pleased, and in that sense as he pleases; but he does not do it freely, for it is the only thing he can do. To the freedom of a living agent, therefore, the twofold power is requisite; the power to the act and the power from the act. Confinement, limitation to a unit, circumscription, necessitation, excluding power for alteriety, is fatal to the liberty of the agent in the external and voluntary act, and by parity in the internal volitional act. To act as we are pleased, to act willingly and to act freely, are not always one and the same thing.

Mr. Hobbes's definition is, therefore, doubly incorrect as applied to an agent's Will. It has a false exclusion or internal impediment; it is a power solely to and not from the particular act, and so is wholly inapplicable to a volitional agent, and therefore is no freedom debated in this discussion. And moreover failing to meet the demands of the moral sense, it is in every respect excluded.

THE SAME REFUTATION

Under the same refutation we bring Professor Haven's[9] definition of freedom: "Any faculty of mind or organ of body is free when its own specific and proper action is not hindered." The will of a necessitated agent, we reply, may be unhindered in "its own specific and proper action," and yet not be responsibly "free." He may want that power upon which such freedom is based; the power over and above his necessitated "specific and proper action"; the power, namely, of performing the conditions of is responsible being, in obedience to a requirement contrary to the stronger motive force. He is not free to perform his moral obligations as a responsible agent.

III. To the Edwardian definition of freedom of Will as the power of doing as we will, our objection is above stated, that it is not located in the Will. To this objection it is replied, and by Edwards himself, by running the Edwardian into the Hobbesian; "to will is in fact to do something; it is to put forth a volition; and so the freedom of the Will by this definition fairly is the 'power to will as we will.' " And thence it is deduced that the choosing at all is choosing freely; freedom and volition being identical. We thereto admit, as of Hobbes' definition, that this freedom is indeed located in the Will, but deny that it is a volitional or more than a mechanical freedom. For,

1. As we have already shown, the assumption at its base, that freedom is "the power of doing as we please" or will, is entirely untrue. A man may do as he pleases, and yet not be free, both because his antecedent pleasing is necessitated, and because he is limited and circumscribed to the course with which he is pleased. Power both pro and contra, power to the thing and from the thing, is requisite for the liberty of a free agent. Power, then, to the given volition, and from the volition, and to a reverse volition, must exist, or the agent is not free in the volition. It is an error to call an agent volitionally free unless he has power for either one of two

---

9. Joseph Haven (1816–1874), was professor of Intellectual and Moral Philosophy at Amherst College.

or more volitions. The above pompous challenge of Edwards is, therefore, we think, fairly met and invalidated. But,

2. According to necessitarianism all actions, motions, or states of being are equally fixed, and so equally free. Impediments, intrinsic or extrinsic, are only modifications of that action which finally and really results; that is, they are causes by which the final action is really shaped. The real action, as so shaped, then, takes place without prevention or impediment; that is, takes place freely. So, in the final and absolute, all action is by this equally free. To speak of a free action, then, distinctively, is absurd. There is no such distinction to mark by the word. A free action is simply an action. The adjective "free" would, then, be inert and void. It would be used in a senseless sense. And a word without meaning, and adding no idea, is not a word, but a mere sound.

The voidness of the term appears by this further consideration. The power to will as we will, is simply the mechanical power for a thing to do as it does; to be as it "be's." Now there is nothing whatever that lacks such notable power and freedom. A mental perception, a sensation, or a clock-stroke, is as free as a volition. A bar of iron, a block of wood, a cube of granite, has that quality. The railcar is free to run solely as it runs, the prison walls to stand as they stand, the marble monument to lie as it lies. All the physical machinery of the universe has the liberty to be solely as it is, to operate as it operates. The figures of geometry are all equally free. The square is free to be quadrangular, the circle to be round, the globe to be globular. And this freedom of the Will, which is boasted by Edwards as the loftiest conceivable, is just the freedom by which whatever is, is and must be.

PHRASE 'TO WILL'

Or if the phrase "to will as we will" means, as it is sometimes made to mean, to put forth a volition which is under necessitation to be what it is from a previous volition, responsible freedom is excluded. That previous volition is under necessitation of a previous volition, and so we are in each volition necessitated by an infinite series of anterior necessitating and necessitated volitions. The same necessitative result follows if we suppose the volition is as some fixed antecedent, whether such antecedent be a "choice," an "inclination," a "wish," or a "please." If such antecedent is a necessitated result of antecedent circumstances or inalternative causation of any kind, freedom does not exist. For if each and every antecedent in the series, however long the series be, is fixed by its predecessor and fixes its successor, the whole train is necessitated, and the putting forth of the last volition, the one in question, is anteriorly fixed. And a volition whose putting forth is anteriorly fixed to a unitary result is not free. The agent possesses not the power to will otherwise in the case; the power from and obligation to will otherwise are impossible.

Professor Haven teaches that circumstances decided and fix the inclination, the inclinations fix the choice, and the choice fixes the volition; and then the freedom of the Will consists in the absoluteness of the subjection of the volition to the fixation by the choice. The more absolute the limitation, the more absolute the freedom. Circumstances, inclination, choice, and volition, are four ninepins in a row; No. 1 knocks down No. 2, No. 2 knocks down No. 3, and No. 3 knocks down No. 4. The freedom of No. 4 in its falling consists in the absoluteness of its being knocked by No. 3 as that is by its row of predecessors. Professor H. holds that it is no matter how the agent comes by his inclination; the only question is: Is he at liberty to be controlled by it necessitatedly, as the ninepin is by its predecessor? Certainly such reasoners ought to see that to subject the Will to a previous necessitative causation, which is itself necessitated, is the annihilation of alternativity. It forecloses the power *from*. The lengthening of the series is but an infantile attempt at relief by pushing the necessitation a little back, and so out of view. They might just as wisely declare first as last, that the Will is in its simple acts fixed and circumscribed to a solely possible volition.

And that is the freedom of a mechanism. Just as a clock hammer possesses in its given antecedents no power for a different stroke instead, so the agent has no power for a different volition instead. The agent can in the given case give none but one solely possible volition, just as the clock hammer can give none but one solely possible stroke. This is true of every volition that ever takes place, just as it is true of every clock stroke that ever takes place. It is true of the entire series of volitions of every single agent, as it is true of the entire series of the strokes of every single clock. Just as, should a clock have an eternal existence, each stroke would be a solely possible stroke, so should an agent have an eternal existence, each volition would be a solely possible volition. As the clock could not, in a single one instance of the infinite, help giving the given stroke, so the agent could not in a single instance avoid giving the given volition. If the volitions were all wicked, still, the agent gives the only that is solely possible. No sinful volition that ever takes place could in the given antecedents have been withheld. No sin ever committed could have been helped or avoided. Sin and damnation are as inevitable to the sinner as the clock stroke is to the clock.

A clock hammer can give a different stroke, if it inclines or is moved to. That is, it can strike differently sequently upon different antecedents. Just so, necessitarians admit that the agent can will otherwise if—the antecedents are otherwise. That is, he can will differently in different cases; which nobody was ever so unwise as to deny. Thus to our making a man's Arminianism or Calvinism depends on his answer to Fletcher's question, "Is the Will at liberty to choose otherwise than it does, or is it not?" Professor Lawrence, replies "A man is at perfect liberty to choose otherwise than he does, if he wishes to."[10] A clock hammer is perfectly at liberty, we reply, to strike otherwise if it is inclined to. But Professor L. teaches, with all other necessitarians, that this anterior "wish" of the agent is just as absolutely necessitated and controlled by antecedent causes, as this inclination of the clock-hammer is controlled by its antecedent mechanical causes. Each lies as a link in the chain of necessary causations. So that the volition, in the given case is as solely possible as the clock stroke in the given case; and we have just the mechanical freedom to and not from. And that excludes all responsibility, and makes a just retributive divine government impossible.

Freedom is as much contradicted by a Law of Invariability, that is, a law by which all Will invariably does obey the strongest motive, even though able to do otherwise, as by a law of Causation. If the invariability is formulated as an anterior fact, strictly absolute and universal, pervading all actual and possible cases, then by the law of contradiction the counter exception becomes impossible. Thus it is claimed by some thinkers that though the Will possesses power for choice against strongest motives, yet that choice will never be used. If that never is an invariability, as truly in itself universal as the law of causation, the usage of the power of counter choice is impossible. It is incompatible with an absolute universal contradictory fact, and cannot take place; and that the reverse of which cannot be, is a necessity. A power that cannot be used, a power not in the power

---

10. Edward A. Lawrence, "The Old School in New England Theology," 324.

of the agent for act, is no adequate power in the agent at all. It exists in words only, and can be no satisfactory basis of responsibility.

Indeed, this case of a Will under Law of Invariability to obey strongest motive, with a so-called counter power never to be used, is a case under law of causation. The Law of Invariability existing, the anterior strongest motive is the cause why the act is one way rather than another. The Law of Invariability must ever be made true. Obeying it, the Will must obey the strongest motive. Just so far as the absoluteness of the Invariability is assumed, just so far there is causative necessitation, and the counter power has no actual existence.

MAN IS REQUIRED

When, finally, a man is required by the Moral Law to will otherwise than he does will, the question must, we say, be answered: Has he the power or freedom to will otherwise? It does not suffice for the demands of our moral nature to tell us that he has a freedom post-volitionally to do what he wills; nor that he can will otherwise if antecedent circumstances are otherwise; nor that he is free from all impediment external to himself; nor that he has power to will according to the strongest motive; nor that he has power to will as he does will; nor that freedom and volition are the same thing. For all these get not beyond the freedom of a mechanism to a thing without the freedom of an agent from as well as to. The simple question is: Is he so limited in power in the given case to the one solely possible choice or volition as not to be free to volitionate otherwise instead, or does he possess a power of disjunctive volition, so that he is free to choose either one of several ways? Choosing thus our own issue, as is our right, we affirm under requirement of the moral sense, as against necessity which denies, that there does exist in the agent a freedom of just this kind.

The terms opposed to this liberty of "doing or willing as we will," Edwards thus specifies: "One is constraint; the same is otherwise called force, compulsion and coaction, which is a person's being necessitated to do a thing contrary to his Will. The other is restraint, which is his being hindered, and not having power to do according to his Will." (50)

From these definitions it follows that the highest motive, however absolutely it may cause the volition to be what it is, can never be said to compel it to be what it is. For compulsion is always exerted upon something exterior to the Will, but in opposition to the Will. The Will is never itself compelled by motive force, for the motive in securing the existence of the volition precludes the idea of any opposition of the Will. The case resembles creation, in which the created object takes its entire existence from its Creator, and thereby receives its whole vitality in perfect subjection and submission to the creative power. The words "compel," "constrain," and "restrain," thus presupposing an opposition of the Will, would properly be limited to designate a force upon our extra-volitional parts or powers. Thus we may compel a person corporeally to yield, to love or hate us, to believe or know a thing; but we cannot, by any motive, be said to compel one to choose a thing.

This sharp distinction, however, when peremptorily asserted, incurs the same confusion (as we shall elsewhere notice) between the most common meaning of a word and the most proper. A less common meaning of a term is often as truly, if not the more proper meaning. Men may often have occasion to use terms in their least proper sense. Men have more need to talk of doings than of willings; of what they can do if they will than of what they can will; of what compels them to do in spite of their Wills than of what compels their Wills to choose. Hence, though "compel" most frequently, if not the most properly, applies to force upon body against Will, yet phrases like "cloud compelling Jove," "by dying love compelled," show that the word is most expressively and correctly used in application to force upon inanimate objects or motive force upon the Will. Such words, indeed, imply opposition. But that opposition may be either the vis intertioe of matter compelled to give way, or the counter force of motive compelled to be overcome, or that resistance to change that is always presupposed when we speak of a cause exerting power to effectuate an event of body or mind, which otherwise by the law of continuity would not take existence.

However, to designate bringing a volition into existence by causation of motive, it may be wiser to use other terms. For this purpose we accept the words to cause, to fix, to necessitate, to secure; by all of which words we mean to express causation, or creation of the consequent volition in the absolute sense, excluding in the given case the adequate power in the agent for the volition to be otherwise, or not to be at all.

"The fates lead the willing, but drag the unwilling," Fata ducunt volentem, nolentum trahunt. But a deeper fate allows no nolentem. It pre-forms and in-forms, and so secures the volition and precludes the nolition, as to rule the man, not against, but through the Will, by ruling the Will. It secures the act by securing the volition. That volition is as truly secured as if created in the mind by Omnipotence, for even Omnipotence could do no more than secure the existence of the act precluding the power of any alteration. It does not matter whether the external act is secured through the volition by an immediate omnipotent agent, or by a sufficient fixing finite cause; for the latter totally excludes all counter power, and the former cannot exclude it more than totally. Nor can any effect take a greater amount of causality, even from infinite power, than is just sufficient to its own production. Our cup can take but a cup full, even from the ocean.[11] To force the agent against his Will is a powerful securing of his act; but to cause his act, precluding the very power of a counter volition, is a still deeper necessitation.

ETHICAL RELATIONS

In regard to the ethical relations of free volition of a counter volition, three things are to be noted:

1. Though the question of volitional freedom is awakened by the moral intuitions, and receives its clearest elucidation from instances of moral alternative, yet the freedom of the Will itself is not to be held as confined to the ethical sphere. The Will is as truly free in the secular and non-ethical alternatives of life as in the moral.

2. The freedom of the Will forms the terminal point as we ascend in our inquiry from effect to cause in search of the location of responsibility. The volitional sins of a necessitated agent are what he cannot help. He could not volitionate otherwise. The secured originative causation must be traced further back than himself, and so the responsibility. But the alternative agent who sins with full power otherwise, has brought an un-necessitated, unnecessary evil into the world. He need not do it. He is its first necessitating unnecessitated cause. Nothing back of him has caused or made it necessary, and so nothing back of him is responsible. He has taken into himself all the anterior causations and influences, and by his own transmuting and originating power has created out of them a new and evil existence in the world. Every free agent is thus an original cre-ator even out of nothing. But for him and such as he, there would be no

---

11. In relation to a different subject, Dr. Whichcote, of Cambridge, says: "The ocean can *but* fill the vessel, which a much less quantity of water can do." See Benjamin Whichcote, *Moral and Religious Aphorisms*, (Norwich: Printed by F. Burges, 1703), 46.

guilt in the world. And just so far as the volition is the necessitated result, however intrinsically evil, of anterior or surrounding circumstances, just so far the individual stands morally excused.

3. A moral and responsible volitional act can be performed only by an existent free volitional agent; and once done, by the very necessity of existence, it can never become undone. It thence forever becomes historically the inseparable fact and attribute solely of that agent, and the fact of its performance can never be literally transferred to any other being or personality. In the personality exclusive of that agent the moral sense sees an axiomatically inhering responsibility, guilt, merit, or demerit. Consequent and correlative to that merit or demerit, the moral sense affixes an ethical desert of reward or penalty. And as the fact of the agent's act is nontransferable from one agent to another, so the merit, demerit, reward, or penalty, is ethically nontransferable. Punishment and guilt, therefore, are no more transferable than personal identity. When an innocent being is said to suffer the punishment of a guilty being the language is conceptual, and not barely literal and true. The innocent being is still innocent, and he endures what to the guilty agent would be punishment, but to him it is only consequent though substitutional suffering.

III

Volition Not Always Preceded by Emotion

M R. LOCKE HELD THE doctrine that uneasiness is the necessary ante-cedent to every volition:

> Good and evil, present and absent, it is true, work upon the mind; but that which immediately determines the Will from time to time to every voluntary action is the uneasiness of desire, fixed on some absent good, either negative, as indolence to one in pain, or positive, as enjoyment of pleasure. That it is the uneasiness that determines the Will to successive voluntary actions, whereof the greatest part of our lives is made up, and by which we are conduct-ed through different courses to different ends, I shall endeavor to show, both from experience and the reason of the thing.[1]

Again:

> For good though appearing and allowed ever so great, yet till it has raised desires in our minds, and thereby made us uneasy in its want, it reaches not our will; we are not within the sphere of its activity.[2]

If this is indeed true, action is born of misery. All energetically ac-tive beings must be unhappy, and the more energetic the action the more intense must be the stimulant by which they are urged and chased.

Post equitem sedet atra cura.

A perfectly happy being must be a perfectly stagnant being. God and holy angels must either be as tranquil as the sleeping deity of Epicurus, or as unhappy as the evil omnipotence of Manes.

---

1. John Locke, *An Essay Concerning Human Understanding* (Philadelphia: Troutman & Hayes, 1853), 160.

2. Ibid. 165.

Sir James Mackintosh, Upham, and others, maintain that the volition must ever be preceded by an emotion of desire.

Mackintosh writes:

> We can easily imagine a percipient and thinking being without a capacity of receiving pain or pleasure. Such a being might perceive what we do; if we could conceive him to reason, he might reason justly; and if he were to judge at all, there seems no reason why he should not judge truly. But what could induce such a being to will or to act? It seems evident that his existence could only be a state of passive contemplation. Reason, as reason, can never be a motive to action.[3]

THE CLEAR DECISION

On the contrary, it is the clear decision of consciousness that the reasonableness or the intellective perception of advantage to one's self or another, or the perception of accordance with a previous purpose, or the intuitive perception of right, may so come in immediate contact with Will as to be the motive of volition.

1. The reasonable, we submit to every man's consciousness, is not choosable simply because it is desirable, but also because it is reasonable. The reasonable, as reasonable, is a reason or motive for action. The reasonable is not only desirable, but it is eligible, choosable. I may choose a thing simply and solely because it is reasonable, and not because it is desirable. I may choose the reasonable in preference to the desirable. I may be in a state of purpose to choose not the pleasant, not the desirable, but the reasonable.

2. If emotion is an antecedent condition to volition, we might suppose, according to the usual reasoning of necessitarians, that the stronger the emotion the surer the volition. If a less emotive object prevailed by so much as the emotion was less, by that much there was choice without emotion. By that much the Will acted from emotionless intellection. Now it is certainly very common for men to choose a distant interest apparently without emotion, and appreciated by but the driest calculation in preference to a matter of present emotive enjoyment. By the usual modes

---

3. Sir James Mackintosh, *A General View of the Progress of Ethical Philosophy, Chiefly During the Seventeenth and Eighteenth Centuries* (Philadelphia: Carey & Lea, 1832), 84.

of necessitarian reasoning this is proof positive of the greater motive power of cold intellection over emotion.

3. But an intellectively perceived advantage to another is an ample motive for energetic volition. An emotionless old man may plant trees whose shade he never expects to enjoy, coolly and simply for the advantage of posterity. A man may perform an act for the benefit of the antipodes that he has never seen, because he perceives it to be a choosable thing that they should be benefited just as coolly and clearly as he recognizes that a circle is not a triangle.

4. A being may will purely because he knows and sees it to be right. Right, as right, simply cognized, is motive upon Will without any intervening condition. The perception of obligation may be obeyed as a perception. It has a claim that can be measured and accepted as motive force. There is weight and power for action in it as a matter of moral calculation.

5. The doctrine that the Will chooses only in behalf of agreeable emotion forms a fair basis for the selfish system of morals. Upon that basis it may justly be said that whatever benefaction we confer upon others we confer purely and solely for the emotive gratification it affords to ourselves.

6. But a large share of the great sum total of human volitions is put forth purely from a perceived accordance with a general anterior purpose. I have a purpose to write through the words and letters of a line or page; every letter is the product of a volition; but so far as I can see, the whole train of volitions is a perfectly emotionless one, each volition obeying the general purpose; the mind, indeed, being in a permanent state of willingness. So far as I can see, the whole process is transacted between the intellect in a certain state of quiet purpose and the particular volition. A bookkeeper in casting up a long row of figures exerts at least one volition at each figure as soon as his eye has perception of its shape and identifies its meaning. Between this identification and the volition he is conscious of no emotion intervening. The whole is a dry emotionless process. Besides, our volitions are as infinitesimal, we might say, as the ultimate atoms of matter, and as infinite in number. In writing this page there is a volition for every turn of the pen in every letter, so that the pulsations of Will, like the pulsations of sound, fuse into a flow. If, therefore, emotion precedes volition, emotion is fused into a simply animate and living state of mind, and the doctrine is lost in the fusion.

7. Are the men of most energetic and powerful action the men of the most excitable desires? They are, indeed, men of the strongest purpose, of the most unflinching determination; but the energy of their volitions is surely not to be measured by the turbulence of the emotions by which they are preceded. The question, be it marked, does not concern the strength of the constitutional appetites of the man, but the intensity or overflowing of the immediate emotion; and so viewed, it may be held as a general rule that the men of strongest volitions are men of the least perturbable emotion. As there is a dry light, lumen siccum, of the intellect, so there is a dry force to the volition.

From all this we conclude that pure intellect, without any intervening emotion, does come as motive-force in immediate contact upon the springs of volition.

IV

Freedom of Will Causationally Presented

FREEDOM OF THE WILL, as distinguished from necessity, is usually defined to be that power by which it may put forth either of several volitions, or in causational terms, that property of the volitional cause by which it produces either of several possible effects. It is an either-causal power.

But to a full development of these definitions an exposition is requisite of the terms: cause, power, necessity, and certainty.

A *cause* is a subject by whose existence another subject comes into existence, or may, without contradiction of any truth, be conceived to so come into existence.

Power is that element in a cause by which the effect comes into existence, or may, without involving contradiction, be supposed to come into existence.

If power is a clear, valid, cognizable idea of a true reality, then its absence or non-existence is an equally valid cognition. We have, therefore, the following precise and cognizable definition of necessity and its cognates.

Necessity in a thing is the non-existence therein of adequate power for the thing to be otherwise than it is. Necessity of particular existence is the non-existence of adequate power to exist otherwise than the one sole given way. Necessity of a causation or an action is the absence of power of non-causation or non-action, and of all other causation or action than the one sole given mode.

That is usually said to be necessary in which the opposite or alternative cannot be conceived. It would, perhaps, be more accurate to say that a thing is necessary that we positively and compulsorily conceive cannot be the different or opposite of what it is. This conceiving of the impossibility of the diverse arises not so much from the law of our minds as from the nature of the necessary subject itself. If it can be said to arise from the law of our minds, it is from that law by which our minds see things as they are; the law that our perceptive intuitions must be controlled by the object intuited. We see this impossibility of opposite, because it is a reality before our view.

All necessity is one—the impossibility of being different. This may exist in different classes of objects; and thus a classification may arise which may be useful in itself, but must not be mistaken for a classification of varieties of the necessity itself. The impossibility of an opposite may exist in matter, in chemical affinity, in magnetism; but that does not give rise to an essentially different material necessity, chemical necessity, or magnetic necessity. There may be the necessity of a clock stroke and of a volition; but these are not two kinds of necessity, but the same necessity in two kinds of operation.

The necessity may exist in different sorts of connection between two things, yet the necessity is not different, being still the impossibility of the diverse. So, between 2x2 and 4 there is a necessary connection; and between the pressure upon a clock hammer and its stroke there is a necessary connection. These are very different connections; but their necessity is the same, namely, the impossibility of the opposite.

We have as yet seen no satisfactorily complete and exhaustive classification of those entities, truths, qualities, connections, etc., which, as we necessarily see, cannot but be. Sufficiently complete for our purpose may be a division into entities and relations, which may be either primordial or derived.

I. By *entities* we mean whatever is cognized by the intuition as a simple and single reality. And among the primordial of these, are the self-existent, time, space; and we are inclined to add in mathematics the point and the line. These are primordial in the sense of being unoriginated and eternal. Among the derived or originated entities, which have a beginning and yet become necessary, are all facts or events, which, being once done, remain facts and done forever. There is no possibility that they can become never having been done, and so they are under a necessity of existence.

II. Among the *relations*, which are primordially and eternally necessary, are the relations of geometry, of number, of right and wrong. Indeed all creation must take place in accordance with their presupposed existence, and be subject to their application and laws. The special application of these relations in the created objects is not primordial, but has beginning.

The popular distinction of moral and natural necessity is a distinction not in the necessity itself, but in the class of subjects to which it belongs. There is no intrinsic moral necessity other than mere moral obligation. I am obligated by the law of right, but not necessitated. The right act is what ought to be, not what must be. There is no impossibility of the opposite of Right, for there is plenty of Wrong. On the other hand there is no necessity that is not natural, that is, existing in the nature of things. The connection of causal necessity existing between a motive and a volition necessarily consequent, is as natural as the connection of causal necessity existing between the pressure upon the clock hammer and the stroke. A man may be naturally necessitated to will what is morally right; but that would be not a moral but a natural necessity. It is the object of the volition that is here moral; its necessity is natural.

FALLACIES OF NECESSITARIANISM

The fallacies of necessitarianism, in regard to power, are numerous, deceptive, and pregnant with absurd consequences. Thus:

1. Necessitarians confound power for some other thing with power to a given thing. A power to see the planet Herschell is no power to talk with its inhabitants. A power of muscle to strike, or of brains to think, is no power whatever of the soul to will. So the power to do as we will is no freedom or power in the Will to will otherwise than a sole way, nor even a freedom or power to will at all.

2. Necessitarians confound a power with the power to or from a thing. A power is often only a part, and an insufficient part, too, of the power. The power to do a thing is the complete and adequate power, which is requisite to responsibility. Where an act requires for its fulfillment several concurrent or constituent powers, each one of these may be deceptively so affirmed as to signify the adequate and responsible power. A fluent elocutionist has a power to deliver an extemporaneous oration, and yet not the power, for he has not the intellectual capacity to think it. So power of Will and power of post-volitional motion are both concurrently requisite in order to the complete performance of a one voluntary act. If a writer, therefore, should say, because a man has a power, intellectual or corporeal, for the act, that the man has the power to perform

the act, he might deceive his readers. He has a power; he has powers; he has faculties; but he has not *the* power; that is, he has not the complete adequate power unless there is also "ability" or power in his Will for the requisite volition.

We shall usually in this treatise use the prefix adjective *adequate* in order to guard against this ambiguity.

3. Necessitarians confound the power, that is, the adequate power, for a thing with adequate strength. An ox has adequate strength to execute a minuet as truly as an opera dancer, but he has not the power. So the living body of a man has ample strength to perform all that his Will shall dictate; but it has not, therefore, the power to do so without the volition, any more than a dead body. So there may be physical strength in an agent, and even in his Will, to put forth a different choice in the place of the one he does put forth; but neither he nor his Will has, therefore, the power.

4. Necessitarians confound a faculty for any kind act with the adequate power for a specific exercise or performance. A faculty for language is not necessarily the adequate power to speak French; the faculty of sight is not adequate power to see stars by daylight. The faculty of thought, of emotion, of Will, does not necessarily imply an adequate responsible power to repent, to serve God, to be perfectly holy.

5. Necessitarians confound the power for a thing with the conditions of the power. Legs are a condition to the full power of walking, but not the power itself. So, a will or an inclination is a condition to the power of corporeal action; but a will, a choice, or an inclination, is no more the power itself of action than legs are the power of walking. Yet, strange to say, important parts of the necessitarian system of theology are founded on this confounding of volition, or, as they call it, inclination with power.

PROFESSOR HAVEN'S WORK

Professor Haven, for instance[1], in discussing the question whether we can do what we have no disposition, or choice, or will to do, decides that the answer depends upon whether or not we consider disposition, choice, or Will to be identical with power. If the two are identical, then want of choice, he thinks, is want of power; if not, then want of choice, etc., is no

---

1. James Haven, *Mental Philosophy Including the Intellect, Sensibilities and Will* (Boston: Gould and Lincoln, 1857), 551.

want of power, and my body is able to act without choosing to act. On all this we remark that the identification of choice and power is absurd; that the definition by which the identity is either denied or affirmed is quite as absurd, and that the inference he draws, namely, that if the two be not identical, then we can corporeally act without choice to act, is as absurd as either, both as an inference and as a supposable fact. For,

1. Disposition, inclination, choice or Will, is not power, any more than it is space or substance, though it be the condition of power. Disposition may intrinsically have power or intensity; its presence may occasion, or be the condition of, power; but to identify it as power itself is as irrational as to identify substance with space, or concrete with quality.

2. The definitions intended by Professor Haven, either to include or exclude this identification, are both absurd, and about equally absurd. Power he first proposes to define as denoting "all that is requisite to the actual doing of a thing." Then my legs are power of walking; for they are requisite to the actual doing of the thing. Then I am myself the power of walking; for a walker, an agent, is necessary to the walking. This definition includes as power the agent, the instrument, and all the conditions, both to the doing and to the power of doing a thing. As instruments, inclination or choice is not the power, but the condition requisite to the power of doing a thing. So far as inclination or choice is not power, Professor H. infers that a man has power to act without choice. What a man can do with choice he can do without choice. By that same reasoning I can prove that a penniless pauper can pay the national debt of England. For money is not power; and so what a man can do with money he can do without money. If with money he could pay the national debt, then he can do it without money!

But a narrow definition, he tells us, limits power "to denote all that is requisite to the doing the thing, provided we please or choose to do it." Then, again, my legs are the power of walking, and my eyes the power of seeing, and my nose the power of smelling. That these and all other organs, and all choices and volitions, are conditions to the power of acting, is perfectly plain; we should not have the power without them; but they are not the power itself. The power exists, consequently, upon them.

3. But Professor H. argues: If choice is power, then I have not the power to act without the choice; but if choice is not power, then I have the power to act without choice. But how, Professor, if the choice should prove to be not the power itself, but, what is plainly the fact, the condition

requisite to the power? Plainly, if the condition requisite to the power is wanting to the agent, the act cannot be done, for want of both condition and power; that is, the choice is not power, yet the corporeity has no power to act without the choice to act. We should like to see any necessitarian gentleman, who says, "choice is not power, and so I have power to get up and walk across the floor without any choice or volition whatever," perform the feat. If pure corporeity has this power of action without volition, a dead body may leap from the dissector's table and march off without even intending it.

In every voluntary external action two facts must ever unite, each possessing a constituent power, namely, the Will, and the extra-volitional, which, though it includes mind, we will embrace under the term corporeity. To say that either of these are power, instead of saying that they possess power, is a confusion of terms. Both factors must combine, and the power of both factors must be ready to cooperate, in order to the existence of the one complete adequate power for the entire composite act. It is then false to say that the corporeity has the adequate power to the act in the absence of the Will in its full power of action. No less false is it to say that the Will with its full power can perform the composite act without the corporeity in its adapted power.

EXPOSE THE FALLACY

And hereby we may expose the fallacy of those necessitarians, with Edwards at their head, who tell us that men do in ordinary language say and hold that if an act or object is physically or corporeally in their power, so that the act is doable provided they have the will, then the act or object is completely in their power; so that ability has no reference to Will, and power or ability is not, in strict propriety of speech, requirable or predicable of Will. A single rational reflection ought to tell those thinkers that the thing properly called power, and ordinarily styled ability, is as truly needed, and exists in the Will to enact a volition as in the corporeity to obey the volition and enact the voluntary motion. When men speak as if all the power required to the composite voluntary movement is merely in the corporeity, the power correspondent in the Will is tacitly assumed as understood, and as of course.

My power to will being implied silently, then a thing or act is in my power if it be corporeally so, and then nothing is needed but the will or volition; I can then do it if I will. But, on the other side, I may tacitly assume the corporeal power, and from that standpoint I may say that all that is wanting to the full performance is the ability or power to will. And from such language taken by itself it might be argued that power is not required or predicable of the corporeity. Ability, in the strict application, would belong to Will alone. A thing is then held to be in a man's power, provided there is power in the Will, just because the full possession of the corporeal power is quietly presupposed. Really and truly, then, power ability, with all the cognate terms, as can, possible, able, etc., is as truly affirmable or deniable of Will as of any other part of our nature.

What gives all the plausibility to the notion that ability or power is affirmable or deniable of the post-volitional or voluntary act solely, and not of the volitional act, is the fact that men have far more occasion to speak of what they can do if they will than what they can will. Practically, men much more often discuss their power to execute than their power to choose. And they are so constantly in this position of silently assuming their power to will, and requiring and predicating the power of the corporeal or post-volitional alone, that Edwards and other necessitarian metaphysicians stand up and most unwisely say that ability has no proper predicability of Will at all.

The definitions thus far given embrace the following postulates:

1. Not every cause is inalterable or unipotent, that is, possessed of power to no other than one sole effect.

2. Causes, in reference to possible and actual effects are either adequate or resultant. A volitional cause may be adequate to an effect, yet that effect may not result; it is therefore, to that effect, not a resultant cause. This difference relates not so much to the nature of the cause as to the fact of the sequence.

3. Non-existence of a volitional effect is not absolute proof of non-existence of volitional power in the agent for that effect.

4. Non-exertion of power is not identical with non-existence of power.

5. The physical effect is always the measure of the intrinsic physical casuality; but the volitional effect is not the measure of the intrinsic power, causation, or objective influence.

Freedom of Will Causationally Presented

These postulates may be shaped in the following antithetic:

Canons

Of non-volitional or necessary causation.	*Of volitional or non-necessary causation.*
I. Every non-volitional event has its necessary cause.	I. Every volitional event has its resultant cause.
II. Every necessary cause is unipotent, that is, has its own solely possible effect.	II. Every volitional cause is alternative, that is, has either of several effects possible.
III. Every non-volitional event that fails to happen, fails for want of a cause. For every no-event there is a no-cause.	III. Non-occurring volitions do not prove non-existence of adequate cause. Not for every no-volition is there a no-adequate cause.
IV. The effect is the absolute measure of the intrinsic power of the cause or influence.	IV. The result is the measure of merely the assignable power of the adequate cause or influence.

Dr. Reid said the following about exertion of power (connected to our fourth postulate):

> Active power therefore is a quality in the cause, which enables it to produce the effect. And the exertion of that active power in producing the effect is called action, agency, efficiency. In order to the production of any effect, there must be in the cause, not only power, but the exertion of that power. For power that is not exerted has no effect. [2]

The Younger Edwards responded:

> Therefore if we be the efficient causes of our own volitions, as Dr. Clarke, Dr. Chauncy, etc. held, we must not only have a *power* to produce them but there must be an exertion of power in order to the production of volition. This exertion is doubtless an exertion of the will. Thus we run into the infinite (causation) series several times mentioned. [3]

---

2. Thomas Reid, *Essays on the Active Powers of the Human Mind* (London: Printed for Thomas Tegg, 1848), 252.

3. Tryon Edwards, *The Works of Jonathan Edwards D.D.*, 1: 335.

But the act, and the exertion of the power for the act, are not two independent acts or effects. Every act is performed in the exertion of the power for the act. The exertion of the power is the drawing upon the energy that the act requires for its performance. It is the manner or condition through which the act is performed. The phrase is a statement of the relation that the performance of the act bears to the inherent power.

Of the term "certainty," the etymology (root word *certain* is derived from Latin *certus*, which is akin to the Greek *krinein*) shows that its primary meaning is subjective. It exists in the mind rather than in the object. When my judgment of the reality of an externality is so firm as to be exempt from all doubt, there is a mental certainty. The certainty is nonetheless real though the object turn out to have been unreal. That is, I may be perfectly certain of a thing and yet be mistaken.

EXTERNAL ACTUALITY

Objective certainly is the external actuality corresponding to and verifying a correct subjective certainty. The actuality or object may be also a necessary object; nevertheless its certainty and its necessity are nonetheless different things. The thing may be necessary by the simple necessity of existence; but the idea of its necessity and its certainty are two distinct ideas. By its certainty it is able to correspond and answer to the mind's reliance that it is so; by its necessity it is unable to non-exist. Mere mental certainty cognizes that a thing is, not that it must be. To cognize its necessity requires a pure intuity over and beyond the simple perception that it is.

Pure certainty in a future event is the future fulfillment of the event, implying simply that while power exists for it not to be, it yet ultimately will be. For it is plain that in this there is no contradiction. If of several possible events one will be, then the certainty is nothing more than just that it will be. And surely the supposition that several events are possible does not contradict the idea that one of them will, in the ultimate become actual. Nor does the fact that one will be contradict the idea that several are possible. It differs from necessity in that the latter negates the idea of diverse alternative or plural possibilities. Objective certainty of a future event is the future fulfillment or will-be of the event. Subjective certainly is the conception or view in the mind of that objective pure fulfillment or simple will-be.

The future objective certainty of a free volitional act, being a pure will-be without the must-be, has no degrees. A will-be cannot be more or less certain. But the corresponding pure subjective certainty, perfect and without degrees, the human mind does not possess. Credence or reliance is the more proper term for our subjective view of a non-necessitated fulfillment. To mere humanity there is no objective certainty in a free volitional future event. Perfect subjective certainty corresponding to the pure objective, which among diverse possibilities will be, belongs to the divine prescience alone.

Certainty, as above defined and distinguished from necessity, is the conceivable correlative of an alternative will. It is the proper predicate or epithet for that volition, which will in a given case be put forth by a will by definition able to put forth other instead. They reciprocally presuppose each other. He who cannot admit that volition can be put forth with full power to have withheld it cannot conceive of simple certainly. With him certainty is necessity. His will-be is a must-be. The result is fatalism.

Some leading philosophers have rejected the term and the idea of causation, and have substituted in its place an invariable sequence, which is as reliable in their view as the continuity of causation. The connection in such case of antecedents and consequences is therefore properly held to be as inevitable as the connection of causes and effects. The Law of Invariability is here as absolute as the Law of Causation, and chance or atheism would as soon follow the supposition of failure in one as in the other. The connection is, therefore, not a connection of certainty, but of necessity. Where such an invariability exists it contradicts and excludes all idea of failure, or possible variation, or power of alternativity, or contrariety. Absolute universal invariability, as axiomatic as causal succession, is in contradiction with power of exception or alteration.

V

Edwards's Synthesis of Definitions Reviewed

A DOCTRINAL SCHEME MAY be framed with a set of definitions dovetailed into each other with so exact a mutual fit, that the very coherency and structural exactness of the system of terms may seem to demonstrate the truth and solidity of the doctrine. Yet each definition may covertly so include more than truth, or an essential idea may be so excluded from the synthesis, that the doctrine may be imperfect or false. The terms must not only exactly fit each other and form a doctrinal structure, but they must fit the truth of things; and they must, without omission, include and fit to everything requisite to the true and complete synthesis. By transgression of these principles Edwards's synthesis of definitions becomes an artificial framework in which the whole question in debate is anticipatively assumed.

By that synthesis necessity is held and defined as comprehending and identical with all existing relations; certainty is identical with necessity; and contingency is held equivalent to chance, to no cause, and so is excluded as absurdity. Now the very question being whether all relations are necessary; whether all certain future events are necessary; and whether contingency is not a valid idea of the understanding; a cool assumption of the result in definitions must be exposed by an analysis of the nomenclature.

I. Edwards, first, rejects a true and adequate definition of necessity. "Here I might say that a thing is then said to be necessary when it must be, and cannot be otherwise. But this would not properly be a definition of necessity or an explanation of the word any more than if I explained the word *must* by there being a necessity. The words *must, can, and cannot*, need explanation as much as the words *necessary* and *impossible*, excepting that the former are words that children commonly use, we know something of the meaning of, earlier than the latter." (30)

We reply, 1. There is no truer test of a definition than this that it reproduces in the mind the clear and precise idea for which the term stands. That the definition be in words so familiar that it creates the idea, even in the minds of children, is a real perfection. It is a decided proof of the universality and indestructibleness of the idea as defined. It is fair ground of suspicion against a theory that it discards the clear for the obscure. Moral philosophers, after a world of recondite explication, find that no term or definition more clearly creates in the mind the precise idea of moral obligation than the verb "ought," and have even found for this purpose the awkward noun "oughtness" a most expressive formation. Just so we may say that certainly or simple future fulfillment has no better designation than simple will-be; and necessity cannot find in all language, a simpler or more unmistakable exponent than the terms "must," "must-be," or "mustness."

Perfectly untrue is the assertion that "must" as much needs a definition as necessity; since "must" in every mind creates the exact idea. This fact is acknowledged even in faulting the term, and is the very charge brought against it. It is the more obscure term that always needs defining, and of which the plainer term is the definition, and the plainest the best. And if so, the only word in the language that can precisely define necessity is *must*, and this neither needs nor can receive a definition except by a synonymous word or phrase.

Equally inadmissible, therefore, is the objection that "must" may be defined by necessity as well as necessity by must. All words are interchangeable with their definitions; all words and their definitions mutually define each other. Associate with a word its synonymous formula, and that to any given mind will be the definition that is best understood. Even Edwards's definition of necessity will be found to be better defined by the word than the word by the definition.

II. Edwards next propounds a definition that gets no further than the definition rejected.

If, however, clearness to a plain or childlike mind is a fault in a definition, the definition of necessity, by Edwards, is in this respect to a high degree unobjectionable. "Philosophical necessity," he says, "is really nothing else than the full and fixed connection between the thing signified by the subject and predicate of a proposition which affirms something to be true." (34)

Edwards certainly does not here say what he means. He surely cannot mean that necessity is the connection itself, but a quality of the connection. The connection is a necessary or fixed connection. The connection and the fixedness or necessity are two things. The necessity is to be found as a property in the idea or reality of the connection.

This is not so much definition as exemplification. It does not so much tell us what necessity is as where it may be found. What it is may still be a dark question; for it may not be so easy at a glance to tell by description or synonymous terms exactly what the necessity is that resides in the connection between subject and predicate. Nor is the darkness much illumined by the adjectives "full" and "fixed," unless "fixed" means necessary, which forces us into the circle of defining a thing by itself. Edwards, however, aids our difficulty by subdividing into three heads his exemplification of this necessity in connection, namely: 1. Things may be connected in and of themselves as mathematical relations, etc. 2. Necessity may exist in the connection between a thing and its existence. 3. Necessity may exist between cause and effect.

VARIOUS EXPRESSIONS

Now the various expressions designating the necessary element under these three heads form his real definition of the thing, as may be seen by the following exhibit: 1. "They may have a full and perfect necessary connection in and of themselves, because it may imply a contradiction or gross absurdity to suppose them not connected." (35) "It would be the greatest absurdity to deny" "the sum of all contradictions," "it is necessary," "fit, and suitable." Under this head comes mathematical and all self-evident truths. These are the only definitions or equivalents of the necessary element Edwards furnishes in the first head of exemplification. 2. The connection with existence of a thing that has already come to pass, and can never not-be, "may be fixed and certain," "made sure," "made certain and unalterably true," "fixed and decided," "impossible that it should be otherwise." These phrases are the real designations of necessity in the second. 3. Connection of antecedent with consequence, or cause and effect, by which the latter is necessary "consequentially." This is "a necessity of consequence." Under this head all so-called "certain" events are by him ranked;[1] that is, all future event, including all acts of the Will, and it is

---

1. Those who claim for Edwards a maintenance of a certainty of future acts of the

upon this necessity rests the great debate. Cause and effect are "firmly and surely connected," "fully and thoroughly" "made sure." After having rejected the simple "must" as too childish for a definition, Edwards gives a list of descriptives like these!

After having rejected the ordinary definition as a mere interchangeable equivalent, he furnishes nothing as a substitute but a catalogue of synonyms. They get not one hair's breadth beyond the simple must. And what is more to our purpose, there is not one in his circle of identities that goes one hair's breadth beyond our definition, that "necessity is the non-existence of power to be or operate otherwise," but is the quality of what "must be"; and "that it should be otherwise involves contradictions," and so it is "fixed," "made sure," etc.

"The fixed and full connection" between the significate of a subject and predicate, he tells us, is necessity, or at least has necessity for a quality. But every connection is a full connection; for that which is only a part of a connection is less than a connection, and so no connection at all. "Full," therefore, is superfluous, and may be omitted. Looking, then, between the subjects and predicate we find that necessity is just fixed connection, or rather the fixedness of the connection. So that necessity is fixedness. By whom or by what fixed is not said. But if we can conceive a connection, and then conceive that connection to be fixed, and then can isolate its fixedness, we shall have shaped to our mental view the Edwardian notion of necessity. Ask Edwards at last what necessary means, and he can only answer, "fixed," "made sure," "fixed and certain," "sure and firm," "contradiction to be supposed otherwise," etc.

This definition nevertheless assumes in the next place, the necessity of all known actual relations. Things, between which any relations or connections actually exist, may be the subject and predicate of a proposition affirming something to be true. When there is such a connection, according to Edwards, then the thing affirmed is necessary. Let the subject, for instance, be a modest man, and the predicate be is to commit a future murder; if the copula is affirmatively true, the future fulfillment it

---

Will as distinct from necessity will please here take note. Edwards expressly maintains, in his chapter on Foreknowledge, that the necessity of *every* future event foreknown, whether volition or mechanical effect, comes under as strict a necessity as a *past act*; and a past act, he here says, having "made sure" of its existence, is *necessary in itself.* Of a future and a past event alike he affirms that their necessity consists "in the present impossibility of non-existence of the event." (181)

seems is necessary. Now this is denied. The connection of the man with the future murder, even though he by action ultimately proves its affirmation true, is not a necessary connection. The logical copula then simply expresses certainty. That is, it gives notice to the mind to feel that repose that is consistent with the view of a future fulfillment which, while there exists power for it not to occur, will occur. And this not necessity. The definition, therefore, is false.

III. Edwards next, for a purpose, overstates the difference between the popular and the philosophical use of the terms.

"The word *necessary*," says Edwards, "is a relative term, and relates to some supposed opposition made to the thing spoken of, which is overcome, and proves in vain to hinder or alter it. That is, necessary, in the original and proper use of the word, which is, or will be notwithstanding all supposable opposition." (31) " . . . We are accustomed, in the common use of language, to apply and understand these phrases in this sense, etc. And if we use the words as terms of art . . . this habitual connection of ideas will deceive and confound us in our reasonings," etc. (32)

EDWARDS ASSERTS

The purpose for which Edwards asserts this relative meaning of the word, and expatiates on its inveterate influence, is to provide a reply at the set time to the Arminian objection against the moral responsibility of a necessary action. Men bring to volitional necessity, he will tell us, the notion, long established by habit, of necessity or compulsion against the Will, and thus attribute to necessary volition that irresponsibility which belongs to compulsory involuntary action.

But the importance attributed by Edwards to the plurality of meanings of the words necessity, impossibility, etc., is excessive and capricious. Few words in any language are absolutely single in meaning; there is no reason assignable why the different meanings of these words should be so strangely and inveterately undistinguishable.

Edwards's account both of the "original and proper sense of the word," and of the "proper use of language," as having some reference to an opposed Will, is, however, wholly incorrect. Reference to an opposed Will is, in the large majority of its applications, in the popular as well as the philosophical, so accidental or so remote as to form no proper characteristic of the word.

1. The "original and proper sense" of the word may be in some degree tested by its etymology. If the derivation is correct that deduces it from *ne* and *credo*, its primitive meaning is unyieldingness. Now a thing may be unyielding to a Will or to a thousand other things. A rock may be unyielding to the waves, a tower to the storm, the clay to the sun. A Will itself may be unyielding to something else, as a temptation or an obstacle.

2. Nor has the "common use" of the word any proper reference to an opposed Will. In its most ordinary use the word necessary is equivalent to requisite—requisite to an end. Thus, light is necessary to day; heat is necessary to the fusion of metals; moisture is necessary to vegetable growth; air is necessary to animal life. The necessity in such cases is the necessity of condition to result, and exists whether Will be involved or not. In these cases quoted there is little or no reference to Will, and that little is rather to Will accordant than to Will opposed. Nine-tenths of all its popular uses are of this nature, and bear no reference to voluntary opposition.

3. Popular language approaches more nearly the philosophical meaning in the words impossible and cannot than in the word necessary. They have, too, a more frequent reference to opposed Will. Frequently we say we cannot do a thing however much we will it. And things are impossible to us in the same sense. Yet Edwards states, far too unqualifiedly, that "*impossible* is manifestly a relative term and has reference to supposed power exerted to bring a thing to pass which is insufficient for the effect." (30) Strictly in accordance with the philosophical sense excluding all reference to opposed will or exerted voluntary power, a man of common sense would use these terms in phrases like these: it is impossible that nothing should produce something; a thing cannot be and not be at the same time; it is impossible for two and two to be five; it is impossible that space and substance should be identical; it is impossible that two moments of time should change their order of succession. These and thousands of other instances that might be quoted wholly excluding any antithesis to Will, amply prove that such a meaning is perfectly familiar to common language, and the idea perfectly familiar to the common mind. They also show that between necessity without any reference to Will, and compulsion against Will, there is no affinity that perplexes the most ordinary mind to distinguish.

IV. Edwards lastly identifies certainty with necessity. "Metaphysical or philosophical necessity is nothing different from (objective) certainty."

That statement, we reply, can be true only on the assumption that certainty is a synonym with necessity. Edwards' metaphysical necessity is, as will appear in due time, the necessity of a fact whose diversity is impossible, is unthinkable, is infinitely contradictory and self-explosive, is a causeless effect. If there be a certainty different from necessity, this is not that certainty, but necessity. If necessity and certainty are synonyms, the statement is worthless; if not, it is untrue. The real fact is abundantly evident that with Edwards certainty and necessity were essential synonyms, the former being occasionally called in as the less repulsive term. When he says that any necessity is nothing more than certainty, he means not the Arminian's certainty but the necessitarian's certainty, which is indeed necessity. The proper subject of the epithet necessary, and so of both terms, is, according to his words, as quoted in our first extract in this chapter, that which "must be and cannot be otherwise," a definition he condemns, not as untrue, but as a mere convertible.

EVENT IS ACCIDENTAL

"Contingent," according to Edwards, implies that an event is accidental, in the sense that its connection with its cause being unknown, its occurrence is unforeseen. "But the word *contingent*," Edwards adds, "is abundantly used in a very different sense; not for that whose connection with the series of things we cannot discern so as to foresee the event, but for something which has absolutely no ground (cause) or reason with which its existence has any fixed and certain connection." (39) If this means that any anti-necessitarian writers use the word *contingent* in the sense of causeless, we know not, nor does Edwards inform us, who those writers are. But we venture to imagine that Edwards imputes to them rather the meaning that their views seemed to him to involve, than that which they consciously affixed to the word. Our own use of the word appears in its proper place.

The very nomenclature, therefore, of Edwards, as a whole, excludes freedom at start. Certainty=necessity is one side; contingency=no-cause=chance=zero is on the other. The two embrace all eventuality without any intermediate, and freedom is nowhere. And when the exigency of the debate compels him to get up and define a freedom, then freedom=the absolute subjection of being and action to the causations of necessity.

VI

Conditions and Limitations of Will's Free Action

WHEN WE SAY THAT Will, or the self in willing, is sole cause of its own volitions, there is, nevertheless, one clause properly to be added, and always to be implied, namely, Will, in its proper conditions. And this leads to the discussion of the conditions or occasions and limitations of free action of Will. The necessitarians insist there is no consistent and maintainable difference between cause and occasion or secondary condition.

Edwards says of *cause*: "The word is often used in so restrained a sense as to signify that only which has a positive efficiency or influence to produce a thing or bring it to pass. But there are many things which have no such positive productive influences, which yet are causes." (68) He instances as real causes the absence of preventives. The absence of the sun is a cause of the failing dew in summer, and of the freezing streams in winter. Mr. Mill maintains the same doctrine, including the absence of preventives under the term cause. He further adds: "The state of the whole universe at any instant we believe to be the consequence of its state at the previous instant; insomuch that if we knew all the agents which exist at the present moment, their collocation in space and their properties, in other words, the laws of their agency, we could predict the whole subsequent history of the universe."[1] From which it would seem to result, that every previous thing is the cause of every subsequent thing, and everything that does not exist is the cause of everything that does exist!

So far, however, as Will is concerned, perhaps a clear and permanent distinction may be drawn between cause and condition. The only difficulty of distinguishing subsidiary occasion or condition from cause arises

1. John Stuart Mill, *A System of Logic, Racionative and Inductive, Being a Connected View of the Principles of Evidence and the Methods of Scientific Investigation* (London: J.W. Parker, 1851), 199.

from the fact that from different standpoints different antecedents become principal and cause; so that cause and condition are ever exchanging place with each other. Thus, of the death of Caesar, from one standpoint, a man may say that the sword of Brutus was the cause, and all other antecedents were conditions. From another standpoint another man may say that Caesar's ambition was the cause; another that a conspiracy of senators was the cause and all other antecedents were conditions.

Where, however, there is a kind of cause, simple and elemental in its nature, whose direct and immediate effect is also always of one and the same simple and elementary sort, and is produced solely by that single species of cause, that cause may be always considered as sole cause, and all accessories as secondary conditions. Will is such a cause and volition is such an effect. Will is a simple elementary cause, directly productive of the simple elementary effect of volition alone, and of nothing else; and volition is the simple, elementary, and sole result of Will alone. Of volition Will is sole cause; of Will volition is sole effect. All other antecedents are conditions, in accordance with whose existence Will causatively acts. If, therefore, we have drawn an invariable line of distinction between Will as cause of volition and all other antecedents of volition, we are freed from all ambiguity of an ever-varying sense of the word cause.

CONDITION DEFINED

A condition may be defined as that attendant upon the direct cause without whose existence the cause is not to be conceived as resultant, but with whose existence the cause is still conceivably non-resultant. A condition enables but does not secure result. A volitional cause, or Will itself, does not differ from a volitional condition in the certainty or necessity of the result; for the cause or agent potential to causation may exist and the result not eventuate. The difference is that the volitional cause is always one, namely, Will, and produces the act by direct power resident in itself; whereas the motives are of variable nature, and only indirectly related to the result.

The conditions of all volitional action may be reckoned to be three: an Object or direction of action, Mental Comprehension, and Motive.

1. There can be no action, and therefore no volition without an *object*. The direct object of the volition is properly the post-volitional act

that the volition produces; but there can be no volition without also an object, or at least direction of the post-volitional act.

2. *Mental comprehension* is a condition; by which we mean that the objects and sphere of action must be within the knowledge, the recollection, and the reach of the attention. A volition for an inconceivable action, an unknowable direction, or for an unknowable action, is impossible. In order to have a choice, the alternatives of choice must be before the mental view.

3. *Motive* is usually considered as a condition to the possibility of a volition by the Will; that is, it is frequently affirmed that men never act without motive. It may be conceded that motive is a usual antecedent to volition, but the strict universality of the antecedency may be doubted. The motive is that on account of which (propter), or in accordance with which, a volition is put forth. But, as with the word cause, so with the word motive, an extension is often made in the use beyond the definition. The motive is not only actual but potential. It is not only that in view of which the volition is put forth, but also that in view of which the volition is able to be put forth. The motive is usually some quality in or attendant upon the object of volition by which it commends itself to the faculty of the mind other than the Will. Thus the pleasant flavor of an apple is that quality in the object why it is chosen.

The motive may be considered as objective or subjective. The sweetness, as existing in the apple, is the objective motive; the sweetness, as a conception in the mind, is the subjective motive. Or ever the feeling of desire, awakened by the flavor, may be considered as the subjective motive.

It is from the motive that the direct object of the volition normally draws its eligibility by which it becomes the object. It is not the bare object itself that is willed, but the object as invested with the motivity borrowed from the collateral motive. Hence, it is not far from truth to say that it is the motivity in the object that is essentially chosen and is the real object. Thus, if I choose a rose from the motive of its sweetness, it is the sweetness in the rose which is most truly chosen, and the other constituents of the rose are chosen as embodying, or attached to that motivity. If I choose to walk into the garden for the same motive, every step is willed as embracing the same motivity, and not one step would be taken which is not invested with that motivity. Hence, the motive is chosen in the choice of the object. The choice of the object and of the motive is one and the same thing.

The Will may be subjectively, and in its own intrinsic nature, free, while objectively it may be limited and necessitated.

1. There may be no external motives in a given direction. So a person may be objectively incapable of sin from the absence of all temptation. He may be objectively unfree to do good, and so be wholly depraved because he is out of reach of a single attractive object of good. When there are no motives within reach, save in one direction, the Will may be objectively unfree.

2. There may be but one external object or direction, actual and known, of action, and so of volition. In such a case the Will, though its intrinsic nature is unchanged, and is truly in its proper conditions free, yet is objectively circumscribed and rendered unfree. It can act but in one sole possible way. Objective volitional freedom requires external plurality or alternatives. But when there are two possible courses, non-action may be in fact a third course.

We have then here the limitations by which the freedom of the human Will is circumscribed. There can be no direction of volitional action that is not within the mental view, under the possible mental attention, and, normally, also commended by motive. When therefore, we say that a free Will puts forth a volition with a full power otherwise, we are always to understand it with a qualification, namely, a free Will in its proper conditions.

This remark obviates the misunderstanding of the Younger Edwards, who supposes that we imagine that the volitional faculty accounts for a volition without any postulate of conditional circumstances:

> The man who is the subject of a certain volition had the power of will long since; yet it never produced that volition, we may suppose, till this moment. What is the cause or reason that it produces it now and not before? To say it does it, because it will, is to say either that this volition is produced by another preceding, which runs into the infinite series, or that the power of will, or rather the man in the exercise of that power, is the subject of volition, which is mere trifling. On the whole, the existence of a power of will in a man will no more account for any particular volition of which he is the subject, than the existence of the man will account for the

same volition, or the existence of a ship carpenter will account for the building of a certain ship.[2]

But, like all other causes, a volitional agent, in order to become an adequate and resultant cause, needs to be placed in the proper causal conditions. The powder causes the flash, but not until the spark is applied. So the volitional agent cannot will until the objects and the alternatives of volition are before his view. He then becomes an adequate cause for either of the alternatives that may result. The carpenter cannot build the ship until the object, motives, and alternatives are before him. But the objects and alternatives no more cause his volitions than the ship creates the carpenter.

MOTIVE CALLED CAUSE

It need not be denied that motive is sometimes called cause, and that words are used both as nouns and verbs, implying a causative relation between the supplying of motives and the complying act that results. It is often said of a man, "This made him do thus;" that induced him to act differently. A tempter or seducer who furnishes motives to sin, in compliance with which destruction is incurred, is said to cause the sin and the destruction, to involve in guilt, and to ruin the victim. A person who supplies instructions and motives to good which, if followed, result in excellence and happiness, is said to cause the excellence and to produce the happiness. This is said with that popular looseness which belongs to the word cause, and to most causative terms. It arises from the external relation of antecedency and sequence, which present the obvious objective appearance of true causation.

This popular use does not assume to decide anything as to the intrinsic psychological nature of the relation. Yet how truly consciousness distinguishes between motives and causes (or between the two classes of causes) is clear, from the fact that a man seldom says that a motive "caused me to do thus," or that such or such was the "cause why I choose thus." Every man assigns not a cause, but a reason why he wills a given way. And if any one truly interrogates consciousness, why he rejects the word, it will be difficult for him to refuse to answer that the word cause is too mechanically necessitative a word, or not to feel that there is a conscious difference between a cause and a reason for action.

2. Tryon Edwards, *The Works of Jonathan Edwards*, 1:332.

The sense of responsibility, too, is grounded upon the assumption of this difference. When the tempter presents the motive before his victim, which he accepts to be his own ruin, the offerer of the motive is a sharer of the guilt. Yet, strictly speaking, he is not sharer in the guilt of the victim's act. Each party is responsible for himself and for his own act: the tempter for his presentation of the motive, the victim for his acting in compliance with it. The heinousness of the act is indeed to a degree a measure of the aggravation of the tempting presentation, especially where it was legitimately calculable and so intentional. Yet the seduced sinner is not the less completely responsible for the full enormity of his compliant crime, on the plain principle that the motive did not necessitate the act; that the motives being all the same, he could have willed wholly otherwise; and that the full causation of the deed took a needlessly effectual origin in himself. And this brings us back to the axiom of universal common sense, that the sin taking its primordial origin unnecessarily from the free agent, the agent is, therefore, wholly and solely responsible. For the proper act the responsibility, as well as the unnecessary causation, takes its beginning with himself; nor is it derived from, nor does it reflect back upon, the tempter or the creator. The tempter has, indeed, his own crime to answer for. The Creator has none.

Not only of individual volitions, but of the course of large masses of men we assign causes. We find causes of events in history; and these causes are simply motives that act in totality of individual Wills. In these so-called causes, necessitative and volitional elements variously blend. So far as they are purely and alternatively volitional they are not necessitative.

VII

Anterior Standard of Accordance

AFTER EXTERIOR FREEDOM HAS been defined to be the "power of doing as we will," both the freedomist and the necessitarian are much inclined in a similar way to define the freedom of the Will to be "the power of choosing *as*"—something. The volition, forsooth, is as the last dictate of the understanding; as the greatest apparent good; as the choice, wish, inclination, bias, or making up of the mind; as the sum total or balance of the entire anterior man; as the strongest motive; as it pleases. Each and all alike of these formulæ may be used to fasten the Will with an iron link to an iron pillar. The simple truth is that the volition is not as any one thing whatever of a single previous fixed nature.

Freedomists themselves, to indicate the idea of free volition, nevertheless originally used some of these formulæ that have served the purpose of necessitarianism so well. That the agent "chooses as he pleases," has an obvious sense quite different from "chooses as he is pleased." The former has an active free look that suggested a freedom, which it does not quite unequivocally express. Necessitarianism, in its habit of appropriating terms that have an exterior show of freedom with an interior necessity in them, has availed itself of this formula to mitigate verbally the hardness of its dogma. The formula that one chooses as he pleases may mean simply, and was used by freedomists to mean, that the Will chooses accordantly with some, or any, previously perceived chooseableness or eligibility; with some motive, that is, though not a sole possibility.

The word "pleases" may designate any or either one of several favorable views in favor of which the Will alternatively and independently of causation or invariability chooses. In such cases the free Will accorded with a particular motive uncaused by any controlling power, just as it self-determinantly "pleased." Each motive or anterior favorable view for either one of several courses furnishes you an "as you please," the volition

55

in favor of either motive would be "a choosing as you please;" by that very accordance it becomes the preferred motive, the, strongest motive, the prevalent motive, the what you think best, the greatest apparent good, etc., etc. Similarly necessitarianism has appropriated to its own fatalistic sense the formula that the volitional power wills as it wills.

Both these formulæ, when used by freedomists as phrases of freedom, mean to exclude every extraneous necessitation or law of invariability to a sole volition, and to affirm that the source of the Will's action is its own self-contained, independent power. The Will, thereby, it is said, wills not as something else wills or causes it to will, but as its own intrinsic alternative power; it wills as itself alone wills or pleases. In this last term *wills,* the very unnecessitated free forthgoing of the act, unlike an act of any other cause, was intuitively recognized by the speaker as intrinsic in its very conception. This recognition of intrinsic free spontaneity, in contrast with the inalternativity of mechanical action, in the very conception of Will induced also the phrase that the agent acted as he willed or pleased. This is a phraseology used by the ancient writers with the unquestionable purpose of excluding the idea of unitary necessitation.

NECESSITARIANS CAUGHT

But the necessitarians caught at the phrase "wills as it pleases," interpreted it to mean duplicate volitions ad infinitum; and the phrases have been abandoned. Over this abandonment necessitarians indulge a jubilation. "The old advocates of the self-determining power," says Dr. Pond, "used to admit freely that the mind chooses because it will choose; it puts forth voluntary" (volitional) "exercises, because it will put them forth. But our modern defenders of this kind of liberty have grown more wary. They are afraid, as they well may be, of Jonathan Edwards." And, doubtless, as the pillaging process goes on, by which necessitarians capture through special definitions the nomenclature of freedom, not only the terms freedom, self-determination, but any words or phrases we can invent, as alternativity, counter power, etc., may be loaded with a fatalistic meaning and compelled to surrender. We may then be "wary" and chary of their use, and task our power to invent new unequivocations, which in turn may have to undergo the same dexterous verbal petit larcenies.

So Origen is quoted by Edwards from Whitby[1] as saying, "the soul acts by her own choice, and it is free for her to incline to whatever part

1. Daniel Whitby (1638–1726) was an English clergyman and theologian in the

she will." With Origen for the soul thus to "incline" or will as she wills, is to will independently of any anterior necessitation, or of anything but the Will. Thus also Justin Martyr is quoted by Whitby as saying, "We Christians do not think as do the Stoics, that all things are done according to fate; but that every man does well or ill according to the freedom of his will or choice." In this expression Justin, without doubt, includes in the doing well or ill the volition itself; and that volition is accordant with the freedom of the Will. Even Whitby himself says that liberty is a power of acting from ourselves, or doing what we will; where the acting and the doing both include the volition, and the phrase *we will* excludes the control of any power but Will. This sort of phraseology is verbally inexact; but there can be no doubt that it was intended when used, not merely by Whitby, but by the fathers of the Christian Church for the first three centuries, to express the exclusion of necessitation from the Will in its volitional action. But what will, in the minds of many, cover their errors with excuse, is the fact that both the elder and the younger Edwards, as well as jubilant Dr. Pond, were guilty of the oversight of calling a volition a voluntary act; whereas it is the corporeal act consequent upon the volition that is voluntary, and not the volition itself.

We find a vicious circle in Dr. Samuel Clarke's formula that the last dictate of the understanding decides the Will.[2] Undoubtedly the Will decides immediately after the last mental act previous to its volition. The fact that the Will decides renders the previous mental state or act last. But so far from being true that the last previous mental state decides the volition, the truth is that it is through the volition that the agent decides which is the last. That dictate of the understanding becomes the last by act of the Will. The Will decides not only the which, but the when; and by deciding the when, it renders the immediately previous the last. It is not then that the last dictate of the understanding decides the Will; it is the Will that causes the dictate to be last.

The phrases used to indicate a previous mental making up that necessitates the volition elucidate nothing. That antecedent making up of the mind is itself, in its terminal point, volitional; being simply a predetermination or resolution that at the proper moment a given volition shall be put forth. That is, it is a previous volition that I will subsequently put

Church of England and known for his strong anti-Calvinist tendencies

2. Samuel Clarke, *A Discourse Concerning the Being and Attributes of God* (Glasgow: Printed for Richard Griffin and Co., 1823), 90.

forth another volition. What is commonly meant by this making up of the mind, is the comparative survey through the intellectual and moral faculties and feelings of the alternatives and a decision by the Will, settling the question by the formation of a purpose or standard determination, the nature of which is discussed in the proper place in this book.

To say that we will as we choose is to make one volition accord with a previous volition. To say with Professor Lawrence that we will as we "wish,"[3] inasmuch as that wish is a fixed object secured by anterior necessitation, is to fasten the Will again to an iron post. We often will as we know we ought, not as we wish.

GIVEN VOLITION

It is said that the judgment, a given volition, is on the whole best and is what the Will necessarily chooses. But, alas! Every feeling claims that its alternative is on the whole the best. Desire, if relying listened to, affirms that its object is best of all, and best on the whole. Conscience, the moral feeling, affirms that the right course is on the whole best. Expediency affirms that the most profitable course is on the whole best. Aesthetic affirms that its beautiful object is best on the whole. A previous choice or a wish affirms itself best on the whole. Reason, judgment, affirms that a rational course is on the whole best. These are all parties, and none are final judges. Among them all, the man makes his choice, and that choice is the true decision of the contest, the first and last strike of the balance.

Professor Haven, after having subjected all our volitions to causation by anterior choice, and all choice to causation by anterior circumstances, considers the question: How then can we exercise a responsible power over our future volitions? To this he makes this ludicrous reply: that it can be done "by shaping your character, which is under your control." Shape your previous character, that is, to higher good and your future volitions may be directed to higher good. But on his doctrine of my having in the past exercised the solely possible volitions, any different shaping of my character has been out of my power. I can neither in the past nor the future rise to any higher level of volitions than a fossil reptile imbedded in a rock could rise to a higher stratum.

Our conclusion is that neither any antecedent intrinsic strength of motive or class of motives, nor an antecedent standard of accordance,

3. Lawrence, "The Old School in New England Theology," 324.

can be assigned as furnishing a limitative law of the action of Will to sole result. But if the choice or sequence of volition is regulated by no Law, it is replied, it must be lawless and out of nature, a mere thing of chance. And this will be said not only by those who claim the Will to be controlled in its sequences by necessary causation, but by those who affirm invariable sequences and are ready to deny that such invariability has the quality of Law.

If we reply, Law in all cases must be held to determine the particular consequence of the antecedent in all possible sequences, if it is such an expression of the order of sequence as that the consequence in the sequence is ever and always individually fixed, then it must be admitted that counter alternative choice must be a choice outside of Law. But if Law may be defined as an expression or description of the true nature of all sequences, then an alternative choice is ever within Law. When before the Agent there are the alternatives B, C, or D, the agent is circumscribed by Law to these alternatives, but not by Law to a sole one. That is the full extent of the Law in the case. The non-resultance of rejected possible volitions is not a case of Lawlessness, for Lawlessness is the absence or default of Law where there should be Law, and is contrary to the nature of things. But such non-result is a case of limitation of the actual extension of Law existing in the true and essential nature of things.

VIII

Schematism of Conscious Free Will

PERSONALITY, PERSONAL IDENTITY, OR Self, is a simple substratum, directly known or intuited by the consciousness, which no analysis can explain. Nor can we explain how to the self, as to a center or nucleus, the faculties exist. All the facts that present themselves to our experiential observation may, however, be stated in proper sequence.

1. By consciousness we note the operations of our own mind, and learn to classify them into intellections, sensibilities, and volitions. 2. We are, from direct cognition, compelled to admit the existence of a central self or soul, which consciousness calls "I." 3. We are with equal irresistibility compelled to admit that for each specific class of our classified mental operations there is a power or ground upon which they are based, which we call a Faculty. 4. Consciousness finds in her *I* a sense of appropriation by which the self claims all the operations and faculties to be its own. Of the operations, the conscious self says, I feel, I will, I think; and the same conscious self says, My sensibility, My intellect, My will. 5. As in the self there is found a sense of receptivity by which certain operations are recognized as incoming, such as the sensations and impressions; so others are felt to be outgoing, as the perceptions, affections, passions, and desires. 6. But, besides both these classes, there is what we call a sense of the free activity, by which we feel that not only the act goes forth by a capability but is put forth from the central self power. So that all our mental operations are threefold, either incoming, outgoing, or forthputting.[1] And in

---

1. Dr. Day in opposition to the claim that action is attributable to Will alone, asks, "Is there no activity in the passions?" Or in "reading?" Or "thinking?" There may be action, we reply, that is forthgoing action; but there is *forthputting action* only just so far as there is Will or volition, separately, or blended with the other action. Jeremiah Day, *An Inquiry Respecting the Self-Determining Power of the Will or Contingent Volition* (New Haven: Herrick and Noyes, 1838), 161.

this feeling of forthputting there is the half-latent, yet diffusive sub-sense that in such putting forth there is exercised the creative, directive power, including the equally possible withholding. For of the directing, shaping, and creating of the volition, the possible withholding is in fact a part. So that the full amount of the sense of putting forth is, that it is done with the full power of otherwise doing or not doing. There is a freedom both to and from the act. 7. The volition so put forth is claimed by the self to be preeminently its own; for its putting forth as it is or withholding, the self acknowledges the unique commensurate responsibility.

THE ISSUE AND ARGUMENT

We have thus far, as our Part First, stated the nature of the freedom of the Will as opposed to Volitional Necessity, and as required, in our estimation, by the doctrine of Responsibility. The form of the argument upon this issue is this. Through our Part Second, assuming the reality of this Freedom, we show that it is not invalidated by the Necessitarian Argument; and in our Part Third that it is established by its own Affirmative Argument.

The Necessitarian Argument Considered

SECTION I

The Causational Argument

I

The Necessitarian Paralogism

I T HAS BEEN SAID that the sum total of the arguments for necessity, especially in the treatise of President Edwards on the Will, consists in the
application in all its phases of the axiom that "every event has its cause."
But perhaps a closer analysis will show that the necessitarian argument
is founded not upon this axiom, but upon the assumption of another
proposition that is neither equivalent to this axiom, nor in itself axiomatic and self-evident, nor justifiably assumed without proof, namely, the
proposition that "every cause is nonalternative or unipotent"; that is, that
every cause will produce but one sole possible effect, to wit, that effect
which always follows, and no other.

It is implied that, in volitions or physics, for every infinitesimal point
of effect there must be the correlative sole infinitesimal point of cause and
vice versa. This is identical with the ordinary physical maxim that "like
causes produce like effects." This maxim is the precise contradiction of
the proposition that "some causes (namely, volitional causes) are alternatives or pluripotent"; that is, "capable of putting forth either of several
effects." Now the assumption of the above necessitarian proposition is the
assumption of the whole point in question. If it were granted, the whole
discussion is foreclosed before it starts.

That the maxim that "every cause is unipotent" is not self-evident;
that it is not, like the maxim that "every event has a cause," granted by
every honest and intelligent mind as soon as its terms are fairly understood and fully weighed, may appear from the following consideration.
Let us suppose the existence of two or more individuals so precisely alike
in all qualities of character, that in a given set of circumstances, they are
each a reduplication or repetition of precisely a similar volitional experiment. If there is within them the power of alternative choice, there is no
proof, from the nature of the cause (though there may be assumption),

that each will put forth precisely the same volition. And this not because of any chance, but from the most opposite principle—the mysterious responsible *self*. It is from the fact that, however alike, each is a distinct responsible Ego; and that in each responsible self is the equal power of alternative choice.

We can recollect but one passage in which Edwards hits upon the thought of directly proving, as well as assuming, that a volitional cause is unipotent; and even in that, as usual, he assumes the point to be proved. Omitting clauses irrelevant to the present purposes, and directed to a point to be hereafter discussed, we quote the passage: "That the soul, though an active substance, cannot diversify its own acts . . . is manifest by this, that if so, then the same cause, the same causal power, force, or influence, without variation in any respect, would produce different effects at different times." (79) That is, if the soul can diversify its own acts, the same cause, in possession of the same power, can produce diverse effects; in other words, if the soul can diversify it can diversify; if free Will is, then it is. We avow both antecedent and consequence, both being the same. Our view (which seems not to be invalidated by the above argument) implies that in the soul is a sum of power, by different exertions of which it can produce different acts. The soul, with its power, is "without any variation in any respect" until the initial instant of such exerting. The power for either exertion is power for either act; and the soul, in view of a given set of motives, possesses one sum of sufficient power for either.

EDWARDS ADDS

"But if it be so," Edwards adds, "that the soul has no different causality or diverse causal force in producing these diverse effects, then it is evident that the soul has no influence, no hand in the diversity of the effect, and the difference of the effect cannot be owing to anything in the soul, or which is the same thing, the soul does not determine the diversity of the effect." (79) That is, if it is not by a diverse causal power in the soul that the diverse effect is produced, then it is produced by nothing in the soul. Why not? Why may it not be produced by the same causal power in the soul, and yet be produced by "something in the soul?" We should suppose that the two things not only could agree, but also were identical. If there be, as we affirm, in the soul the power of producing either of several effects, then that same singular, or unchanged power, can "determine the diversity of the effect," can fix which effect shall exist, and either effect would be from something in the soul.

Why, according to Edwards, does the soul require diverse causalities, or causative powers, to produce diverse effects? Plainly because a single causality, or causal agent, can produce only a single and sole effect, is unipotent. How is it shown that a single causality is capable of but a single effect? By assumption only of the thing to be proved. And this is the bottom, the fundamental assumption on which necessitarianism is based. This it does not prove, but takes for granted, and uses to prove the system. But it is, also the sum total of the system itself; so that the system is assumed to prove itself. The premise and the proposition are identical—an elaborate paralogism.

It is no doubt undeniable that if all cause is unipotent, then any supposed diverse effect is superfluous, and so causeless. Causation then runs in single direct lineages; and every event lying out of the inevitable direct line is parentless, and cut off from possibility. If every cause has its one sole possible effect, any other supposable effect is one too many; it is severed from any cause, and drifts loose in the world. Now Edwards first assumes unipotence to prove diverse effect causeless and then proves unipotence by the causelessness of diverse effect.

We also make our counter assumption. In our very definition of freedom of Will we assume in the volitional sphere the inapplicability of the maxim that "like causes ever and always produces like effects." We assume that either one of several effects is legitimate from the same cause. And while we admit that in non-volitional causation the law that "every event must have a cause," means that every event must have its own peculiar cause, adequate for itself alone, in volitional causation an event may have a cause adequate either for it or for other events; and whichever event exists, the demands of the laws of causation are completely satisfied. If these assumptions, made in the First Part of our treatise, can hold good against the objections met in the Second, they will scarce need the affirmative argument of our Third to establish their validity forever.

II

Cause of Particular Volition

AGAINST ALTERNATIVE CAUSATION THE main amount of necessitarian argument may be reduced to the four following questions:

I. What causes the Will to act?

II. What causes it to put forth the particular volition; or the particular volition rather than another?

III. Why does the volition (or rather *nolition*) for which there was adequate cause not take existence?

IV. What cause for this contingent diversity of happenings (by which result for which there is adequate cause) does and does not take existence?

These questions we shall consider in their order.

I. To the preliminary question: What causes the Will to act? It is competent to reply that every agent in his proper conditions is under a general necessity of action, even while free in the particular choice. Thus an agent with three alternatives before him must choose one of the three or refuse to choose either. But this refusal is but a fourth alternative, and the refusing act or nolition is as true a volition as either of the three. So that the necessity is that he is compelled to take some one of the four; the freedom lies in his equal power of selecting either one of the four.

II. But what causes the Will to put forth the particular volition and no other? This is the crucial question that constitutes, it is supposed, the vital force of the entire necessitarian argument, which it claims as the unanswerable point, and by the complete answer of which it must confess itself conquered. "The question," says Edwards:

> is not so much, How a spirit endowed with activity comes to act, as
> Why it exerts such an act and not another, or why it acts with such

70

a particular determination. If activity of nature is the cause why a spirit (the soul of man, for instance) acts and does not lie still, yet that alone is not the cause why its action is thus and thus limited, directed, and determined. Active nature is a general thing; it is an ability or tendency of nature to action, generally taken, which may be a cause why the soul acts as occasion or reason is given; but this alone cannot be a sufficient cause why the soul exerts such a particular act, at such a time, rather than others.[1] (77)

So also Dr. Day in his work on the Will:

> Some writers speak of the power of willing, as being the sole and sufficient cause why the mind wills one way rather than another. But it is evident that the mere power of willing is not, of itself alone, even the reason why a man wills at all, unless the term power be used in the broad and unusual sense which includes every antecedent on which his willing depends. Is a man's power to walk the only reason why he actually walks? Does a man always speak when he has the power to speak?[2]
>
> But whatever may be assigned as the reason why he wills at all, the main inquiry will still return upon us: Why does the mind will one way rather than another? Why does it choose one object rather than its opposite? An equal power to will any way indifferently, is not surely the only ground of willing one way rather than another.[3]

To this we reply, 1. Though a general activity or power is a general thing, and accounts only for action generally, yet a particular power or cause is a particular thing and accounts for a particular action; and moreover an alternative power or cause is an alternative thing, and accounts

---

1. We shall here note, as in many other instances, how preposterous the pretense that Edward does not teach necessity, but only certainty. Edwards here argues that the motive sustains to the particular volition the absolute relation of cause and effect. It is necessary in order to the existence of the particular volition; and when it exists *it not only negatively renders other volition causeless and impossible, but it positively secures, causes, and necessitates the particular volition.* If there be any certainty distinct from necessity, this is not that *certainty* but *necessity.* There can be no stronger proof that Edwards excludes not merely the use but the existence of contrary power. His necessity is *certainty* just because *his certainty is necessity.*

2. Jeremiah Day, *An Inquiry Respecting the Self-Determining Power of the Will or Contingent Volition,* 47.

3. Ibid. 48.

for the coming into existence of either one of several effects. And that is the thing to be accounted for, and so at once and for all the crucial question is answered.[4*]

IMPERFECT CAUSE

"A general activity" or cause is an imperfect cause inadequate to any specific effect without the addition of some further causal or conditional element to render it particular and possibly resultant. When it is thus made specific and possibly causative of particular effect, the question may still remain to be settled not à priori, but experientially whether the cause be unipotential or adequate to an effect solely possible, or whether it may account for either one of several results.

And in the latter case the existence of the single result and the non-existence of the others are as truly accounted for as in the former. For a cause capable of either effect is in nature as in our definition, the cause of whichever effect results. If consciousness cognizes a class of causes of which each one is a sufficient cause for either of several effects exclusive of opposite effect, then whichever effect results has a sufficient cause for its existence excluding all effects contradictory to itself. If there be a cause as fully sufficient for either of several effects as a unipotent cause is of its own sole effect, then whichever effect results has as sufficient, as full, as complete and adequate a cause as any physical or necessary effect whatsoever.

2. Every cause, like every other thing, is to be tested by the conditions of its own existence and nature. A unipotent cause is to be held to the conditions of its own nature. An alternative cause also must be held only to the conditions of its own nature; it cannot be held impossible because it does not comply with the conditions of unipotent cause. If a cause is by the condition of its own nature sufficient for either one of several effects, then either one of those several effects may be brought into

---

4. "The particular determination is accounted for in the very quality or attribute of the cause. In the case of a physical cause, the particular determination is accounted for in the quality of the cause, which quality is to be necessarily correlated to the object. In the case of Will the particular determination is accounted for in the quality of the cause, which quality is to have the power to make the particular determination without being necessarily correlated to the object."

This thought was, we believe, first introduced into the discussion in Henry Tappan, *A Review of Edwards's 'Inquiry into the Freedom of the Will'* (New York: J.S. Taylor, 1839)

existence in accordance with the conditions of the nature of that cause without requiring it to fulfill the conditions of another kind of cause. Now the necessitarian repudiates the alternative cause because that fulfills not the conditions of unipotent cause. He infers that because a unipotent cause cannot produce other effects than one without the introduction of a new antecedent, therefore an alternative cause cannot; and therefore an alternative cause cannot exist.

But experience may show a class of causes from which either one of several effects may result, without the introduction of any new antecedent. In such a case, therefore, to demand a new antecedent, that is, to ask what causes the particular volition, or what prevents the counter, is illegitimate. It is to require conditions not belonging to the nature of the subject.

And this reasoning is good for whichever of the several alternatives occurs: for C as for B or A. If C results, then the assignment of an alternative cause of which C is a possible alternative effect, is just as true an accounting for C as if it were the result for which we can assign a general cause rendered unipotent by the addition of the requisite causal condition. The same assignment is as good for B or A as alternative results of the same alternative cause.

3. Let us divide all causes into partial and complete, adequate or sufficient. A partial cause is that antecedent, or number of antecedents, necessary to a given effect, but insufficient to the effect without some further element added. It needs something to cause it to produce the effect. Thus powder is but a partial cause of flame, but not an adequate or complete one. And it is properly asked what causes the powder to produce the flame, and the proper answer is the spark. The rail car is a partial cause of locomotion; and when it is asked what causes it to move, the answer is the steam power. A complete, sufficient, or adequate cause comprehends all the constituents requisite to the effect. The adequate cause existing, the effect is possible to exist. Thus the powder and the spark combined are a complete cause of the flame; the car and the steam power produce motion. It is absurd to ask or assign any additional cause for the existence of the effect of a complete and adequate cause. For the complete cause, with all its plural constituents, produces its effect uncausedly, though there may have been influences previously. The complete cause existing, the existence of the effect is finally accounted for. Requiring additional cause

73

would be asking what causes cause to cause? What causes causation? The cause exists and the effect arises; and that is the ultimate.

Now of its own effect, *Will*, in its proper conditions, is not a partial, but a full and adequate cause. Put your finger upon any effect (volition) and ask, What caused this result exclusively of the others? And the reply is, The Will, or the agent in willing. Ask then what fully caused the Will in its conditions to cause the volition and the reply is, nothing. However, in the case of the volitional decision to repent, God's prevenient grace does exert an enabling influence on the will. John vi, 44; xvi, 8-9. An influence is not the same as a determining cause or partial cause. The will is still free to go in alternate directions.

GRACE OF GOD

Furthermore, the grace of God frees the Will from being completely bound by sin since the Fall, but it does not determine or cause which way the Will volitionally decides. Even for a pagan, the Will is free to choose between sin, relative human good or repenting to become a Christian.

Or if the question is: In general, why did the Will in equipoise choose thus rather than otherwise? The reply is, because the Will was a complete and adequate cause for that choice rather than another; and when an adequate cause is assigned the Why is answered. In nonalternative causation, the Why is indeed to be answered by furnishing the additional element that renders the cause adequate. In alternative causation there is no need of furnishing additional causality, for by its nature alternative cause furnishes adequacy for either; and for either over, or rather than, the other. In either alternative or non-alternative causation, when the sufficient and adequate cause is assigned, there is an end of all questions, the "whys"? "wherefores"? and "what causes"?

It is in fact not true that "a general power" is truly the power—that is, the power adequate to the effect. It is only part of such a power, and must wait until the other part is supplied before it is the power relatively to the effect. When, in the proper sense, the power exists, the effect is accounted for. If a unipotent power, the one effect is accounted for; if an alternative power, either result is accounted for. If the unipotent cause exists, the solely possible effect must result. If the alternative cause exists, either alternative effect may result, and one of the several must. And these two exhaust all causality and all eventualities.

III. But be it admitted that a full and perfect cause accounts for the particular volition transpiring; was there not also a full and perfect cause for the counter volition? If so, what was the cause of its not coming to pass? If the alternative Will is capable of either of several effects, what causes an alternate effect?

If this has not been satisfactorily answered in the preceding remarks, consider the following points:

1. A particular volition implies and includes not only the actuality of itself, but the negation of the counter volition. Particularity coming into existence is itself exclusive of all those counter. Hence, if the actual particular volition is accounted for, the non-existence of the counter is accounted for, and the whole is accounted for.

2. The same reply is ready to be given for the rejection of the counter as for the actual particular volition. The said rejection is then to be viewed as the volitional act to be accounted for; and the same reason is to be given. The Will in its proper conditions is a full and perfect cause for the volitional act in question, namely, the rejection of the counter.

3. Our very definition of a free Will is, a power of choosing in a given direction, with a full power of choosing otherwise. Now the rejection of a counter for which there is full power, in giving forth the actual, is included in the very idea of a free Will. To deny the possibility of this is to assume the point in question. Thomas Hobbes wrote:

> I hold that to be a sufficient cause to which nothing is wanting to the producing of the effect. The same is a necessary cause. For if it were possible that a sufficient cause shall not bring forth the effect, then there wanteth somewhat that was needful to the producing of it, and so the cause was not sufficient; but if it is possible that a sufficient cause should not produce the effect, then is a sufficient cause a necessary cause. Hence it is manifest that whatsoever is produced is produced necessarily; for whatsoever is produced hath had a sufficient cause to produce it, or else it had not been, and therefore also voluntary actions are necessitated.[5]

That, we are here told, "is a sufficient cause to which nothing is wanting to the producing the effect." That is, in other words, an adequate volitional cause is one to which no power is wanting for the forthputting of effect. It is a true proposition. But it does not necessarily follow that this adequate cause will be a resultant cause as we have noted in the Second

5. Thomas Hobbes, *A Letter About Liberty and Necessity*, 8–9.

of our Postulates: "The same is a necessary cause." Not granted; but let us hear his reason why it is "necessary." "For if it be possible that a sufficient cause shall not bring forth the effect, then—what follows? It follows, we think, and is true, that there may be a sufficient or adequate cause which does not put forth "the effect"; that is, the given sole nonalternative effect. It follows as we have stated in our Postulates, that there may be a volitional adequate cause for an effect not resultant in that effect, but in some other effect for which it was equally adequate.

But Hobbes's inference is, "then there wanteth somewhat which was needful to the producing of it, and so the cause was not sufficient." It is not admitted from the fact "that a sufficient cause shall not bring forth the effect" that "then somewhat" of power, sufficiency, or cause was wanting, "so that the cause was not sufficient."

It merely follows (according to our Canon III) that "Non-occurring volitions do not prove non-existence of adequate cause. Not for every no-volition is there a no adequate cause." For an alternative cause may non-produce an effect for which it is sufficient, by producing the other effect for which it is equally sufficient. What is "wanting" for the non-produced effect is not power, but (Postulate IV) exertion of power.

SUFFICIENT CAUSE

A sufficient cause, Mr. Hobbes argues, uniformly produces; for if it ever produce not, it is not a sufficient cause, and being uniform it is necessary. Substitute our other term, namely, adequate cause; and let us say: A free, conscious, adequate cause does not uniformly produce the required possible result; for there may not be a particular result, and yet the cause be consciously adequate; hence an adequate cause is not always a necessary, but often a non-necessary, alternative free cause. Hobbes will then have stated the necessary causation of physics; we shall have stated the free causation of Will.

The argument of Hobbes is essentially adopted by the Princeton Essayist: "If it (the contrary choice) is not made, then those conditions were wanting in it [the Will] as a cause which were indispensable to the effect, and in the absence of which it was not adequate to the effect." (254) This assumes, with Hobbes, that there are no "sufficient" or adequate yet non-resultant causes; and that the absence of volitional result is demonstrative proof of the absence of volitional power.

Edwards uses an argument somewhat similar, drawn from the necessary dependence of the effect upon the cause. "If," says he, "the event be not connected with the cause it is not dependent on the cause; its existence is, as it were, loose from its influence, and may attend it or not, it being a mere contingence[6*] whether it follows or attends the influence of the cause or not, and that is the same thing as not to be dependent on it. . . . So far as an event is dependent on the cause and connected with it, so much causality there is in the cause and no more."

That all effects necessarily depend upon their causes, and if they exist are necessarily connected with their causes, no one denies. 1. Every physical cause and effect are so necessarily connected that with either existing, the other exists. 2. It is admitted that in the order of nature, so soon as a thing begins to exist, so far as it does exist, it necessarily exists, since it is impossible for the thing done to become not done. This necessity is consequent and subsequent in the order of nature to the existence. 3. It is granted that every volitional effect which comes into existence is "connected with its cause," is "dependent on its cause," derives its existence from its cause, and would not exist as it does without the cause. 4. But it is not admitted conversely, that the volitional cause depends on the effect, so but that it can exist in all its fullness and completeness, without producing that effect; or that it is necessitated to the effect. The proof is demanded that an agent cannot exist with full power to an act, without performing that act. The proof is demanded, but has never been furnished, that an agent may not be a sufficient or adequate cause without being a resultant cause.

If it is said that a cause without an effect is no cause at all, it is again merely a verbal argument. We may define cause to be that in which power to the effect exists, and the argument is voided. We may affirm that a cause potential to an effect it does not produce is still to be called thereto a cause.

IV. But, finally, if adequate causes are not uniformly and necessarily resultant, if adequate cause sometimes produces and sometimes produces not, or what is the same thing, can be conceived as producing or not pro-

---

6. Let the reader note here that Edwards places volitional causation on precisely the same ground as mechanical. There is no "contrary power," no mere "certainty," no "always can but never will cause otherwise." Alterability is non-dependence of effect upon cause; it is "a mere contingence," that is, "no cause." The dependence is just commensurate with the causality. Nothing can with more mathematical accuracy exclude "contrary power."

ducing an alternative effect, necessitarianism holds all to be at loose ends. It asks, What cause for this contingent diversity of happenings (by which result for which there is adequate cause) does and does not take place? Thus Edwards says,

> If there be any event which was not necessarily connected with the influence of the cause under such circumstances, then it was contingent whether it would attend or follow the influence of the cause or no; it might have followed and it might not when the cause was the same, its influence the same, and under the same circumstances. And if so, why did it follow rather than not follow? There is no cause or reason for this . . . What can be the cause or reason of this strange phenomenon, even this diversity, that in one instance the effect should follow, in another not? It is evident by the supposition that this is wholly without any cause or ground. Here is something in the present manner of the existence of things and state of the world that is absolutely without a cause. (112)

Doubtless this is a melancholy "manner of the existence of things and state of the world"; and perhaps our reply will in no degree relieve it. For, 1. It seems a little hard to be required to furnish a cause—that is, a general and uniform cause—for a diversity, we might say an infinite diversity, of particulars. Diversities countless in number may have a countless number of particular causes, tedious as well as difficult to enumerate. 2. To the argument of, How can the diversity found in alternatives be accounted for, we return a retort. How can we account for the uniformity found in unipotency? How can cause be necessitated to one effect? What forbids alternative effects, and limits and binds and imprisons cause down to one result? Here is a thing to be accounted for "in the present manner of the existence of things and the state of the world" which no man has ever yet accounted for. That includes this uniformity—this unipotency—by which every particular causality, physical and spiritual, finite and infinite, is fastened to one solely possible effect.

FOUND THE FASTENER

And when we have found the fastener, what fastens the fastener? The chain of fate fastens all things, but what fastens the chain of fate? If over the entire whole of things, through immensity and through eternity, the iron casement of necessity is fast bound, to tighten everything in its place, what holds the particles of the casement in cohesion, and what tightens the tightener? What necessitates necessity? The casement needs another iron layer, and another in an infinite series of adamantine strata; and is then never secure, for there must be no outside layer. For what holds the outside stratum, and what holds the whole infinity of adamantine strata in cohesion? What holds the essence of deity together, or gives omnipotence its strength, and causation its causality?

In short, alternatives are as easily accounted for as unipotence, diversity as uniformity. It is as easy telling how cause diverges as converges. A priori both are equally difficult and equally easy. One can be accounted for as much and as little as the other. Both can be accounted for by the same verbal solution. The uniformity as well as the diversity must be verbally accounted for by saying, Such is the nature of the case—there are two classes of causes; in one lies the power, I know not how, to terminate in one sole effect; in the other, I know not how, lies the power of terminating in either of several effects. And thus the necessitarian is answered by being shown that his own doctrine involves all the difficulties he objects to us. And since it is agreed that these difficulties are not recognized as such by any reason or philosophy, the arguments of necessity, based on causation, disappear.

There remains one causational argument more by which President Edwards maintains the necessity of volitions, and which will require but a brief consideration. Every effect, he argues, is necessary; being absolutely produced and modified by its cause. Volitions are an effect; and as such are passively modified, and therefore absolutely necessary.[7*]

Now this may be fully granted without at all touching the question of the freedom of the agent who produces the volition. A volition, as a fact brought into existence, has indeed no freedom. It must take existence as it is brought into existence. It is a produced entity, and not a living principle. It did not make itself, and could not prevent its own existence, or make itself otherwise. But the liberty resides in the free agent, who was able to produce that or other volition instead. It does not follow that because the volition must come into existence just as the agent brings it into existence, that therefore the agent cannot bring it any otherwise into existence, or could not have brought forth another volition instead. The necessity comes into existence after the free causation, which brings both the necessity and the volition into being together. A free volition is so

---

7. Let the reader note that this argument assumes pure necessity; not any mere certainty in any sense distinct from inalternative causational necessity.

called, not because, as an abstract caused fact, it has intrinsic freedom, but because it is brought into existence by a free causal agent.

So also reasons the Younger Edwards: "Unless they (events) take place absolutely without a cause they are effects; and every effect necessarily follows its cause." (1: 398) If the phrase, "necessarily follows its cause," means that the effect truly takes the shape and quality derived from its causation, it is true; but this proves not that other effect instead may not have been produced by an alternative causal power, adequate to the other effect instead. He further reasons, "if the mind cause its own volitions it necessitates them into existence" (1:399); but that proves not that the mind is necessitated to necessitate them into that particular form or specimen of existence.

The same error of locating the freedom in the act as it receives existence from its cause, instead of in the free agent, is committed in the Princeton Essayist, who makes it the foundation of a fallacious argument: "If such an action as is possessed of such qualities, and no other, is free, it follows that if a given choice be free it must be such an action and no other." That is, a free act must be just such an act as it is and no other, and is therefore necessary. But we reply, that makes no difference with regard to the freedom of the agent, whose freedom consists in the power for this or for either of several other acts. Whichever act he produces must indeed be just such an act as it is and no other—it must be itself and nothing else; it must be free and not necessitated; but that does not prove that the agent could not produce other acts instead.

If the reply is that still the agent must be possessed of certain qualities and no other, the reply is true, but worthless. The agent must, in order to be a free agent, possess the quality of freedom. In other words, it is logically necessary in order to his being a free agent that he be a free agent. Whatever is, is.

The writer adds: "In order to freedom in the manner and quality of an action there must be a necessity as to its event; a necessity that it be as it is and not otherwise." If this means that there is necessity in the agent to produce but that sole event it is denied. If it means that the event must take existence as the agent causes it to receive existence, it is true but worthless. A dead fact cannot possess power to unmake, transform, or substitute itself; nor does any theory we have maintained attribute to it such power.

In the same paragraph this writer affirms, as a "fundamental position of Calvinism," that "in respect to the choices of moral agents there is freedom as to the manner, and necessity or fixedness as to the event." But, we ask, is there any less fixedness or necessity according to necessitarianism in the "manner" than in the "event"? Does not necessitarianism as truly limit the mode as the fact? Would not an act performed in a different manner be a different act? If there be a greater freedom in the choice of the manner than the act, would that not require two choices for every act, one for the manner and one for the act? Or what kind of a freedom is that which consists in performing a fixed act in a manner as fixed as the event?

If there be no self-determining power in the manner of the action, no power of alteration of manner of action, no power of contrary choice, then there can be no more fixedness or necessity in the event than in the manner, and no more freedom in the manner than in the event. And if the fixedness and necessity of the event are the antithesis and exclusive of freedom in the event, then that same fixedness and necessity are the exclusive of freedom in the manner. Both in the event and in the manner, then, there must be a necessity excluding freedom.

CAUSAL MAXIM

Leibniz[8] had a variation of the causal maxim upon which he much prided himself, namely, that "nothing takes place without a sufficient reason." Herein he misuses the last word of the maxim, "reason," by transferring it from the subjective to the objective. A reason is not the external or physical antecedent of the result. It is always something within the mind. When not a motive for a volition, it is a premise for a conclusion, or an internal accounting for, perhaps an external fact, by the mental assignment of its external cause. Yonder water wheel, whirled by a stream, is not whirled by a reason; it is not so reasonable a being as to be moved by any reason whatever. The water is not a stream of reason; it brings not a reason to bear upon the wheel. But when I am asked why the wheel revolves, I assign the fact, that the cause, water, exists, to account for the fact that the revolution exists. That is one fact, the existence of the wheel, taken into the mind as premise or reason, enables me to see that another

8. Gottfried Liebniz (1646–1716) was a German rationalist and mathematician who wrote on a wide variety of subjects.

fact, the revolution, is a commensurate result. The perception of the fact is a reason for the affirmation of the conclusion.

But in volitional language there is a reason for action, which is not a cause. The cause is the agent or Will; the reason is that on account of which the agent acts or wills. To class this reason under the term cause is the gross sophism of Edwards; to class it under the same term as cause is made to bear, is the more delicate but just as deceptive sophism of Leibniz.

As to the maxim, Nothing takes place without a sufficient reason, let us ask, What is the sufficient reason for a sufficient reason's being necessary? What is the sufficient reason for a sufficient reason's accounting for everything? What is the sufficient reason for a cause producing effect? By what sufficient reason is all cause limited to one sole effect? What is the sufficient reason why the march of cause and effect never stands still? If every cause is limited in physics to one sole effect, what sufficient reason is there that a volitional cause may not produce either of several possible effects? And if either one of said possible effects results, what is the sufficient reason why that cause should not be adequate cause and sufficient reason for that effect?

These questions are properly answered by saying that mind must stop at the boundary line of experience and intuition. It must take laws and not attempt to throw anticipatory injunctions on the nature of things, nor try to project its inquiries beyond axioms and settled universal processes. Nothing takes place without a cause—without a sufficient reason being assignable. But suppose our experience and intuition affirm a sphere of conditions in which a one sufficient reason will account for either of several results; neither result would then eventuate without a sufficient reason; for either result actually eventuating, the actual sufficient reason is the amply accounting reason. Then as before, the mind must accept the laws and limitations that this experience and intuition impose. Questions must stop when our investigations strike against a wall of solid reality.

Leibniz's reply is: "A man never has a sufficient reason to act, when he has not also a sufficient reason to act in a certain particular manner." This is simply an authoritative assertion of the point in question; that is, it is a blank denial that there may be in condition a sufficient reason for either of several results. It is merely a statement of counter issue, for which we want and forever must want the argument.

III

Boundary Lines of the Unknown

T HE CONCLUSIVENESS OF OUR reasoning in the last chapter may appear more decisive if we duly consider what are the limitations of human knowledge, what questions in philosophy are legitimate, and of what questions no answer can be required because the answer lies in the domain of the Unknowable. It will be perhaps ascertained that no unanswerable question can be propounded to the side of Free Will that is not equally a poser for the side of necessity. The difficulties on both sides are identical, arising alike from our incapability of knowing the interior nature of causation.

Hamilton[1] affirms that Free Will is to be believed; although it cannot be conceived because the human mind cannot conceive the beginning of motion. For that same reason, we reply, necessity cannot be conceived; for we can no more conceive the initial point of effect springing forth out of a necessary cause, than of effect springing up from an alternative cause. Effect is ever born in darkness; and all movement is mystery. What has ever given to the cause of necessity an apparent victory has arisen from the fact that it has taken its turn to ask the question, *How*, just at the boundary line of that unknowable, which conceals the answer equally for both sides.

It is just as difficult to answer how unipotent cause is limited to one sole effect, as how alternative cause is capacitated to either of several effects. And when from the difficulty of answering this question, Edwards affirms that alternative effect is effect without cause, he forgets that unipotent effect is equally effect without cause. And when again Edwards assumes from the same difficulty that alternative volition can be put forth only by a subsidiary volition to fix its particularity, he forgets that unipotent causa-

---

1. Sir William Hamilton (1788–1856) was a Scottish metaphysical philosopher.

tion, whether finite or Infinite, requires a similar subsidiary causation to limit its unipotence and ascertain its fixed effect.

And this may be the place to notice a profound difficulty stated by Sir Hamilton against Cousin's theory of volitional freedom (which is essentially our own), that "divorcing liberty from intelligence, but connecting it with personality, he defines it to be a cause which is determined to act by its proper energy alone."[2] This may be an overstatement of the difficulty in our theory. By our doctrine of motive influence, as hereinafter stated, we profess to maintain a freedom that is not "divorced from intelligence." But letting that pass, our present purpose is to state the proper retort. All power is blind; all knowledge is impotent. How then, even in the constitution of the Infinite Being, does blind power recognize the dictates of intelligence and guide itself in absolute submission to its absolute impotence? Or how does the impotence subdue absolute power, which is unable to recognize its dictates, to its own control? Here, then, is a divorce of intelligence and force whose interaction, though they can never be explained, must ever be accepted.

PERSONALITY FORMS

If it were said that Personality forms the medium of transition by which power and intelligence come into contact, we rather reduplicate the difficulty. How do power and intelligence come into contact in the personality so that intelligence, which is impotent there, controls power; and power, which is blind, appreciates and obeys intelligence? And how does thought become fixed to substance so as to inhere? And how do the faculties fasten upon the self as upon a bare and rigid nucleus? We ask not these questions for their own sake. Their only purpose is to show that the difficulty is equal for necessity and for freedom. And yet if a complete answer be impossible, we may bring our conceptions perhaps as near as possible to a satisfactory state by the following statements:

1. By the division of faculties, admitted by modern necessitarians and by Sir Hamilton himself, into intellect, sensibilities and will, the Will is as truly divorced from feeling and intellection as by our doctrine of freedom. By that division the Will can neither think nor feel. It has neither eyes nor heart. It is simply a projectile lying between the opposite

2. Sir William Hamilton, *Discussions on Philosophy and Literature, Education and University Reform* (New York: Harper & Brothers, 1853), 43.

faculties to whose forces it yields with a mechanical exactness. It can never be explained how this blind insensate projectile, Will, is able to appreciate and know when the exact measure is furnished so as to obey it, nor how intelligence that is impotent can master and secure obedience. And then, assuming that this projectile may appreciate and obey, we can no better conceive it as appreciating a fixed measure and obeying with a mechanical spring, than as appreciating and obeying a variable measure with a contingent, living, freely selective elasticity, and from its own self-activity. Freedom is therefore no more a divorce of Will from intelligence than necessity.

2. Perhaps it further relieves the difficulty of a true conception to remember that this division is truly nothing else than a classification of operations of the single agent. Will therefore is simply a fact that an intelligent agent chooses, and that he has power so to do. Volitions are therefore intelligent acts, put forth not by a blind, but an intelligent cause. Nor does our view of freedom make them less intelligent than does necessity. We suppose the agent to act in full view of all that intellect or all that feeling can present, yet with a power lying in his nature of responsibly choosing and deciding for either of their presentations. Freedom, therefore, is again no more a divorce of Will from intelligence than necessity.

IV

Freedom Involves Not Atheism

IN AN ELOQUENT CHAPTER on the argument for Theism, Edwards maintains that inasmuch as alternatives of choice involves maintenance of an event without a cause, the logical result is Atheism. His followers, even to the present day, are accustomed, with an air of taunting classification, to tell us that Edwards demonstrated necessity against Arminians, Pelagians and Atheists.

The heroic hardiness that thus classifies freedomists with Atheists or infidels illustrates the proverb that "Fools fear nothing" to any man who will consider the fact that there is not perhaps a single unequivocal advocate for alternative Will on record in ancient ages or modern who was an Atheist.[1] And though Edwards has laid open the route and made its breadth conspicuous to the world, by which transition from freedom to Atheism is made, not the first man has ever been found to travel the road from either to the other, so as to become a sincere atheist as a result of his freedomism. The admission of the validity of the syllogism is not clearer from exception than the rejection of this logical transit. Nor do we need any better proof than this argument of the utter abstractness of its proposer, or any more clear illustration of the entire want of intuitive

---

1. Epicurus alone is a cited case to the contrary. Yet had Epicurus been like one of the Christian fathers, a desirable authority, how easily would Edwards have shown the identity of that philosopher's opinion with his own! The words of Lucretius expounding Epicurus, "ducit quemque voluptas," are a true equivalent of the Edwardean liberty, "doing as we please." That the Will is "fatis avolsa" implies merely its exemption from the line of purely physical causation. The *clinamen, or* bent of the Will, is expressly assigned by him as in the line of nonalternative causation, for the very causational reason assigned by Edwards:

> De nihilo quoniam fieri posse videmus—
> Nothing can spring from nothing.

sympathy that the intellect of Edwards, with all its acuteness, possessed with the true "universal common sense of mankind."

Enlarging our previous statement, we may now say that it will be very difficult to find exception to the rule that all Atheists, Pantheists, Materialists, and professed Fatalists are necessitarians. From Leucippus and Democritus, through Spinoza and Hume, down to d'Holbach and Comte, the whole mass, one and all, will agree with Edwards in maintaining the absolute universal necessitation of all events, whether volitional or non-volitional. The doctrine that one principle of causation or fixed invariable sequences rules all things, material or mental, and all events of Will or of physics, is central with the d'Holbachian Atheism and Edwardean Calvinism.

And at the present age especially, the same principle rules with that school of godless naturalism which threatens to overwhelm the thinking world with a base materialistic and lawless antichristianity. The very principle that Edwards and his followers endeavor to install in Christian theology, in order to rescue us from Atheism, is found by the mass of deniers of God, and immortality, and the soul, and the asserters of irresponsibility, and of death an eternal sleep, to be cognate to and congenial with their own unhallowed systems.

We assert no theory, no rule with exceptions, but a universal fact; a fact that demonstrates our results, that the entirety of that class of antichristian thinkers take the necessitarian side. They do so because logically and morally necessity belongs in their system, and freedom of the Will does not. The doctrine that there is no soul and no Will exempt from that same invariable sequence that rules the domains of physics, that there is no God who does not come under the same inflexible nonalternative law with matter, levels the whole into one system of fatalistic materialism. The subjection of human volitions to the same law eliminates responsibility, dispenses with retribution, divine government, and human immortality. And it is a memorable point in modern intellectual history, that when the European mind lay stagnant in the black quagmire of the sensual philosophy of Condillac and his brother materialistic Atheists, the first omens and the first start of the reaction in the hands of Maine de Biran, Royer Collard, and Victor Cousin, were the conception and development of the idea of Will, of active Power, and of Alternative Freedom.

As we have before said, it is the moral consciousness that rouses the question of freedom of Will. It is from the demand of the ethical intuitions, requiring a base for the sense of responsibility. It is from the high promptings of the soul refusing to be laid by dynamical law to the level of dead nature, and claiming the dignity of a self-determining personality. And that same sense of responsibility that demands freedom for its base looks forth and upward to immortality as its ultimate. And the same sense of responsibility that demands freedom for the agent demands a God as the executor of responsibility. Nor from any other quarter than from this high Personality within which the moral and free nature blend, can we find, out of Revelation, any valid proof of the moral personality of God; that is, any finite model for the idea of a true and real God at all.

The affinity of Edwards's system with the naturalism of Lord Kames early encountered his book on its first arrival in Scotland; and Dugald Stuart informs us that its effect in that country has been deleterious within the range of his observation. Its accordance with materialistic forms of Unitarianism, patronized by Belsham and Priestley as well as with the worst forms of Universalism and Parkerism in our own country, is beyond our dispute. Far be it, however, from us to intimate that the Christian surroundings with which Edwards and his followers have encircled their central fatalism, are at all congenial with the religious view and feelings of these various classes of errorists.

The charge of denying the axiom that every event must have a cause has been made against the advocates of freedom by a late lively writer and disciple of Comte, George H. Lewes:

> With respect to one class of phenomena, more than half of the thinking world is firmly convinced that every effect does not imply a cause. The class of phenomena referred to is that of human volitions. All those who espouse the doctrine of Freedom of the Will declare that all our volitions are self caused; that is to say, our volitions are not caused by anything external to themselves, not determined by any prior fact.[2]

1. Now it is untrue that freedomists are firmly convinced that every effect does not imply a cause. They maintain the maxim of requisiteness of cause for effect as firmly as Mr. Lewes, and make careful provision for the strict universality of the maxim. They affirm that every unipotent effect implies a unipotent cause, and every alternative effect implies an al-

---

2. George H. Lewes, *A Biographical History of Philosophy From Bacon to the Present Day* (London: G. Cox, 1853), 4:132.

ternative cause, and that neither of these effects can take place without its appropriate adequate cause. The averment that both these effects equally require a cause, and that the causes assigned are adequate, and all that the nature of things requires, does not imply an effect without a cause. All that Mr. Lewes is authorized by fact to say is that freedomists assign for a certain class of events causes that he, not they, excludes from the class of causes. The issue is not as to the affirmance of the maxim, but as to their success in finding for it a legitimate fulfillment. To assign a false cause, or even a cause that is not a cause, is not to deny the need of any cause. The real issue is whether alternative causes are cause; whether a class of alternate causes exist. 2. Unipotent causation and alternative causation differ, not in the requirement of an antecedent, but in the extent of the possible area of the effectuation. For instance, the unipotent cause being A, the solely possible result B constitutes the entire possible area of the effectuation of this cause A. But of the alternative cause N, there are the possible results, X, Y, and Z, disjunctively taken. This resultancy of X, or Y or Z disjunctively, is the extent of the possible area of the effectuation of N. The difference then is in the extent of the area of effectuation; but of either area there must be its own antecedent, A or N. Neither alternative of the disjunctive area, X, Y, Z, can any more come into existence without a cause than the inalternative area, B.

Assuming X, Y, Z to be the only alternatives before the Will, all other courses are excluded by a decisive and genuine necessity. The Will is then closed in to these sole avenues of action by an adamant wall. Any action in other direction would be out of the conditions of volition, and would be event without cause. All the contingency, that is, non-necessity there is, lies in the alternativity of these directions. And as the total of the diversity of these directions, as been shown, as much requires a cause for its existence as a single nonalternative result, that totality is kept under the control of cause. The scope of freedom is therefore circumscribed within an outer boundary of impassable Law, and the Divine Ruler is thus enabled securely to admit a domain of freedom, dependent on cause circumscribed by Law, yet within its scope perfectly alternative in action.

Edwards maintains that not only every event but every modification of an event must have its own peculiar cause. And this is fully admitted, and is shown to exist in every alternative effect. But what Edwards further claims is that every modification must not only have its own peculiar cause, but also a cause that must be inadequate to be the own and peculiar cause of an alternate effect instead. But he does not show that this last claim is necessary to the requirement of a cause for every event. If either of two possible events springs from a given cause, certainly it springs from a cause, and so is not an event without a cause. Nor does such a supposition imply that any event could originally spring from non-existence without an antecedent, since even alternative effect and every alternative area of effectuation requires its own existent antecedent. It admits no result without a cause, no volition without a Will, no deed without a doer, no creation without a Creator.

In conclusion, let it be again noted that Edwards holds that motive is so absolute and nonalternative a cause of the one particular volition that the supposition of a counter-volition is with him identical with the supposition of an effect without cause. That is, for contrary volition there is no causality or power. For the particular sole volition there is the direct necessitative causation. This is no mere certainty distinct from necessity, but necessity itself. It supposes not the non-usage, but the non-existence of contrary power.

V

What Is the Use?

IN DISPROOF OF THE existence of "the power of contrary choice," it is sometimes asked, "What is the use of a power that is never used?"

We reply: 1. The argument lays only against a particular mode of expressing the alternatives of will, namely, the phrase "power of contrary choice." Should we say that freedom is a power of choosing either of several ways, then the question loses its force. The man has the power either of several ways that he may choose one as well as another, or another as well as the one; and this may be far better than to be limited to one solely possible choice.

2. The objection in fact assumes that there exists before the volition, a class or sort of motives or powers the Will will not use. It means this or it means nothing to the purpose. Now there is no such class previous to the volition. The unused possible volitions become a class consequently upon the volition. It is the volition that makes the class or sort. The assumption that there is a sort or class of volitions never used is untrue.

It is true that if Leibniz, Dr. McCosh, and others' view be correct, that although there be "power of contrary choice" it will never be used, inasmuch as the Will will always choose for the strongest motive, then there is an antecedent unused class. There is then a specific faculty given never to be used. It may well be asked what is the use of it, since by a law of correlation there is but one real object of choice.

3. The use or advantage of a power is that it may be used, especially if an advantageous use of it be before the agent. If a wrong course for instance, is before him, it is of vast importance that it be not necessitative to be chosen; but there is also in power an alternative of right, that he may choose it whether he will or not. If a right course is before him, having a wrong alternative from which he is excluded by neither necessity nor law of invariability becomes a trial of virtue, without which moral merit could

never truly exist. That these opposite alternatives in the absence of such exclusion are not used, does not destroy their use.

4. To the question: What is the use of a faculty that is never used? It is a sufficient reply to say that the existence of such a faculty, unprevented by law of necessity or invariability, is a necessary element of the existence of a free agent, without which there could be no just divine government. The use of such a power, therefore, is to render a divine government possible! And surely that is a very great use.

Somewhat similar to the above necessitarian argument drawn from "use," is the following drawn from the Baconian philosophy:

> Adhering to this Baconian method of philosophizing by induction of facts, what legitimate evidence is furnished of the existence of such a faculty of contrary choice as we are now canvassing? That men choose as they do choose all admit, and of course maintain the existence of a faculty adequate thereto. But that they choose the contrary of what they choose none contend. How then can they contend for the existence of a faculty in all respects adequate to do what confessedly is never done?[3]

We reply: 1. The Baconian philosophy abundantly maintains a power and faculty for the happening of things that never have happened. One signal instance lies indeed at the basis of that philosophy, namely, the assumption of the permanence of nature. The past has happened, but the future has not. Yet of the future the Baconian philosophy holds that it will be analogous to the past. The future never does and never will happen, but only the present. The actuality of the fact takes it out of the category of the future, just as the actuality of a volition takes it out of the category of the contrary; so that the future and the contrary are alike excluded from possible experience, and from all possible experiential proof of power alike for either. But as the Baconian philosophy allows an intuitive recognition of a power or faculty for the unexperienced and unexperienceable future fulfillment of a fact, so may it for the alternativity of a volition. One is a permanent non-existent ahead; the other is a permanent non-existent at our side. There may, therefore, be a true Baconian recognition of a possibility or faculty for "what confessedly is never done."

2. Every man assumes intuitively and necessarily before the exertion of every volition the existence of the power for its exertion. Otherwise

---

3. *Princeton Essays*, 253.

he would not attempt it. But that contemplated volition does not and has not existed. It is future, and no future is ever actual. It has never been and never can be experienced. This necessary anterior assumption of power, then, for a putting forth of volition never yet experienced, is according to the Essayist's reasoning anti-Baconian and false.

VI

That Alternative Volition Is Chance

IT IS SOMETIMES OBJECTED that not to be governed, meaning neces-sitated by some external cause operating upon our volitions, but to act solely from the self, is to be governed by chance. Says the Princeton Essayist: "How can it (the Will) make any first choice between objects in a state of perfect equipoise between them? . . . Or could such motion be referred to anything besides the purest contingency and haphazard, or possess any property of a rational and accountable act?" (255)

1. Alternative volition, we reply, is not by chance or haphazard, but by the free origination exerted by the Self in the proper conditions, un-necessitated by any anterior or exterior forces, putting forth action, con-sciously in its own. If any thinker can form no third conception which is neither necessity nor chance, but free originating personality, he seems to us to need the creation of a new idea in his mind. He stands much in the condition of the old moral philosophers perpetually resolving the idea of right into utility, happiness, greatest good, until Butler[1] arose to con-vince them that right is nothing but right. His maxim was "Everything is itself, and not something else." So these thinkers need to understand that unnecessitated self-originated volitional action is not something else, as chance or haphazard, but is simply itself, volitional freedom.

2. If, by chance, these thinkers mean the total absence of cause, in-ternal or external, for effect, that is untrue; for there is all the cause that in the nature of things can be or need be. For if it is claimed that by our view the soul puts forth volition without a cause of putting it forth, or that the soul puts forth a particular volition without a cause causing it to put forth that particular volition, we answer, there is all the cause that the nature of

---

1. Joseph Butler (1692–1752) was an English bishop, philosopher and theologian.

94

causation require in order to a full and complete causation in the cause. As has been shown in the proper place, there is here no cause because, by the true principle of causation, no cause is needed.

3. Instead of being governed by chance, haphazard, or caprice, we may more properly say that the unnecessitated volitional self governs caprice, preferring it, bringing it into existence, shaping, limiting, completing its character, or rejecting it and acting the contrary. When the caprice is fully accepted, and constantly and habitually acted, it is indeed conceived as becoming the master. But that mastery is accepted, chosen, created, and so far forth governed by the self. The course of caprice, or order of law, or lawlessness, is freely, unnecessitatedly, and so responsibly selected by the agent.

4. But if the soul does cause its own volitions, without any necessitating cause back of itself, and so acts uncausedly, it is asked: By what is the mind governed? There are reasoners with whom this is an inveterate question: What governs men's Wills? The impulses of their nature look for freedom; but their theory assuming that Will must be governed, that is, absolutely ruled and limited in the most infinitesimal movement, they vainly seek for freedom in some cause that can thus govern them, and yet leave them free. They seek a contradiction. Just so far forth as the Will is free, we reply, it is not governed at all, but acts from itself, freely and independently.

Government is limitation; and exactly so far as it extends is the exclusion of freedom. In the point and space of freedom there is the absence of restriction. The self does indeed create, bring into existence, shape and limit, and in all these senses necessitate and govern its volitions. But back of the self there is not, nor is there needed to be, by the true laws of causation, any cause causing self to cause volition to be thus or so.

5. The ascription of free volition to haphazard or chance stands in striking contradiction to that moral consciousness by which the soul affirms that its responsible actions are unnecessitated, put forth with power to have done otherwise, yet are of all actions most truly personal, appropriable by, and imputable truly and justly to, the self alone. Where the consciousness acknowledges responsibility, it denies chance, abjures necessitation, and affirms free self-origination. Where there is responsibility thence is the causation, and there the freedom. That independence of all necessitative causation by which the self originates its own responsible action is indeed unique and singular among things; as unique as respon-

sibility itself. The self can lay no blame on contingency, nor on incoming causation, nor on necessitation, since itself is the sole source, and thereby solely responsible for its acts. For not obeying the divine command, it cannot plead that a stronger causation from without placed the obedient volition out of the power of the Will. For the criminal volition, it cannot plead that a stronger force from without necessitated by absolute causation the putting it forth. The power and the accountability are precisely commensurate. Self is solely and uncausedly the cause; and self is solely responsible or meritorious.

6. In the failure of Logic to identify free causation with Chance, recourse is next had to imagination. Freedom is idealized as an omnipotent "no-cause" and this contingency is personified into a goddess rivaling Fate herself. Thus philosopher Isaac Taylor[2] makes a free agent exclaim, "Wherever and as long as my conduct is governed by reasons and motives, I cheerfully consent to be treated as a responsible agent . . . But not so in those dark moments when the fit of contingency comes upon me; then I am no longer master of my course, but am hurried hither and thither by a power in the last degree capricious, whose freakish movements neither men, nor angels, nor the Omniscient himself can foresee . . . It is the unalienable condition of my existence to be governed by a power more stern and inexorable than Fate herself. Alas! Contingency is mistress of my destinies." To say, we reply, that the agent, who solely shapes his own acts, unobliged by any force from without, is "no longer master of his own course," is a self-contradiction.

It is to say he is not master of his own course because he, and nothing else, is master of his own course. He is master of his own course in the purest sense of the terms. To act and to Will from self alone surely implies the completest mastery in the self. For the soul in the necessitarian sense to be "governed by reasons and motives," that is, necessitatively fixed ever and always by a particular stringent motive force occurring, excluding all power of choosing otherwise, is to be governed by something out of the self, by the not-self, and to be at the mercy of contingent external incoming forces. If the strongest happening motive is for wrong and death and hell, there is no power for choosing right; the incoming foreign force fixes the choice and the destiny; and if any rational man can "cheerfully consent to be treated as a responsible agent" without the power of choos-

---

2. Isaac Taylor, *Essay on the Application of Abstract Reasoning to the Christian Doctrines* (Boston: Crocker and Brewster, 1832), 96.

ing right, he is welcome to his very irrational "consent." Our moral sense accepts no such decision.

This "fit of contingency," as before shown, is in the agent's power to accept or reject. He is free to it or the contrary. The "fit" never "comes" unless he brings it. It does not necessitate him by a stronger irresistible impulse. He is not "hurried hither and thither by a power" from without. Whatever hurrying is done, is done by himself. If to be controlled by solely the self is to be controlled by contingency, then we have the absurd equation self=contingency.

A contingency by which the agent is "hurried hither and thither by a power," and is "governed by a power" that is "in the last degree capricious," so that he is "no longer master of himself," is not freedom but necessity. It is necessity from without the agent himself. It differs from the more regular kind of necessity by being incalculable and violent in its successive causations.

Necessity is one conception; Contingency is a second; Free Agency is a third. Necessity is the control of the soul in volition by some foreign causation. Contingency (in the sense of chance) is the loosening of the volition from all, even the soul's causation. Freedom is the control of the act by causative self. In the first an external accident is master; in the second nonentity is master; in the third the master is the agent himself.

The Psychological Argument

I

Self-Determination, Infinite Series

THE QUESTION IS ASKED, "What determines the Will?" That this is an awkward question is evident from the fact that its consideration must be preceded by the previous question: What does this question mean?

"By determining the Will," says Edwards, "if the phrase be used with any meaning, must be intended, causing that the Will or choice should be thus and not otherwise." (18) That is, causing the particular volition. And that question has already been amply discussed.

The phrase "self-determining power of the Will" we generally avoid, not from anything Edwards has argued against it, but from its own inherent ambiguity. The term "self" in the phrase may refer to the agent, to the power, or to faculty of Will. The word "Will" also may signify either the faculty, or as it often does in Edwards, the act of the volition.[1] These last two significations produce questions of very different meaning, requiring very different answers. If, according to the latter signification, the question is: What shapes, particularizes, individualizes, or specificates the volition? The answer is, The Will. If, according to the former signification, the question is: What causes the Will to specificate the volition? The demand is for a very different answer. We are called upon now, as formerly, to furnish a cause back of the Will causing it to specificate; and we answer as before, the cause is nothing at all. The Will in its conditions is a full and adequate cause accounting for the effect, and no adequate cause needs any other cause to make it effective. It causes a particular effect uncausedly, though as we have acknowledged, the prevenient grace of God does work

---

1. From this term arises also the fallacious remark of Professor Bledsoe, that the volition "is not *determined*; it is simply a determination." Albert T. Bledsoe, *An Examination of President Edwards's Inquiry Into the Freedom of the Will* (Philadelphia: H. Hooker, 1845), 228. The remark is founded on the double meaning of the word "determine" as it signifies either to *limit* or to *resolve* or *purpose*.

to persuade the will in the issue of repentance and salvation. This is not the same as causing, however.

Upon the ambiguous term and the usual maxim that the Will determines itself, Edwards founds a lengthened and intricate argument that freedom of the Will involves the consequence that every volition requires an infinite series of anterior volitions to bring it into existence, thus reducing the doctrine to an absurdity. It is important here to remark that inasmuch as this argument, held as it is to be complete demonstration, does in the view of Edwards, exclude all alternative liberty of Will from the universe, and even from possible conception, it must be held to establish the very strictest and most absolute necessity, and not a simple certainty in distinction from it.

CERTAINTY DIFFERS

So far forth as certainty differs from necessity, this is necessity and not certainty. It stands, therefore, in inflexible contradiction to the declarations of Edwards, (421 and elsewhere) that it "is called by the name necessity improperly," and "is more properly called certainty than necessity." By his own definition necessity is that which is "fixed," "made sure," and "absurd to be supposed otherwise." And surely nothing, even in mechanics, is more properly the subject of these predicates than that connection between the Will and particular volition from which all alterations are so perfectly excluded that it is not only impossible that they should exist, but impossible that they should be conceived to exist. Contrary choice is not only an impossibility but an unthinkability. Nor is it competent for Edwards first to prove the sternest necessity, and then out of his abundance to fling in a share of his conclusion and diminish it down to certainty, any more than Euclid may demonstrate that the square of the hypotenuse is equal to the squares of the two opposing sides, and then graciously compound for the conclusion that it is equal to just a square and a half. When we are told therefore that Edwards is "careful to say" that he holds only certainty, we reply that it is of no consequence what he says, provided we know what he proves, if he proves anything.

Edwards bases this celebrated argument upon a gratuitous supposition of his own in regard to the mode by which the Will determines itself. "If the Will, which we find governs the members of the body, and determines and commands their motions and actions, does also govern itself, determines its own motions and actions, it doubtless determines them the same way even by antecedent volitions." (58) By this gratuitous assumption every volition of the Will is held to be, like the body, governed by a preceding volition; but that volition is governed by a preceding volition; that by a preceding; so that by computation every volition is preceded by an infinite series of volitions; each one of which series has its own anterior infinite series, with branchings backward into infinities of infinities. Edwards expands the argument through nearly three pages, demonstrating, with many a labyrinthine fold, over and over again, that "this Arminian notion of liberty of the Will . . . is repugnant to itself and shuts itself wholly out of the world." (60)[2]

The answer we have already given to the question: What determines the Will? if valid, empties their famous demonstration of all substance, leaving of it nothing but a very loud reverberation. If the Will is determined by nothing whatever, then it is a superfluous benevolence for Edwards to furnish us the method by which it is done. If it is not done at all, we may venture to assume that it is done in no way at all. If done in no way at all, then it is not done by an antecedent volition, and consequently the entire tail of the infinite series is completely cut off.

Should the question be asked: What causes an alternative adequate cause to produce or cause a particular effect? The answer might be: It causes itself; and then instead of a self-determining power we should have a self-causing power in every cause in order to causing an effect. The answer, though awkward, would nevertheless be true; provided it does not imply in such self-causation any new antecedent element; for that would bring in the infinite series. All that could be meant by the answer is, that it belongs to the very nature of cause to bring itself by its own inherent force to the production of the effect.

2. The argument of the infinite series, so formally framed by Edwards to prove the absurdity of alternative Will, might be paralleled about as effectively in relation to the obligation to right, to consciousness, to cause, and to the possible exertion of power. Why am I obliged to do *right*? Because it is right. But why am I obligated to regard that right? Because that right is right; and so on forever. Consciousness is to know that I know; but I cannot know that I know unless I know that I know that I know, etc. Cause in order to an effect must put forth a causative act; but that causative act being an effect requires a previous causative act, and that a previous, and so in infinite series. There can be no power unless there be the power to exert that power; but that exertion is an act requiring a previous power to exert it, and that exertion a previous, *ad infinitum*. Whether these are not as valid arguments as the infinite series of Edwards, and what their validity is, let the reader judge.

Edwards proceeds to "invent" several "evasions," as he is pleased to call them, and graciously bestow them on the Arminians. Not one is identical with the reply we have here furnished and we cannot therefore accept the donation. The reader who chooses to examine them will see that we have no need to analyze their logic. But there is one we may notice with reference to the above distinction between the different imports of the question: "What determines the Will?" The distinction truly lies between making specific the volition, which is done by the Will, and causing the Will to make specific the volition, which must be done by an entity back of the Will, but which we deny to be at all required. Edwards supposes us to adopt the "evasion," or answer "What determines the Will?" He does this as follows: "The exertion of the act is the determination of the act; for the soul to exert a particular volition is for it to cause and determine that act of volition." (64) This reply makes us understand the question to be: What makes specific the volition? And our answer would be the Will. Edwards in refutation of this reply attempts to make the due distinction between the two meanings of the question and fails. He charges that in this reply "the thing in question seems to be forgotten."

He says: "The very act of volition itself is doubtless . . . a coming to a choice between two things or more proposed to it." (65) And now comes the distinction. "But determining among external objects of choice is not the same with determining the act of choice itself among various acts of choice." (65) But the choosing between external objects and the determining the act of choice being both not back of but in front of the Will, cannot be and are in no way required to be different things. That is, no "determining the act" is required different from the choosing of the object. The difference of the object secures, and is one of the constituent peculiarities of, the particular choice. If there be three objects, A, B, and C, the selection of either object will secure the specific particularity of the choice. All the difference between the choices will be that A, B, or C will be chosen. Choosing the object is the shaping and bringing the choice into existence. Both choosing the object, and the determining the act of choice, implies that the meaning of "What determines the Will?" is, "What makes specific the volition?" The answer is, The Will; and to make specific the volition is all it has to do.

But in the very next sentence Edwards vibrates back confusedly to the other meaning of the question. "The question is," he says, "What influences, directs, or determines the mind or Will to come to such a conclusion or choice as it does?" (65) Here the question is made to demand a cause back of "the mind or Will," causing it to make specific the volition. Our reply is as before. Nothing does, or is required to cause the Will, previously, to make specific the volition; and that breaks Edwards's cobweb. He goes on to ask, "Or what is the cause, ground or reason why it concludes thus and not otherwise?" (65) We again reply, No prior "cause" is required; the word "ground" here is ambiguous, and demands no answer; and the "reason" or condition is, the motive, which, as is elsewhere shown, is no necessitative cause for the particular volition.

Edwards continues to say, "Now it must be answered, according to the Arminian notion of freedom, that the Will influences, orders, and determined itself thus to act. And if it does, I say it must be by some antecedent act." (65) But, we reply, as our "notion of freedom" requires no anterior causing or ordering of the Will to act, as we hold the Will in its condition to be a complete cause acting uncausedly, there is no requisition for any "antecedent act." And so again the necessitarian cobweb is broken.

DIVINE LAW

As has been before remarked, when the Divine Law requires that an agent choose otherwise than he does choose, the question arises, Has he power in the case to choose otherwise than he does choose? The question supposes that the choosing otherwise would be simply an act of choice. Whichever way the volitional action is, it is an act of choice and nothing more. Though there be power of choosing either way, yet whether it chooses this way, or that way or the other way, all it does when it acts is simply and solely to choose, and nothing more is required. If the Will chooses otherwise than a supposed way, there is in that cause no more choosing to choose than if it chose the supposed way. That other choice would be as simply a choice as the choice actually put forth. Whichever way it chooses there is simply a Will putting forth a choice. And the simple question is: Has the Will power to put forth either simple choice? To which our reply is affirmative. And having the alternative conditions before it, endowed with power for either way, whichever way it puts forth it does so without needing or having any causation back of it. There is a power of choosing either one of several different ways, and the exercise of it is the choosing either one of these ways.

To a statement of Dr. West, who says, "the sense in which we use self-determination is simply this that we ourselves determine"; and that we are "the determiners in the active voice"; the Younger Edwards replies that Dr. Edwards perfectly agrees with such a view:

> We grant that we are determiners in the active; and yet assert that we are determined, or are caused to determine, by some extrinsic cause, at the same time, and with respect to the same act. As when a man hears a sound he is the hearer in the active voice, and yet is caused to hear the same sound by something extrinsic to himself. (1:327)

We pass by the fact here, that by this statement the volition is rendered as necessitated as the sensation. The true difference between the two is, as we maintain, that the determined act of hearing is performed without, and the determinate act of volition is performed with the power of other action instead. Both may be in the active voice; but both are not active with an alternative power.

Again, the Younger Edwards propounds the following dilemma: "If we cause our volitions at all, we cause them by a previous volition, or without such a volition." Undoubtedly. And the horn we accept is "without." "If we cause them by a previous volition," then follows the infinite series. "If we cause them without such volition, we cause them involuntarily, without any design, any motive or agency." No volition, we reply, is voluntary, but volitional. But then an alternative volition such as we state it is without "any design, any motive or agency," is not admitted, and is without proof.

II

The Nature of Motive Influences

THE TERMS DENOTING THE comparison of motives, especially as used by necessitarians, are derived from various physical sources. The favorite descriptive terms are the weightiest motive, the strongest motive, the highest motive. Thus the dimensions of material objects and the forces of physical dynamics are ascribed to mental operations. They are endowed with an exact mathematical commensurability; and were our faculties sufficiently clear and penetrating to ascertain with sufficient precision, we should be able, it is assumed, to label antecedently the proper motive as, relatively to the given Will, "weightiest," "strongest," "highest."

And in this superior power of perception consists the nature of the divine foreknowledge of human actions. God's knowledge of the future depends on the causative series of results. Omniscience travels through the future on the bridge of causation. Surely the physical nature of the very terms used should warn these philosophers of the danger of error. Certainly the application of mathematics to quantities and weights of thought is a very questionable dogma. Nor is there any reason to know or to suppose that any more acute power would enable us to detect what does not belong to their intrinsic nature. The qualities of thought, like other qualities, may be comparable without being commensurable.

The comparability of motives may be supposedly as ascertained either from extra-volitional or from volitional sources.

Thus we may compare the different degrees of excitement in an emotion, a moral feeling, a desire, a fear, a sense of obligation. Some we may know to be prevolitionally and intrinsically more intense than others. Impressions made by external objects upon the mind are comparable; and where the external object is itself mathematically commensurable, there arises the most plausible appearance of a mathematical commensurability in the impression. A thousand dollars may make a stronger impression on a miser's mind than can nine hundred and ninety-nine dollars and ninety-nine cents, and that greater impression may, for aught, we know, be pronounced arithmetically exact in its surplus. But prevolitional impressions are not so properly motives in themselves, but in their relation to the Will.

What is in truth meant by the highest or strongest motive must be derived from the Will itself; and thence we have this definition, all-important to this discussion, that the so-called strength of a motive is the comparative prevalence that the Will assigns it in its own action. Or, otherwise, it is the nearness with which the Will comes to acting according with or to it.

Volitionally considered, (the only true mode of consideration) the so-called strength of a motive may be again defined as the degree of probability that the Will will choose in accordance with it or on account of it. And it is most important to remark that the result is not always, nor in most cases necessarily, the highest probability.

The Will may choose for the higher or for the lower. And as the Will may choose for a lower rather than for a higher probability, so the Will may choose on account of what is called antecedently a weaker over a stronger motive. And hereby is once for all established the difference between mechanical force and motive influence, that whereas in the former by necessity the greater effect results from greater force; in the latter the less is possible from the greater, the greater from the less.

HIGHEST PROBABILITY

That result is not as the highest probability is shown in the Doctrine of Contingencies or Probabilities. The chance may be improbable and yet prove successful. So the volition calculably improbable may become the actual. On the contrary, there may be the highest probability and yet a failure. And this is equivalent to saying there may be the strongest motive and yet the Will rejects it. Aggregate calculations are in a degree reliable in practice; and yet individual results are fallible. A margin of so-called reliable certainty there is, that is of probability, so strong that a quiet and settled reliance is practically reposed upon it. For life is practically based on probabilities. But when the probability is raised so high that it is absurd to expect that it is ever reversed, we arrive at necessity.

The intrinsic strength of a motive antecedently to its effect in volition must consist in the strength of some prevolitional mental operation; that is, in the intensity or excitement of some previous feeling or the positiveness of some intellection. It is only through these that any motive can be called intrinsically strong antecedently to the Will. It may, then, be granted that where there is an opposition of motives, the probabilities are as the above-named intensity or positiveness. Yet, as we have already illustrated, the result is not always as the strongest probability, that is, as the intrinsically or prevolitionally strongest motive. Relatively to the prevolitional faculties, the strongest motive often fails; relative to the Will, the strongest motive is but another term for the accorded motive.

That a six may be the next cast by a player at dice may be a fair probability. That it should occur twice in succession is improbable; but though the stronger probability is against it, it does and may occur. Still stronger is the probability against its occurring thrice; but against that stronger improbability it is yet a possible result. Four and five are increasingly improbable, and possible in diminishing and doubtful degrees, and can hardly be supposed able to happen. At six or seven perhaps the probability is held to have ceased; and as the synthesis of causes exists in the cosmos, possibility is excluded and absolute necessity prevails. So under a certain state of intense prevolitional strength of motive it may be in the highest degree probable, affirmatively or negatively, that a given volition will be put forth, and yet that highest probability may fail. The probability may diminish and reversely be opposed and yet succeed.

Against increasing balances of improbability the event may occur, but with diminishing possibility. But when the point is attained, though but indistinctly visible to observation, at which it is true that such a choice never would be made by any rational free agent either actual or possible to exist, necessity commences and normally responsibility is at an end. When from the very nature of things a choice is such that, though the conditions be repeated an infinite number of times, it is self-evident or intrinsically a fact that no Will would ever put it forth, as true a necessity is attained as rules over matter, or over the passive operations of mind. It is in this interval of area, between opposite necessities, where events may overrule probabilities that freedom and responsibility exist. As human perception covers a narrow interspace between two unknowables, so human freedom covers a narrow interspace between two necessities.

It may indeed be said that at each single throw the upturn of a six is possible, no matter how many times it has been repeated; and as it is possible each single time, so it is possible an infinite number of times. Distributively (as the logicians say) or individually, this may be admitted to be true; and yet it is collectively untrue. Each particular case is held possible, but not all the cases together. More than a given cycle of cases (whose terminal point cannot be exactly fixed) cannot be. We know this comprehensively, because we know that such is the synthesis of causes and causations in the system of things that an adamantine stoppage exists at some point.

It may be true that in a system of probation an agent may be able to do right each time and yet may not be able to do right collectively through all time. In the presence of some constant powerful temptation, from which he is never protected a moment, an agent may be able to resist each time without the ability to resist through the whole. And so Wesley reasons against Taylor, that Adam's one sin did not prove him depraved; for any one sin may be committed by a pure free agent; but why is it, he asks, that all sin universally and constantly? This is not solved by saying a pure free agent may sin any one time, therefore he may sin all times.

What is distributively true is not therefore collectively true. The supposition that an infinite series of sixes might be cast with a perpetually decreasing probability down to the infinitely small, yields no result. A power infinitely small for a volition would furnish no basis to the view of common sense of responsibility.

The contingency thus calculable is in reality grounded in Will. For casting a six is the result of a certain method of motions by the player. A series of minute and unseen volitional and muscular causations makes the result come about. Could the same method be performed any number of times the same result would follow. The method being produced by the volitions, the contingencies are all really based in the Will of the player. Strictly, then, there is external contingency, but no intrinsic chance in the matter. Though, phenomenally, freedom is thus illustrated by chance, their bases are different. A chance event is one whose cause being concealed is but uncertainly calculated; a free volition is one whose alterability, and so measurable incalculability, is grounded in the agent's nature. The illustration of freedom from chance, indeed, has but a negative value, as showing that Edwards's application of the logic of mechanical dynamics to Will is not the only possible method of reasoning. Thereby our thought is enabled once for all to emancipate the sequence of motive and volition from Causative Necessity or Invariable Law.

The maxim that "the effect is the measure of the cause"[1] has a double meaning, and is, under limitation, true in both. The effect may be the measure of the cause either intrinsically, or as conventionally assigned. In the former case the effect is not only the measure, but also the manifestation of the antecedent intrinsic amount of causation. Every infinitesimal addition or subtraction of intrinsic causality has its necessary showing in the effect. Such is the fact in all cases of physical or non-volitional causation. The effect, on the contrary, can be only a conventional or assigned measure, when there is no exact intrinsic proportion in the causality, and the effect is merely an assumed test of its greater or lesser amount. The greater or lesser amount of the matter, or contents, making up the antecedent condition does not always show itself in the result. Here the result is no measure of the intrinsic antecedent force, but is held so arbitrarily because there is no other measure. In the physical instance the anterior causality measures out the fixed proportional result; in the volitional the result creates all the measurement there is for the antecedency. More properly we may therefore say that in the former case the antecedent causality is the fixing measure of the effect; in the latter the result is the conventionally assigned measure of the antecedent influence.

APPLY THESE VIEWS

We are now able to apply these views to illustrate the nature of what are called motive influences, in relation to Will. As Will acts more or less in accordance with such influences, there is a due propriety in saying that influences act upon Will. But there must be most clearly understood, as resulting from our statements thus far, the distinction between a physical force and a volitional influence.

A physical force is the same as a physical cause, or rather it is as causation acting to produce effect. Its effect is the fixed and proportional manifestation of the real and intrinsic causation. A certain amount of force manifests itself in a certain amount of effect.

A volitional or motive influence has not in the result any absolute and precise proportional manifestation and fixed exhaustive of its intrinsic amount. Its connection with result is contingent. That is, the greater

1. Edwards, 97.

intrinsic intensity constitutes an external probability of the proportionate result, yet neither the necessity nor absolute certainty. For, as in the doctrine of contingencies, as already illustrated, the greater probability may fail, the lesser probability may result. This establishes a doctrine of contingent motive probability.

This contingent character of motive influence is correspondent with the alternative character of that which is its sole possible object—Will. An alternative Will and a contingent motive influence are correlatives. They mutually explain and sustain each other. To admit either is to admit both. And so a unipotent Will and a necessary motive influence are correlatives. He who is compelled to admit one is compelled to admit the other. It will be a mere controversy about a word to say that an influence that does not produce some result is no influence.

That may be legitimately called an influence that is conceived as potentially such though contingently. That may be legitimately called an influence, it is important to add, which is conceived as possessing an intrinsic probability for result, though the higher probability be a contingency for which there exists power of failure. If so, then contingent motive influence is established, and the doctrine of volitional necessity is at an end. The relation between physical force and effect is necessity; the relation between motive and volitional is contingency.

These views illustrate our use of the term Contingency. We do not call the action of Will contingent, but rather free. The word Contingency, by habitual association, approximates so near the idea of accident that it should scarce be made the characteristic term for volitional action. It implies a sort of blindness in its subject, which may not improperly be attributed to motive, in its influence toward Will, but not to the Will, that is, to the agent himself. Or, we may say, that while freedom is the intrinsic quality of the agent in volition, contingency is the exterior view of the same thing. To us, as we contemplate it from without, the act which is free is phenomenally contingent, for we are previously uncertain which way it will turn. To the motive itself the result is contingent, for the motive is blind, and its success may or may not result.

It may be granted that where a given course is urged upon the Will by some highly excited-feeling antecedent, or by some moral obligation, or by some reasonableness, or some calculable interest, there may be in each of these antecedents an intrinsic comparable strength constituting an anterior probability, which the mind admits, that the choice will accord with it. The probability, however, is the stronger may fail and the weaker prevail. The probability may be so strong as to produce that feeling of subjective repose called assurance, reliance, or, less properly, certainty, and yet fail. It is not until the condition of motivation is such that it is true that all Will as Will would decide but a given way, that necessity commences and responsibility ceases.

A volition, a train of volitions, may be so probable as to be reliably certain that is, probable, and be practically far beyond all rational doubt before it becomes metaphysically necessary. We rely on the undoubted purposes of others in many cases with as much repose as we do upon the stability of physical objects and causations without confounding the practical reliability of the former with the absolute necessity of the latter.

THESE ELUCIDATIONS

From these elucidations we have the following results:

1. The apparent contingencies of human action are explained, being verified by their bases in the very nature of Will. Human behaviors are truly to our eye externally or phenomenally made up of certainties and uncertainties blended or alternating. This contingency arises in the category of chances from our ignorance of the causes; and it arises, in the case of Will, from the very intrinsic nature of the causes. There is a phenomenal resemblance; but the essential base is different.

2. Will is made to appear, as it reveals itself in consciousness, not a bleak, mechanical thing. It is not a projectile made to protrude or withdraw, as by a spring, according to the rigid forces that propel it. It acts, in the natural alternations of the soul, with a free living power.

3. We have the explanation how motives have a living and proximately calculable influence on action without fastening or locking its movement as with an iron bolt. We see how appeals to feeling, to reason to conscience, are reasonable appliances, and rightly expected to impress the mind and reach the Will, without squarely producing in it a fixed motion according to the proportion of solid momentum applied, or securing it as a fixed invariable sequence. We see how the strongest appeals and the most powerful impression may meet with prompt repulse from no other assignable cause than a determinate Will. Hereby we are presented in theory with a view of the things, creating in our minds precisely the

same impressions that naturally result from the contemplation of their reality in life.

These principles furnish us with solutions of many of the sophisms of necessitarianism.

1. We may test Edwards's doctrine of the "fixed" gradational antecedent strength of motives. "There is," says he, "such a thing as diversity of strength of motives to choice, previous to the choice itself." Motives, he proceeds to argue, have an antecedent "strength" because "they do previously invite, induce, excite, and dispose the mind to action," or to "volition previous to volition itself," and that previous "strength" is causation and the effect is necessary upon the cause. That there are differences of intensity of feeling, of clearness of intellectual conviction, or solemnity of sense of moral obligation, prevolitionally existing, we may abundantly admit. How far these are of a commensurable nature, reciprocally, we discuss in the proper place. These prevolitional conditions, we also admit, may, by their different degrees, produce a greater or lesser probability that the Will will accord to them what is the only test of motive-force, the prevalence by volition. Nevertheless the result is not always as the greatest antecedent force equals greatest probability of the volitional accordance. The highest of the motives may fail, the lower motive may prevail, and Edwards' causational argument of necessary effect fails.

2. We may solve the problem, considered by Hamilton insoluble, of the Will's being able to choose against a stronger motive expressed even in an arithmetical form:

> On the supposition that the sum of the influences (motives, dispositions, tendencies) to volition A is equal to 12, and the sum of counter-volition B equal to 8, can we conceive that the determination of volition A should not be necessary? We can only conceive the volition B to be determined by supposing that the man creates (calls from non-existence into existence) a certain supplement of influences. But this creation, as actual, or in itself, is inconceivable, and even to conceive the possibility of this inconceivable act we must suppose some cause by which the man is determined to exert it. We thus in thought never escape determination and necessity. It will be observed that I do not consider this inability to notion any disproof of the fact of free will.[2]

----

2. As quoted in Albert T. Bledsoe, *Theodicy: or Vindication of the Divine Glory* (New York: Carleton and Phillips, 1854), 156.

No creation or calling power from non-existence is, we reply, needed in the case. The numerals 8 and 12 are but representatives of the different degrees of anterior probability that the Will will decide in favor of A or B. It is a chance as two to three that the agent will decide for A; but this does not settle the question, as in a counter action of mechanical forces. The weaker probability may, in strict accordance with the Doctrine of Probabilities, receive the accord of the Will; and B may, without any contradiction to any existing truth, be chosen. What is wanting is not creation of new power, but use of power already in existence.

3. We may furnish a rational solution to the question: Can an agent choose without a motive? The cases of no motive may be reduced to three classes: 1. Where the opposite alternatives are perfectly and so equally valueless; 2. Where, they are equally valuable; and 3. Where there is value, and so motive on one side, and all the no-motive is on the other side. A). Where there is no value, and so no motive on either side, it is a balance of zeroes. Yet from the very definition of free Will that it is the power of choosing either of several ways, as well as from the fact that non-action is impossible, and a choice between the zeros is necessary, this case becomes a balance of not only improbabilities, but of probabilities. It is equally improbable, that is, equally probable, that the Will will select either one. And this selection of either one, actually made, would be a choice without a motive. B). Where the value and so the motive on each side is equal, there is motive for each, but no motive for either over that of the other. Here the probabilities are equal, and, as before (like a case of equal probability of casting a six), the result either way is accordance with reason. Such a balance of equal forces in physics would prevent action; in volition there would be action without antecedent predominant motive. C). Where the alternatives are unequal, as zero against 2 or 3, the probabilities are all on one side, and a possibility only on the other. The no-motive is a zero, its alternative is a unit; and for that unit the chance is equal to just the possibility or probability that an improbability will result. As the 2 or 3 increases, the improbability converges to and finally may arrive at necessity. It is at this necessity that the impossibility of choosing without motive is absolute. Such a state of motivity for good, for instance, insures an entire depravation—a total depravity.

4. Arminians, Edwards argues again, admit that motives are necessary to choice; but what motive can there be for choice for a lesser motive? He claims, hence, to exhibit a clear Arminian contradiction. For

Arminians hold that the Will cannot act without motive, and yet really hold to a case of acting without motive; for what motives can there be for acting contrary to the strongest motive? We here do not avail ourselves of our showing that we hold not the doctrine that Will cannot act without motives, nor of our future showing of the antecedent incommensurability of most motives. Our business now is to apply the solution derived from the doctrine of probabilities. The choosing for the weakest motive is nothing more than choosing according to the lesser probability. And then the question: What motive can there be for acting in favor of weaker motive? This is just equivalent to the following question: What probability can there be of an event in favor of a lesser probability?

STRONGEST MOTIVES

The strongest of the motives has only the highest of several probabilities in its favor. Yet as the event may actually accord for the lower probability, and there is a probability that it will, so the volition may actually accord with the weaker motive.

5. Edwards still further argues that the weaker motive not only affords no motive for being chosen, but it really affords a contrary tendency. In such case the Will would choose not only without motive but contrary to motive. So far as the motive is less, so far there is from it a contrary influence. But such, we reply, would be simply a case of superior counter probability. Let the influence of one motive be 8, and of the other 6; the superior probabilities would be 8 to 6, and yet the 6 and not the 8 against the contrary tendency may result.

6. Edwards puts the case of a man with two different foods before him, with a superior appetite for one, and every other motive perfectly excluded; there could be no motive, he argues, for choosing the inferior, and he would choose the superior necessarily. The comparison of motives would, we reply, be as in the preceding paragraph. As to the choice, there is either a certainty, or rather reliable probability, that he would choose for the superior motive, or, at the proper point of increasing probability, a necessity.

7. Similar was the reasoning of the Younger Edwards against West, who admitted that Will could not choose unless the object had something in it "eligible"; that is, unless there was some quality constituting a motive for it. Then, replies Edwards, the Will cannot choose for a lesser

motive, for that would not be "eligible." And yet, we reply, though not on the whole "eligible," the object may have in it something that is "eligible," and that single item of eligibility is motivating. There then arises between the two motives two counter probabilities, of which, again, according to the theory of probabilities, the lesser may prevail.

8. The Younger Edwards asks whether "when several motives are proposed to a man, he sometimes passes by the most persuasive, and follows the least persuasive? If so, what is the motive in this case?" (1:352) The term "persuasive," we reply, expresses not so much a relation to the Will, as to the feelings. That an object is more persuasive to the feelings, does produce a higher probability that the Will will choose in accordance with it as motive. Yet, as before shown, the higher probability may fail, and the lower meet with accordance. To ask what is the motive for this choosing for a lesser motive, is to ask again what is the probability in favor of a lesser probability.

9. These views show the futility of an argument by the Younger Edwards to prove the necessitative character of motive influence. "To be influenced by motives is to be really and effectually influenced, just so far as the influence is exerted by them at all. And so far as he is influenced or persuaded by them, so far he is governed and determined by them. For that is what we mean by a determination by motives." (1:380) "To be influenced by motives," and to "be really and effectually influenced," we reply, are not one and the same thing in any sense suitable to Edwards' purpose. To be "effectually influenced" must mean, to suit his purpose, to be so influenced as that the effect is resultantly secured and accomplished. But we have already shown that the agent may be prevolitionally influenced by motive objects, nay, may be most strongly influenced by them, and yet the influence is not effectuated in the result. The result is not the measure of an antecedent intrinsic force, and so is not necessitated.

10. These views show the fallacy of Edwards's argument by Approximation, or rather Recession. (265) Inducements, he argues, may be presented so strong as to be "invincible," which he apprehends Arminians would hold "destroy liberty." Then he infers if "invincible" arguments "destroy liberty," half as strong will half "destroy" it, a quarter a quarter, and so on. The destruction of liberty will be in proportion to the amount of motive. This reasoning, we reply, is parallel to the following argument: "If, at a certain limit, approximating probabilities merge into necessity, then half that approximation destroys half the probability,

a quarter a quarter, and so on. The destruction of probability will be in proportion to the approximation." But the approach of the probability of the given volition to necessity does not diminish the liberty or the power for a counter-volition. It is simply a diminution of the probability of its exercise, which diminution may be cancelled by the free volitional act.

FREE VOLITION

The increase of difficulty for a free volition or for any action is not equivalent to a diminution of power. Suppose a person able to lift a hundred pound weight. He has more difficulty in lifting fifty than in lifting ten; and yet he has just as truly and just as much the power to lift fifty as ten. He has the full complete power of lifting ninety-nine pounds. And so difficulty for free volition is no diminution of power. In the overcoming of that difficulty is the probation and trial of virtue. That difficulty is no otherwise a diminution of liberty than as a requirement of effort. In such effort, and in the abolishing by effort all difficulty, and making the right easy, natural, and finally necessitative, all probationary virtue lies.

In his chapter upon this point Edwards adds three corollaries, the first of which alone requires attention. In this he argues that if motives are not necessary causes, producing volitions securatively, then exhortations, the presentation of inducements and reasons, in order to bring about desired choice, are all in vain. To which we reply, as before intimated, that the common sense of men does not consider exhortations as producing volitions necessitatively, destroying all power of counter choice in the cases in which they are complied with, but as being contingent influence, probable with given intrinsic force, to result in choice, yet leaving a possibility of counter choice. This view of the matter leaves full scope for the reasonableness of exhortations, for the probable calculation of contingent results, and for the free play of alternative Will. And such are the plain truth and nature of the case.

Motives are not in their nature compulsory, or securative of a necessary effect, destroying all counter power of choice. So inducements offered or influence brought to bear by the divine administration or by the operations of the Holy Spirit, i.e. prevenient grace, normally leave in the agent the power of otherwise choosing, and of successfully "resisting the Holy Ghost." It is of the very nature of probation that no influences shall be applied to the Will that the Will possesses not full power at its own responsibility to reject and nullify. The whole world has the full power to reject God and his Gospel; and the reason why the world is not now holy is, not that God has withheld anything of all that the laws of free probation permit, but that men in the use of alternative power, with full volitional ability to do otherwise, do restrain the progress of truth, the operations of the Divine Spirit, and the course of Grace.

Calvinists often claim that the prayers even of Arminians presuppose that God may at any time consistently with his administrative system convert any man they are praying for, or even the world, at any moment. But in this matter Calvinists truly contradict themselves. They pray, as the result often shows, that God would do contrary to his own sovereign election. Their prayer, though itself decreed, is often against God's decrees. They pray that God would act contrary to the strongest motive; which they say God has no moral power to do. That is, they commit these contradictions unless all prayer is considered as offered under the proviso that what is asked for be consistent with the Divine Will, and is in fact asked for so far only as is allowable by the fundamental laws of God's administration. Not my will but thine be done, tacitly or expressly limits and underlies every true prayer.

And such a proviso as fully explains the prayer of the Arminian as of the Calvinist. When an Arminian prays that God would awaken the public mind to repentance, or convert an individual, or spread his Gospel through the world, and turn all men's hearts to righteousness, he thereby expresses his earnest desire that such things may be accomplished in accordance with fundamental laws. Just as when he prays that a temporal blessing may be bestowed, as health restored, or life preserved, he usually expects no unequivocal miracle, but trusts that it may be done in such way as Infinite Wisdom may devise in accordance with the constitution of things; and that on condition of his prayer it may be ordered otherwise than if such prayer were not offered. We know not how far the prayer of the saints is a condition to the goings forth or putting forth of God, nor how fully he requires the co-operation of his Church, in order to render possible such displays of his truth as will convince the unbelieving, and such impressions by his Spirit as the free wills of men in process of time will, it is foreseen, accept and obey. Certainly man's Will and not God's remissness has prevented the complete good of the world. Of the world, God truly speaks when he asks, "What more could have been done to my vineyard, that I have not done in it?" Isai. 5:4.

III

Commensurability of Motives

Volition as Greatest Good

THAT MOTIVES PREVAIL BY their antecedent strength so that the strongest is ever victorious, just as the heaviest weight must always turn the scale, is the doctrine of necessity. It assumes an exact and infinitely perfect antecedent commensurability as a certain fact. How true this assumption is, is worth an examination.

In regard to commensurability, things may be divided into two classes, those measurable by each other and those that are not.

To the first class belong things of the same denomination, as dimension with dimension, weights with weights, and abstract numbers with abstract numbers. And when objects of this class come before the mind there is an antecedent commensurability of motive, which on the doctrine or probabilities, renders the result reliably certain or probable, and even necessary.

Where in opposite scales of choice before a miser's attention there are ten dollars and a thousand dollars, every other inducement being excluded, there can be little or no doubt which he will choose. It is a condition of motive balance in which all Wills would choose alike. There is an exact intrinsic commensuration between the two objects, establishing an antecedent subjective probability amounting to reliable certainty, and perhaps to even "secured certainty" or necessity that the agent will choose in a particular way.

To the second class belong all those objects of different denominations, or received by the mind through different senses, faculties, or impressibilities.

There is no commensuration or comparableness between a pound and a rod; between the brightness of the day and the force of magnetic attraction. Still less commensurable are comparing material things with mental: as the weight of a rock and the honor of a gentleman; the hardness of iron and the sternness of Cato; the length of a walk and the glory of a victory.

It would not afford much sense to say that this night is as dark as this rose is odorous; that this timber is as solid as this woman is beautiful; that this fruit is as sweet as that crime is wicked; that this truth is as clear as that desire is strong; that this music is as sweet as that duty is binding; or that this color is as deep as that action is honorable. And yet these comparisons may represent the balance of opposite motives antecedent to volition.

A cold intellection is not intrinsically commensurable with a deep emotion; nor a sentiment of taste with a feeling of moral obligation; nor a physical appetite with a sense of honor or duty. These influences receive their degree of prevalence, and consequently their comparative so-called strength of motive, from the Will.

This class of cases makes clear to our consciousness the fact that the volitional preference assigned to the motive is the actual so-called strength of the motive. Nor is there any force in the assumption that if our faculties were keen enough we should be able to see that even these were intrinsically mathematically commensurable. What we should see were our perceptions omnisciently clear is not so certain. But we venture to believe that we should see in our responsible volitional nature the power to choose independent of the exact control of motive necessitation.

But to all this the objection is sometimes made that prevalence is the sole proof of greater antecedent weight or force even in mechanical dynamics. We only know, for instance, that a certain steam pressure is cause of the motion of a locomotive only by the motion itself. We know that the stroke of the hammer is cause of the entrance of the nail only by the sequence. To this we reply:

1. The intuitive common sense of all mankind cognizes matter as intrinsically inert and dead.[1] It possesses no intellectual power to discover and select a direction of action, and no inherent force to move itself if it could select. In all these respects, we find it contrasted with mind, with

---

1. This, with some subsequent passages, was written before the dynamic theory of matter had become a topic of discussion. The writer has seen no ground to change the opinion here expressed. The next sentence is valid in its argument on any theory of matter.

which we can intuitively contemplate as the seat and residence of both selective self direction and dynamic self activity.

2. As matter is thus inert, it moves only by forceful impact from without. A body moving against it must propel it. Mind thus does cognize the propelling and the motion as cause and effect, and recognizes cause and effect as moving from behind onward. And as the moved body is inert in itself, the mind is compelled to hold that it is passively caused to move, and that its motion is not independent and concurrent, but dependent, proportioned, and caused. It is the antecedent that effectuates the consequent and makes it be; not the being that makes that the antecedent.

3. Of the same sort of matter a given bulk and density possess with uniform exactitude a given weight and force; so that weight and force are seen to be intrinsical, and the movement of the impelled body to be a proportionate and necessary effect. By induction the same law is extended over all cases, and natural philosophy constructs her system on that conclusion, with full confidence in the results.

4. To all these views of material motion as an effect of impulse from without, there is no contradiction, either from consciousness, experience, or moral sense. Whereas in Will, consciousness finds self-activity, experience finds incommensurability of motives, and the moral sense denies necessitated volition.

OTHERS HAVE ARGUED

Others have argued that we have the same proof that volition is the exact effect of motive force, that there is that perception, is the exact effect of the external object. To this we reply, consciousness and the moral sense present the most positive contradiction. One of the strongest proofs that Will is free we derive from the conscious feeling of the nonalternatives of perception as compared with the alternatives of Will. Let our readers on this point consult our chapters on the Responsibility for Belief, and on the proof of Freedom from Consciousness. And this conscious difference between perception and volition furnishes an à fortiori proof for the difference between matter and Will.

A due consideration of this antecedent incommensurability of motives may aid in deciding the question whether Edwards's maxim is true, that the volition is always as the greatest apparent good. By this is meant, let us carefully concede, not necessarily, the greatest actual good, nor the greatest absolute good; but what appears to the given mind at the moment the greatest good within its survey. According to this maxim it may be said that the particular motive receives from the prevolitional faculties its decision and character, as greatest apparent good, according to which Will always decides.

To which we reply, that the prevolitional faculties do receive and compare the different eligibilities presented as commensurable or incommensurable, or as in one point or another preferable; and there are particular motivations for which we may calculate a higher or lower degree of probability of their receiving the volitional accordance; and yet is matter of both observation and consciousness that, while the judgment has decided that a course is for the greatest good, even contemporaneously, with that judgment, the Will often does, from the suggestion of some inferior motive, decide against that acknowledged greatest good. In such a case, the necessitarian will indeed reply, "Yes, but then that inferior motive was to the mind at the moment the greatest good." That, we reply, is a paralogism. It is the regular necessitarian dodge. The Will, forsooth, chooses for the greatest apparent good; for it is of course the greatest apparent good if the Will chooses it.

The intellectual and volitional actions described by the poet Horace said:

Meliora video, proboque

Deteriora sequor,

The better I see and approve, the worse I follow, were perfectly simultaneous. Even while volitionally preferring the worse, he prevolitionally preferred the better. There being *meliora,* he could see only by comparing the two; and it was while so comparing and seeing that he chose the *deteriora.* He chose for the weaker motive, and for the lesser apparent good relatively to his mind at the moment of choosing. He made up his mind prevolitionally that the *meliora* were the greater good; he made up his mind volitionally by choosing for the *deteriora.* President Asa Mahan[2] truly remarks, "How often do we hear individuals affirm, 'If I should follow my feelings I should do this; if I should follow my judgment I should do that.' " That feeling and that judgment present motives often intrinsically and entirely incommensurable; whence, then, the decision but from the Will?

---

2. Asa Mahan (1799–1889) was an American Congregational pastor and the first president of Oberlin College.

A Southern planter, let us suppose, sees that the approaching rebellion will be his absolute ruin unless he escapes, which he can do with all his property and ultimate honor. Yet he determinately says, "I go with my State." He sees that such course is not to him the greatest apparent good, but the greatest possible ruin; yet he chooses it so seeing—knowingly chooses what is no apparent good at all. So far as the motives were commensurable he doubtless chose for the weaker against the stronger. An Edwards might ask: What motive had he for so choosing against the stronger motive? It might be replied: None at all, yet he so chose.

If any assert that the most intense and exciting desire or other emotion is intrinsically the strongest and always determines the Will, that is denied as contrary to experience. Quiet judgment or duty often gains the day over the highest human feeling. So the boy required to stand the fire by his father's command until devoured by the blaze, willed the calmest duty against the highest torture. The Indian wills the coolest intellection in spite of the highest agonies. The Wisconsin boy who, when required to recant a true statement, expired under the infliction of repeated whippings, persisted in the utterance of truth against the highest possible immediate motive.

How often are men of intensest passions accustomed to subdue their storm by the stern imperative of Will. How often are we called upon to suppress every variety of emotion, grief, joy, love, anger and laughter by the central volitional energy? So striking an instance of this was Socrates, that when a physiognomist told him that his distinguishing features showed him to be a natural profligate, the philosopher admitted that he was so by passion and good only by Will. In such cases it is the volitional power that strikes the balance, and not the judgment, for the very contest is between judgment and feeling. Judgment is not the judge, but one of the parties.

If any one asserts that the firmest and coolest intellection prevails, every deliberate sinner who, knowing and believing that an endless woe is the penalty, commits sin on the slightest temptation is proof to the contrary. A moment's gush of feeling overthrew the life purposes of Coriolanus, the legendary Roman military hero; while Brutus sacrificed the deeper sense of parental feeling at the requirement of cool calculation.

The very strongest moral obligation, fully acknowledged and most deeply felt, is made to yield to the slightest desire, interest, point of honor, or aesthetic gratification. The preference of less to greater, even as they confessedly appear to the individual mind at the moment, is here often pre-eminently marked.

If any say that the strongest motivation prevails because that is strongest which the Will chooses, he gives up the question. If by the strongest motive is meant simply the motive chosen, then to say that the strongest motive prevails is only to say that the motive chosen prevails, or the motive chosen is the motive chosen. It concedes our position that the strength of a motive is the comparative prevalence that the Will in its own action assigns to it, or is the nearness to which the Will comes to acting on account of it. Men, thereby, do not always choose what they most desire, nor what they think best, nor what they think they ought; but for these or some other eligibility; and for whichever eligibility they choose, that, forsooth, is the strongest motive.

That motives are not subjectively and intrinsically commensurable, either geometrically, or arithmetically, is confirmed by the doctrine of contingencies. Suppose two players at dice, one of whom has two sixes and the other has three. The goodness of their chances therefore is as two to three. That is, the latter has one third a better chance than the former. His lot is as a motive that is one third better than its opposite. Yet though the better chance has the higher probability than the other, yet it may fail and attain but an inferior result. Therefore, the so-called stronger motive may fail of its comparative result. When compared in regard to their results, they are utterly incapable of exact commensuration. There is no adding them so as to produce an exact sum; there is no subtracting them so as to obtain a precise remainder; there is no commeasuring them so as to obtain exact comparative magnitudes. Their true superiority consists in their prevalence; which the volition does not reveal as occultly intrinsic in them, but creates. Opposite probabilities are comparable, but not with absolute exactness commensurable.

NON-COMMENSURABILITY

This non-commensurability of motives appears in various phases of life. A self-interest and a sense of the heroic stand before the agent's attention; there is no intrinsic commensurability; is it not the Will that decides between them? A man will sacrifice property, life, every selfish interest, and encounter the most terrible forms of danger from a point of honor. Another man will say, "Burn my private property if it will serve the public good." Doubtless, as has been elsewhere shown, some basis for the possibility of such acts must be found in the character; but a large share of that character is formed by the volitions, and a large amount of solution of the immediate acts must be found in Will.

Leibniz illustrates the freedom of the Will from that eager spontaneity with which men seek after happiness. It is necessary; yet how free! But happiness is by no means the summum bonum, the polestar regulating all our volitions. Bishop Butler[3] and Dr. Chalmers[4] have well shown that we have other than selfish feelings. A man loves a thing itself; not merely the happiness he gets out of the thing. He may love, not the happiness, but the thing. A mother loves the well being of her child, not because it will make her happy, but because it will make her child happy. Though she was to know that well-being but for one moment of her existence, how much more of her own happiness would she sacrifice than could be crowded into that moment of calm intellectual knowing that the child's well-being was secure. So in myriads of instances sacrifices of selfish feelings of interest must be looked upon as instances disproving the doctrine that our own happiness is the generic motive moving all volitions.

"However, it may be requisite," says the Princeton Essayist, "in order to men's being responsible, that they be able to do as they please or choose, yet who will claim that is deemed necessary that they should have the property of choosing the exact contrary of what on the whole appears to them most eligible and desirable?" (254)

We "claim" this very thing. If God, for instance, commands the agent to choose the very reverse of what appears "most eligible and desirable," (a frequent case), every man of sane moral and common sense would affirm that power to that reverse is "necessary" in order to responsibility for not choosing that reverse. If moral obligation require a choice contrary to the apparently "most eligible and desirable," then there must be power for that contrary choice. Otherwise there is requirement for the performance of the impossible, which is infinite injustice, and penalty for the necessary and inevitable act, which is the most appalling fatalism. It will indeed be doubtless replied, "If God's command be obeyed, then God's

3. Joseph Butler, *The Analogy of Religion, Natural and Revealed* (London: Printed for J., J., and P. Knapton, 1736)

4. Thomas Chalmers, *On the Power, Wisdom and Goodness of God, as Manifested in the Adaptation of External Nature, to the Moral and Intellectual Constitution of Man* (London: William and Pickering, 1833)

command will have been the most eligible and desirable." But does not this logician see that he is landed in the old paralogism? The most eligible is chosen, because the chosen was most eligible. The volition is the test of the eligibility.

Since the prevolitional views and feelings are thus, as motives, to a great degree incommensurable, whatever previous "making up of the mind" precedes a given volition that assumes and is based upon their commeasurement must itself be, as has been before said, at least in its terminal point, volitional and free. It must assign the commeasurement, and fix the advising and balance of the intrinsically incommensurable but comparable and opposing motives. Here plainly a vital point of volitional freedom lies. It is not by perception merely that a set of motives intrinsically incommensurable are commeasured; but it is the Will that assigns the balance of the motives, and often furnishes a determination or purpose as to further volition.

A thing or act may appear in many respects most eligible and desirable on one side, while another thing or act may appear most eligible and desirable in many respects on the other side. There may be no intrinsic commensurability between them; and between these two the agent through the equipotent Will makes his decision. It was with a full perception of strongest motive—strongest, that is, in different respects—on both sides that young Solomon chose "an understanding heart." (1 Kings 3:9) It was with a full comprehension of the comparative superior inducements in different respects of either side that young Hercules, in the apologue of Prodicus, chose the offers of Virtue rather than of Pleasure. It was with a vivid view of strongest motives on opposite sides that Caesar chose to cross the Rubicon. There were counter alternatives, and according to our definition the agent put forth the choosing volition with full power of reverse choice instead.

IV

Motives No Necessitative Cause of Volition

B Y THE PRINCIPLES THUS far ascertained we meet the arguments assuming that motives are causes that necessitate volitions.

I. The assumption that for the Will to act in accordance with a motive, and for it to be caused to act by the motives, is essentially the same thing.

Edwards writes: "It comes to just the same thing: to say, the circumstances of the mind are such as tend to sway and turn its inclination one way, is the same thing as to say, the inclination of the mind, as, under such circumstances, tends that way." (263)

The two things are very different. It is one thing to say that the extrinsic "circumstances" impose a necessitative fixation upon the Will to tend a given way; it is another thing to say that "the inclination of the mind," that is, the Will, "under such circumstances," with full power, normally exercised, of tending either way, "tends that way." It is one thing to say that the exterior object secures the volition, excluding power from the Will, to will otherwise; it is another thing to say that in full possession of power to will otherwise, the Will acts in accordance with the exterior object. It is one thing to say that the external presentation fixes the Will to a given act; it is another thing to say that the Will, in presence of several equally possible alternatives, acts for that external presentation. The former of these respective couples of phrases affirms that motive fixes the Will, that the relation of motive is the relation of limitative cause and effect, and that the motive secures the particular volition as its one solely possible result. The latter affirms that the relation of a given motive to will is that of condition to one among several other possible results.

Between the so-called "tendency" of a physical object to a given movement and a tendency of the Will to a given direction there is a wide difference. The tendency of the physical object is in fixed proportion to the forces applied, and is the inevitable result of those forces. The tendency of a tower to lean is in precise adjustment to the measure of opposite forces that press to a downfall or sustain its erectness. The tendency of the Will to a given direction is simply the degree of probability that it will act in that direction of which the result is fully able to be no exact measure. The tower acts in precise fulfillment of the strongest force; the Will acts in no precise fulfillment of the strongest probability. With the tower there is no possibility for the strongest force to fail; with the Will there is full adequate power for the strongest probability to prove null.

II. The assumption that motives are causes that necessitate volition. The following is one of many passages by Edwards to this effect:

> If every act of the Will is excited by a motive, then that motive is the cause of the act of the Will. If the acts of the Will are excited by motives, then motives are the causes of their being excited, or what is the same thing, the cause of their being put forth into act and existence. And if so, the existence of the acts of the Will is properly the effect of their motives. Motives do nothing as motives or inducements but by their influence; and so much as is done by their influence is the effect of them. For that is the notion of an effect, something that is brought to pass by the influence of another thing. And if volitions are properly the effects of their motives, then they are necessarily connected with their motives; every effect and event being, as was proved before, necessarily connected with that which is the proper ground and reason of its existence. Thus it is manifest that volition is necessary. (126)

And again the following:

> And besides, if the acts of the Will are excited by motives, those motives are the causes of those acts of the Will which makes the acts of the Will necessary; as effects necessarily follow the efficiency of the cause. (266)

The points here made are:

1. That as volition is produced or excited by motive, so the relation of motive and volition is that of nonalternative cause and effect.

2. To arise from the "influence" of motive is to be the nonalternative effect of motives.

3. To be the effect is to be necessarily caused; the relation of cause and effect being a necessary relation.

4. Therefore volition is necessarily caused by motive.

Before directly meeting these points we may note that it will not do to say that all this necessity is really but "mere certainty," that is, any certainty distinct from the most absolute necessity.

ANY NECESSITY

If there be any necessity which is different from certainty this must be that very necessity. For it is that necessity that exists in the relation of nonalternative cause and effect. And it consists in the non-existence of power for the effect to be without the cause, or to not be with the cause, or to be otherwise than caused. It is not the mere non-usage but nonexistence of such power. This relation is just as necessary as any other causal relation whatever; for Edwards claims that if it can be loosed, every other causal relation will be loosed and atheism will result. So that it is as strong and immovable as any causal relation in the universe; and all things fall to pieces if it is in the least degree softened or invalidated.

To the above points we now state our counter points.

1. Motive and volition do not stand in the relation of nonalternative cause and effect. Of volition the cause, the sole cause, is Will. Motives are collateral conditions without which there is no adequate power for the volition to be; with which there is adequate power for the volition not to be. The relation therefore is not "fixed"; the antecedent motive does not "make sure" the enacting of the volition; the relation is not that of necessity. Notwithstanding the motive, the Will in projecting the volition is non-necessitated and free.

To say "the acts of the Will are excited by motives" is scarcely correct; for feelings, not volitions are the object of excitement. But it is untrue that for motives to excite the volition is the same as for the motive necessitatively to cause the volition. For the motive is only the occasion, and all its acts of excitement amount to no more than this, that they stand as probable conditions opening the way toward which the Will thereby acquires opportunity to act with full adequate power of not acting. And this is very far from being "the cause of their being put forth into act and existence."

2. For the volition to arise from the influence of motives is not the same as to be the effect of motives. To be the effect of motives, in the Edwardean sense, is so to depend for existence upon the motives that for the motives existing there is no adequate power for the volition not

to exist. As motives, then, are no cause of volitions, so volitions are no effect of motives. Volitions are what follow, and are the results, or events of motives, not their effects.

3. The relation of cause and effect is not (so far as Will is concerned) a necessary relation. The affirmative of this proposition is assumed by Edwards as universal, not only in physics, where its universality is admitted, but in volitions. On the contrary, we exclude it not only from motives in relation to volition, but from Will as nonalternative cause of nonalternative effects. The relation between motive and volition we hold to be contingency, which in itself is blind; the relation between Will and volition we hold to be alternativity, which is not blind. The Will is cause and not the motive, not because the relation of necessity exists in the relation between Will and volition, but because the position of Will is central and constant, while that of motive is subsidiary and transient; and because the Will is the controlling conscious self in the exercise of direct power in producing volition. The volition, though the effect of this power, inasmuch as it is able to be withheld, is not necessarily caused.

4. Nor is volition the necessary result of the motive. If, though the motive exists, there is full power for the volition to exist or not exist, arising from the causative power of the Will, then the relation of the Will to the motive is not necessitation, and the volition is not necessary. If there is the higher probability that the motive will result in the actuality of the volition, and yet the higher probability yields to a lower counter probability, then the relation between motive and volition is not that of necessity.

III. The argument by pseudo-synonyms.

Edwards argues from a series of equivalent terms in the following manner:

> If motives dispose the mind to action, then they cause the mind to be disposed; and to cause the mind to be disposed is to cause it to be willing; and to cause it to be willing is to cause it to will; and that is the same thing as to be the cause of an act of the Will. And yet this same Mr. Chubb holds it to be absurd to suppose motive to be the cause of the act of the Will. (143)

But the question is not whether motives cause the soul to will, but whether the cause is necessitative. Words expressive of causation, both nouns and verbs, we have in the proper place stated, are with allowable impropriety applied to designate the influence of motive upon Will, without deciding that they express more than contingent condition. Motives upon the individual Will or upon the Wills collectively of whole masses, are frequently called cause, actual or potential, whether the action really follows or not. If a given motive condition is accorded with by the Will, it is a resultant cause; if it is not accorded with, it may still be called a cause, adequate and potential, yet not resultant.

IV. The Argument from Approximation.

Edwards argues that "when motives are very strong all will allow that there is some difficulty in going against them. If they were yet greater, the difficulty would be stronger. Unless, therefore, men have an infinite power of resistance, the motive influence might be so strong as to be impossible to be resisted." Such is the argument by approximation. We remark:

1. If the influence is solely on one side and no alternative is present before the mind in the opposite direction, it has already been stated in the proper place that there is an objective-limit to freedom in the case. If there are opposite motives, then influence, however great, cannot be infinite; for it is only the remainder after the opposite has been subtracted.

2. The amount of motive influence must be also measured by the receptive capacity of a finite being. Only an infinite capacity can receive an infinite amount of motive impression, and that same infinite capacity aided by an opposite motive (which is always to be supposed) can resist it. Human experience amply shows that the human Will can, with motive opposite, resist the utmost motive influence that human capacity can receive. Mrs. Hemans[1] has celebrated in verse the boy Casabianca, who was stationed upon shipboard and charged by his father not to leave his post. He firmly maintained his stand, even though the fire raged before his face, and perished in the flame, a martyr of constancy. He withstood the most immediately intense and powerful motive that could be brought to bear upon the human Will.

HOWEVER STRONG

But the motive, however strong, unless it is of such a force, or of such suddenness of shock as to expel and exclude all counter motive, or so decisive that all Will as Will would choose in accordance, and so produce an objective necessitation, leaves the freedom untouched. Between the

---

1. Felicia Hemans (1793–1835) was an English poet, whose works appeared in nineteen books.

motives within these limits there will still arise counter probabilities, to which the law of probabilities will still apply, that the higher may yield to the lower.

V. The notion that not to be causatively necessitated by strongest motive force is an irrational exemption from all motive influence, and is to be insanely loose from all reason.

By what can a man be better governed, it is asked, than by the highest reason? To be governed otherwise is to be the subject of folly. And to be no way influenced by it, which, according to free-willism, must be the perfection of freedom, would be a complete exemption from sense or reason. The highest freedom would therefore be the most complete idiocy.

If, we reply, by the highest reason is meant the motive apparently to the individual most strong, brutes, fools, and madmen are, by the necessitarian theory, as much governed by it as anybody. And this, by any theory, is the obvious fact; for the volitions of such persons very much resemble the mechanical movement under strongest motive-force that necessitarianism implies.

If by highest reason is meant the absolutely truest wisdom, there can be nothing higher and better, or more unlike idiocy or madness, than to act, as a free agent, according to its influences. As a free agent, we say, for if it is as a living sensitive automaton, fixedly giving forth the motions, corporeal or volitional, precisely according to the motive-force applied, then there can be something better and nobler, of which this is but the mockery. There can be a true free agent, willing, with power otherwise, most freely, for the true highest reason.

The highest reason is often, necessitarianism being judge, to the individual the lesser motive. Necessity in such a case excludes him from the highest reason and shuts him to the opposite. Freedom is the condition of choosing according to the highest reason, even though against the relatively strongest motive.

VI. The sum of contradictions.

Edwards thus sums up the opposite sides of Mr. Chubb's statement of free will:

> And if we compare these things together we have here again a whole heap of inconsistencies. Motives are the previous ground and reason of the acts of the Will; yea, the necessary ground and reason of their exertion, without which they will not be exerted, and cannot in the nature of things take place, and they do excite

these acts of the Will, and do this by a prevailing influence, yea, an influence which prevails for the production of the act of the Will, and for the disposing of the mind to it; and yet it is absurd to suppose motive to be a cause of an act of the Will, or that a principle of Will is moved or caused to be exerted by it, or that it has any causality in the production of it, or any causality to be the cause of the exertion of the Will. (143)[2]

The "heap of inconsistencies" lies in the supposed contradiction between the two members of the sentence lying before and after the phrase "and yet." But taking the words "cause" and "causality" in the latter members of the sentence in the necessitative sense, both sides are consistent and soundly true. Motives may be "the previous ground and reason of the Will, yea, the necessary" (in the sense of requisite) ground, etc., without which the Will act not. They may excite by a prevailing influence, which prevails for the act; they may be fully and freely acted in accordance with; "and yet," astonishing as it may seem, the said motives may still not be the necessitative causes of the volition. They may still be sidelong conditions, without which the Will cannot act; with each one of which there is a probability, more or less strong, that the Will will act accordingly. The probability though superior may fail by the Will's acting not accordingly, or the inferior may prevail by the Will's acting accordingly. And so the motive, though a requisite condition, is not a necessitating cause.

---

2. For the philosophy addressed by Edwards here, see Thomas Chubb. *A Collection of Tracts on Various Subjects* (London: Printed for T. Cox, 1754). Chubb (1679–1747) was a prominent English deist.

V

Uniformities of Volitions

As FREE WILL HAS been viewed by those who have little studied its nature to be synonymous with lawlessness, so on the other hand the impossibility of lawlessness and the actual experience of uniformities of volition both in the continuous life of one individual and in the aggregate of masses of men, are held by some as demonstrative of necessitarianism.

A Napoleon through a whole career puts forth an entire series of volitions in conformity with one great predominant purpose. A jailer's will is, practically, as reliable as the dungeon walls. An army with the uniform and concurring will of its hundred thousand soldiers is the despot's reliance for the stability of his throne. A uniform number of suicides in a given community, a uniform number of letters passing through the post office, in the course of several years marks the uniformity of human volitions. On all this I remark:

1. The very definition of a free Will is in proof that uniformity may be its course as truly as variety or irregularity. If the Will can choose either way, it can choose in a uniform way. If it can choose lawlessly, it can also choose a rule, and ever after put forth its choices in accordance with that rule.

2. In our chapter upon the conditions of Will we have in effect shown causative limitations by which however subjectively free, it is objectively unfree. Thus much uniformity is accounted for.

In accordance with principles previously laid down, uniformities of volitions may be considered as taking place from positive reasons or negative.

The positive methods consist in the influence of motives, which we define as consisting in the probabilities with which the Will is likely to choose in behalf of such motives. The greater the probability, therefore, the more conclusive the explanation of the fact of the uniformity. The uniformity may be calculably so probable as to be practically, though not absolutely, certain or necessary. Empirically, though not incontestably, the uniformity may be general if not universal.

The negative method by which volitional uniformity takes place consists in the mental exclusion of all attention to or thought of a counter course or alternative. This is a strictly necessitative limitation in the given case, drawing an impassable boundary line around the area of volitional freedom. If there is no adequate power in the given case of bringing within the knowledge or mental comprehension other than one course, volitional freedom is limited to that one course and there arises an absolute necessity.

We may specify four generic cases in which one or the other of these two methods takes place, namely, corporeal nature, dispositions, standard purposes, and habits.

Without adopting the theory of *unisubstanceism* (one substance) as held by Spinoza,[1] we may maintain the very fact that substance itself, lying at the basis of all agents, forms a most generic basis of unity and uniformity. But, in addition, all human agents being corporeal, with a corporeity the same in nature, as if all were organic structures made from the same material, possess a still more specific ground of natural and necessary uniformity. To this bodily basis belongs a set of natural properties as of mere matter, a higher set as of corporeal matter, and a still higher set as of corporeal organism, in all of which all bodies agree and are uniform. These bodily organisms, as they blend with mind and unite with soul, furnish a large nature base for an immense amount of uniform phenomena. Corporeal form, strength, and peculiarities shape a large number of the actions and habits of men. Hereditary constitution, national peculiarities, and personal idiosyncrasies modify a large part of our manners, movements, impulses, and mental tendencies. This corporeal basis receives a large share of its fixed nature at birth, and the born material does, through all the changes of age, receive from surrounding circumstances its shaping, as a cast is modeled by its mould. Such is the lowest, the nature formation, upon which as a primitive the successive strata of character are formed.

---

1. James Buchanan. *Modern Atheism: Under Its Forms of Pantheism, Materialism, Secularism, Development and Natural Laws* (Boston: Gould and Lincoln, 1857), 147.

By *dispositions* we mean the entire set of primitive prevolitional mental tendencies in the natural constitution, as well as all those that have grown, or been acquired, upon this constitutional base. The intellectual views and beliefs, the emotional susceptibilities, the desires and appetites, the moral sensibilities and tendencies, the nervous and sensorial excitabilities, the corporeal appetites, all combine to furnish motives, amid which the Will decides. And as these different constituents exist in different force in different individuals, so there exist accordingly greater or lesser probabilities that the choices will or will not take place in given directions. As a practical rule, it may be laid down that where there is no prevolitional propensity of some one or more of these kinds, there will be no corresponding action. As a practical rule, too, where given propensities are strong and temptations constant in a given direction, a reliable certainty of yielding action arises, which bears an exterior resemblance to necessity. The individual who resists once, twice, or thrice, yet is exposed to a perpetual temptation of intense character against which he can interpose no excluding barrier, is worn out, and seems as if he were not to possess the amount of resisting strength to maintain a perpetual warfare and a perpetual victory. However volitionally free such an agent may be intrinsically, the probabilities of his sinlessness are likely to be in inverse proportion to the continuity of his exposures.

CORPOREAL NATURE

These prevolitional tendencies, with their corporeal nature base, when intensely favorable to evil in their character, and accepted by the Will, constitute the fountain of which evil conduct is the stream. If all adequate possibility of interposing good motive into the mind is wanting, then, by the very laws of mind, there is likely to be an absence of volitional freedom for the good.

If such is the state of the dispositions that the love of God cannot be a motive of action then there results a state that may be called total spiritual depravity. Where this exists a spiritual renovation is needed, either by injecting the possibility of spiritual motive into the dispositions, or by a correction of the dispositions themselves, or both. And this is done by the Holy Spirit. Where such a state of dispositions or surrounding circumstances, or both, exists as that moral motive cannot be interposed as a ground of action, then we have a moral depravity or lawlessness.

Where the absence of the possibility of motive for good, and so of action, is from the first moment of volitional capability necessitated, there can be no moral probation, responsibility, or just penalty. Where the possibility once existed and has been freely and positively banished by the agent, the responsibility remains. Where it has been congenitally non-existent, but has been graciously placed within the reach and freely rejected, the responsibility remains. Where the depravity is congenital, yet the offer for its regeneration is freely presented but the retention of depravity is freely preferred, then it is ratified, sanctioned, and responsibly appropriated.

Habits are uniformities of action that may be said to grow upon us by repetition. They are uniformities of volition, too and are often performed with so little deliberation as to acquire a resemblance to instinct. Positively, habit arises by the influence of the same recurring motives for which the Will will act. These motives are brought up by the laws of intellectual association of time, place, objects, and causation. Natural impulses seem to spring up in the being, physical and psychological, suggesting the usual volition. Meantime, negatively, counter motive and counter thought are gradually more perfectly and constantly excluded. No other than the given way is imagined or enters into the mind. And thus the volitions move, as in a passage way walled upon either side. The wall is an amalgam of blending freedom and necessity.

Habit, being self-formed, however strong, seldom or never ceases to be volitional and responsible. Even should the circumscribing wall become hardened to a "fixed" necessity, responsibility can perhaps never terminate. No man can build up a palisade to exclude himself from the path of righteousness and then excuse himself for not treading therein.

Standard purposes are volitions adopting an extended course of volitional actions, and to which, in consequences, an extended number of volitions subordinate themselves. They are plans, enterprises, and resolutions, determinations, which contemplate and include a due number of volitions in obedience to themselves. Yet it is important to note that these standard volitions do not of themselves directly and of their own power necessitate the subordinate volitions. A man is free in carrying out his plans and resolutions. The existence of the plan as a permanent standard motive furnishes the probability, more or less strong, that the subordinate volition will sustain it. The motive may be so permanent and strong as to create a firm reliability that the subordinate volitions will accord. Indirectly, the counter motives may be excluded so as to leave the mind completely shut up to the positive motive, and a necessitation is superinduced. Men, thus, may be so absorbed in their plans as to cease to be free, alternative agents. But they seldom or never thereby lose their responsibility.

Men put forth at given points of their lives decisive volitions to which their whole subsequent history becomes more or less subordinated. A person engages in a profession, contracts a marriage, undertakes an enterprise, becomes absorbed in a study, which may be a life-long matter. But lesser standard purposes there are, covering a much briefer line of volitions. A man takes a journey of a few hours, undertakes a brief essay, or manufactures a single article. The number of subordinate volitions herein included is far larger than might at first be imagined, but small in comparison with our life-long settlements.

INCLUSIVE PURPOSES

But there are lesser inclusive purposes still, which are occurring every hour and moment of life, to which their little sets of minor volitions subordinate themselves. We cannot walk across the floor, or eat a meal, or read a page, or even write a single alphabetic character, without a purpose fulfilled by lesser volitions. How numerous and rapid the volitions by which a lady executes her purpose of playing a tune upon the piano! Indeed, as the tones of music are a succession of infinitesimal pulsations or vibrations, melting into each other so as to form a flow, so most of our courses of action are formed of a series of infinitesimal volitions.

Maxims and opinions may be volitionally so adopted as to become standard purposes. An opinion may be theoretically believed with no practical effect until the Will has adopted it as a reason of action. A man may disbelieve the Christian religion, and yet may act his disbelief so little externally that it may be supposed by his acquaintances that he is a theoretical believer until he commences a course of open opposition. A large share of education consists in the volitional adoption of maxisms and principles as fundamental and permanent grounds of action. Repentance and reformation are the adoption into practice of a belief of the badness of sin, and the preferability of a right cause. By means of all those fundamental adoptions a character different from the first and natural constitution is with more or less completeness newly formed.

So largely and effectively do the dispositions, the habits, and the standard purposes influence the volitions, both by position and impulse, and by excluding counter courses from the view, that the agent, however intrinsically and by nature free, is to a great extent objectively unfree. Perhaps of many lives, if not most or all, a full analysis would show that a large majority of the volitions are thus objectively not free. And this very consideration may serve to explain the error of many thinkers in too hastily inferring that all volitions are unfree, and that the agent is not free intrinsically and by nature. They select a few cases that are in fact cases of objective necessitation, and draw the rash induction of necessity over all volitions, human and divine. A large number of the test instances selected in the argument between freedom and necessity may be cases of necessitation from the above-named influences, and so may be hastily held to decide the question. The observation of an inquirer may rest mainly upon volitions of this class; and so he may fall under the impression that life is ruled by necessity. The true ascertainment of the sorts of choices hemmed in by objective limitation, may serve as the proper guard against these heedless generalizations.

Thus, if we have rightly traced the process, is constituted character. Upon a basis of corporeal, physiological and mental nature are overlaid a primary superstratum of dispositions blending the native and the volitional, and a secondary formation of generic purposes wholly volitional, and formed by repetition into a tertiary of habits. And thus we have in his mingled constitution of necessitation and freedom an agent prepared for daily free responsible action. The question arises not only how far this character is necessitated, but how far it is necessitative. How far is the character a fixed antecedent, limiting and unipotently excluding all but a sole volitional result?

At start we may repudiate all such one-sided and extravagant statements on this subject as the following from the Princeton Essays:

> All will doubtless admit that, although the natural faculty of Will exerts the choice, the direction of that choice under given outward motives is determined not by the bare natural faculty, but by its moral state. Thus the faculty of the will equally in good and bad men exerts their volitions; but their moral goodness or badness determines the direction and quality of those choices. (255)

If this indeed is true, then all the actions of a holy being must be necessarily holy. How, then, the first holy angels sinned, how the first Adam fell, how the second Adam was really tempted, how a holy universe originated transgression, it would puzzle the Essayist to tell. If his doctrine is true, the sinful being must as necessarily emit sin as the charcoal emits its black shade and the holy being must as necessarily shed holy effect as the diamond radiates the bright beam. All moral change for either good or evil in the finite agent must be by reconstruction from an arbitrary interposing omnipotence. From the omnipotent first cause all secondary causes must receive the necessitating causation of their good or evil effects. Evil as well as good finds from this awful doctrine the primordial, necessitating, intentional cause in God. And yet, contradictorily, this is impossible; for God, being holy, can cause nothing unholy, and so no sin can be caused by him.

LARGE ADMISSIONS

In the first place, large admissions may be readily made in favor of the actual power of the past over our present actions, as well as over the permanent nature of our future action. It may be, so far as it extends, a real causation, sometimes a necessitation, limiting the free future fulfillment. Or it forms a basis of probable, often of reliable, but not incontestable calculation. Our everyday life in its details is more or less voluntarily and volitional surrendered over to its influence.

1. A character may be formed with a mind so wholly circumscribed within a circle of sensual feelings and conceptions, selfish and corrupt maxims, sordid purposes and habits, that complete inventory of the thoughts is depraved, and no honorable or truly ethical volition is within the catalogue of possibilities. Of such a character it may be said, without our being obliged to define whether it is a cause of necessity or reliable certainty, which he cannot will nobly or rightly. On the other hand, another character may be formed, by a noble course of self-education, by the continual rejection of the sensual, selfish, and sordid, and the constant adoption of the honorable, the intellectual, the just, and the independent; so that, finally, everything mean or depraved is spontaneously rejected, the motive of its presented alternative being impossible, or repelled by mental exclusion; and the man's admirers shall say with possible truth

that it is impossible that he should have descended to a particular vile action. These are the causes of reliable probability, possibly of necessity.

Comparatively few, however, in all probability, of these are causes of unequivocal necessity; few or none perhaps there are of whom such an impossibility can be affirmed in regard to every form of excellence or unworthiness. Even the very permanence of the constitutional base, both on the worthy and the unworthy side, secures to a very great degree the power of motivation in opposite alternatives, and maintains a foundation for a reversal of generic determinations, of life-laid plans, and long indulged habits.

There is plentifully in the history of free agents such a thing as "acting out of character." There is often the action, great or small, which reverses the record of life or a protracted course of action. He who well watches his neighbor, however blind he may be to his own practical self-contradictions, is sure to find, even in the life most even in its great outline, plenty of minor inconsistencies. Or as Müller well says, that both our observation and our subject's temptation may occur just at the moment of one of his great volitional turning points.[2] From the apostacy of the first angels, and the Fall of man through the whole course of human history, we have innumerable instances of revolutionary volitions, not only out of the previous character, but shaping a new character. The one disastrous sin of Moses, the one great complicated crime of David, the apostacy of Solomon, the wisest of men, are all proofs how, not only in contrasted traits, but in revolutionary acts, a man may be

The wisest, greatest, meanest of mankind.

2. Cases of apparent necessary action from antecedent character are often solved upon the principle of contradiction. A man can neither be nor do contradictory things at the same moment. He cannot at once maintain and abdicate a given character.

That original thinker, Buffier, supposes the question: Can a sage enact the mountebank in the public street?[3] Fenelon had decided it to be a moral impossibility; yet defining, in an undertone, this impossibility to be only a very difficult thing that might sometimes be done. Pe`re Daniel

---

2. Julius Muller, *The Doctrine of Sin* (Edinburgh: T. & T. Clark, 1868)

3. Claude Buffier, *Traite des Premieres Veritas et de la Source de nos Jugements* (Paris: Chez la Veuve Mauge, 1724)

had decided that from want of motive the thing could not be done by a true sage.

Mr. Buffier decides that the man could play the buffoon, but yet the playing buffoon by a sage could never be done. Why? Because the buffoon player by the very act is no sage. It is the impossibility of incompatibility or contradiction. Whichever side is assumed excludes the other. Ice cannot be melted, for to be at once completely melted and ice is a contradiction. The carnal heart cannot be subject to the law of God, for the heart when conformed to the law is no longer carnal. Carnality and conformity to holy law are a contradiction. So a perfectly chaste woman cannot be a prostitute; nor a truthful man a liar. And when from long observation of a woman or a man we feel confident of the character, we take, inductively, the affirmative that they are permanently chaste or truthful, and with some generous hyperbole we pronounce in the instances that she cannot be immodest, and that he cannot have grossly lied. It is in this principle of contradiction that terms of power or want of power are extensively used where many have supposed there is only want of willingness. This point we discuss in another place.

3. From the very nature of this formed character we expect the immediately future action to be in accordance with it. And this not because the coming action is necessitatively shaped by the character, but because visibly the character is as the sum total of the actions. Or rather upon a correct view the character is an amalgam of the free volitions and the prevolitional dispositions as contemplated together. When a volition comes unexpected and out of character we accept it, correct our previous estimate of the man, and add the new fact into the sum total of which his visible character is made.

But the power to predict action from previous character is often overestimated. Hits of that kind, instead of proving the completeness with which it can be done prove the very reverse, for it is the extraordinary character of the hit that makes it impressive. The knowledge of the style of action to be expected is usually very generic, and leaves a very broad play for varying particulars. When it is specific, it is of some single trait or two that streaks through the action of life. We have a clear idea of a lady's style of motion, even in casting a dice; but how totally we fail to predict what depends upon the character of the motion, the particular throw she will turn up.

Of the nearest friends with whom we associate, and whose character of mind, and habits, and peculiarities we best understand, while we can give some general account and make some fair general predictions, yet how utterly will we be at a loss, ordinarily and every hour of the day, to tell what will be the next immediate action, or how they will choose in given circumstances. You cannot conjecture with any confidence, usually, what, with the circumstance before you, will be the words your most familiar friend will next pronounce.

GENERICALLY PREDICT

You can but very generically predict in the morning what minuter motions, steps, and walks your bosom friend will, even in a give set of circumstances, perform during the day. In all life, character, course of action, there is variation ever more widely varying, opening new traits to view, defying all mechanical calculation, and attesting the reality of freedom.

4. Statistics are cited by necessitarian writers showing that in Paris the amount of crimes, even those crimes that may be especially supposed to depend upon individual peculiarities, is annually nearly equal. This is held by many to be an arithmetical demonstration of the doctrine of volitional necessity. But,

1. It does not appear why this might not as truly be the case on the doctrine of freedom as the doctrine of necessity. In the calculations of contingencies, as we have very fully said, while results of compared large aggregates, in the same conditions, may approach equality, the contingency of each individual case remains still a contingency. If our best illustration of the contingencies of freedom is drawn from the laws of Probability, what is more reasonably to be expected than that the most perfect alternating of individual Will should result in a degree of aggregate uniformity? So, though large aggregates of free volitions, surrounded by the same round of motives, may approach equality, the freedom of each individual Will remains.

2. This uniformity of statistics can be true only so long as the aggregate character of the city remains contingently the same. It amounts to this, then, that where the aggregate character remains the same, the number of individual crimes will be about the same; and when the number of individual crimes shall change, the aggregate character will change. That is, the aggregate character is made of individual facts. A city is thus

like a stupendous individual, whose stages of development are on as stupendous a comparative scale as its magnitude, but which in its life of centuries within its compass of surrounding influences acts with its full measure of limited freedom. Its free development is partly a sum total of individual freedoms and partly organic in character.

3. But while such statistics show that freedom often operates in the aggregate very much by rule, we are confident there are others which are, or might be kept, that exhibit freedom in its full variations. Accurate church registers, kept by permanent pastors, show very different numbers of conversions per year. Some seasons surely are remarkable for a much greater religious interest than others. The number of public general prayer meetings in New York City has greatly differed in different years. Other seasons are specially marked by an extraordinary number of strangulations or garrotings. Particular periods occur of specially numerous suicides, fires, or steamboat or railroad accidents. If uniformities, thus, prove necessity, these irregularities must equally demonstrate freedom. From all this we conclude that while it is not to be unexpected that freedom should result in great aggregate uniformities, there are ample enough varieties to vindicate the Will from the imputation of necessity.

VI

Double Volition

FALLING BACK UPON OUR first definition that free will is competent to choose either of several objects, each several object stands before the Will, being an object only as invested with the motivation. Therein the Will chooses, by its own one act, either one of the several objects, with a stronger probability perhaps arising from the motive of choice for one over another, yet with the full possibility that the counter of that one may be selected.

The freedom lies in the agent in the motive conditions, at the initial spring of the volition, so that the volition is called free because it springs from a free cause, that is, a free agent. The particular object chosen receives its prevalence from the Will and by the choice; so that taking the word Motive in the sense of prevalent motive, there is a truth in the maxim that "it is the Will that makes the motive." For though the choice is subsequent to the perception of the eligible or potential motive quality in the object, and may be called an alternative consequence of it, it is that subsequent choice itself by which the potential motive becomes actually prevalent motive, that is, by which a motive becomes *the* motive.

The motive is often an agreeable or otherwise eligible quality in the object chosen. An apple is chosen for its sweetness as motive, a rose for its beauty, and a perfume for its fragrance. At other times there is a separate motive-object that invests the object of choice with its motivation. The game is the motive for which the sportsman chooses a gun. Money is the object for which the laborer toils. Yet after all these, motive-objects lend their motivation to the choice-object and thereby render it the choice-object. It is the motivation by which the object of volition becomes its object. The motivation is the true object in the object and is really chosen in it. Necessitarians say we choose what we think best; and if so the said best is ever both the true motive and object, one and the same. So that

146

ever and always we truly choose the motive when we choose the object, by one and the same act.

These views may refute the imputation by Edwards against a certain freedomist, Mr. Chubb, of really holding that in every volition we first choose the motive for the volition and then we choose the volition. Mr. Chubb holds language like this: "Every man has power to act or to refrain from acting, agreeably with or contrary to any motive that presents."[1] "Every man is at liberty to act, or refrain from acting, agreeably with or contrary to what each of these motives considered singly would excite him to."[2] "Man has power, and is as much at liberty to reject the motive that does prevail, as he has power and is at liberty to reject those motives that do not."[3] These are perspicuous statements of the truth of the matter. But Edwards imputes to them the doctrine that the Will first by one volition chooses the motive to which it will yield, and then by a second volition acts from the motive. Thence would follow not only that each volition is duplicate, but that each of every duplication is also duplicate ad infinitum.

EXCELLENCE BORROWED

The eligibility, motivation, or excellence borrowed from the motive-object is or becomes a quality in the object or alternative of volition. It inheres, as quality, and goes to make up the object. Now surely it is very absurd to say that it requires one choice to choose the quality, and another to choose the object. The object with its qualities stands as alternative with others before the Will; and the agent chooses with full power of choice for either. So that Mr. Chubb is correct in saying, "Every man has power to act (volitionally) or to refrain from acting, agreeably with, or contrary to, any motive that presents." And this does not imply that there must be duplicate volitions, the one to choose the motive and the other to choose the object.

---

1. Thomas Chubb, *A Collection of Tracts on Various Subjects*, 2:27.
2. Ibid. 28.
3. Ibid.

VII

Activity No Passivity

SOME ADVOCATES OF THE doctrine of volitional freedom have made it a part of their argument to maintain that there can be an activity without a passivity. Taking the liberty that every writer has the right to assume of defining his own terms and adhering to his definition in the present discussion, they have limited the terms *act* and *action* to the exercise of the Will. They have thence maintained that there is such a thing as action that is no passion, an agent who is not a patient, a mover who is not moved, a doer who is not caused to do.

In reply, Edwards maintains sternly that there can be no agent who is not caused to act, and who so far as caused is not a patient. Every mover is caused to move, and he moves only as he is moved to move. To move and to be moved are but opposite sides of the same thing. There is no movement that is not being moved. All agents act as they are caused to act; activity and passivity are inseparable correlatives.

How strict a fatalism this is, and how truly Edwards, who maintains it, is a fatalist, and how his argument excludes not merely the use but the existence of power of counter choice, we need but leave the reader to decide. Every agent and every Will is but a term in a series of inflexible causations; the volitional is as fixed as the material term or unit in the series. The dynamic series is just as rigorously exact, just as absolute a necessity in contradistinction to certainty, in volitional agency as in mechanics or any part of natural and physical forces.

If our view of volitional freedom is true, there is action where there is no passion. There is such a thing as an uncaused causal act. It exists in the Will putting forth its alternative volition. The Will in its proper conditions is a full and complete cause uncausedly effectuating the particular volition. In the particular act, in the putting forth of the volition there is a causative producing that is uncaused by anything beside or back of Will, and which, as has been shown, the laws of causality do not require to be so caused. A unipotent cause must in its every particular action be caused to put forth that particular effect. But of an alternative cause either one of several particular results may be the effect without any antecedent to cause that alternative cause to produce that particularity. Here, then, is so far an agent not a moved patient, an activity without a passivity, and that without any harm to the laws of causation.

"And this implies," says Edwards, "that action has no cause and is no effect; for to be an effect implies passiveness, or the being subject to the power and action of its cause." Undoubtedly, the "action" is caused by the agent in bringing it into existence; but the agent is not caused to bring it into existence. The action, indeed, as the receiver of existence, as the abstract fact produced, is necessitated to undergo the agent's causation and come into being. But the agent is patient to no anterior cause necessitating bringing the act into existence. There is an agent, no moved patient.

EDWARDS CONTINUES

This "notion of action," Edwards continues, "implies that it has no necessary dependence or connection with anything foregoing; for such a dependence excludes contingence and implies necessity." (282) Undoubtedly, the act or deed is dependent on the agent for its existence. As a condition to the fact's existence, the factor's existence is necessary; in the sense, however, of requisite. The deed could not exist without the doer, or the volition without the willer. But this proves, not conversely, that the agent could not exist without the volition, the potential factor without that particular fact. Nor does it touch the question whether the agent, putting forth the particular volition, may not be a cause uncausedly producing effect, and so may not be an agent who is no moved patient.

The final argument of Edwards on this point, that freedomists require that free choice must be put forth by previous free choice, comes under his old fallacy of the infinite series. His argument here is in form of a dilemma. Free choice must be chosen by free choice, and that is infinite series; or the mind is made subject of free choice without any free choice in the matter, and that is necessity. Very well. It then follows, and this is all that follows, that the agent is necessarily a free agent. For, to be the subject of free choice, is to be a free agent; to be so without any previous free choice of our own is to be necessarily a free agent. But that proves not that the free choice itself is in its particularity necessitated. It still leaves us an agent, no moved victim. There is a free cause which causes a particularity without being caused to cause it and without needing any cause of its causing.

The acts of a free agent are, therefore, not a fixed term in a necessary series. They are not in the line of fixed nature. They are not, like a mechanical operation, a moving as moved. Inevitable forces do not rule all things; necessity is not master of the universe; fatalism is not lord of God and man.

From what has been said above it may appear that there is some difference between saying that the Will acts on account of a motive, and saying that the Will is governed by the motive. Government, just so far as it goes, implies limitation, control by causation, non-existence of power but to a fixation. It implies in the Will passivity without proper activity; that the activity is only passivity, caused motion rather than free action. No doubt limitative causation (and so irresponsibility) rules the main part of our nature. But just where is the alternative action of Will the limitation force approaches but does not touch? The Will freely acts on account of the motive but is not governed by it.

VIII

Determination from Indetermination

F ROM OUR DEFINITION OF freedom of the Will, that it is the power of choosing either of several alternatives, it will follow that before the putting forth of the given volition there is a state, during a longer or shorter period, of deliberation, balance, or equilibrium. This state may last but an indivisible instant, and terminates at the initial point of the volition. The commencement of the volition is the close of the indetermination. In this case, as in all other cases of cause and effect, the effect goes forth, or rather is put forth, in a manner not to be explained, from a quiescent cause.

This state of indetermination of the Will has been called indifference, and hence the phrase, liberty of indifference; but as it is the act of volition which terminates the balance and creates the difference, the state previous to the volition may truly be called a state of volitional non-difference rather than indifference. The non-difference is not in the prevolitional faculties, but in the Will. But inasmuch as at the present day the term indifference is exclusively applied to the feelings or prevolitional operations its use is likely to mislead .The so-called liberty of indifference is the liberty of a Will existing in such a state of previous indetermination as that it possesses full conscious power to choose either of several ways.

This non-differentiation of the Will prior to the given action, and while it is quiescent as to the particular volition, is perfectly consistent with the abundant existence of differentiations in the prevolitional mental elements. In the intellect, conscience, emotions, desires, there may coexist plenty of inclinations, predispositions, tendencies, preponderances, and preferences, either way or both ways. All these might exist and fluctuate with terrible energy without the existence of even the faculty of the Will in the soul.

This statement of the coexistence of prevolitional preferences with a non-differentiation in the Will, will solve at once much of the necessitarian verbal argumentation in which the term "inclination" is made to play an ambiguous part. Thus the Princeton Essayist says, "For if the Will be in a condition by which it is fitted or liable to turn either way, then it cannot be already inclined by a preponderating bias in one direction: for this is but saying that it chooses the contrary of its own preference."

"Inclination," we reply, may be either volitional or prevolitional. In the latter case it is fully consistent, and may be coexistent with a "condition" of the Will's being able "to turn either way." If by "a preponderating bias in one direction" is meant what we have elsewhere called a permanent state of purpose into which the agent has been resolved by a previous volition, then, as has been explained, that purpose or "bias" simply constitutes a motive, which will come into view when the question of change at any time rises before the Will.

ORDINARY OCCURRENCE

The change of such a "bias" is an ordinary occurrence in the operations of the human mind. It is a choosing by the agent of "the contrary of its own preferences" previously existing. True it is, the Will cannot choose the contrary of its own volition; for a volition proper is an instantaneous act, and such choosing the contrary would imply the coexistence of contradictory volitions. But the moment the volition has passed, having placed the mind in a state of determinate purpose, such purpose, as above said, becomes simply a motive against change by the Will, and not a necessitative exclusion of change.

The inclusion by Edwards of all our active sensibilities under Will betrays him in the conjuring up of imaginary contradictions, such as (100) "to prefer contrary to its own preference, or choose contrary to its own choice"; "to prefer and not to prefer at the same time, or to choose contrary to its own present choice." That such contrary matters do coexist in the mind we trust has been amply and satisfactorily shown.

In his chapter upon Liberty of Indifference, Edwards makes the following points: 1. He assumes that the "indifference" preceding the volition is a self-balanced inertness, a deadlock, a complete blocking of the whole being. From it, therefore, he argues that no action can take origin. 2. This indifference must be not partial, but total and absolute so that no action to produce volition can co-exist with it. 3. He assumes the necessity of producing volition by a previous producing act, which must, by self-contradiction, be put forth within the stagnant indifference. 4. The freedom=indifference and the volition must coexist, which is a further contradiction.

1. Upon the first of these points we remark that the Will, or the volitional agent, is not a powerless, indifferent, inert substance, in perfect stagnation; but a full, free, complete and adequate causal power in the proper conditions for the alternatives before it. It is not a state of powerlessness, but the seat of primordial power, the type whence, perhaps, our primitive idea of power is obtained. We know nothing of power except as the basis and source of action. Wherever we see the action, or by experience recognize the antecedents of action, unipotent or alternative, or by consciousness recognize the sense of the interior causal capacity for action, we locate the power. Before action that power is in apparent repose. Before the flash, at the contact of the powder and spark, there is the instant of indifference, but from this indifference the action takes its causal origin. Yet in this equilibrial instant, the powder plus the spark are a cause of a sole effect, just as the agent in his proper equilibrial conditions is a full, complete, adequate, alternative cause of either of several effects. There is no more inertness, or powerlessness or mystery in the one case than in the other. The assumptions of Edwards would prove that the repose of even physical cause could never awake. Cause would forever cease to go forth, the universe of things would stand still, and activity would forever die out.

2. To the full existence of equilibrial freedom, it is not necessary, as Edwards claims, that a complete expurgation should be made of all preferential, prevolitional feelings, views, or motivities. It simply implies, as we have already shown, that anterior to the choice the Will is, in its proper conditions, an agent or power in an indeterminate state, and that the determination or particular volition takes origin from this previous state, just as all causational action takes origin from a previous inaction—inaction, that is, as to that particularity. If there exists previous preferential feelings, or previous predeterminations or prepossessions, these do not destroy the liberty of the ensuing volition. They are not contradictory of the "indifference," or deliberative equilibrial state of the Will previous to the action. They only constitute motive influences in favor of some one of the alternatives or other, and these influences are simply among the

conditions of volitional action. And these motive influences do not impair the liberty; they only constitute a probability that the Will will act in accordance with them; yet the higher probability may be rejected. They simply increase the number of motives. Between acting in accordance or against them, there is still a freedom of Will.

3. The old sophism that a preceding volition is necessary to produce a free volition here recurs. Edwards requires that "the Will, while it yet remains in perfect equilibrium, without preference, determines to change itself from that state, and excite in itself a certain choice or preference." (105) The agent, we reply, in view it may be, of a variety of preferences, before it has decided, and is yet "in equilibrium," does (not "determine to change itself," "excite itself," etc., but) in full power for either volition, puts forth one of the volitions that are in power. The equilibrium in the order of nature precedes the volition, the indecision precedes the decision, and the indetermination precedes the determination, just as the quiescence of cause precedes the effectuation. The volition then put forth is not a determination, previously, to change itself, but is itself a change; the change and the volition upon its object being the same.

Nor is the non-differentiation of Will before volition a stagnant idiocy or unconcern in regard to the alternatives. Edwards argues copiously that such indifference cannot even "begin" to act so as to originate volition. If such "indifference" is indeed a dead impotent stagnation, such an argument would be conclusive. But the case is that of power. It is simply the condition of an agent before action in which resides the element of power of or for action. That so-called "indifference" is simply the equipotence for action in either of several directions. How absurd to say that an agent who possesses the power for action cannot act or "begin" to act! That the Will does in presence of alternatives, and in this state of so-called "indifference," or weighing of alternatives, possesses full power for action, is a matter of universal consciousness.

4. Nor will necessitarianism gain much from this notable axiom— "every free act is done in a state of freedom, and not only after such a state." (102) "It will not suffice, that the act immediately follows a state of liberty; but liberty must continue and exist with the act." (103) That is, as Edwards maintains, inasmuch as Arminian liberty consists in "indifference," therefore choice and indifference=freedom, preference and nonpreference, volition and non-volition, by the Arminian hypothesis, must exist at the same moment; which is a contradiction. "How ridiculous

would it be for anybody to insist that the soul chooses one thing before the other when at the same instant it is perfectly indifferent with respect to each." (103)

Now these things "are very inconsiderately spoken." The doctrine of free Will doubtless requires that the volition should spring from a power capable at the point of choice of either alternative choice. But it does not require that freedom to an act should exist after the act itself exists. Freedom from the act is out of the question after the act has taken place. Freedom in regard to the act, or any infinitesimal part of an act, already existing, to cause it never to have existed, is not claimed.

DEED ALREADY DONE

It is not required, as it is impossible, that the deed already done, or so far as done, could be rendered not done, or the fact be made to be no fact. The completed and past act is out of power. But that does not disprove that such act is a fact, now and forever, which was produced by an alternative Will and in that proper sense a free act. Yet although the existent act is no longer in power, freedom still remains as the quality of the Will; which Will is still the antecedent, whence may spring continuous free volitions.

The volition by the very definition of freedom is called a free volition because it receives existence from an alternative cause, namely, the free agent. The freedom lies in the cause, not so properly in the effect. To its being a free volition, it is not necessary, by any definition, or any view of freedom that such cause be able to render it, so far as it exists, not done. It may change it anew, but cannot render it never having been done. Yet the soul was free in its antecedency; and is still free, not to the destruction of the existent, but to the alternative causation of the still non-existent.

It is not true, therefore, that the freedom to a particular act in the order of nature coexists with that act; nor does the doctrine of freedom so require. Cause and its particular effect cannot coexist. In the order of nature the commencement of effect is the cessation of cause. The moment an infinitesimal part or point of effect exists, its infinitesimal point or amount of cause, as cause, has ceased to exist. The object that caused may exist, but no longer as cause. All cause expires in childbirth; but the fact that the effect has once come into existence is indestructible. And so doubtless a free cause in the order of nature, precedes its effect; and as a cause and as a free cause, in regard to the particular effect produced. This is namely, the particular infinitesimal part or point of effect that may be produced; it is no longer a cause or a free cause and so far as produced, the effect is out of power. The freedom to that act lasts so long as the causality lasts, and no longer. And so the free cause as such, in regard to that particular effect, is no longer a free cause; it does not coexist with the effect. And if the axiom of Edwards that "every free act is done in a state of freedom," means that causality coexists with effect, or that the free causation does not precede but coexists with the freely produced effect, it is a sophism and not an axiom.

And yet this does not disprove that the cause in the production was free; nor that it still remains a like cause for future free production. The cause always antecedes the effect of which it is the free producer.

Surely it is not a strange or abstruse idea that the causing of the deed precedes the deed instead of coexisting with it; or that the doer could at the point of choice choose or not choose; or that the choice once made, even though withdrawn or changed, remains as a fact, forever a fact; or that all this is consistent with the freedom of the doer in that choice, or its still permanent freedom for all future choices.

We conclude by calling attention to the fact that the argument of Edwards if it is valid proves not any mere certainty of the volitional event different from necessity, but it proves necessity itself. That is, he proves not the non-usage but the non-existence of any power of different volition or contrary choice. Edwards can affirm that his necessity is certainty only because his certainty is necessity.

IX

Choice between Equal Alternatives

Alternatives may be before the mind so equally eligible that, so far as consciousness may be judge, the Will decides without motive upon its object.

In anticipation, however, necessitarians meet these instances by affirming, first, that these cannot be genuine cases because there can be no volition without motive. Second, volitions without motive can possess no moral character. And third, the cases are of so trifling a character as to be inconsequential in the argument.

The first of these affirmations, though the most influential upon the minds of men, of course takes the conclusion for granted, and proves itself by itself. The whole of this treatise is our entire reply.

Second, that motiveless actions can have no moral character has been too lightly conceded by the advocates of free will. For a person guilty of repeated profanity, or theft, or murder, it would be no defense that the crime was without motive. Indeed, motiveless crimes and sins may be many times altogether aggravated by the very fact that they are motiveless. If the slightest act of sin is an infinite sin, as Edwards holds, then an infinite sin may be committed supposably without a motive.

Third, the minuteness of the action by no means diminishes the importance as a test experiment. The experiment decides, so far forth as the decision of consciousness is clear, that volitional cause is different from any cause in material dynamics. Natural philosophy knows no cause that can act either way in face of an equilibrium. The minutest successful experiment proves the whole doctrine of volitional freedom.

The ability of the Will to choose in equilibrial alternatives establishes the reality of that point of freedom that Mr. Locke and others find in the power of volitional suspension. The Will, say they, often meets alternatives before which it is not necessitated at the instant to decide, but may hold the mind in an indeterminate state; which is doubtless true. But, replies Edwards, in this there can be no freedom; for this holding the mind in suspense is an act, and for the act there must be the motive. But, we reply, if the Will can in any case act by intrinsic power without motive, however minute the case, or however strong the probabilities against it, the reply of Edwards is invalid, and there lies a freedom in this power of volitional suspension.

Each for himself must decide the case. So far as my consciousness can decide, after I have been induced by motives to engage myself in the experiment, I make movements for which the nicest observations of consciousness can detect no motive. Having purposed to move one of my fingers, I detect no motive for the particular one moved. I close both eyes, and can open one of them without motive for either. Pointing my finger over the center of a chessboard, I touch without any individualizing motive a particular square.

PRONOUNCE NAMES

I pronounce names, John, or Thomas, or Samuel, without any motive for the priority of either. I perform these experiments guarding against all the causes of preference suggested by either the Elder or Younger Edwards, and with a clear result. And so far as this is a clear result it is a decisive result, decisive of the whole question. For if any, the slightest volition ever took place without the impelling of motives, necessitarianism is a false system.

And in our individual practical history, how infinitesimal are the beginnings that involve in the long run even infinite consequences. How slight and often motiveless are the acts that give a new turn to our career and a new complexion to our destiny. Nay, the slightest and most motiveless act may produce effects upon the history of nations and change the face of the world.

There are, however, two kinds of equilibrial cases. One is, as we have already discussed, where the two or more sides are equal because they are equally valueless. The other is where both sides have a value and, so far as the prevolitional faculties are concerned, an equal value. It is not to be inferred that because the motives are balanced and no superior strength stands on either side that the importance of the opposite interests is therefore infinitely small. On the contrary, the most momentous value may belong to each. For we know the opposite motives before the mind of Eve may have been subjectively equilibrial, and thus the moral destiny of the entire race may have been decided by a volitional act that was by cancellation without a motive. Caesar paused at the Rubicon; motives of stupendous magnitude held the scales even; perhaps it was Will that decided. So God is conceived as deciding between two undifferentiated points of space by Will.

A theory of equilibrial freedom, called "liberty of indifference," is propounded by Archbishop King with much ability and at full extent.[1] It limits freedom to that class of volitions that the mind puts forth, without any preponderating motive on either side. But it maintains that consequent upon the volition the thing chosen becomes agreeable, and is fully and permanently accepted because it is chosen. He says while in a large class of cases the desires and appetites precede, induce, and determine the Will, in other cases the Will precedes, and the fixing of the appetites upon it follows. Not only are things chosen because they are first agreeable, but things are often agreeable because they are previously chosen. And, thus, a choice without any previous motive, and so perfectly free, creates a permanent motivity in the thing chosen, whereby the consistency of the man is maintained, and he becomes a free creator of agreeableness in objects and happiness to himself.

There are some inconsistencies and crudeness, both of thought and expression, in the details of the archbishop's system.

He made but an incomplete approximation to an accurate expression of the true view when he said, "things are loved because they are chosen." Doubtless this is sometimes, though not uniformly, the truth. But the real fact ordinarily is that the volition determines the mental position. It settles the question of preference between alternatives, dismisses the counter motives from view, and closes the debate. Opposing inclinations, desires, inducements, and feelings of obligation disappear, and that preference to which the Will gives predominance becomes sole and settled master.

The Will passes the mind on to new objects and the discussion of new alternatives. Meanwhile it adds a new and irrevocable fact to the history, perhaps contracts a new responsibility, and often gives a new change to the entire destiny. Whether the choice has been for a higher or a lower

---

1. Archbishop King, *An Essay on the Origin of Evil* (London: Printed for W. Thurlbourn, 1731)

motive, in favor of its moral interests or of its sensual propensities, a self-commitment may have been made that will lead to incalculable results.

The natural cravings and affections usually do form around even the object chosen at first with little or no motive; and there is no want of verifications of the maxim that "things are loved because they have been chosen."

X

Equality of Divine Motives

NECESSITARIANS ARE OBLIGED BY the nature of their argument to apply the assertions of necessity to mind as mind, to Will as Will, to cause as cause, whether finite or infinite. This very boldness enables us to adduce an instance of equilibrial choice of a character so pure and perfect as to give it the nature of a demonstration.

Pure infinite space is everywhere perfectly and absolutely alike. Before creation of any body or substance, there is nothing in one location in space to afford any motive for preference over everywhere or anywhere else. It is impossible, then, for a motive to be offered here for the placing a world or a universe rather than elsewhere. No place or point can therefore be selected, and no universe can be created, because it cannot be located. The same argument applied to the absolute similarity of all points of time would prove the impossibility that the world could be created ever.

This argument assumes the doctrine of Sir Isaac Newton, that the universe is finite. Leibniz denied this upon grounds now altogether exploded, though he admitted the possibility or power in God to create a finite universe. Dr. Samuel Clarke conclusively replied that the very admission that God could create a finite universe is full concession that the universe might be established in particular space without particular motive.[1]

In his reply to the arguments of Clarke and others in behalf of the freedom of the Divine Will, drawn from the equality of different spaces, times, and objects, Edwards maintains that there is a contradiction in the very terms, for things between which there is no difference, whether spaces, times, or objects, are absolutely the same. So to speak of a choice

---

1. Discussed at length in *A Collection of Papers Which Passed Between the Late Learned Dr. Leibnitz (sic) and Dr. Clarke in the Years 1715 and 1716 Relating to the Principles of Natural Philosophy and Religion* (London: Printed for J. Knapton, 1717)

between them is absurd. He thereupon institutes an elaborate argument to make the following points:

I. He confounds resemblance with identity; he confounds difference and sameness in point of resemblance with difference and sameness in point of identity. He invalidates all essential self-identity or individualization in any given unit.

II. He reduces infinite time and space to mere conditions of body.

III. He confounds the abstract qualities of bodies with bodies themselves and their individual realities.

IV. He supposes a false analogy between body and sound.

To all these we offer what we trust are satisfactory replies:

I. There is one sort of difference between objects in respect of resemblance, and another sort of difference in respect to intrinsic identity. These are two different senses of the word *difference*, which, unless we would confound things by words, must be kept separate and distinct. The word *same* is still more ambiguous. We call individuals of the same class or species the same, which is a specific sameness, as, e.g., all human nature is the same. We call a successional aggregate, which is continually changing its constituents, the same; as a river whose waves are perpetually different is the same river; or the human body, though its particles are perpetually substituted; and this is a historical sameness. Two individuals, more or less alike, we call the same; and the resembling qualities of two bodies we call the same, which is the sameness of resemblance. But all these are secondary or transferred meanings. The strict essential meaning of sameness, or identity of an individual, is its essential separate selfhood, by which it is not and cannot be identical with any other thing, but must be itself and nothing else.

Though the words *same* or *sameness* are applied to both, yet resemblance and identity are essentially two very different things. Increase of resemblance is no approximation to identity. Things most perfectly alike are no more identical than things most perfectly unalike. Suppose I have in my right hand an ivory ball, and in my left an iron cube; it is at once seen that the two have little resemblance and no identity. Suppose by power of will I could transform the iron cube to an iron ball of precisely similar size and roundness with the ivory. The two are no nearer identity than before, though far less different in point of resemblance. Increase of resemblance, diminution of difference in point of resemblance, then, is no approximation to identity. Let a second dictum of Will transmute the iron ball into ivory. The resemblance, then, becomes absolutely perfect; the non-identity remains just as absolutely perfect. No change of position could affect their respective identities.

MUTUALLY EXCHANGE

If my hands should mutually exchange them, their reciprocal position would be changed, but not their intrinsic identity. Each had has a different ball in possession from what it had before; different in identity, but absolutely alike in resemblance; and just as different in identity as if there were no likeness in resemblance. Let there be a million such ivory balls, perfectly like, flung in perfect disorder through the sky, and of not one of them would have its identity changed. Unless we allow the confusion, which doubtless would reign in our perceptions at the sight, to disturb our minds, we shall see that although the whole million have no difference in point of resemblance, yet their individual identities are just as distinct and changeless as if there were no resemblance at all.

When Edwards asks, therefore, of two different bodies perfectly alike, "If they are absolutely without difference, then how are they different objects of choice?" the mere play upon words becomes transparent. They are "without difference" of resemblance; they are with difference in identity. They are perfectly alike; they are absolutely non-identical. No exchanges, nor legerdemain, nor confusions of our perception of them, can ever render them not different in identity. And when Edwards adds, "If there be absolutely no difference in any respect," (we do not say there is "no difference in any respect;" we say only there is no difference in the one respect of resemblance) "then there is no variety or distinction;" (336) we reply, certainly there is both variety and distinction in point of identity.

And further, "If there be no variety among proposed objects of choice, then there is no opportunity for variety of choice or difference of determination." (337) There is, we reply, a variety of objects of choice, namely, a variety of intrinsic, inexchangeable identities, that perfectly resemble each other. And it is the absence of difference of resemblance between the different objects that renders each an exact case of choice for one or the other without specialty of motive.

And, again, when Edwards gravely tells us, "For these two different bodies are not different or distinct in any other respects than those wherein they differ; they are two in no other respects than those wherein there is a difference," (341) the remark is neither profound nor pertinent. We grant that bodies are different in just those respects in which they are different, for that which is, is. But that does not show that bodies may not be without difference in point of resemblance and yet with absolute difference in point of identity. "If they are perfectly alike in themselves"— then what? Then they completely resemble in themselves, but are none the more identical with each other in themselves. "For it is difference only that constitutes distinction." A truism; difference in resemblance constitutes one distinction; difference in identity another.

The freedomist proposes the case: Let there be two different objects perfectly alike, and the choice of either must be without motive. For the necessitarian to reply if they are perfectly like and there is no difference, then there is no variety of objects, and so no two or more alternatives to choose from, and therefore the choice is the same, is no reasoning at all. It is a play upon words.

II. The freedomist again argues that all space being perfectly similar, though with an infinite variety of identity, there can be no motive for the selection of one point or portion of space for a creation than another, and hence neither choice nor creation.

In reply, Edwards denies the existence, beyond the limits of creation, of space, of infinite length, breadth, and depth, truly and properly distinguished into different measurable parts. He denies at some length the division of immensity into "miles and leagues" and "sorts of measures." The absurdity of measuring immensity by miles and the absurdity of measuring by miles and the absurdity of measuring eternity by years he thinks to be equal.

In reply we might ask: Would not an infinite number of years be eternity? If so, then eternity can be conceived divisibly, as an infinite number of years, just as well as undividedly, as an endless time. An infinite number of years would be endless time; endless time would amount to an infinite number of years. If an infinite number of years and eternity are not equal, which is the longer and which the shorter?

Space is affirmed by the human reason as being external to the self, and as that in which all body must necessarily be. It is held necessarily to be; for if in thought you abstract from it all body, space is still left; and if you attempt to abstract space, space will not undergo abstraction, but remains. Space is conceived as infinitely extended. For you can in thought fill it with infinite body; it will then no longer be void space, but occupied space.

The extension of the space is thereby measured by the extension of the body, and proved to be infinite. If the body is then removed, there remains an infinitely extended void, an infinitely extended capacity, from which all body, substance, or thing, is absent. Space is, but space can scarcely be said to exist; it is reality, and yet it is the boundless absence of all substance, an infinitely extended nonentity. And because it is nonentity, it is void, and receptive capacity for something.

OUR OWN EFFORTS

We do indeed feel in our own efforts and thought the need of some regulative object from which to calculate directions and distances, in order to determine any particular place in infinite space. When we attempt to identify a point in infinitely pure space, the impression is apt to arise that it is all "the same" and we forget ourselves and reduce infinite space to a sole point, annihilating, by mental withdrawal, all other space. We forget that this "sameness" is such only in point of perfect resemblance, and that our very phrase "immensity of space" is an assertion of boundless variety in point of identity and reality. Were infinite space conceived as filled with an infinite system of stars, then infinite space would be commensurated with an infinite mechanical rotation of heavenly bodies—the infinite by the infinite.

Each star would be in its own place and not in another. If then, every star but one is blotted out and all other space is left pure, that other pure space still exists. And all the points once occupied, though unmarked and pure of all trace, as if no substance had ever been there, still exist as truly as if the orbs were sill there. Blot out that last star, and though there is nothing left but pure void infinite space, its infinitely extended capacity remains, and all the places and points once occupied remain. But those places and points were not created or intrinsically differentiated by the orbs.

All we have gained from them is aid to our thought. The places and points are in the infinite sameness of resemblance but variety of reality, of immensity of space, are conceivably different places and points of capacity for occupancy by substance. One place in infinite pure space is not another place; one point is not another point. Immensity of space is an infinity of singly measurable places which, if occupied, the immensity of space is filled by equal immensity of occupancy.

We could not in that case speak, in Edwards's phrase, of "milesquares of Deity." But as a cubic mile of body can fill and measure a mile square of space, so by mental withdrawal of the body we should have a cubic mile of space remaining.

If all this is true, then prior to all creation there would be in infinite space an infinite variety of determinable spaces, either of which could be occupied by a body. But none would present any difference from any other, rendering it preferable for the occupancy of any particular body. And if no one could be selected by the placer's Will without some superior eligibility over all others, then the Will would be held in immovable equilibrium, and the occupancy of any point is infinitely impossible. We therefore do know (Edwards says) "what we mean if we say the world might have been differently placed from what it is in the broad expanse of infinity." (338).

The above exposition of space will facilitate the true view of time. We do not, indeed, know what Edwards means by saying that eternity, the "eternity of God's existence," for instance, is his "possession of the whole of his unlimited life, together and at once." (337) We can no more conceive how eternity can be condensed to an instant than how immensity can be condensed to a point. If time, as Professor Hickok remarks, presents itself to all minds as a river flowing equally from an infinitely distant source, creation is necessarily conceivable as fixable at a point higher or higher up the stream. The world may be conceived as created at sixty centuries ago; or it may, if geology can ascertain a precise chronometry, be at sixty billions or octillions of centuries ago; or, transcending all point, matter may be held eternal. All required by the freedomist is the conception that of the beginningless stream there are higher or higher points really conceivable, between which, as time is ever alike, there must be a selection, without a determining motive.

III. Having exhausted his logical double-entendres on the words *different* and *same*, as applied to things, Edwards expends a few in application to the qualities of things. Of two perfectly similar particles or atoms he tells us, "The figure is the same, the measure is the same, the solidity and resistance are the same, and everything the same but only the place." (341) We may here, by the way, ask why, by Edwards's reasoning, is not "the place" "the same?" In that, as in every respect specified, the sameness is merely sameness of resemblance; and surely one space is as much another space, as one quality is another quality. The so-called sameness of qualities in different bodies is what we have above defined as specific sameness, namely, that resemblance in the qualities of different objects by which we are able to classify them into species. One body's quality, however like, is no more identical with another body's quality than one man's headache, however similar, is identical with another man's headache. No absolute resemblance of qualities in two different bodies—much less of the substratal bodies themselves—even approximates to an identity. As the bodies are for their resemblance none the more identical, so the qualities are for their resemblance none the more identical than if they had been a contrary sort of qualities.

Edwards puts the case: "Supposing that God in the beginning had created but one perfectly solid sphere in a certain place; and it should be inquired, Why God created that individual sphere in that place at that time? And why he did not create another sphere perfectly like it, but numerically different, in the same place, at the same time?" (346) We reply that to answer these "whys" is to assign a motive for creating the particular sphere, which is the very thing, we argue, that cannot be assigned. But if the question is whether God could have created a perfectly similar other sphere instead, or either one of an infinity of similar other spheres instead, we answer promptly. Yes. And not one of those spheres will be another any more than if they all were of different shapes, colors, and substances.

IV. Edwards next argues that it would be just as rational to ask why a given sound is not by the Almighty supplanted by another sound precisely similar. And he argues that as a perfectly similar sound substituted would be the same sound, so a perfectly similar body substituted would be the same body.

The cases, we reply, are not analogous. It is by the circumstances in the case that the self-sameness of the sound is constituted. It is of the sameness of time, place, material air, impulse, atmospheric motion, sensation, and quality that the sound is what it is. Change either of these and the sound is no longer the same. These being the same the sound could not in the nature of things be replaced with another sound precisely similar by any power, even omnipotence. It is of these that the intrinsic nature and individualization of the sound is made up; and the self-sameness of these is the self-sameness of the sound, which, therefore, cannot be exchanged with or replaced by another.

Dr. Clarke's conclusions, then, remain untouched by the logic of Edwards. All space is perfectly alike; all spaces are different identities. Their different identity creates a plurality of objects of choice; their perfect likeness excludes any superiority of motive. A particular space, therefore, cannot, according to necessity, be selected for creation, and creation is therefore impossible.

XI

Useless Modifications of Necessity

NECESSITATION, SO FAR FORTH as it exists, and Responsibility, are incompatible. This is true regarding: 1. The Source, 2. The Mode, 3. The Point or part of our being necessitated, or 4. The Result. Necessity (not self-superimposed) and responsibility cannot cover the same ground. They cannot coexist; but just so far as one exists it excludes the other. This essential incompatibility is in the nature of things unchangeable and indestructible by any power, even Omnipotence.

1. *The Source.* Whether the source or cause of this necessitation is infinite or finite, God or second causes, a physical or a nonalternative motive force, the non-freedom is the same. A finite cause excludes the contrary power, and an infinite cause can do no more than exclude it. By either cause there is equally only the freedom of the clock-hammer, to but not from. If one non-freedom excludes responsibility so does the other.

2. *The Mode.* Whether by creation, by secondary causation, by birth, by information, or by insertion, necessitation is equally exclusive of freedom, and so of responsibility. A necessity formed within me, or put into me, is no more a non-freedom than a necessity imposed upon or intrinsic in my nature.

3. *The Point.* Whether the point or part of my being upon which the necessitation is imposed is mind or body, intellect, sensation, or Will, the necessitated action of that part or faculty—so necessitated as to be nonalternative to the agent—is irresponsible. A necessitation upon Will to volitionate, upon the muscle to act, upon the intellect to perceive, are alike irresponsible. It is absurd to say that a volition is responsible purely because it is a volition and not something else.

4. *The Result.* Whether the result necessitated to exist is a volition, a nature, a state, a condition, or an action of body or mind, it is in either case equally unfree and irresponsible.

Dr. Emmons[1] heroically maintained that we are free and responsible even though our evil volition was created and put into us. Dr. Shedd rejects that absurdity, but maintains that we are responsible, even though our sin is a necessitated nature. Dr. Pond rejects our responsibility for a nature, and boasts that he ascribes our responsibility not in nature but in action. Professor Lyall[2] abjures necessity from causation, but places responsibility in intrinsic spontaneous necessity of Will to obey motive. Dr. N.W. Taylor rejected all these and placed responsibility in a power of willing either way, which, meanwhile, is secured by a Law of Invariability, or intrinsic spontaneity, to be exerted in but one sole way. All these distinctions are foreclosed by Edwards, who maintains that it matters not to responsibility how we come by our volitions. With Edwards we agree that it matters not how we come by our necessitated volitions—or our necessitated anything else; all alike and equally are irresponsible. Not one of these people has any ground of boasting over venerable Dr. Emmons. That is, the maintainer of responsibility for volition created within us, is no more absurd nor any less justifiable than the maintainer of responsibility for a necessitated nature; or for a necessitated action; or for a spontaneous necessity to obey the given antecedent without existing counter power; or for a spontaneous necessity to obey such antecedent by an invariable non-usage of an existing counter power.

I. Dr. Shedd holds 1. Sin is not so much an act as a "nature" or a "state," and as such is guilty and damnable. 2. This nature is a "product" namely, a product of the human Will; and depravity lies properly "in the Will"; and consists in the Will's necessitated state of ever flowing evil volitions. 3. The Will is not the "mere volitionary faculty," but is inclusive of the affections, emotions, intellections, fused into a necessitated mass; the whole man himself viewed as necessitatively determined in unity to a given and fixed direction. 4. In all this the Will is self-determined; but only as all unipotent cause determines itself in a solely possible direction; that is, the self-determination is a necessary one.[3] But in this most fatalistic view of stereotyped depraved Will, ever by necessity tending to evil,

---

1. Nathaniel Emmons (1745–1840) was a Massachusetts Calvinist pastor who supported the New Divinity movement.

2. William Lyall (1811–1890) was a Canadian psychologist and philosopher who followed the 'Common Sense' tradition.

3. William G.T. Shedd, *Discourses and Essays* (Andover: W.F. Draper, 1862), 219–271.

Dr. Shedd sees something highly consistent with responsibility. At least, it is not so bad as an inserted or omnipotently deposited depravity. It is free (in the sense that necessitated choice or power of choice is freedom), self-determined (in the sense that every material cause is self-determined), originating in Will (in the sense that the Will is the amalgam of all the necessitated faculties of the mind), and is not half so bad as an omnipotently interpolated depraved nature.[4] "Were this nature created and put into man, as an intellectual nature or as a particular temperament is put into him by the Creator of all things, it would not be a responsible and guilty nature, nor would man be a child of wrath. But it does not thus originate."

But if this "nature," intrinsic and necessitated upon the agent by birth, is any more responsible than inserted or in-created "nature," what is the ground for such greater responsibility? Not certainly a greater freedom; for in both cases the freedom is equally the mechanical freedom to and not from the "nature," whether of the "volitionary faculty" or of the whole man determined in unity. Nor, as above premised, does it matter at all whether the cause of necessitation is creation, insertion, or birth; nor what the result; whether an act or a "nature," or an act or nature identified, the responsibility is excluded by necessitation.

REPRESENTATIVE EXHIBIT

II. Dr. Pond tells us that Edwards taught—"in opposition to Arminians, Belgians, and infidels"—that liberty of Will consists in "merely choice or the power of choice."[5] In other words, President Edwards maintained that "freedom is an essential property of Will," just as striking is an essential property of a clock. And he specially boasts that his system deposits freedom and responsibility not in state, nature, or condition, but in "action." And similarly Dr. Hitchcock asks, "So long as they act voluntarily do they

---

4. There is no necessitarian writer, we think, who more unrestrainedly appropriates a freedomistic nomenclature under a special and "private interpretation" to express necessitarian dogmas than Dr. Shedd. See also his *A History of Christian Doctrine* (New York: Charles Scribner, 1863) 15–16. The reason doubtless is, that he unites a freedomistic heart with a fatalistic head, with intuitions tending to the right hampered by a falsifying logic. Why is that necessitarians so struggle to clothe *their* dogmas in our terms, while we so struggle to clear our phraseology from all affinity or resemblance to their dogmas? These verbal appropriations of theirs are the tribute paid by fatalism to freedom; just as hypocrisy is said to be the compliment that vice pays to virtue.

5. Enoch Pond, "Hopkinsianism," *Bibliotecha Sacra* 19 (July 1862): 636.

not act freely?"[6] Freedom and the power of choice are by this identical. A volition however necessitated is free and responsible just because it is a volition and not something else. We remark:

1. This definition voids the word freedom as applied to Will of sense or meaning. If volition, choice, or the power of choice is liberty, then there is no such thing as free choice, for that would be free freedom; nor for the same reason any free power of choice, or power of free choice. There can be no free volition nor freedom of volition. You have said the whole when you have said volition; and the word free prefixed to it is useless, superfluous, and a mere sound and no word. A free volition is a volitional volition. A free volition is as absurd a phrase as material matter. All you can say then is that over and above the being a volition or the power of a volition there is no freedom. The word "free" adds no idea, expresses no individual thought, element, or perceptible quality in the volition. Free volition is just as correct as zero volition.

And so there is no sense in the word "free" as applied to Will. Will is the faculty of volition; free will is nothing more. You have neither added any idea by the epithet *free*, nor particularized an individual idea in the Will. Thought can individualize no point, phase, or property in the subject answering to the term. Abolish the word and no meaning is lost. Predicate or affirm freedom of the Will and you have predicated nothing. You have merely said, Will is Will. To all Dr. Pond's statements, Fletcher, eighty years ago, furnished a concise but most ample reply: "It is not barely the having a Will, but the having free Will, which constitutes us accountable, judicable, punishable."

2. Freedom, say these theologians, consists in the power of willing. Freedom from what? we ask. For freedom is a relative term, implying exemption from something. It can only be freedom from its opposite, that is, freedom from not willing. But in that same method sensation is free—free from nonsensation. Everything is free from its own opposite. And so this definition of volitional freedom makes the Will or the volition just as free as a mathematical figure. If necessitated volition is free why not necessitated perception or necessitated clock-striking?

Why is action any more a freedom than inaction? There is often a delightful freedom in repose; in exemption from the necessity of action. The

6. Edward Hitchcock, "The Law of Nature's Constancy Subordinate to the Higher Laws of Change," *Bibliotecha Sacra* 20 (July 1863): 538.

slumberer after fatigue delights to be free from disturbance. The ocean enjoys a tranquil freedom from storms. And we see not why the exemption of the soul from all choice might not just as well be called freedom as the existence of choice. The clock without a hammer, a stagnant marsh, a block of granite are all free. Each state is exemption from a reverse state.

3. But Dr. Pond considers it (what is here our main point) a great merit in his system to locate responsibility in action, exercise, volition, however necessitated; and not in state, being, or nature. But we reply, as above premised, that under necessitation, it matters not whether it is state, condition, action, or inaction; responsibility is equally incompatible.

FLIP OF COPPER

Would any sensible man give a flip of a copper for choice between damnation for necessary action and damnation for necessitated being? Is a necessitated motion any more responsible than a necessitated quietude? Motion or action is simply change in space or time. Is necessitated change any more guilty than necessitated sameness? Necessitated motion is, in fact, necessitated being; being necessitated to exist in different successive spaces. But why is necessitated being in different successive spaces any more responsible than necessitated being in the same space through successive time? God can as well necessitate me to be a certain thing, and then damn me for it, as necessitate me to do a certain thing and damn me for it.

For herein doing is being; for necessitated doing is nothing but necessitated changing states of necessitated being. Justice can just as readily hold me condemned for a necessary essence as for a necessary quality; and for a necessary quality as for a necessary operation. For a necessary operation is a property, and a property is but the essence manifest. Yonder metallic shrub, shaped by the cunning hand of modern art, standing with its stately stalk, lifts aloft a little wilderness of foliage and vines, most light and airy to the eye; but those clustering festoons and the rigid stalk are, alas! alike—cast-iron! So the stalk of a necessitated nature, and the wildest wreathings of necessitated action, are alike cast-iron—irresponsibly fatalistic. The actions and the being are one inseparable piece, one being, one nature. And this doing-being is created by God; for it is necessitated by him into existence, and to necessitate into existence is to create.

We could as reasonably be held retributively responsible for a necessitated shape of our person as for a necessitated shaping of our actions or motions. One is but a necessitated molding of our body in space; the other is the necessitated molding of our being in space and time.

Dr. Pond says that an African incurs no "guilt" "for the color of his skin," because it is not "action." But the shedding necessitated colored rays from his cuticle is, we reply, as truly "action" as the shedding necessitated evil volitions from his Will. His cuticular pigment can just as easily radiate a white as his volition faculty can volitionate a good. An automaton may just as well be held guilty for being wooden as for projecting his arm in a blow when the spring is touched; that is, as well for a necessitated nature as for a necessitated action.

And so when another writer[7] tells us by way of justifying damnation for a thing decreed in us, that "it is decreed that we be perfectly voluntary" in it; decreed "that we shall act of our own accord;" neither that "voluntary" nor that "accord" is any more responsible than a decreed wart on the face, or a foreordained and secured black luster beaming from the skin. Is a previously decreed volition any more responsible than a previously decreed intellection or muscular spasmodic motion? If God decrees my necessary damnation he may as well secure it through a hempen cord, an electric shock, a muscular movement, or any other necessary thing, medium, or operation as a necessary volition. God may as well secure my damnation without anything voluntary as secure it by securing the voluntary. Securing my volition in order that he may secure my voluntary sin and consequent damnation is about the poorest piece of sneaking despotism that one could attribute to an omnipotent Evil.

III. That same point that volition=freedom, and that necessitated volition is responsible because it is volition and not something else, is thus put by another writer.

1. "There can be no necessity in volition. It is the very opposite of necessity. It is liberty itself. Because volition has a determinate cause which makes it what it is, this does not alter the case. If the cause be a free agent, and the kind of volition be determined by the unconstrained inclinations of the heart, the freedom of our actions is no how affected by this certain connection, between volitions and their cause." So says the Princeton Essayist (277). And yet this writer, who calls volition the very

7. Nehemiah Adams, *Evenings With the Doctrines* (Boston: Gould and Lincoln, 1861), 250.

opposite of necessity, also calls the volition an "effect" of a certain "cause" of which it cannot but be the result, unless he admits, contrary to his own doctrine, that a cause can fail, of its sole effect. But if the volition cannot, but be the solely nonalternative effect of the existing cause, how is it other than necessary? How can it be "the opposite of necessity?"

2. This writer, who talks of a mere "certain connection between volitions and their cause," denies the power in Will to will any otherwise than as we please. That is, as he explains it, the volition has no power to be otherwise than as the prior inclination or mental state. So that by his own express statements it is not a mere certain, but an absolutely necessary connection. But that prior inclination cannot but be the effect of prior causation. The agent comes by birth or creation into existence, and has a first- caused inclination which causes other mental states; the first volition is the effect of the antecedent inclination; and so is the second of its antecedent inclination; and so all the succeeding volitions. And thus each volition of his entire existence lies as a term of a necessary series of causes and effects, all equally certain and equally necessary. If an external physical object strikes the surface of the body, a sensation is a necessary result; of that sensation an inclination; of that inclination the volition; of that volition the external act. If the sensation is the necessary result of the corporeal stroke, and the inclination the necessary result of the sensation, is not the volition the equally necessary result of the inclination, just as the external act is the necessary result of the volition? For why is the sensation the necessary effect of the stroke but because there exists no adequate power in the terms of the series for that result to be otherwise?

EQUAL NONEXISTENCE

But the writer affirms an equal nonexistence of power in the case for other volition. There must, therefore, be in the volition an equal necessity. So that the stroke, the sensation, the inclination, the volition, and the external act are the five links of an adamantine chain of necessity. What sense is there, then, in arbitrarily interpolating the effeminate word *certain* between either two of the links? The volition is just as necessary and just as certain as every other link of the causational chain. What sense, then, is there in his telling us that "there can be no necessity in volition?" All the links are just as necessary as the impulsions of a row of elastic balls, or any other chain of mechanical effects whatever.

3. But he tells us next that the volition "is liberty itself." Then, we reply, it can have no liberty; for liberty cannot have liberty. But if liberty consists in the volition itself, then it does not consist in being the opposite of necessity, for even a necessary volition is a volition, and therefore liberty. The freedom, then, is not freedom from necessity, but freedom from not being a volition. And that notable freedom belongs to every block, clock, or everything that happens to be itself and nothing else.

IV. No truer responsibility can be found in a necessity professedly divorced from cause and made intrinsic and spontaneous in the agent himself. This view appears in the following extract from a book by Lyall.

> Is it causation when the will follows upon desire? It is here, we think that the whole stress of the question regarding the freedom of the Will lies. It does not seem causation in the same sense between the strongest emotion, or the prevailing desire, and will, as between a judgment and an emotion, or an emotion . . . the effect of a conception or judgment . . . . The Will follows reasons, inducements, but it is not caused . . . .[8]

> Even with the strongest motive that could operate, to obey that motive is to be free; it is to will, and that is freedom . . . The will does not determine itself: it may be allowed even that it is determined by motive: but still to will is to be free; or it is to act; and if we attend to the idea implied in action, we have the essence of freedom. What other freedom could be desired? . . . The Will does not control motives: it does not even choose between motives: it follows or obeys a motive, a motive prevailing at the time—the strongest motive; but in doing so it wills, and that is activity, freedom. . . . Freedom is freedom to obey motive—for the Will to obey motive, or to decide in obedience to motive. In that consists essential freedom. . . .[9]

> It (will) is far from the nature of a mere effect . . . It is an effect so far as it is under influence, but it acts under that influence by an activity of its own, derived from nothing without itself.[10]

---

8. William Lyall, *Intellect, the Emotions and the Moral Nature* (Edinburgh: Thomas Constable and Company, 1855), 581. The work is enthusiastically indorsed at full length by the *Princeton Review*, edited by Dr. Hodge; and by the *British and Foreign Evangelical Quarterly*, edited by Dr. Cunningham.

9. Ibid. 582–583.

10. Ibid. 586.

The obedience of Will to motive as here described is obedience by intrinsic necessity. It is intrinsic because it inheres in all Will as Will, belonging to its nature. There is no possible freedom consisting in a power of disobedience to highest motive. Obedience is freedom; and there is no other freedom. It is, therefore, what must be; an inherent intrinsic necessity, or spontaneity.

But it matters not to responsibility whether necessity is from a specific antecedent cause, or is thus spontaneous and intrinsic. Cause can do no more than put into the volition the necessity to exist. That is, cause simply infuses the necessity into Will for the volition; and the necessity thereby becomes an intrinsic necessity in the Will for the sole putting forth. Cause, as has been said, expires as soon as effect exists, but the necessity for the effect to exist even then still remains intrinsic in the agent or subject of the effect. So that, whether by a specific cause or not, the necessity is ever intrinsic. In the one case the intrinsic necessity is caused once for all in the primal causation of Will itself; in the other it waits for the specific cause.

Nevertheless, Lyall's obedience of volition to motivate is, in spite of himself, caused by motive. For by intrinsic necessity it acts according to the motive; and the motive decides and fixes, determines and secures what the act shall necessarily be, and other than which it cannot be. It is the same old clock-hammer freedom—power to without power from. Between the motive and the act the relation is necessitative, for the motive is the antecedent by whose strongest force the act necessarily takes place.

To be an effect is to be determined necessarily in direction and measure by an antecedent. But the result in the case of intrinsic necessity depends upon, is fixed by, the antecedent. But to be necessarily dependent upon and fixed by a previous antecedent is to necessitatively caused by it. The antecedent causes the intrinsic necessity of the agent to act in a certain measure and direction in conformity to itself. In respect to responsibility this necessitation differs not from causation.

XII

Invariable Sequences or Spontaneous Necessity

IT WAS MR. HUME who first performed that analysis by which the sequence of cause and effect was reduced to "a constant conjunction of objects;" and the idea of "cause" or "causation" was placed by him in the category of "prejudices" arising from "custom."[1] So far did he carry his analysis as to invalidate the legitimacy of all assurance that the stated consequence will follow the experiential antecedent. Dr. Brown,[2] taking this theory, identified the connection of cause and effect as mere "invariable sequence;" banished causation from existence; but with at least a less absurd philosophy, legitimatized the expectation of the sequent upon the experiential antecedent, as a valid intuition of all mind.

This theory has been adopted by two very different classes of thinkers. First, is the class which, adopting it with strict consistency, applies it alike to all the dynamic sequences of mental and physical science. Second, are those (generally among theologians alone) who admit causation in the phenomena of physics and of intellection, but exclude it from the sphere of free agency; therein substituting Invariable Sequence. Between these two classes the question is whether or not the causations of physical and volitional action are alike reducible to Invariable Succession. To the former class belongs a large class of naturalistic savants, including the positivists John Stuart Mill and Auguste Comte. To the latter class belongs, especially in this country, the body of necessitarian theologians who desire, in phraseology at least, to recognize the alternative power of the human Will.[3] These two classes in order we may now discuss.

1. David Hume, *The Philosophical Works of David Hume, vol. 4* (Edinburgh: Printed for Adam Black and William Tate, 1826)

2. Thomas Brown (1778–1820) was a Scottish metaphysician who defended Hume's concept of causality.

3. The theory, however, nearly, if not quite coincides with the view of Leibniz. For

I. Mr. Hume congratulated himself (ironically perhaps) upon the result of his analysis as furnishing a termination to the controversy upon necessity. In this fancy he is followed by some of his followers. Mr. Mill, in his confused chapter on Liberty and Necessity, contained in his work on Logic, takes this ground. Necessity, all that there is, simply implies the fact that a volition, like every other effect, is an "invariable sequence" of the existing sum total of "antecedents." That is, did we know all the antecedency completely, we could infallibly predict the consequent volition—we should know how the man will act. And surely, he argues, this sure and invariable future fulfillment ought not to be called Necessity. To which we may briefly reply,

1. That we should be able to predict which way a person will choose from knowing him perfectly, is more than any one is able to affirm. That there is much ground for probable prediction we have fully shown in what we have said upon the Influence of Motives and upon Uniformity of Volitions. But this assumption is, that we only need the perceptive power to analyze the exact interior mechanism of Will, and a perfect motiveometer to take the dynamics of the forces in contact with that machinery, to calculate with as absolute mathematical accuracy the direction and the momentum of every future volition, as we can the direction and momentum of a material machine. This is precise necessity. It finds an agent a true machine. It is based upon its mechanical dynamic. And it is a pure, gratuitous, and most unnatural assumption. If we could clairvoyantly look upon the interior of a man's mental being we might, and if consciousness and moral sense are voracious we should, find a controlling alternative power that would baffle our predictive inferences.

We do not understand that it is by an accurate tracing of cause and a reasoning to effect, that God foreknows the ways in which a free-agent will act, but by the uncaused perfection of his own absolute omniscience.

---

instance, take the following passage:

"Libertas exempta est tam a necessitate, quam a coactione. Necessitatem non faciunt futurtio veritatum, nec praescientia et praeordinatio Dei, nec praedispositio rerum. Non futuritio: licet enim futurorum contingentium sit determinata veritas, certitudo tamen objectiva, seu infallibilis determinatio veritatis, quae illis inest, minime necessitati confundenda est." Gottfried Wilhelm Leibniz, *Opera Philosophica, Quae Exstant Latino, Gallica, Germanica Omnia* (Berolini: S.G. Eichleri, 1840) 660.

Leibniz moreover invented the doctrine of a Sufficient Reason; that is, an adequate antecedent which in physics the subsequent always *must* obey and in free agency *will* obey.

It is not in the divine mind calculation, but pure knowledge, taking in the fact past, present and future precisely in its form and nature. Had we, therefore, power to inspect all the elements of a free agent's nature to the utmost, and power to deduce all the legitimate inferences therefrom, it is neither self-evident nor demonstrable, nor naturally probable, that we should by calculation foreknow the agent's future free act. As a free choice is not a necessary result of a given cause, so a reasoning from non-alternative cause to effect would fail to furnish a sure prediction. To make the conclusion infallible, the result must be a necessitated result. The logical calculator of a free volition would make but a probable guess. Far in the ultimate depths of his being he would find a self-center, capable of projecting action, which, without the intrinsic nature of chance, would be as incalculable as the most absolute chance itself. The contrary of this is mere assumption; of no more value at any rate than our assumption.

OUR VOLITIONS

2. Mr. Mill does not hesitate to admit that our volitions are on par in this respect with mechanical causations, forces, and operations. My choice is, by his view, in given circumstances as "invariably" resultant, and as fixedly as a bullet from a revolver. We are thus again reduced to a mere mechanical freedom, a freedom to the sole but not from. A will is just as free as a clock-hammer and no more. Nay, inasmuch as even mathematical certainty is, in Mr. Mill's view, empirical, he must maintain that the agent puts forth volition, just as fixedly as 2 and 2 become 4. Now all these physical and arithmetical results are, even by Mr. Mill, called necessary. Why not the equally sure and fixed future volition?

3. If it is right to banish that hard looking word "Necessity," a large retinue of words—all the words implying power, efficiency, avoidance, with their contraries, and the auxiliaries can and must—must follow. Nearly every causative verb in the language must either be expunged or adapted to new conceptions. For if there is such a thing as power and such a true word as can, and their negatives, and there is a power to put forth a certain volition, and no power to withhold or substitute it, then we shall want some word to express this unipotence. Whatever word would serve that purpose would soon acquire the rigid features of this word Necessity.

4. Nor are we at all helped by Mr. Mill's substitution of "invariable sequence" and "antecedence" in the place of effect and power. If it is fact that my volitions start up before or in me, as independent events—"sequences"—it helps me not a particle; it distresses me all the more to know that they are "invariable." If I have no power over them except to stand a passive "antecedent," and they come into existence, "invariably" tacked to me, it is very hard for me to be responsible for them. There is only the power to, not the power from. If it is indeed my destiny to be antecedent of a certain set of "invariable sequences," I see not how I can be divinely and justly required to be "antecedent" to another set, over which I have not the least power whatever. Moral obligation to a different course is thereby impossible. I stand a helpless stock for "invariable sequences" to be fastened upon; and neither praise nor blame, merit nor demerit, guilt nor deserts, responsibility nor honor, reward nor punishment, can be for me any just attribute.

5. Mr. Mill doubtless would say that reward and penalty are the inducements, that is, the "invariable" motive "antecedents" for the right series of volitional "sequences." This reduces penalty to a mere expedient—a method—like the application of a sidelong force to right a wrong-going mechanism. The true morale is thus expunged, the expedient alone remains. The theory is saved at the terrible expense of the annihilation of Eternal Justice. A questionable intellectual notion is established, but the moral sentiment is forever invalidated.

To this general head we may conveniently refer the opinions of Kant. This philosopher, dividing our conceptions of things, into the phenomenal or external, or empirical, and the noumenal or transcendental, places all freedom in the latter. The noumenal, concealed in the phenomenal, as the marrow is centralized in the bone, is reached and seen only by the intuitions of pure supersensuous thought. Such thought recognizes that there is this deep intrinsic subphenomenal freedom in man, which forms a just basis for inputation, by our pure moral intuition, of guilt for sin, although all our phenomenal or empirical volitions and external actions are bound to succeed each other by as fated a law of invariable sequence as rules over the mechanical operations of physical nature.

It may indeed be acknowledged in reference to this, that freedom is deeply intrinsic in our nature, and that it clothes itself to the outward glance with a succession of phenomena, very much like a causal succession, very much like the wave evolving wave in the current of a stream. In volitional, as in external nature, there is a large amount of ascertainable causation. In external nature, statics and dynamics are capable of accurate measures of causation in the form of physical force; and where no accurate measurements of causation can be taken, science still has not, from any warnings of consciousness, or of the moral sense, any fear to apply her exact inductions and assume that necessitation reigns absolute. But in the volitional sphere we have not gone far in this direction before awful consequences loom up and stern negatives bar procedure. Plain indications reveal themselves that the laws of so much exact result for so much exact antecedency are no longer fully applicable. Freedom does not clothe herself with phenomena bearing, always and unequivocally, the evident laws of exact physical causational or invariable succession.

VOLITIONAL FREEDOM

But a volitional freedom, be it noumenal or phenomenal, limited to the process of necessary succession causation, is no responsible freedom at all. It is the old mechanical freedom over again, the freedom to but not from. It is freedom to a solely given direction, and so non-alternative. It is Edward's freedom, the power to will as we will. This phenomenal, yet actual necessity of volition, is not a jot helped by laying under it a noumenal freedom; for if that freedom can never give a volition for right against the strongest motive force, what is it good for? It neither furnishes power for the right or responsibility for the wrong. It solves no problem, and furnishes no relief.

II. The second class of thinkers surrenders all events outside the Will to causational necessity, but subject volitions only to the law of spontaneity, or invariable sequence to the highest motive. The Will possesses power, but never uses it, for counter volition. An agent always can, but never will choose otherwise. This they hold to be the true certainty. All volitional certainty thereby presupposes a one particular kind of condition, namely, strongest antecedent motive force, and a particular kind of result, namely, obedience to the strongest motive under a particular law, namely, invariable succession upon major force. Any event or future fulfillment not under such condition or law is absurd chance or lawless uncertainty.

Such Law of Uniformity or spontaneity of obedient action under condition of superior force is seen to be absolute, not merely in all experienced cases, so as to be an induction, but in all possible cases, so as to be seen super-experientially and intuitively true, and therefore it is self-evident and axiomatic. It would be intuitively true, as the contradiction of lawless chance, upon an infinite number of repetitions of an infinite number of cases; so that it is a strictly absolute and true universality. As the sole exemption from a self-contradictory chance, it is (so we infer) a necessity. But by them it is named certainty, and held to be the only true certainty, as distinguished from necessity on one side and chance on the other.

On this theory of so-called certainty we make the following points:

1. The advocates of this view must, with us, refute the main body of Edwards on the Will.

We have shown at the various points that whatever may be Edwards's occasional professions (and he never professes that his necessity is equivalent to our certainty), his argument demonstrates necessity in distinction from certainty, if any distinction exists, and the non-existence instead of the non-use of the power of contrary choice. The certainty to which he affirms his necessity to be equivalent is the necessitarian's, not the freedomist's certainty. His argument demonstrates these or nothing.

At start he excludes "power of choosing otherwise in given cases" as an unthinkability. As we have noted, his argument of the infinite series boastfully reduces the conception of diverse power to infinities of infinities of contradictions. His causational argument knows only non-alternative cause, and the effect of any other sort of cause is a causeless effect. He identifies the necessity of a past event and of a future event as one. His reduction of free Will to atheism proves, if anything, that the supposition of the existence of a power of counter choice logically supposes the non-existence of God.[4] His identification of Will with desire excludes the possibility of a counter volition as truly as of a counter sensation. His argument against liberty of indifference excludes all power for Will to flow but in a certain channel. All activity is with him a passivity. All causality

---

4. In an able article, Professor Park speaks of "the element which Edwards disclosed to the Church, the union between certainty and spontaneous choice." Edwards A. Park "New England Theology" *Bibliotecha Sacra* 9 (January 1852): 212.

But Edwards's certainty is as absolute a necessity as the divine existence. A variation would be a causeless effect.

is exhausted in the result. In none of these arguments can invariable sequence be substituted by a modern thinker without destroying the argument. Withdraw these arguments and what is left of Edwards? A valueless shell from which the kernel has been completely extracted. To deny that Edwards taught pure necessity as distinct from certainty, non-existence as distinct from non-use, is as absurd as to deny that Euclid taught geometry. To demonstrate necessity against the existence of a self-determining power, that is, a power in the self of determining the Will otherwise than a one causal way, is the very object of his entire body of argument. To attribute to a man a doctrine that he does not affirm is bad enough; to attribute doctrines he denies is worse; but what shall be said of the attempt to attribute to Edwards the very doctrines that are the very purpose of his work to demonstrate to be absurd and unthinkable?

For this modern distinction of non-use of contrary power from its non-existence, Edwards had no use. The object of its invention is to reconcile necessity with responsibility; but Edwards had other modes of such a reconciliation, and wholly ignored this. His modes, as in the proper place is shown, were two, and contradictory ones at that. 1. Natural ability, which was either a power to will as we will, and not otherwise (a positive contradiction of the power of contrary choice) or a post-volitional power of fulfilling the volition. 2. A denial that power must underlie responsibility; which is equivalent to affirming that no power of contrary choice is requisite in order to obligation to contrary choice. Edwards would therefore have promptly told these philosophers that their power of contrary choice is as useless as it is absurd. He would have soon convinced them that he was not for them a stronghold or a standard, but an opponent and a foe, without an overthrow of whose positions there is no status for them.

CHRISTIAN PHILOSOPHERS

These Christian philosophers, then, if they are good logicians, must cordially unite with us in the overthrow of nearly the entire body of the argument of Edwards. We both are equally bound to refute his position that there is no power of contrary choice. If our argument on this point is valid, they are bound to sustain it; if weak, to strengthen or to replace it with a better. And that would be an end of Edwards's work as a theological authority. We may, indeed, have a subsequent issue with them, namely, upon another point. After we have together disproved the necessity of Edwards, consisting in the non-existence of power of contrary choice, they may attempt to set up another necessity consisting in a Law of Invariability, a necessity as fixed and as destructive of responsibility as the causational necessity of Edwards. Their issue with Edwards's positions is then succeeded by an issue with us. We deny the necessity both of the law of causation and of the law of invariability.

And when they have cancelled all the arguments of Edwards that rigidly prove the non-existence, instead of the non-use of counter power, their theory of non-use is itself left about proofless. The residuum of Edwards that they can appropriate will be found the least demonstrative part of his argument, a part we trust will have been very amply refuted in this present treatise. A main objection, then, at start against this theory is its destitution of evidence.

2. The doctrine that the Will always can but never will volitionate for weaker motive is supposed by its advocates to be covered by the maxim, which they illustrate by various instances, that many things can be but never will be. That maxim is true, but it does not cover the doctrine. Theirs is a never-will-be of a specific and a peculiar kind, under conditions and presuppositions that nullify the can-be. When a will-be or never-will-be under a certain fixed sort of condition results with absolute uniformity, even upon an infinite number of repetitions of the experiment, including all possible cases, then a reverse can-be—either to the given will-be or given never-will-be—is impossible. The will-be or never-will-be, is, then a necessity, and not a mere certainty. The sort of condition in this present case is the strongest motive; and a certain obedience assumable, invariably and eternally, without exception, even in an infinity of repetitions, is necessity.

The maxim that things can be which never will be is true, for instance, in the following cases, without covering the doctrine of invariability: 1. The free-agent always can but never will contradict or vary from the way that God foreknows; but that, as shown in the proper place, is a case in which a constant cause, Omniscience, ever operates adequately to foreknow the way that with power otherwise will be chosen, and so, without necessity on the choice, is necessity of result and agreement between foreknowledge and choice. 2. God always can but never will do counter to right; but that is simply the firm purpose of one, not of an infinite number of agents. 3. Of all the rejected possible volition or nolitions of all free agents, it is true, each and every one, that it can but will not be; but that is not the infinite repetition of equivalent or identical cases, but an infinite variety of single, peculiar, and individual cases. It is simply a collection of all the cases in which a possible volition is rejected; not of uniform cases under given conditions. But what is affirmed by this theory is that a strongest motive case, repeated an infinite number of times by an infinite number of agents and by all possible free agents, is intuitively seen to be sure of the same result.

It is also said to be true that nobody does as well as he can, and so there is a can-be which never will-be. Distributively or individually, that is not true. People often do do as well as they can. Our Lord testified of one that "she hath done what she could." People sometimes, but not usually, do as bad as they can in the given case. But the maxim may mean, collectively, nobody through his whole life does as well as he can. If that means that free agents, who have the evil and the good constantly tempting them, are in the highest degree likely to choose sometimes one and sometimes the other, that is true. But we have elsewhere shown that it may be true distributively that an agent is able to choose in each and every single instance for the rightest and best without being able to choose always rightest and best. This high collective *can*, therefore, is not true. Mankind cannot choose as well as they can. It is, on the whole, a pure and impossible ideal. Nor is it quite certain that there are none who collectively do not on the whole do as well, at a lower scale, as they can; and who, if they should ascetically strain for a higher *can*, would, in fact, do worse.

3. Pure certainty, as in the proper place we define the word, and as distinct from necessity, is not predicable of, nor to be identified with invariable sequence, or with the relation between the antecedent and consequences of such a relation. This, our pure certainty, is the simple future fulfillment of an event that is possible to be otherwise. Invariability is no element of certainty. Pure certainty is the pure future fulfillment of the event irrespective of invariability. To add that such a certainty is limited to a sole condition of strongest antecedent force, and is ruled and fixed by a law of sequence and to a sole result, furnishes new elements not belonging to the idea of pure fulfillment. This becomes a certainty of a special class of the entire genus, which is really no certainty at all. For if the so-called certain act is formulated by a previous fixed universal law,

selecting a particular set or sort of facts, then to that law it must conform; and that is necessity.

The totality of facts which must be presupposed as taking existence under restriction of this Law of Invariability is an entirely different totality; that is, it embraces facts entirely different from the totality of pure, unrestricted certainty. A Will or system of Wills, producing volitions under a certain law of sequence, would supposably produce an entirely different totality of volitions from a Will or system of Wills producing volitions unrestricted by such law. Any anterior prototype decree, rule, configuration, especially an eternal one, and still more a universal one, founded on the very nature of things, to which the free act, by the nature of the case in all possible instances conforms, causes it to be no certainty but necessity. To be pure certainty the anterior prototype must take its form or configuration wholly from the posterior free act; and if the act must take its configuration from the prefixed prototype, it has no longer freedom, nor pure certainty, but necessity. Such conformity being pre-assumed, the act must be accordant and cannot be otherwise; and that is necessity.

FOR THE CALVINIST

For the Calvinist, however, on the other hand, to affirm the ultimate conforming of the free act to an anterior configuration, which configuration has in truth been antecedently conformed to the free shaping of said free act, to be equally a necessity, is inadmissible. The free act would then only be conformed to a true expression of itself; that is would be conformed to and be itself. But if the anterior configuration take its shape not from the free act, but from some other independent source, be it the divine decree or an axiomatic law, (as, for instance of Invariability) and in order to its own truth, requires the act to conform to itself, the act is not free.[5]

---

5. Park, "New England Theology," says New England Calvinism maintains "that a sinner can perform what a reasonable law requires of him, and [yet] that he *certainly* never will do as well as he can, unless by a special interposition of Heaven." (177) But this "certainly-never-will" is secured by an absolute law of Invariable Sequence, namely, of obedience to strongest motive force, an exception to which would be chance, uncertainty, and atheism. With what truth is it said, then, that the sinner "can" achieve such an exception? Can chance and atheism be made true? Or what practicable basis does such a "can" afford for responsibility, retribution, or theodicy?

Hence the phrase to secure the certainty of a free act is absurd, because contradictory. To secure a thing truly and absolutely is to make an opposite thing impossible. To secure the safety of a sum of money is to prevent the possibility of its abstraction. To secure the impregnability of a fortress is to prevent the possibility of its taking. To secure the certainty of a thing is to preclude the possibility of an opposed or different certainty. Now a pure certainty, as above shown, cannot be anteriorly secured, caused, shaped independently, but as it takes shape from (not gives shape to) the future free act. The true certainty is simply the future fulfillment; and that fulfillment takes its nature and being from (and not vice versa) the free volition. "Coming events cast their shadows before," and it is the event that shapes, secures, fixes causes the anterior shadow, not the shadow the event.

To "secure the certainty" previously to and independently of the event, is to destroy its nature of certainty and make it necessity. To secure it according to a previous universal Law attains a different individual event and a different set of events from the events of a future fulfillment free from the Law. The securing the previous certainty of the event can be done only by securing the event itself in the future by which such certainty is caused or shaped; and to secure the event is to destroy the power of contrariness and transform the whole into necessity. The freedom and responsibility of the act expire in the process.

To secure the certainty of an event is, as has been said, to secure the event itself in the future. This securing the event can only be by a causative influence extending from the securing antecedent to the event itself. This antecedent must both positively fix the event and also exclude efficiently all contradictory events. But that would be a necessitated, not a merely certain event.

A necessitarian writer says: "to say 'an event certainly will take place,' is one thing; to say 'an event must necessarily take place,' is another thing."[6] True. But to say that it is previously secured that an event will take place, that is, that the event is secured to take place in the future, is to say that it is necessitated to take place, that it cannot but take place, and so must necessarily take place.

To bring into existence some event subsequently upon which an agent will perform, with full power otherwise, a volitional act, is not to se-

---

6. Rev. D.T. Fiske, "The Divine Decrees" *Bibliotecha. Sacra* 19 (April 1862): 405.

cure the certainty. A minister preaches a most excellent sermon, and one of his pewholders subsequently blasphemes about it. Now the sermon did not "secure" (that is, render the opposite impossible) either the certainty or the blasphemy. The certainty is not a previously secured matter. It is simply future fulfillment, and takes its existence from the shaping of the free act and from nothing else. But to secure the certainty of a future act by bringing into existence an object or event that includes the future act within the law of invariable sequence is to necessitate that future act. The substituting invariable sequence for necessity of volition does not, consequently, clear the Divine Being from the authorship of sin. God is thereby made to bring the agent within the invariable sequence of sin, which is as true a necessity as the sequences of causation.

FREE ACT OF THE AGENT

Calvinists at the present day define decree or predestination as simply rendering certain the free act of the agent. And by this phrase is meant that God so plans as that the event is brought into the category of invariable volitional sequences, so that a completely new theological nomenclature comes into use, softening their version of predestination in words, but retaining it intact in fact. Thus Mr. Fiske says:

> By the doctrine of divine decrees we mean that God from eternity purposed or determined so to constitute and govern the universe as to make it certain that all events would take place precisely as they do take place.[7]

Additionally:

> The decrees of God are not merely his purposes to permit events to take place as they do. Some hold with regard to the existence of sin, we can only affirm that the divine decrees extend to it in the sense that God determines to permit it, that is, not to prevent it. But the decrees of God are not mere negatives. They are purposes positively to do something, and to do that which renders certain the existence of all events, sin included.[8]

The phrase here to "make certain" is equivalent to "secure a certainty." The phrase to "render certain" is ambiguous. It may signify to cause that

7. Fiske, "The Divine Decrees": 401.
8. Ibid. 404.

an agent will do a thing excluding from him power for any other doing by setting in operation a train of causations securing his act. In that sense we reject the phrase, for the thing is necessity. Or it may mean the doing a thing subsequently upon which an agent will do some other thing. Thus, I may give a servant a direction to do a thing, and he, in a spirit of perverse independence, does the opposite.

Did I cause, produce, create, or make the certainty, or render it certain that he will do so? I think not. Certainty is not a made thing. It is simply this—that he will so do, and all its reality receives existence from the doing, reflected backward. If, however, this is all that is meant by Mr. Fiske, that God does a thing subsequently upon which there arises a volition or act from man, that is what Arminians have ever held. But that is not Calvinism.

The Princeton Essayist (70) argues that inasmuch as the doctrine of foreknowledge concedes that all future events are certain and foreordination does nothing more than to render them certain, therefore there is no difference between the two. We reply, 1. If God renders the future event certain so as to secure its coming into existence, he is made responsible for its existence. To render a thing certain is to secure its existence in the future and so to become its author. The difference then between the certainty of the event secured by foreordination, and the simple certainty apart from foreordination, is that one makes God the author of sin, and the other does not. 2. This securing a certainty secures according to a certain special rule; and so secures a special set of facts, differing from those involved in a simple certainty. Foreknowledge and Calvinistic predestination therefore presuppose different courses of events. 3. By this foreordaining securement of a special set of facts, the facts are made to accord with the antecedent causational securing, and not, reversely, the previous matter conformed to the posterior result.

Dr. Bonar, of Scotland, narrates a colloquial argument to the following effect: You admit that in order to foreknowledge, the future event must be certain and fixed; will you please to tell who fixed it? In this argument the word *fixed* has two separate meanings, namely, as an adjective and a verb. The axioms of mathematics are fixed; will you please to tell us who fixed them? The adjective fixed, as applied to a future alternative act, if properly applied at all, signifies simply certain; that is, the act which of several possible acts will be performed. And that fixed future fulfillment does not need that anybody should fix it. Its future certainty is simply its will-be; and that requires no present cause, nor any cause whatsoever, excepting the future agent who will perform it.

4. Our ground, as already stated, is, that where it is a conceded point that a volition would be put forth in the given or equivalent case, not only by all actual but all possible free agents, the case is not a certainty, but a necessity, and the counter power is an unreality. The case must take its place with all other facts or laws among fixed principles founded in the nature of things.

This fact of spontaneous Invariability must be validly pronounced to be a necessary Law, as absolute and as a necessary as the Law of causation, being secured in fact by necessary causation.

It extends in its true statement not only to all actual, but to all possible cases. If any actual or possible diversity is admitted that indeed alters the case, for we then have a crude freedomism hereafter to be considered. It must be held that God himself cannot create a being who will choose counter to highest motive; for if he can, man should be that being. For man is the being required to act out of that Law of Invariability both by the moral Law and by his own highest well-being. If then such a case as a chooser against strongest motive is impossible to exist even to Almighty power, the invariability covers all possible cases in every part of the universe through absolute eternity and as exceptionlessly as the Law of causation.

NATURE OF THINGS

It exists immutably in the nature of things; and what by the very nature of things exists, exists necessarily, and exists necessarily every moment and in all its individual instances and particular acts. It is not an induction to be held true until contradicted by some counter experience; but an intuition to be held true in all possible cases, the possible counter being intuitively excluded. It is not created and empirical, like the Law of Gravity; but uncreated and primordial, like the law of causation, modifying the nature of creation itself. Like the Law of Causation, it is strictly and self-evidently assumable of all its species of instances. It is then a necessary and absolute Law; and to it as a Law its subjects are subordinated; and to attribute to them a power to break it is a contradiction. You might just as well attribute to non-alternative effect the power to nullify its own causation. No act or event can break into axiomatic Law.

For that which is seen, not experientially and inductively, but intuitively, to be strictly true of all possible cases, universally and eternally is self-evident and necessary. Self-evident, of that is the very nature of intuitive truth, which is whatever is seen, not through media and evidence, but immediately and by its own self-presentation. Whatever is self-evidently true is necessarily true; for the basis of the self-evidence in the thing must intrinsically and necessarily verify the intuition. The intuition is fixedly and necessarily true; and the correspondent fact must be as fixed as the truth of the intuition. An intuitive truth defining the mode of a subject's action is a necessary law, and the action and the law are necessary each, a necessary type and antitype of each other, the necessity of each insuring the necessity of the other. Now what in the present case is thus intuitively seen as universal and eternal in all Will, as Will, is the invariable accordance of all Will with strongest motive force. That accordance, therefore, is necessary. And that necessity stands in contradiction to the power of an opposite fact, a contrary choice. A necessity and a counter possibility cannot coexist.

As a basis for the affirmation of such invariability in the Will, the intuition must cognize in Will, as Will, a sufficient ground, nature, and cause to exclude all opposite or exception. That cause, intrinsic to Will, as Will, must be inseparable and necessary. Its effect, namely, this invariability, is also necessary. For it is, in the nature of things, commensurate, and completely resultant in the effect, in all possible cases, and cannot fail. The counter event is completely excluded, by a cause in its own nature efficient and resultant in all possible cases. The counter is therefore impossible. A will-not-be which is prevented from existing by antecedent commensurate causation, in all possible cases and in the nature of things which cannot be otherwise, cannot exist. A will-be whose counter is by the nature of things efficiently and resultantly excluded in all possible cases, is a must-be. It is a secured certainty=a necessity. And being grounded on inseparable cause intrinsic to and inseparable from all Will as Will, it is a causational necessity.

Lyall's theory is that Will possesses a spontaneous intrinsic necessity to obey strongest motive without a counter power; this theory is that, with a counter power by necessary spontaneity unused, there is a spontaneous intrinsic necessity to obey strongest motive. By both theories there is equally a necessary spontaneity to obey strongest motive. By the present theory there is negatively a necessary spontaneous necessity of non-usage of counter power, and positively a spontaneous necessity to obey strongest motive. And these two are one necessity. But as before argued, a power by necessity unused by the agent is not a power at the command of the agent, and so is truly not in his possession. He cannot do the act, and so his power for it does not truly belong to him.

It is the non-usage of the counter power=the positive strongest-motive volition, which lies in the eternally uniform succession of events; that is, in "the constant conjunction" of Hume, the "invariable sequence" of Brown, and the "unconditional invariable sequence" of Mill. It amounts to this, that the non-usage is the successive event of a given antecedent, unconditionally, in all time and place. How far it, hence, differs from Lyall's spontaneous necessity of action according to cause, or from the invariability of physical events as held by Brown, let the reader judge.

5. The arguments adduced in behalf of this uniformity demonstrate the impossibility of contrary choice, and so demonstrates necessity. To deny invariable sequence, as our freedomism does, it is argued, is to introduce an absurd and inconceivable uncertainty into all volitional events. It dissolves all firm relations and disintegrates all moral system. It abandons the world to random Chance and consequent Atheism. It takes away that fixedness of future events by which they can be the subjects of a sure foreknowledge.

If this argument is solid then all choice is necessitated, and all counter choice is impossible in the nature of things. For chance is impossible. Uncertainty is impossible. The defeat of God's foreknowledge is impossible. Not a single case of chance, uncertainty, or defect of God's prescience is able to occur. The non-existence and contradiction of these is absolute, universal, eternal. The opposite of these, to wit, uniform choice for strongest motive, is therefore an absolute necessity.

If acting counter to the "invariable sequence" is chance, then freedom, consisting in a power of choice counter to invariability, is a power for absurd and impossible chance, and the act is an act of chance. To obey God against the strongest counter motive, is to act chance; and a life of obedience to God's law against temptations sufficiently powerful, is a life of absurd chance. God requires of a man in such a case to act by chaotic chance, and damns him to all eternity because he does not act by chance, but does act as all free rational moral intelligences, God himself included, through all the universe and through all eternity have acted, and ever do and ever will act.

6. Nor does this scheme explain the sense of conscious and self-condemning guilt. All guilt has by it this excuse and justification, that there is no being in the universe, high or low, finite or infinite, that in the same category, namely, of strongest motive, would not commit the same guilty act. Whether the most pious saint or the most abandoned sinner, whether the purest angel or the blackest demon, whether a blended character or an extreme, all alike, high or low, finite or infinite, exercise the Will for the same one highest motive or uniform standard of accordance. The merit hereby of all the good, is not that they would do any better than the worst. It is only their fortune that they are not in the same predicament. Place any other free agent or any other possible free agent in the same category and he would do the same. Guilt is then a matter of position, a thing of accident, chance, or fate. Place any real or conceptual being in the right relation and he is a sinner.

AMPLE PRECEDENT

The sinner, then, has ample precedent for his sin. He is authorized and justified in sin by the sanction of all beings really or virtually in his place. The universe is on his side. His sin has this surpassing excellence, that there is no being, however excellent, wise, or powerful, that would not be in the same category though endowed with the power of choosing otherwise, choose exactly as he does. Sin is, therefore, excellent, being the virtual act of all excellent beings.

And yet how is one agent any more morally excellent than another? All are ready, however endowed with contrary power, to sin just as soon as the proper conditions are presented. The criminal stands on the same ground of exculpation or inculpation as the judge, the sinner as the preacher, the demon as the angel, the Satan as the Messiah. All owe their accident of excellence to their position; all are potentially and virtually alike, good or evil. The transgressor, but for the circumstantial category in which he stands, is as good as the saint, the devil as good as the angel. The culprit can call all beings to acquit him. He has the entire Totality with him. The line of moral distinctions is expelled from the sum of existing things.

This theory is framed for a practical purpose, namely, to evade the intuitive feeling of the impossibility of responsibility for a necessitated act. It thereby admits that impossibility. It is specially framed to enable the necessitarian preacher of righteousness to remove all excuse from inability to do otherwise than sin, even accordance to strongest motive. It is thought, forsooth, to be very effective to be able to say to the sinner, "Plead not the strength of temptation; you are able to disobey the most powerful temptation and the strongest motive, and so are without excuse." This is a "Moral Ability," that is, a claimed Volitional Ability to put forth the required volition, and the preacher is able to use the words of the freest Arminianism. But, alas! This preacher here tells but a part of his story. He conceals what he knows to be fact, what proves this Moral Ability a worthless ideality, and what is the sinner's valid and ample excuse.

Let that preacher tell that sinner, "You are condemned for not disobeying the highest motive because you had the power. It is true, no man ever did use that power, no man ever will. Nor will any being, angelic or archangelic, demonic or diabolical, ever exert that power. Every being that ever did exist, or ever will exist, or ever can exist, will do and would have done just as you have done. I should have done the same, Gabriel would have done the same, Jesus Christ would have done the same, the blessed Jehovah would have done the same. But you, for doing just what I, what Christ, what God would have done, are to be condemned to everlasting death." Surely any sinner would feel it intuitively just to reply, "If I am condemned for doing what all other beings would do and have done, why should not they be condemned with me? How is the throne of my judge less guilty than I?" Go to the sinner, Mr. Preacher, with such a story and you are logically and demonstratively estopped. Go to the sinner with such a story lurking concealed in your theory, and you ought to be estopped, logically and morally; logically because your theory is absurd, morally because your concealment is deceptive.

There is no way of solving the problem of responsibility, justice, guilt, and remorse, than by the hypothesis of a counter power which may be supposed as practically used, in act, against the so-called strongest motive. The proposition that consciousness affirms the prevalence of strongest motive as uniformly our own case, and therefore by an induction always the case of all, can never be proved. I am, as a man, sensible that I choose, or have chosen, against the strongest reasons, against the strongest temptations, and against the strongest moral obligations, and so to all appearance against the strongest motives. No consciousness of mine asserts this invariable prevalence of strongest motive.

7. Against this theory the question lies in full force: What is the use of a power which is never used by any being whatever? The answers we have rendered in our own behalf cannot avail for this theory. It cannot be said that there is no antecedent class of unused motives. For, by this theory, there is antecedently a class that will be used and a class that will be rejected. Nor can it be said it is a power that may be used for a good purpose; for it is useless to expect that such a purpose will ever be attained. Nor can it serve in any degree as a basis for a just divine government; for no divine ruler could ever require an act of righteousness that neither himself nor any possible being in the conditions would ever perform, namely, the act of choosing contrary to the uniform law of motive. Of what use then, is this power tacked to the being? It serves no purpose; it elucidates no difficulty; it satisfied no moral demand; it is not good for anything.

XIII

Counter Choice a Prodigy

THERE ARE JUST A few thinkers who abandon necessity, both causational and uniformitarian, and maintain that counter choice may supposably happen, but nevertheless is an extraordinary or a prodigious situation.

Against such a view we can of course have little argument; for our issue is with necessitarianism, and these thinkers advocate a real freedomism however crude. Edwards maintained that counter choice is unthinkable; the others maintain that it may be held, not only as thinkable, but as often taking place; for extraordinary events in the course of centuries do often happen.

This freedomism, however, can scarcely give a rational account of itself, either to the reason or the moral sense. For if necessity and uniformitarianism are fairly abandoned, and freedom consists in counter choice supposably sometimes made, why should not either alternative be often equally easy, probable, and normal? What reason is there for supposing such choice may happen, which does not indicate that it may ordinarily happen? Moreover, since this view admits that power is necessary to obligation, it follows that the more extraordinary the less the guilt of non-performance. Is it just to require of weak man the performance of the extraordinary? Here these thinkers stand upon an inclined plane, perpetually tending to diminish the extraordinary to justify the divine government, and ever descending to the level of plain freedomism. But as it is of the purely natural man they affirm this freedom, this descent is into old Pelagianism. From this they can be saved only by the Arminian doctrine that, as has been mentioned, grace underlies all our moral probationary freedom; a doctrine that affords a freedomism ample enough for the broadest Pelagianism, and an honor to divine grace that should satisfy the highest Calvinism.

XIV

Volitional Powerlessness or "Moral Inability"[1]

THE NECESSITARIAN HAS DEMONSTRATED to his own satisfaction that for volition, even for right, against strongest motive-force, there is in the agent no adequate causality or power, and that such volition would be what, through a forcible illogic, may be called a causeless effect; and this non-causality-in-Will =volitional powerlessness he is pleased to style "Moral Inability." The common sense of mankind then demands what obligation there can be upon any agent or cause to produce, without causality or power, an act which is best expressed by an illogic in words, because it is a contradiction in thought and in thing.

1. His answer, according to Edwards, should be that no power to an act is necessary in order to have obligation; no power from an act in order to have responsibility or guilt. His maxim is, no matter how we came by act; if it be ours, the merit or demerit is the same. When, therefore, he proceeds to furnish the underlying power upon which responsibility is really based, he contradicts himself. The whole procedure of furnishing any ability whatever for the act in order to have obligation is absurd. It is affirmed that responsibility is without a basis of power and yet has a basis of power. We will call this contradiction No. 1.

2. But when he proposes to furnish an underlying power for the required act, of course it must be what he proposes to furnish, namely, an ability for the required act. It must not be some other ability, and for some other act or thing. Now, what he is to furnish is the ability for the volition required.[2] But what does our necessitarian do? He is compelled

1. In necessitarian nomenclature, "Moral Ability" is *the power to will, which equals volitional ability* or power. "Natural Ability" is the subsequent power to obey or fulfill the volition=post-volitional ability. A man wills to strike by a "moral ability;" the arm executes the blow by a "natural ability."

2. Edwards says: "*The Will itself*, and not only (merely) those acts which are the effect

by his own great demonstration to admit and maintain that there is no causality, power, or ability in the Will ("Moral Ability") for the volition required. And so in lieu of that he proceeds to say that though there is in the Will no power for the volition—no Moral Ability—yet there is out of the Will in the agent a power—"Natural Ability"—for obeying, fulfilling, or post-volitionally executing the volition, provided it could and did exist. The man who has not the power to will is responsible because he has power to externally do—if he did will. This, we say, is furnishing a power for the act required that is not the power for the act required; and this we label contradiction No. 2.

This second contradiction is self-evident. The thing claimed to be furnished is a power for a given volition; but the very point, aim, or gist of the whole necessitarian argument is to demonstrate that no power for the given volition, the sole power required, can exist; and for that power he substitutes a power not in the Will, nor for a volition; but it is a power out of the Will and for a post-volitional and ordinarily a mere corporeal, material act. Now this, we say, is a self-evident contradiction. It is a power furnished that is in the Will, but is not in any sense in the Will; it is for a volition, which is in no sense a volition.

If the power is not in the Will it is not anywhere. Nowhere else can there be any power to the purpose. It might just as well be a power in the Pleiades as even in the agent out of the Will. And if it is not for a volition, but for something post-volitional, it is nothing to the case; nothing in the world is done. It might, so far as human responsibility is concerned, be a power in the Pleiades to discard gravitation.

3. But there is a self-contradiction No. 3. This "natural ability" is the power in the agent to fulfill the volition; but what volition? A volition that not only does not and cannot exist, but which it is the very purpose of the entire necessitarian argument to prove to be unable to exist. The proffer of this natural ability is to furnish a power in the lieu of that demonstratedly impossible volition. The external, or post-volitional fulfillment is furnished under the very presumption of the absence and impossibility

---

of the Will, is the proper object of precept or command . . . The motions or state of the body are matter of command only as they are subject to the soul, and connected with its acts. But now the soul has no other faculty whereby it can, in the most direct and proper sense, yield to or comply with any command but the faculty of the Will . . . Other acts, that are not acts of the Will . . . are obedience or disobedience only indirectly, as they are connected with the state or actions of the Will, according to an established law of nature," etc. (228)

of the very volition it is to fulfill. Necessitarianism first demonstrates the impossibility of the volition, and then proposes to base responsibility on the power to fulfill or obey that demonstratedly impossible volition. The fulfillment is post-volitional with no possible volition before it. It is the fulfillment where there can be nothing to fulfill, and is in fact proffered because there can be nothing for it to fulfill. The very fact that there is no possibility for the volition is the reason why its imaginary fulfillment is proposed as a most solemn reality—a basis for a most momentous responsibility.

NATURAL ABILITY

Both the exercise and the existence of this natural ability are a causeless effect. The exercise of this ability would be a causeless effect, because as necessitarianism itself demonstrates, its solely possible cause, the antecedent volition, cannot exist. The exercise must be the effect; the antecedent volition the cause; but the antecedent volition necessitarianism has shown to be itself a contradiction, and so an impossibility. The exercise then would be an effect without a cause. And equally the power for such exercise—the "natural ability" itself—must exist only as effect without cause. Without the existence of that same antecedent self-contradictory volition, the power for its fulfillment has no existence. The self-contradiction is the cause; the power to fulfill it is its effect. No "natural ability" to fulfill a volition against strongest motive ever did or can exist except as a causeless effect, the self-contradictory consequence of a self-contradictory antecedent.

If anyone wishes to know how contradictory, self-explosive, self-expelling from existence, unthinkable and idiotic a thing necessitarianism holds that antecedent to be, let him read Edwards's famous demonstration against the self-determining power. And then let him mark that it is upon the power and act consequent to that contradictory, unthinkable self-determining act as antecedent, that Edwards bases human responsibility. Now if such is the nature and character of the antecedent, what must be the nature and character of the consequence—the necessitarian base of human responsibility? It requires that power and act of "self-determination" that Edwards so scouts to bring "natural ability" into existence. The whole, then, of that renowned demonstration against "self-determination" is an equally strong, and still stronger demonstration against "natural ability"—still stronger, for the self-determining act, with all its absurdities, must exist in all its completeness and finish, before the "natural ability" can begin to take existence.

There must exist in the agent the adequate causality, namely, the antecedent volition, or there cannot exist in him the effect, namely, the post-volitional, corporeal, or intellectual ability, that is, the "natural ability." And if there cannot be the "natural ability," that is, the causality for the post-volitional act, then there cannot exist the causality for the required post-volitional act. Necessitarianism, therefore, builds responsibility on a basis which she has previously utterly and overwhelmingly destroyed. She thereby overwhelms herself in her professed effort to furnish a power for obligated act. She sinks by her own self-contradictions back into her position that an agent is required to act without power for the act required; that a cause is obligated to produce a causeless effect.

Where there is no moral ability there can be no natural ability. Where there is no power to will, there is no power to execute the behest of the will. That behest cannot be obeyed if it cannot exist. If there be no adequate power for the given volition, there is no volition to obey, and so no power to obey. An impossible volition cannot be fulfilled. If a man through counter motive-force has no power to will otherwise than sin, he has no subsequent power to do otherwise than sin. If a man has not the power to will right, he has not the power to act right. An agent can perform a bodily act only through his Will. And as it is a universal law that no agent can do what he cannot will, so it is a universal truth that where there is no power of will, there is no bodily power to fulfill the volition that cannot exist. What a man cannot will, that he cannot do. That is, where there is no moral ability, there can be no natural ability. Hence it is helplessly absurd to propose "natural ability," in the absence of "moral ability," as a ground of responsibility.

XV

"Moral Ability" as Treated by Edwards

To clearly state this notable necessitarian theory for the solution of responsibility for necessitated volition is to make bare its absurdity. It is tolerated only when wrapped in ambiguities of phrase. Edwards's definition, for instance, of his moral inability or necessitarian volitional powerlessness, which he believes overwhelmingly demonstrated to be produced by counter strongest motive-power, comes (Part I, sec. 4) when he meets the question of responsibility. In its case this is a signal instance of the "use of words to conceal thoughts."

He does not tell us, as a definer should, what this necessitarian powerlessness or non-causality from strongest counter motive-force is; but he professes to tell us in what it "consists"; and yet he really does not tell us in what it "consists"; he only tells us upon what conditions it exists, or by what it is caused. He tells us it "consists" (45) "in either, 1. The want of inclination, or, 2. The strength of a contrary inclination, or, 3. The want of sufficient motives in view to induce and excite the act of will, or, 4. The strength of apparent motives to the contrary." The whole four of this amusing enumeration of particulars is embraced in the last; namely, in the strongest counter motive-force. The quadruple consists of two couples; the two members of each couple are the same thing; and the two same things are finally the one same thing; and that same thing is the strongest counter motive-force. The first couple is the "want of inclination" to a given act or "strength of contrary inclination" against it. But these are the same thing, for strength of contrary inclination is want of favorable inclination, and where they amount to a moral inability the mind is under strongest counter motive-force. The second couple are one; namely, a mental condition of subjection to strongest counter-motive-force. So that in all cases subjection to strongest counter motive-force is the condition, volitional powerlessness to the required act is the result.

The act cannot take place for want of cause or because strongest contrary causation makes it impossible.

Edwards himself indeed reduces the four to "inclination." But "inclination" cannot in any case be the inability itself, but the condition of the inability. Inclination can reach the will only through or as motive; and the inability is the result of motive, namely, of the counter motive-force. The inclination is therefore one or two steps prior to the inability, and not identical with it.

Of the instances Edwards gives, a single one will furnish exemplification to our agreement: "A woman of great honor and chastity may have a moral inability to prostitute herself to her slave." (45) That is, according to necessitarianism, such is the permanent state and correlation of motive with her mind, that there is not in it the causality for the volition, so that the volition would be a true instance of causeless effect. If so, then we say that the external act would also be a causeless effect. So that if there is no moral ability, there is no natural ability. If the absence of motive, or force of counter motive, renders the volition impossible, the absence of volition renders the external act impossible. What she cannot will, that she cannot do. It is simply the impossibility of an event without a cause; the universal impossibility that a fixed train of causes and effects should run off the track.

It is true that in the frame of the above-mentioned lady there may be corporeal strength for the act named, if the other requisite causalities were present. But that is only one constituent of the necessary adequate power. It is, as is elsewhere shown, only a power in the sense of a part of the power; it is not the underlying adequate power, sufficient for the effect, of which alone the requisition for responsibility can take cognizance. The act is not responsibly possible without that totality of causal constituents requisite for its existence.

MORAL NECESSITY

Into this so-called moral necessity or moral inability, by which this lady is powerless to the named volition, there must not be incautiously infused any infinitesimal particle of Arminian contingence. Necessitarianly speaking, it is as fixed as the motion of the planets in their orbits, when all the forces of attraction and repulsion are in their well-adjusted play. It is fixed by that professedly demonstrated absurdity of a self-determining power, or power of diverse choice, than which no mathematical necessity, no necessity of the divine self-existence can, according to necessitarianism, be more fixed.

Edwards, indeed, graciously tells us that volitional or "moral necessity may be as absolute as natural necessity"; that is, as physical or mathematical necessity. But there is no "may be" about it. All necessity is absolute and equally absolute. There can be no tight and loose necessities. Necessity is perfect, and has no degrees. It is the non-existence of adequate power to be otherwise, and non-existence cannot be graduated. There can be no fractions of nothing. Moral, that is, volitional necessity, physical necessity, (with all its sub-classes of mechanical necessity, chemical necessity, magnetic necessity, electric necessity, etc.), and mathematical necessity, differ only in the final points connected not in the absoluteness and fixedness of the connection. Certainly if any other necessity is a soft necessity, this volitional necessity, according to Edwards, with his demonstrated infinities of infinities of absurdity, even in the conception of a diverse or self-determining power, is quite as absolute as the most absolute in the catalogue. And it is by that so-called necessity that the lady in question has no power either moral or natural for the wickedness named.

We have remarked that much of the necessitarian language on this subject seems used, unconsciously, we presume, to conceal thought. We now say that the very terminology is false and deceptive. The terms "moral" and "natural" as thus applied to ability and inability convey, especially to the popular mind, false ideas, and are among the misleading ambiguities that should be banished from any metaphysical or theological nomenclature that aims at precision.

This moral inability, so-called, is in the Will; it is therefore a volitional inability, powerlessness, or non-causality. Natural ability is made to cover the whole field of our nature outside the Will; it is therefore an extravolitional or post-volitional ability.

The apology framed by Edwards for these terms may excuse the user, but does not authorize the use. He admits that his *moral* is as truly natural as his *natural*; and his *natural* he might admit to be as truly moral as his *moral*. But he tells us that nature being observed to be "in a settled course," "the word nature is often used in opposition to choice." But that is a very untrue statement. The word "nature" is no ordinary antithesis to "choice." God and nature, man and nature, grace and nature, are normal antitheses, but not choice and nature.[1] And what aggravates the falsity of this antithesis is the fact that the term *nature*, as used in this terminology, is made to embrace with external nature man himself—except his Will. It is the Will versus human and universal nature. That is, every other part of man is nature, is of a piece with external nature. But the Will is not natural and is no part of even man's nature!

These terms, *natural* and *moral*, as thus used, are no exclusive antithesis; that is, they do not exclude each other. Many things are both moral and natural. Why should natural be opposed to Will when the Will is as natural a power as the intellect or the corporeal strength? The volitions are as truly natural as any bodily act. The Will is a natural part of the human soul. The ability or inability of the Will is a natural ability or inability. There is no faculty more natural than the Will, or that stands above it, or antithetical to it, as more eminently natural. On the other hand, to make moral= volitional is absurd; for many acts of the Will belong not to the sphere of morals. They are not moral or ethical acts, and therefore they exert no moral ability; and so again the power to will is not a moral but a natural ability. A large share of our volitions are wholly unethical. So that this volitional ability, unless conferred by supernatural grace, is always most truly a natural ability.

This misuse of terms infringes upon and tends to supplant their legitimate application to their proper significates. There is a proper natural ability, moral ability, and gracious ability, to which these terms should be exclusively applied.

Natural ability or abilities include all the abilities or powers with which a man is born or into which he grows. Natural is hereby often antithetical to acquired. The term *ability* includes capabilities of body or mind; of mind including intellect, Will, or moral sense.

Moral ability, being a species under natural ability, is every power of body or mind viewed as capable of being exerted for a moral or immoral purpose.

Gracious ability is an ability, whether of body or soul, conferred by divine goodness over and above the abilities possessed by man by nature, that is, as a born and growing creature.

---

1. A theory by Dr. Bushnell perhaps contains an attempt to inaugurate this antithesis. But it identifies choice, not as moral, but as supernatural. See Horace Bushnell, *Nature and the Supernatural, as Together Constituting the One System of God* (New York: C. Scribner, 1858)

Language, we repeat, may be so used as to conceal thought, and this may be done with great unconscious skill. Edwards, after having demonstrated positively, in behalf of the doctrine of necessity, the non-existence of power of volition against strongest motive-force, having named this no-power moral inability, next proceeds in behalf of the demands of responsibility to declare that this moral inability is no inability at all! This denial is in fact nominal and of the word, but is so phrased as to seem real and of the thing. Thereby necessity is really saved, and responsibility is saved in words; for while a no-power is demonstrated, an inability of some sort may be denied, as well as some sort of ability is affirmed.

EDWARDS SAYS

The word *inability*,[2] Edwards says, more properly belongs not to the Will, but to the subsequent powers of fulfilling the Will's command. There is no verbally proper inability in the ruffian's Will to withhold the ruffianly blow, or in the drunkard's Will to reject his cups.

To this we reply, 1. Whether "the word 'inability' " is the proper term to designate the powerlessness or non-causality in the Will to volitionally counter strongest motive or not, is irrelevant to the case; the only question being whether such powerlessness is fact. And as it is the whole purpose of the necessitarian argument to prove that it is fact, it is the same as the question whether necessitarianism is true. If necessitarianism is true, then such powerlessness is fact. Blocked by counter motive-force, the ruffian's Will and hand are equally powerless for the blow, the drunkard's for the cup. As the entire body of Edwards's argument, if it proves anything, proves it true, it is altogether irrelevant for him to state that a particular word is not the right name to call it by.

The applicability of a particular word has nothing to do with the question of the real existence of the fact that this necessitarian powerlessness really exists, and is the negation of all basis for just responsibility. Volitionally and muscularly powerless, no agent could be required to act

---

2. "The word *inability* is used in a sense very diverse from its original import. The word signifies only a natural inability, in the proper use of it; and is applied to such cases only wherein a present Will or inclination to the thing, with respect to which a person is said to be unable, is supposed. It cannot be truly said, according to the ordinary use of language, that a malicious man, let him be never so malicious, cannot hold his hand from striking, or that he is not able to show his neighbor kindness; or that a drunkard, let his appetite be never so strong, cannot keep the cup from his mouth." (48)

or not act. The term *inability* at any rate is so far suitable and pertinent as that it calls up the actual fact as it is asserted by necessitarians to exist. And being by them selected, it is very inconsistent in them to criticize it; and it is palpably deceptive to so repudiate the word as to seem to deny the thing.

2. Either there is this powerlessness to will, and so to volitionally counter strongest motive-force, or there is not. If there is not such powerlessness against such force, then there is a true and real adequate power to volitionally counter strongest motive; that is, there is that famous "self-determining power" so scouted by necessitarians, that "power of contrary choice" which is the contradiction and overthrow of volitional necessitarianism. And then Arminian freedomism is true, and all the demonstrations of Edwards roll up into vanishing vapor. It is to demonstrate this point, namely, that there is not the adequate power in Will to choose counter strongest motive-force that Edwards wrote his book. That is the very doctrine of Necessity. But if there is, according to necessity, that demonstrated powerlessness and non-causality against motive-force, then let the necessitarian stand to it. Let there be no wordy legerdemain, no verbal denials that there is an inability in the Will because "the word" inability, "in the proper sense of it," is applicable solely to the consequences of Will, which denials are accepted by the unwary as equivalent to an affirmation that there is a power in the Will, and consequently in the results of Will, which is ample base for responsibility.

But Edwards next proceeds to maintain that the terms *power* and *ability* are here inapplicable, because they are not properly applied to will or choice, but to the powers and actions subsequent to choice. Such a thing is, in strict language, held to be in power, if the post-volitional capabilities are able to fulfill the Will or volition if present.[3]

So far as this argument is merely verbal, dealing with the application of a term, it has no validity in determining the reality of the irresponsible powerlessness. So far as it is a real argument, it is a most unconscionable statement that power and no power are attributable to the post-volitional

---

3. "In the strictest propriety of speech, a man has a thing in his power if he has it in his choice or at his election; and a man cannot be truly said to be unable to do a thing when he can do it if he will. It is improperly said that a person cannot do those external actions which are dependent on the act of the Will, and which would be easily performed if the act of the Will were present." (48) This and the quotations that follow in this chapter are successive sentences in the closing passages of Edwards's chapter on "Moral Inability."

powers alone, and not to Will; and that they are not predicable of the agent as inhering in the Will. We affirm, in contradiction, that a man's will may truly be said to be without power, or unable, or under inability to choose. It is rightly said that he cannot choose for want of power to will, and that he cannot do, or move, or corporeally act, because he cannot choose to so do, move, or act.

1. If human language affirms that "a man has a thing in his power if he has it in his choice"; common language herein is Arminian. Human language does hold that "a man has a thing in his power if he has it in his choice"; but human language does not affirm that he has it in his power by having it in his choice, if the choice itself is a causeless effect, and so out of his power. What Edwards does is to clap necessity upon will, and then appeal to our natural, spontaneous consciousness (which is Arminian) that our free will is free will in proof that a necessitated will is free will. It holds a thing in his choice to be in his power, because it holds his choice to be in his power. The external act is in the power of his choice, and the choice is in the power of the man; therefore, the external act is in the power of the man. Hence the human consciousness is herein Arminian. And if the thing be commended by the weaker motive, and still be in power, then common language and common sense hold that the choice for a weaker motive is in power.

2. But a thing is not in the choice or at the election of a man, when to choose that thing would be an effect without a cause, or when the very principle of causation itself secures another choice, and so another act, and therefore annihilates all power or possibility to this. For certainly nothing can be in the power of an impossible choice; and a choice that would be a causeless effect must be an impossible choice. 3. It is, in spite of Edwards, very properly said "that a person cannot perform those external actions which would be easily performed if the act of the Will were present," provided there exists no power for the act of the Will, that is, provided that act of the Will were a causeless effect. 4. If some other causation than the influence of counter highest motive, as mesmerism or fascination, were to exclude the power to a volition, it would be immediately seen and confessed that there would be no power in the corporiety to perform the unwilled act. Of a man without power to choose a thing—as against counter strongest motive-force—it is not true that "he has it in his choice or at his election"; for an impassable gulf lies between him and that choice. It is certainly most true and properly said, "that a person cannot

do those external actions which are dependent on the act of the Will, and which would be easily performed if the act of the Will were present," whenever there is in the person, from strongest counter motive-force, no adequate power to will. For the subsequent acts of the volition cannot be performed without both the power of volition and the exertion of that power. The power of volition is a causal condition, requisite in order to the existence of the power of post-volitional action; and when the condition cannot exist the result cannot exist. What a man cannot will, that he cannot do. Where there is no power of Will, there is no power of action consequent upon Will.

SEPARATING OUR NATURE

Separating our nature thus in two factors, the Will and the subsequent post-volitionality, it is plain that in each factor there must be its own adequate power for its required action, and there must be cooperative exertion of each power of the composite action of both. There must be power in the Will for volition; there must be power, also in the post-volitionality, whether body or mind, for obedient execution of the volition. It is surely untrue to say that the power of each is not requisite for the composite action of both. Taking standpoint, indeed, with either one of the above two factors, and tacitly assuming its adequate power, a man may say that all the ability is to be required solely in the other factor. Taking thus standpoint with the Will, a man may say that the thing is in his power if he can post-volitionally fulfill the Will's behest—just because he tacitly assumes his own power of Will. And as men are practically most obliged to discuss what they can externally accomplish, assuming their power of Will, so they talk, without express reference to Will, as if the corporeal or post-volitional thing were in their power if there is corporeal or post-volitional ability to perform it. But they surely do not mean that, without any volition or power of volition, their corporeity is able to start up of itself and perform the thing unwilled. They do not deny the requisiteness of the power of Will; they assume that power to exist, ready for action in the proper conditions; and that all that is now wanting for full composite action is corporeal power. For taking the contrary standpoint, with the corporeity, and assuming its adequate conditionality, the same man may say that the thing would be in his power, provided he had the ability to will it. And from that standpoint it is right to say "that a person cannot perform those external actions"—for want of a power of Will—"which are dependent on the Will, and which would easily be performed if the act of the Will were present"

A man can truly "be said to be unable to do a thing"—for want of a power of Will—"when he can do it if he will." For what a man cannot will, that he cannot do. What a man cannot will, he can neither will nor do. The terms *can* and *cannot*, *able* and *unable*, *ability* and *inability*, are thus with quite sufficient accuracy applicable to either, and the idea conveyed is not the less true because the phraseology is not normal. But whether the term is or is not verbally accurate; there is affirmed by necessitarianism a powerlessness in the Will for volition against strongest motive-force, to which the necessitarian has affixed the term moral inability, which negates all basis of human responsibility.

And note, it is in the absence of the requisite causal conditions necessary to the result (namely, of power of Will), that necessitarianism requires the result to be possible. Its defender cannot say that he only asserts or requires the resultant power or possibility under assumption that the causal conditions all do exist and are present. He is assigning natural ability as a ground of responsibility in the absence of moral ability. That is, he is assigning the power of post-volitional corporeal action in the absence of power to will that action. Its very object is to find ground of responsibility in an admitted case of non-existence of power to will, and finds it in the power of external action in that same instance of no-power to Will. We are held to be obligated to perform an act, because forsooth, we possess power to perform it without power to will. That is, we are obligated to bring into existence a result for which the requisite conditions cannot exist. That is, we are obligated to produce an effect without cause, a deed without the power of doing.

FURNISH A POWER

And inasmuch as this is the effort of necessitariansm to furnish a power adequate to responsibility, it admits for the time being that adequate power is requisite to responsibility. And yet it offers no power that exists. It offers only the impossible power of doing a thing without the power to will it; of effecting a thing without a causal power; of producing a result without the existence of the necessary conditions. That is, necessitarianism acknowledges the requisiteness of the power but furnishes none.

A command, let us say, comes to me from God requiring a volition contrary to the strongest motive-force. But I have no power of contrary choice; contrary, that is, to the highest motive-force. Now what adequate power have I to obey this divine command? I have no power in the Will, for that would be the condemned power of contrary choice. I have no such power in the body, for the body cannot move where there is no volition, much more where there is no power of volition. There is no power, then, either in soul or body, by which I can obey the divine command. And every case of actual sin is a case of this kind. Every case of actual sin is a case in which counter motive-force, that is, counter causation, excludes, first from Will and then from body, all adequate power to obey the divine command. Sin always occurs, a thing the sinner cannot help. God's command is always disobeyed because it cannot be obeyed. No agent ever sinned who had, in body or in soul, the adequate power not to sin. Men are always damned by God for not doing what they cannot do; or for doing what they cannot help doing. God first puts in motion those causations that cut off the volitional power of obedience, and then damns a man to all eternity for disobedience! All this "to the praise of his glorious justice!"

Though our Calvinistic friends say that we have no moral ability, that is, ability in the Will, for the right volition, yet—something supplies the want of it—namely natural ability, that is, ability in the body. But, alas! Just when the moral ability is wanting, always and ever, the ability in the body, which is to supply the deficit, is wanting too. A most villainous ability surely is that which always, and forever and ever, steps out just when it is wanted! It not only does not stay, but it does not be. It steps not only out of reach but out of existence. What a man cannot will, that he cannot do. That is, where there is no "moral ability" there is no "natural ability."

Edwards adds, "It is in some respects more improperly said that he is unable to exert the acts of the Will themselves; because it is more evidently false with respect to these that he cannot *if* he will." (49) But there is no "if" allowable in the case; the case being that of counter causation excluding both the "Will" and the "if." Edwards, in his chapter on the self-determining power, has professedly demonstrated that the very conception of this "he will" with the "if" before it is infinitely and infinitely absurd. And the conditional "if he will" being absurd, any consequent power of Will as basis of responsibility is absurd. It is not "improperly said that he is unable to exert the acts of the Will themselves," because the very "if" which supposes them possible in the case is absurd. A stone may start up and fly, if it will; but the very *if* being absurd, the consequence is equally absurd.

Last comes the cap to the whole climax of absurdity. "There are," Edwards concludes, "faculties of mind and capacity of nature, and everything else sufficient, but a disposition: nothing is wanting but a Will." (49)

Now, in every sense of this triply ambiguous dictum, it is, on his own necessitarian hypothesis, vitally and fatally false. If the wanting "Will" means the volitional faculty of the man, the constituent power to will in the human soul, no man, not even the vilest sinner, wants that integral part of the man. If it means the disposition, or temper of heart, or "inclination," not only is that wanting, but, what is very much more, and the very gist of the difficulty, the power to the "inclination," or temper, or disposition is wanting. If it means that the volition merely is wanting, that is as momentously untrue; for it is the power to the volition that is wanting.[4]

---

4. It was to meet the moral demand for *power* in such cases that the doctrine of Invariable Sequence, discussed in a former chapter, was invented. Its maintainers "can preach moral ability" to will against strongest motive! Alas! It is by an absolute universal law an unexercisable power; a power not in the possession of the agent; no power in him at all. Such a power furnishes no escape from the argument of these chapters.

XVI

"Moral Ability" as Homiletically Treated

THE CLOSING REMARK OF the last chapter exhibits a radical error running through all the necessitarian utterances on this subject. It is the confounding the want of the act with the want of the power of the act. It is the confounding of the absence of inclination or volition with the absence of the power of or for the inclination or volition. And the reason, or rather motive, of this perpetually cherished fallacy is obvious. Ignoring the fact that not the act but the power of the act is wanting evades the negation of responsibility. The mere act may be wanting and the responsibility remains.

The power of the act is wanting and responsibility disappears. But the necessitarian is unjustified in thus substituting the want of mere act for the want of the power. It is founding responsibility upon a falsification of facts. If the strongest motive-force must prevail, as every efficient cause must produce its effect, if the self-determining power is infinitely absurd as in any physical cause, if the power of contrary choice is inconceivable, if a choice countering strongest motive-force is an event without adequate causality, then there is a powerlessness, a non-causality, of the Will to choose in the case just as absolute as in a physical agent to produce a causeless effect, and not the mere absence or withholding of the act of choice.

The most melancholy point in these systematic misstatements of fact is that they are introduced by the preacher and practical pastor into his sermons and his dealings with men's souls. Thereby the minister of Christ becomes, unconsciously and unintentionally, we gladly admit, an equivocator and a sophist. We wish herein to indicate the sad mismanagement by which the case of God and righteousness is betrayed, and the best of the argument yielded to impenitence and sin, in order to clear the way of truth to the consciences of men, and to render the labors of such a minister more successful in subduing their hearts to the obedience of the faith.

To exemplify these equivocations we take some passages from a sermon of the excellent Dr. Wardlaw in which the fallacy appears in its various forms.[1]

1. Substituting the want of the act for the want of power for the act.

"To say you would believe if you could is not only not true; it is the precise opposite of truth. The plain truth is that you could believe if you would; there being no one thing whatever that prevents you from believing but the want of Will; nothing between you and pardon but the want of Will to have it in God's way—that is, freely, and in connection with holiness, with newness of life."

AMBIGUOUS USE

We find here the same ambiguous use of the word "Will" for volition, as in Edwards; and the same assumption that what is wanting is the mere act, instead of the power of the act. Yet so long as the counter motive was strongest, that is, so long as the adverse volition really existed, Dr. W., as a necessitarian, was obliged to admit that the power did not exist. He was, therefore, requiring an impossible act, a causeless effect, which his audience could deny to be just. The advocate for God is a sophist, and his reasoning a fallacy. The best of the argument is with the sinner.

2. Confounding the faculties of the mind with the specific power in the faculty for the required particular act.

"You have all the natural faculties and powers that are necessary to constitute a ground of accountableness. You have the natural powers required for considering, understanding, believing, choosing, loving and hating, speaking and acting—and moreover, for asking."

The sinner may have all these faculties, including that of "choosing," but while counter motive is strongest he has not the adequate power in the faculty for the required choice. There is a faculty of choice, but it has not the specific power to choose the thing. If adequate power must underlie obligation there is no obligation to the required act. The best of the argument is again with the sinner. The cause of God is mismanaged and betrayed.

---

1. Alexander C. Rutherford, *Lectures on the Doctrine of Election* (Philadelphia: Higgins and Perkinpine, 1854): 199–205. Rutherford quotes Wardlaw's sermon at length.

3. The identification of power and no-power, ability and inability, with inclinations, dispositions, and their opposites.

"So far from being unable, in any sense that palliates your unbelief and impenitence—your inability, rightly interpreted, resolves itself into the strongest mode of expressing your culpability and guilt. For what does the word mean? Simply the strength of your antipathy to God and to goodness. Your inability to believe is only another phrase for your aversion to the truth of God. Your inability to 'repent and turn to God, and do works meet for repentance,' what else is it, less or more, than your fondness for the service of sin and of the world, and your unwillingness to relinquish it? What is it but that you cannot give up the world—you cannot renounce your favorite sins."

Here, inability is identified with an "antipathy," an "aversion," and a "fondness." Now these "inclinations" are no power or want of power; for power is an attribute, and these are subjects of an attribute. Inclinations are the result of a want of power superinduced by strongest counter influence resistlessly producing the inclination. They are also a cause of inability, or the absence of the conditions of ability, when they exclude power to a given volition. But they cannot be the inability itself. And as necessitated, and then necessitatedly necessitating, they are equally irresponsible.

But Dr. W. here identifies this necessitated inability with "culpability and guilt." He could do this only on the assumption that power to a different course was requisite for responsibility for their actual course. He must deny that they are irresponsible for the absolutely inevitable. And thus his gospel is at issue with the surest moral intimations of the human soul.

XVII

"Moral Inability" as Expressed in Ordinary Phrase

THIS IMAGINARY "MORAL INABILITY" has been found also in one of
the ordinary modes of expression in which we at first view seem to
affirm a mere unwillingness or opposition of Will by terms that signify
want of ability. Instead of instituting an analysis to ascertain the psychological solution of this fact, these theologians have grounded upon it that
most unscientific identification of inclination with power which we have
exposed in the proceeding chapters.

We give the grounds of this verbal argument in the words of Dr.
Pond:

> We find it in all books, and in reference to all sorts of subjects; so
> that those who are inclined to repudiate it find it next to impos-
> sible to succeed. The *me dunamai* of the Greek, the *nonpossum*
> of the Latin, the *ne puis pas* of the French, the little *cannot* of the
> English, are continually used in two different senses: the one what
> is called a moral, the other a natural ability; the one a mere inabil-
> ity of disposition and Will, the other an inability extraneous to the
> Will,[1] and over which the Will has no power. We ask a pious friend
> to lift for us a thousand pounds. He replies, 'I cannot do it.' We ask
> him to go to some place of amusement on the Sabbath; he replies
> again, 'I cannot do it.' In both cases he pleads, and pleads properly
> (as terms are used), an inability. But who does not see that here
> are two kinds of inability? Our friend has no natural power to lift
> a thousand pounds. He could not do it if he would. He has the

1. Suppose, then, the command is to *will right*, and we have only this natural ability,
"extraneous to the Will." Are we morally obligated without any power intrinsic to the
Will to *will right*? If yes, then, contrary to what is said below, we are obligated to do what
we have no power to do; for certainly a power "extraneous to the Will" is not a power to
will. If no, then no volitional sin was ever committed; for all such supposed sins are committed under strongest motive, and without power to will otherwise. And if no volitional
sin, then no sin at all, for Dr. P. makes sin consist in volitional "action."

natural power to comply with the other request, and only lacks the willing mind. . . .[2]

Joseph's brethren hated him, and could not speak peaceably unto him. (Gen. xxxvii, 4.) 'We cannot but speak the things which we have seen and heard.' (Acts iv, 20.) 'I have married a wife, and therefore I cannot come.' (Luke xiv, 20) In each of these cases there is obviously no lack of capacity, of natural power. The inability is wholly of a moral nature, the inability of Will. . . . Natural ability has respect to the natural capacity or faculties of an individual.[3] Moral ability has respect to the disposition, the concurrent Will, or (which is the same) to the predominant motive, with which the Will always coincides. . . .

Besides, this kind of ability[4] constitutes the ground and the measure of our moral obligation. We are morally bound to do, and God justly holds us responsible for doing all the good which he has given us the natural ability, the capacity to accomplish. As God has given us our faculties, he may justly require us to exercise them all in his service. And this is all that he can justly require. Should he command us to exert powers which he has not given us?[5]

Now upon a little analysis it will perhaps be found that this so-called "moral cannot" does express a true inability, a natural inability, a physical and metaphysical impossibility, and as perfectly absolute a powerlessness or non-causality as nature or thought affords. All the cases that can be quoted belong to the impossibility that both sides of a contradiction should at the same instant be true, the impossibility arising from incompatibility. In all cases if one side of a contradiction is assumed as true—whether it actually is true or not, whether the truth is real or conceptual, removable or irremoval—the opposite side of the contradiction is pronounced impossible.

And even if the contradiction is but a pretended one, still it is a natural, logical, and metaphysical impossibility that is intended. If a certain course is held as so fixed that it cannot even be discussed or held ques-

---

2. Does he not, Dr. Pond, according to necessitarianism, lack the power of the willing mind?

3. Is not the Will a natural faculty?

4. And why not the other kind too?

5. Enoch Pond, "Hopkinsianism": 652–655. If, then, he has never given us power to *will* right against strongest motive, can he "justly require" us to will right against that strongest motive? Must not the strength of the motive furnish the measure and limit of the obligation?

tionable, then surely the opposite course is excluded as incompatible and so impossible. If I assume it as a settled point, not to be called in question or at all considered, that I am to remain in my study and write a chapter of manuscript, I shall tell my friend who invites me to a pleasure-ride that "I cannot go." For I assume it a fixed fact (however volitionally removable it may really be) that my person is to be in my chair; how then can it be in the carriage? Or how can I will that it be so?

By such a reply the refusal is based upon an assumption presupposed (whether validly or not) to be immovable, and the acceptance is excluded as an incompatibility, and so an impossibility, for which there is an "inability." "Ye cannot," says the Savior, "serve God and Mammon." (Matt. vi, 24) That is, assuming that we serve God, then we cannot serve Mammon; and assuming that we serve Mammon, we then cannot serve God. "Ye cannot," says the apostle, "drink of the cup of the Lord and the cup of devils." (1 Cor. x, 21) And, therefore, whichever they should do, by the law of contradiction they could not do the other.

Thus assuming that God has laid down unchangingly the laws of nature, we say with reverence that he cannot restore our departed friend to life, or cause a child to be a man in a day. We mean not that he cannot violate or change these laws. But tacitly assuming that he will not, then either of those things are impossible, because they are contradictory and incompatible. So assuming the eternally unchanging truthfulness of God as beyond all question, we affirm that he cannot lie.

MAY BE A FALSEHOOD

The assumed side of the contradiction may be a falsehood, a removable state of things, or an immutable fact and necessity. The condition to the impossibility or "inability" is the presupposed (not always the actual) immovability of the assumption; the impossibility lies in the incompatibility between the assumption and its opposite.

Thus God commanded Samuel to go and anoint David king; the prophet replied in his unbelief, "How can I go? If Saul hears it he will kill me." (1 Sam. xvi, 2) The prophet's double assumption that Saul would kill him, and that he was bound to keep out of danger, was false; but nevertheless, being silently assumed as true and settled, his going is impossible.

"How can ye believe," says the Savior to the Jews, "who receive honor of one another, and seek not the honor that cometh from God?" (John v,

44) The assumed and real condition of the mind of the Jews was voluntary and removable. But their tempers remaining as they were, and presupposed as not to be removed, the two things were incompatible.

A circle, presupposing the figure remains unchanged, cannot be an angle. Here both a contingent and a necessary matter is assumed, namely, the unchanged self-sameness of the circle and its properties and the impossibility lies in the incompatibility of the two figures. But the impossibility is in itself no more absolute than in the previously adduced examples.

So the texts quoted by Dr. Pond. Joseph's brethren "hated him, and could not speak peaceably unto him." (Gen. xxxvii, 4) Their hatred being presupposed as complete and firmly settled is incompatible with peaceful speech. Perhaps they could have renounced their hatred; perhaps it was a psychological and a natural impossibility to do so; for we cannot always by any volitional or other natural power control our feelings or change our tempers. It may therefore have been an instance of the assumption of an unchangeable fact. But at any rate the sacred writer gives us a clear idea of its all-controlling intensity by assuring us that it was utterly incompatible with a peaceful word. "We cannot but speak the things which we have heard and seen." (Acts iv, 20)

The not speaking and the fixed feelings prompted by the things heard were incompatible, perhaps intrinsically and irremovably, and perhaps not. "I have married a wife and cannot come." (Luke xiv, 20) The presupposed and settled plans, purposes, feelings, and arrangements attending the matrimony, one or all, by incompatibility excluded his coming. In all these cases, and in every case of this class, one side being assumed as settled and of course, for the other side there is a "lack of capacity, or natural power."

And so of the supposed extra-scriptural instances of Dr. P. To lift a thousand pounds, and to break the Sabbath, the former by reality and the latter by assumption of the contradictory, were equally and equally naturally, physically, and metaphysically impossible. The latter was an impossibility by the law of contradiction, perfectly absolute in itself, though apparently not absolute because the assumption was of a removable fact. Equally natural and equally absolute, and on the same principle, is the impossibility of the leap from the precipice.

This class of linguistic expressions then does not indicate that inclination is itself power, or that there is any propriety in the distinction proposed between moral and natural power. Universally they indicate a metaphysical and logical impossibility existing between a presupposition and its contradiction.

The Theological Argument

I

Foreknowledge and Predestination

INTELLECT AND WILL WE are obliged to recognize in the divine Personality as truly as in the human. They are there as distinct as God's attributes of omniscience and omnipotence. And as foreknowledge belongs to the intellect, and foreordination to the Will, the former being perception and the latter volition, there can be no excuse for confounding the two or not recognizing their wide diversity. And as intelligent volition or any real volition is preceded by perception, so God's foreordination must be viewed as being preceded by foreknowledge.

Besides, as God's foreknowledge, being but a particular phase of his omniscience, is an attribute, and is of the essential attributes of the divine nature, so it must in the order of nature, even if both are eternal, precede foreordination, which, being a volition, is an act. Even in the depths of an antecedent eternity, as an eternal cause must be held in logical order to be antecedent to its eternal effect, so God as omniscient and therefore as foreknowing, must be held to be antecedent to God as acting, willing and foreordaining. It is indeed, impossible to conceive the Deity as acting or willing in unintelligent darkness. The knowledge of all future fulfillments, possible or actual, even of his own divine actions, must in the order of nature precede the actions themselves. And as we purpose to show that the freedom of an act is not affected by its being the object of foreknowledge, so the freedom of the divine predeterminations is not restricted by the previous existence of the divine prescience of them.

In foreordination or Calvinistic predestination the divine volition is logically antecedent, and the event predestinated is immediately or mediately consequent. Predestination is as an antecedent stereotype, to which the consequent total complex of events must conform. The consequent complex must conform to the antecedent stereotype; not, as in foreknowledge, the stereotype to the complex. Foreknowledge takes shape from the fact; the fact takes shape from the predestination. Calvinistic predestination is the causative, logical, and chronological antecedent of the fact, foreknowledge is the chronological antecedent, but logical and causational consequence of the fact.

If the stereotype conforms to the complex, then the complex is foreknown first, and then willed, which as between foreknowledge and foreordination concedes the former. It supposes that God foresees man's sin and ratifies it. The future fact is first overlaid with foreknowledge, and then that foreknowledge is overlaid with predestination, and thereby with necessitation. Ironically, it implies all the dependence of God upon man of which Calvinists object to Arminianism. It incurs all the charge of making God the authorizer of sin, which can be truly made against the Calvinistic version of predestination.

DISTINCTION BETWEEN DECREES

The distinction between "Causative" and "Permissive" decrees, if the latter signifies God's volition to permit or not prevent the free act of the free agent, is the Arminianism of Arminius himself. With it we have no controversy; for it appears in the proper place to be the very doctrine maintained in this treatise. But we may here note that by the proposition that "God foreordains whatever comes to pass," it is the event that is foreordained or decreed, and not its permission; so that such foreordination cannot be a mere "permissive decree."

Against the doctrine that foreknowledge precedes predetermination the following is the argument:

> The foreknowledge of actual future events is not an essential attribute of God. We can conceive of him as a perfect God without it. If he had not chosen to create a universe he would still have been God. But in that case there would have been no future events. Foreknowledge must be distinguished from knowledge. The latter is an essential attribute of God, and extends to all possible existences; but the former can extend only to things which will actually exist. It therefore must first be determined that events will be, or there can be no foreknowledge of them. They must be transferred from mere future possibilities, which are objects of Gods knowledge, to future certainties, before they can become objects of his foreknowledge. But this transfer can be made only by the Will of God. He alone can determine whether a thing that may be will

be. His determining purpose must precede and be the ground of its certainty. Therefore, God as decreeing must be conceived of as preceding God as foreknowing, and hence it is perfectly legitimate to reason from his foreknowledge to his decrees. [1]

The fallacies, as we esteem them, are here so numerous that we now address them: 1. God cannot be conceived "as perfect God" without a foreknowledge of all future possibilities and actualities. Whatever of the future is certain reflects its certainty back into the essential, eternal omniscience of God. If omniscience is an attribute of God, the knowledge of all future fulfillments is an attribute of God; and that is foreknowledge. 2. If God had produced no future events, then he would have eternally foreknown the absence of all future events. It is not the knowledge of future events exclusively, but the knowledge of all future fulfillments, all that the future does or does not contain, which constitutes foreknowledge. Foreknowledge is omniscience comprehending the future. 3. Foreknowledge differs from knowledge just as much as a thing differs from itself. The knowledge of a future event or a future no-event is just as truly knowledge as the knowledge of the past or present. Omniscience includes all three. "Known unto God are all his works from the beginning of the world." (Acts xv,18) 4. If "it must be first determined that events will be," then, as that determination is an "event," so that event must be foreknown in the essential omniscience of God. And that comprehensive event being foreknown, all the events it comprehends must be foreknown. 5. And this "transfer," being an event, must be foreknown; and it must, before that event, be foreknown into what "probabilities" and into what "certainties" the transfer is made. 6. The certainty of the "purpose" itself does in the order of nature precede the "purpose" whereby the "purpose" is foreknown in the essential omniscience of God, which, "in the order of nature" precedes all volitional acts, even of God himself. That "certainty" is not antecedently grounded or caused by any previous act, since it consists in the pure future fulfillment of the certain event, and has no ground except in the event of which the fulfillment is predicable. 7. If God's omniscient foresight of all that is or is not in the future is the effect of God's determination, then an attribute of God is created by an act of God.

If God's foreknowledge depends on his determination, and must wait until after its existence, then he can have no foreknowledge of his own

1. D.T. Fiske, "The Divine Decrees," 415.

acts, and must wait for present or post-knowledge of them. And, finally, if God can be a "perfect God" without "the foreknowledge of actual future events," then he can be a perfect God with omniscience empty of facts. His omniscience, then, instead of being an actual knowledge of future fulfillment, would be only a capacity for knowing, and not the knowledge itself. From all this it follows that of all future fulfillments, whether events or non-events, whether necessitated facts or free acts, it is an essential attribute of God to possess an eternal knowledge.

II

Reconciliation of Free Agency and Foreknowledge

THE ADVOCATES OF CALVINISTIC predestination and necessity maintain, with great show of logic that free agency, as we hold it, is inconsistent with God's foreknowledge. A finite agent, they maintain, cannot possess power to do otherwise than God foreknows he will do. Nor can any event be otherwise than God foreknows and so contradict his foreknowledge. We address our argument to this point.

I. We may first remark that our view of free agency does not so much require in God a foreknowledge of a peculiar kind of event as a knowledge in him of a peculiar quality existent in the free agent. This is a point apparently much if not entirely overlooked by thinkers upon this subject.

Power is a substantive quality intrinsic in the agent possessing it. It is a positive element in the constitution of the being. To a knowing eye it may be perfectly cognizable. If any power is planted in an agent, God, who placed it there, must know it. And if that power is, as we shall assume to have proved, a power to do otherwise than the agent really does do, God may be conceived to know it and to know it in every specific instance. That is, God knows in every case that the agent who wills a certain way possessed the elemental power of choosing another way, or several elemental powers of choosing several other ways. God may know the way in which the agent will act, and at the same time there may be seen by him in the same agent the substantive power of acting otherwise instead. The two facts, namely, that he will act thus, and that there resides in him the power of other action, may be seen at the same time by God and be mutually consistent with each other. God's foreknowledge, therefore, of the volition which will be put forth is perfectly consistent with his knowledge of the agent's power of willing otherwise. That is, prescience in God is perfectly consistent with freedom in the finite agent.

Surely if an agent can will either one of several ways, God may know each one of those several ways; and if of those several ways there is one that the agent will will, God may know which that way is. His knowing the way which, of the several, the agent will choose does not negate his knowing that the agent possessed powers for either of the other ways. For all those powers are simply positive elements in the being of the agent, which God is certainly to be conceived as able to know.

This view reduces the whole question to discussion of man's nature, or the proper analysis of the nature of a free agent. It becomes a discussion not of the metaphysics of events in regard to their necessity or possibility, but of psychology or anthropology, or rather (what is of momentous consequence in the controversy) the psychological investigation and decision to overrule and predetermine the metaphysical. If there is, in the free agent, ascertainable by psychology, or required by intuition, or supposedly seen by the divine eye, the power of putting forth the volition with full power of alternative, then God knows that power. And, then, God knows, or knows not, the agent's future acts. If he knows them not, his foreknowledge does not extend to all free acts. If he does know them, then he knows what future act will be, while there is full adequate power for it not to be.

If these views are just, the question is settled. The free agency of man is consistent with the foreknowledge of God. What is true of one free agent may be true of all. Agents, acts, and events may exist, free in their character, which are known of God in perfect harmony with their freedom.

COROLLARY RESULTING

As a corollary resulting from these views, we note that an agent may be supposed to possess a power of acting otherwise[1] than the way that God foreknows he will act. The proposition that an agent cannot act otherwise than God foreknows he will act is not clearly certain, nor possible to be proved. He can act otherwise, for there is seen by God in him the element of adequate power for other action. And yet God will not be deceived; for such is his perfection of knowledge that it is known to him which power of action will be exerted. So that there is a perfect compatibility between

---

1. Of course in all such propositions as this we mean otherwise instead or substitutively, and not two opposite ways at the same time.

the two propositions: an agent can act otherwise than the way that God foreknows; and God can never be deceived in his foreknowledge.

II. There is a class of thinkers who avoid the difficulty of reconciling foreknowledge with free agency by denying the existence or the possibility of the foreknowledge of a free or contingent event. They affirm that a free act is, previous to its existence, a nothing, and so not an object of knowledge. The knowing it, therefore, supposes a contradiction. And as the impossibility of performing a contradictory act is no limitation of Omnipotence, so the impossibility of a contradictory knowledge is no limitation of Omniscience. Undoubtedly this view would be preferable to the admission of predestination, provided it solved the difficulty and was necessary to its solution. But it may be doubted both whether it is necessary, or whether it solves any difficulty.

Whether there is any foreknowledge or not, it is certain that there will be one particular course of future events and no other. On the most absolute doctrine of freedom there will be, as we shall soon more fully illustrate, one train of choices freely put forth and no other. If by the absolute perfection of God's omniscience that one train of free events, put forth with full power otherwise, is embraced in his foreknowledge, it follows that God foreknows the free act, and that the foreknowledge and the freedom are compatible. The difficulty does not indeed lie in the compatibility of the two. The real difficulty (which we distinctly profess to leave forever insoluble) as may soon more clearly appear, is to conceive how God came by that foreknowledge. But that is no greater difficulty than to conceive how God came by his omnipotence or self-existence. It will be a wise theologian who will tell us how God came by his attributes. It will require a deep thinker to tell how the universe or its immensity came about by its real or actual deity; or how the present self-existent came to be, and no other.

III. Freedom, in every individual case, as we have defined it, implies, that of several possible volitions, one and no other will take place: one in opposition to many—numerically; one in opposition to any other instead—alternatively. And so of a whole series of volitions, namely, of the entire existence of any free being, temporal or even eternal, each volition and the entire series of his individual volitions, though possible to be otherwise, yet each will be one particular way. Certainly, when we define that a free volition is one which is or will be put forth one way, by a will able to put forth some other way instead, we do not deny that such particular one will be put forth; nor that such ones, infinite in number, through a whole series endless in length, will be put forth. And so we may affirm of the infinite number of individual volitions of each of an infinite number of free agents, in one vast totality—interweaving in mutual correlations with each other, in infinities of infinities—that while there is power that each volition should not be, yet each and all will be in its own one way, and not another instead. Such a free totality can be viewed simply in itself as being just as free as if it were unforeknown; just as free as if there were no God to foreknow it. So the freedomist, with perfect ease and consistency, is enabled in conception to survey the one great free whole of all future volitions as a valid conception. And he can speak of it, and argue about it as that one which in each particularity could not be, and yet individually and wholly will be.

This conception of a system of free alternatives stands opposed to the conception of a universal system of absolute necessity, as taught by Edwards; of which every event is a fixed product of fixed causes; and the totality, one solid fixation of which it is a contradiction to suppose, that either for the whole or for a single item of the whole, there is the least possible power[2] to be otherwise. Of the former, the entirety, all the elements are pervaded by the will-be, and yet the can-be-otherwise; the other by the must-be and the can-be-no-otherwise. The former is pure certainty; the latter is necessity.

Opposed, secondly, to this free volitional totality is a totality ruled in its events not by the law of causation, but by a previous law of Invariable Sequence, to which by the very nature of things all volitional events conform themselves according to the same conditions of comparative strength of antecedents, and with the same absolute Uniformity. This claims to be a totality of simple certainty, but upon false grounds. Simple certainty, unrolled by previous fixed and fixing law, belongs to the volition which, with full alternative power, will be by the agent ultimately put forth. This Uniformitarian law, if it is what it claims to be, an absolute invariability, requires and secures that the volitions and the totality should be configured as necessarily to its own previous type as does the law of Causation. It secures a different set of individual volitions from the ultimates of free alternatives, but identical with those of causative necessity. It excludes from the agent, if not the intrinsic power of putting forth a different voli-

---

2. For according to necessity the effect is always the measure and the exhaustive of the power. The totality of events is the exhaustive of the totality of power.

tion, certainly the exertion of that power. And when we understand that to put forth that different volition would be to annul an axiomatic law, we shall conclude that the power itself does not and cannot exist.

CERTAIN TOTALITY

Opposed, thirdly, to this simply certain Totality is the Totality of Calvinistic predestination. According to this the divine Will, not relying on foreknowledge of the future fulfillment, selects and predetermines it, contradicting and excluding the possibility of a substitute alternative, and causatively securing the identical event. In foreknowledge the divine cognizance is shaped by the future event; in Calvinistic predestination the event is shaped by and to the predetermination. Even if by some inexplicable coincidence, therefore, the event predetermined is in all cases the very event at which the alternative Will would ultimately arrive, still the very moment it becomes predetermined the power is foreclosed, contradicted, and causatively excluded for it to be otherwise, and the agent is no longer a free agent. But a predestination based simply upon foreknowledge is not the actually maintained predestination. In Calvinistic predestination the totality and the individual events, predestined in order to be foreknown, are originated and stereotyped, not by the aggregate of free agents, but by the Predestinating Volition primordially causing the efficient finite causes to cause, and the effects to exist.

That supposed Divine Volition by which all events are said to be predetermined or predestined cannot include less than those three things: first, origination of the event; second, exclusion of every contradictory or preventive alternative; and, third, securing of the identical event. The event must of course have its first conception in the divine mind, and be fixed upon by the divine Will, and that must be the first intentional cause of its existence. For if the divine Will predetermines the act, it cannot stand inert but in a causative relation to the event. Unless causative of the event, it is a brutum fulmen, a blank, and a nothing. Next, the divine Will as cause must pledge itself, and efficiently secure that no adequate contradiction prevents the identical event; by which all counter cause or contrary choice is rendered impossible. And, third, as cause the divine Will is pledged to secure positively that the identical event in the identical way comes into existence so that the actual future is solely possible, is necessary, and must be. Less than this Calvinistic predestination cannot

be. And through whatever secondary causes or agents the events are effectuated, one thing is self-evident, that the divine Will is perfectly and
intentionally its responsible author. The first cause is responsible cause for
the last effect.

IV. We have then before us the true distinct conception of a free totality of free volitions: the infinite, universal, eternal system of free events,
which while they are each one able to be otherwise than thus, yet will
freely be thus; and while they are able to be thus, and truly will and do
be thus, are able to be otherwise than thus. Now of this free totality, thus
clearly, we trust, conceived, our doctrine affirms that it exists in the prior
omniscience of God, and is the very future totality that God foreknows.
It is that grand totality (each item of which will be with full power otherwise) that is the totality embraced in God's foreknowledge. And just
because it is this grand free alternative totality that stands included in
God's foreknowledge, therefore God's foreknowledge embraces a grand,
free alternative totality. That is, God foreknows an infinite amount of free
acts that will be put forth with full power of alteration. That is, God's
foreknowledge of the act is perfectly consistent with freedom of the act.
And that is, finally, that God's foreknowledge of the act neither makes nor
proves its necessity.

Of this free totality, let us suppose there actually existed before its
commencement, a perfectly accurate record of its future fulfillment. It
would be a most wonderful thing. If that record were on the tablet of the
Divine Mind, it would be one among the many wonders of God, above
the power of human reason to conjecture how it came to be. But such a
record would not at all change the nature of the future free totality. By the
supposition, it is the free totality that is on the record, and not the fated
totality.

That is, it is the totality that ultimately will take place, though there
is full power with each volitional act for another to take place, which is on
the record. There is full power for other than the recorded events to take
place; just because it is the events that will take place though, there is full
power for other events, which are the recorded. If that record is the divine
Prescience itself, then its full possession of the accurate future fulfillment
of all free volitions is fully consistent with the full power of their being
put forth otherwise. The entire system of free agents is fully adequate to
bring into existence an entire totality of acts different from the foreknown
future free totality. Nay, there is power existent in the entire system of free

agents for an infinite diversity of free totalities; and we may add that there may be in the first progenitors in that system adequate power for the generation of an unlimited diversity of totalities of free agents themselves.

ALLEGORICAL TABLET

Of our allegorical tablet, above supposed, the apparently contradictory propositions are true: 1. That it is absolutely impossible that its record should not be true; and yet, 2. That it is perfectly possible that the events it contains should not take place. The first of these two propositions is true; for by the very supposition the one actual future event amid the many possible future events, is the event that is recorded with absolute accuracy. The second is true, because by the very supposition every event recorded is an event for which there is an existent power that it should not be. From the very nature of the record it is impossible that it should be changed and impossible that it should err. Yet it is perfectly possible (for where there is power for the different, there is possibility for the different) that the event should be otherwise; and between these two statements there is no contradiction.

V. That the freeness of the act is not affected by the consideration of its being foreknown of God, may appear from the fact that both may be viewed as independent, yet coinciding facts. We can conceive of the freedom, first abstractly from all foreknowledge, or foreordination. There, is, as before remarked, a large class of thinkers who deny foreknowledge, and contemplate the field of free events as spreading out, uncovered by any prescience. Nay, an Atheist is fully able to conceive a world of free agents without any omnipotent personal first Cause. At any rate, it is fully possible for our mind first to posit a world of free agents, who put forth a limitless totality of free volitions, in full power for other volitions instead. Such a totality may be viewed as being just as free as if no deity existed to decree or foreknow them.

After the conception of this totality has been fully formed and amply contemplated, we are fully able to conceive, additionally, that a foreknowledge existing incomprehensibly to us, may take just this totality into its comprehension, without producing the least change in its free nature. The foreknowledge has (unlike Calvinistic predestination) no causative influence on the free event to change or destroy its freedom. It is a free totality in the first stage of the above conception; it is a free totality in the second stage. It is a free totality that is presupposed; it is the same free totality that is foreknown. That is, there may conceivably be a foreknowledge of all the free acts of all free agents without at all affecting their freedom. God may thus foreknow all that the whole universe of free agents will do without any contradiction to their free agency.

VI. If it is true that an agent this moment puts forth an act in the full possession of a power for contrary act instead, then the doctrine of freedom is just and true. But the proposition that such an act will be put forth—namely, an act put forth with full power for contrary—though unknown to any human mind, was true a moment before the alternatives arose. Were the proposition declaring which act will be thus put forth, with absolute accuracy affirmed one moment before the alternatives arose, such a proposition, however undiscoverable by the human mind, would be perfectly true. Such a proposition, affirming, with perfect accuracy, which act would be put forth by an agent possessed of contrary power, would be true not only a moment, a year, but a whole eternity before its occurrence.

And the truth of that proposition from all eternity is fully consistent with the doctrine of freedom. That is the truth of the eternal proposition that the agent will certainly, unfailingly act thus and thus is fully consistent with the proposition that there was full power in said agent to act oppositely instead. And if the eternal truth of that proposition is thus perfectly consistent with its capability of being altered, so must the knowledge, the eternally anterior knowledge of that truth, be so consistent. If the proposition may be eternally true consistently with its alterability, it may be eternally known with its alterability.[3] Consistently with that, it may be written on the divine mind; it may be written upon the pages of the prior eternity, upon the firmament of heaven, upon the surface of the primitive rocks, upon the pages of the prophetic word. If on any of those tablets every future volition of every future free being were minutely recorded, it could neither make nor prove any change in the nature of its freedom.

From these views, two inferences may be justly drawn.

1. The prophecies of Scripture, were they ten times more numerous and explicit than they are, furnish no argument for necessity or Calvinistic predestination. Men are adequate to falsify both divine foreknowledge

---

3. But not also eternally decreed consistently with that alterability; for, while knowledge has no influence on the act or event, a decree is causative, securative, and fixing of the act.

and divine prediction. The free agency of Jesus was uncontradicted by the predictions of his conduct. He himself affirms his own full power to falsify the predictions of the Old Testament. His mind could fully comprehend the relation in which he stood to prophecy, to divine foreknowledge, and to the divine purposes, and recognize his obligation to fulfill them all. Men know not their relation to foreknowledge; and although they possess adequate power to act otherwise than the foreknown or predicted way, yet whichever way they do really act, omniscience will be beforehand with them, and fully and accurately foreknow it. Hence no argument could be drawn from the prophecies of Holy Scripture, to prove the predestination of human actions or the necessitation of human agents.

2. If by setting a train of causes in motion the future existence of a particular living free agent is absolutely secured a thousand years hence, its contradiction being absolutely excluded, his existence is a necessity. If that agent in a given case is able to will either of several ways, there is no need of a present causation to make it certain which he will do. The agent, by his act in the future, makes all the certainty there now is. It is by and from that act solely thus put forth that the present will-be of the act exists. He will put forth his act unsecured by any present nonalternative making or securement. Whichever act he puts forth it is true that he will put forth; and that now unmade will-put-forth is all the certainty there is. It is by that putting forth solely that the present will-be is true. All the certainty there is, that is, all the will-be about it, depends upon, and arises solely from the free act of the agent himself. It is simply the present uncaused will-be of an act which can otherwise be. Certainty, therefore, is not a previously made, caused, or manufactured thing.

As to the "certainty in things themselves," of which Edwards talks, I pretend not to know what it means if it means anything else than the will-be of the thing. But if it is anything that previously fixes the sole one way of the thing, thus making it a solely possible future fulfillment beforehand, that is no pure certainty, but a necessitated certainty, a pure necessitation.

III

Edwards's Argument for Necessity from Foreknowledge

VII. THE FIRST AND main argument of Edwards (whose logic we now propose to discuss) against pure foreknowledge may be thus abbreviated.

An event connected by a tie of necessity with another absolutely necessary event is itself necessary. But a future volition is an event necessarily connected with a past and therefore necessary event, namely, God's foreknowledge; therefore the future volition is necessary. The foreknowledge of God, being past, has already made sure of its own existence, and cannot but be, and is therefore necessary. With this past and so necessary foreknowledge, the future fact is connected by the necessity of knowledge, and is therefore necessary.

The necessary connection of the free volition with the past omniscience, is the weak point of this argument. Such necessity requires indeed that the foreknowledge should, in order for its accuracy, know the right fact; and not that the fact must accord with the foreknowledge. The necessity lies not upon the free act, but upon the foreknowledge. The foreknowledge must see to its own accuracy. Pure knowledge, temporal or eternal, must conform itself to the fact, not the fact to the knowledge. Knowledge, by its very nature, accepts the fact as it is; it does not shape the fact to itself, or require the fact to be configured to its own type. All the necessity of connection there is between the divine foreknowledge and the event is this, that it is necessary—in the sense of prerequisite—in order to the accuracy of the divine foreknowledge, whichever act the free agent with full alternative power puts forth, to have in possession that act, and no other instead. But that is no necessity on the act. The rightness of the knowledge must be seen to eternally before the act. The act is bound by no necessity to conform to or be connected with the knowledge. It is perfectly free to contradict the knowledge, and the knowledge must take care of itself.

The act can be as it pleases, and the knowledge must conform. The act is under no necessity to agree with the knowledge. And these relations are essentially the same whether the knowledge is temporal or eternal. If the knowledge is absolutely eternal in the past, and is pure knowledge, it must as truly be conceived as conformed to the fact, and not the fact to it, as any knowledge of the present instant. How such knowledge can come to exist, receiving beforehand the independent self-shaping of the fact is not the question. It is now enough to maintain that such is the intrinsic relation between fact and knowledge. There is, therefore, no connection between divine foreknowledge and the free act imposing any necessity upon the latter.

VIII. Upon the more minute points of his arguments we may next note:

1. Edwards reiterates, with some attempt at emphasis, the terms "infallible," "unfrustrable," and "indissoluble." We admit that omniscience is infallible, in the sense that it cannot err, and therefore will have the right fact; and unfrustrable, in the sense that it cannot be frustrated, because it cannot err; but deny that between the foreknowledge and the act of the agent power the connection is necessary or indissoluble. The foreknowledge is infallible because in possession of the truth of the future fulfillment. But the agent-power is not necessitated to produce the act which is foreknown to be true. For the true future fulfillment, foreknown as such, is true not necessarily; but made true by a power adequate to make it not true. Between the foreknowledge, therefore, however fixed, past, made sure, infallible, or unfrustrable, and the event or act which will be put forth, there is no such necessary indissoluble connection as necessitates the act to any particular conformation. And the argument of Edwards to that effect is a failure.

CONTENT OF KNOWLEDGE

By the *content* of a knowledge we mean the matter or matter of fact, as contained in the mind, which makes up the knowledge, and of which the knowledge consists. Now Edwards thinks that in divine foreknowledge there is an "indissoluble" connection between this internal content and the external act, requiring the latter to conform to the former. But there is not. There is an "indissolubleness" requiring the former to conform to the latter; but that is bound to have been taken care of an eternity ago, and the present free act has no concern with it, and is bound by no necessity to it.

2. Edwards says: "And so does certain foreknowledge prove that now in the time of the knowledge it is, by some means or other, become impossible but that the proposition which predicates future existence on the event should be true." (181) Edwards is here certainly mistaken. A proposition affirming a certain future fulfillment is perfectly consistent with the power for the fulfillment to be otherwise. That such a proposition is certain does not prove the necessity of its verification. Such a proposition cannot, indeed, be true and false at the same time; but it can be true in full consistency with the existence of a power adequate to make it false. That the proposition is certain does not prove the non-existence of the power, nor the impossibility of its exertion, but simply that it will not be exerted. The proposition simply affirms which of several powers will be exerted, and which of several possibilities will become an actuality. But that is not affirming but there were the other powers and the other possibilities in the case.

Indeed, in a true view of the case, we may say that the agent is able to falsify that proposition, by which the divine foreknowledge affirms that a particular act will be put forth. If the divine foreknowledge is not falsified, it will not be because there is no full power for such falsification in the free agent. The foreknowledge secures itself against falsification, not by limiting the power of the agent, but by allowing him its full exercise in putting forth either one of several possible acts and conforming its own pre-perception to that one. It remains, therefore, still true, that while there is in the agent full power to falsify the divine foreknowledge, the foreknowledge can fully guard itself from the exercise of that power, and maintain the requisite necessity, that the accuracy of omniscience should be absolutely perfect.

3. "To say the foreknowledge is certain," says Edwards, "and infallible, and yet the connection of the event with that foreknowledge is not indissoluble, but dissoluble and fallible, is very absurd." a) The foreknowledge, we reply, is infallible in the sense that it will not fail of the truth; whichever is truth will and must be infallibly known. Yet inasmuch as "the event," that is, the act, is not necessarily the truth or true act, the connection between the event and the foreknowledge is "dissoluble and fal-

lible," in the sense that there is full power for another event or act instead, and to say that is not "absurd." b) There is, says Edwards, a "necessary connection between a proposition's being known to be true, and its being true indeed." As just shown, a proposition may be "known to be true," it may be consequently "true indeed," and yet not necessarily "true indeed." There may be power for it to be made untrue. c) "If there be an infallible knowledge of future volitions," Edwards adds, "the event is necessary; or, in other words, it is impossible but the event should come to pass." There may be an infallible knowledge of future volitions; yet the volition infallibly known may be one put forth with full power for other volition instead. The infallibility consists in the fact that of either put forth, the knowledge will be accurate. Nor is it "impossible but that the event should come to pass;" for the very event infallibly foreknown is an event for which there was a power adequate for it not to come to pass. d) "If it be not impossible but that it may be otherwise," he adds, "then it is not impossible but that the proposition that affirms its future coming to pass may not now be true." The word "may" here is ambiguous. It may imply subjective uncertainty arising from ignorance, as "the thing may be so for aught I know," and in this sense it is here inapplicable. It may imply a power for either way. In that sense it is here true. It is not impossible but that for the proposition that affirms a future fulfillment, there should be a power adequate to render it "now untrue." It is true not for the want of power to make it "now untrue," but because that power will not be exerted, the very act foreknown being the one for which the power will be exerted. So that it correctly follows, and is true, that "it is not impossible but that there now should be no truth in that proposition which is now infallibly known to be true." The proposition is infallibly known to be true, not because it is impossible to be untrue instead of true, but because it is true. It is true, though there exists a power adequate to make it untrue instead. The knowledge has truly in possession that future fulfillment, which the agent, possessed of power for either of several future fulfillments, will produce.

IX. Origen is quoted by Edwards as saying, "God's prescience is not the cause of things future, but their being future is the cause of God's prescience that they will be." To this view of the matter, which has been commended by Arminians, (and we indorse it with them), Edwards furnishes two answers: 1. If foreknowledge does not make future events necessary, or impossible to be otherwise, it proves them so; and 2. It is as strong arguing from effect to cause, as from cause to effect. If foreknowledge is a fixed effect of things future, then the future act, being alleged as its cause, must be equally fixed.

GOD'S FOREKNOWLEDGE

God's foreknowledge, we reply, neither makes the future event necessary nor proves it so. The event foreknown is the resultant or ultimate act put forth by an agent possessing power for a different act. The fact that an agent, or an infinite number of agents, perform an infinite number of acts, with power in every instance for other acts instead, does not disprove that such acts will be put forth. And certainly the fact that those acts are foreknown no more proves than it makes them different from what they were before, namely, the free acts of free agents. They were each able to be otherwise, and they were all able to be otherwise; nevertheless, of all possible ways they are thus, and as thus are foreknown. But their being foreknown neither takes away their freedoms nor proves it gone.

Nor, assuming that the foreknowledge is the effect at which the free act is the cause, does the fixedness of the eternal effect, namely, the foreknowledge, prove the fixed necessity of the cause, namely, the act. For whether the act is free or necessitated, its eternal previous effect must be equally unvarying. If my present free alternative act sends back, in the very process of being freely performed, its eternal image of itself into the depths of the divine omniscience, it sends it back, with no trembling line, a true image of itself—a free alternative act. It creates in the divine mind an eternal unchanging perception of itself as it is, a free act. If the divine omniscience is supposed to have truly ascertained and taken possession of the true free future fulfillment, what demand can there be for change or unsteadiness in its eternal pre-perception? When once right it would be its business forever to stay right, and be forever immutable in its rightness. If the ray of the divine eye is once "fixed" upon the free act, it should forever stay fixed.

Edwards makes the supposition, so fully made by us, that the future action may be written in a book, as, for instance, in prophetic prediction, and draws the inference of necessity. "If so then it is impossible it should ever be otherwise than that that predicate and the event should agree; and this is the same thing as to say it is impossible but that the event should come to pass; and this is the same thing as to say that its coming to pass is necessary." (185) The agent-power, we reply, is not necessitated to make its act to be the act with which the predicate affirmed by foreknowledge agrees. The foreknowledge must take care of itself. All the impossibility there is that "it should be otherwise than that the event and the predicate should agree" must be secured by the care of foreknowledge to get the right event under its predicate. So long as that is duly taken care of the disagreement between the predicate and the event is sufficiently "impossible," and the freedom of the agent is not thereby affected.

Edwards flings into a variety of forms the reiterated argument, or rather assertion, that foreknowledge demonstrates the necessity of the future fact. "I freely allow that foreknowledge does not prove a thing to be necessary any more than after-knowledge; but then after-knowledge, which is certain and infallible, proves that it is now become impossible but that the proposition known should be true . . . And so does certain foreknowledge prove," etc. (181) After-knowledge, we reply, embraces a fact in which there is no power to cause to be no fact, or to make to have been not done; for the past is out of power. The fact accomplished can never be made no fact. The past fact has an intrinsic necessity of its own, the necessity of already secured existence; and that is a perfect necessity whether known or not. But for the future possible fact there is an adequate power for rendering it otherwise than it will be.

X. Edwards considers the notion that God *is above the conditions of time*, and endeavors to show that it demonstrates necessity. This notion is that there is "no succession of time to the divine mind," "no fore-knowledge or after-knowledge," but that all is "an eternal now." (184) Edwards endeavors to appropriate this notion to the purpose of his argument, first, by the maxim we have already considered and, we trust, refuted, that "knowledge proves necessity of the thing known." God, he says, "always sees things just as they are in truth;" of which we have no doubt, and hence infer that he sees a free act to be a free act. But Edwards infers, "hence there never is in reality anything contingent in such a sense as that possibly it may happen never to exist." But it may still be true that a thing may be contingent in the sense that there is full power for it not to be.

Edwards thus puts the point of his argument: "If, strictly speaking, there is no foreknowledge in God, it is because those things which are future to us are as present to God *as if they already had existence.*" (184–185) In regard to free future acts, the palpable error of Edwards occurs in the italicized words; in place of which should stand these words, as if they were now transpiring. Events viewed as if they already had existence are, virtually, past and gone, not now and present. It is the becoming of all acts that the "eternal now" of God supposes; not the have become. It is as if God were a person now present looking upon the free act as now alternatively being performed. That now-being-performed act reflects itself into the divine mind just as it comes into existence; and just according to its nature is free, and under condition that other acts instead were in power and possible. And so the act is not necessary, and is divinely seen to be not necessary.

ETERNAL NOW

The "eternal now" supposes that God is as a man who stands in the sunlight of a clear day and "now" watches a leisurely walker directing his steps in whatsoever path he pleases, looking to any point of the compass, employing his hands in any business he will. Neither the sunlight, nor the ray of the watcher's vision at all limits, circumscribes, hampers, or destroys the freedom of the traveler's movements. The vision of the watcher takes in the free action just as it transpires. God's mind, according to the "eternal now," is like this mirror, before which I may stand. Every movement of my head, hand, body is reflected with perfect accuracy according as that movement is by me freely and alternatively made.

The image in the mirror does not shape or constrain the movements of my choice, but accepts them in all their freedom, and represents them precisely as they are successively becoming. My free act causes the reproduction in the mirror; the mirror does not cause a necessitated act. If the conditions of time, as Edwards allows, may be, even for argument's sake, considered as supposably non-existent to God, then his mind, filling eternity, must be considered as ever present at the moment and mirroring the acting, not the act; the thing as under the doing, not the thing as done. And not one free act alone, or the acts of one free agent, but the totality, are all mirrored in the divine mind, in their present tense, just as they are when they transpire, free and alternative. The divine knowledge takes them, not makes them.

If the act is thus, then thus does the divine mirror receive it; if otherwise, then otherwise. The act could have been otherwise than it is mirrored; for were it otherwise, then the mirroring would be otherwise. The act causes the mirrored reflection, not the reflection the act. The mirrored image conforms to, is shaped by, the presented object. Supposing, then, omniscience to be above the conditions of time, it is a present mirror, a divine transparency, taking in the reflection of the act as the moving of the act presents it. And thus in the pure, perfect, infinite, boundless light of God's omniscience is the limitless Totality of all free acts coming into existence. It neither makes the act unfree nor proves it so. Whatever freeness may be in the nature of the act remains unchanged.

XI. As regards the individual human being, the doctrines of Calvinism and of foreknowledge may be illustrated by the following two views:

1. Before every man at his birth (according to Calvinism) is a certain course of actions, which by an infinite causation it is secured that he must take, all others being decretively and causatively excluded. In this statement predestination, necessity, and fatalism coincide.

2. Before every man at his birth, according to foreknowledge, there is a course of actions, which he will choose among many others equally in his power of choice, and from which he is not excluded by antecedent causation.

Both these cases agree in the future fulfillment of some one course, but differ in the nature of the agency that produces the course.

Now it would seem that if by some perfection of the divine nature there should exist a tablet, upon which were written, without any connection with the course, except the most truthful agreement, the exact details of this case No. 2, it would prove nothing as to the intrinsic capability in the man of taking any other course. It would amount to this, that the course which, in full possession of ample power to choose any other course, he actually will choose, is the course that is written. The existence of such a tablet would certainly not affect his freedom. Nor would it disprove his freedom; for any theory of freedom admits, not only of one man but of all free agents, there is a certain course he or they will, freely and alternatively, of all others take. And if by supposition that is truly the one recorded, the existence of the tablet from a million years ago, or from all eternity, neither makes nor proves the actions of the agent to be not free.

The difficulty, then, is not to tell how our freedom is consistent with foreknowledge. It is to tell how God is omniscient. We shall not trouble our mind with that inquiry.

IV

Calvinistic Predestination: An Unnecessary Hypothesis

CALVINISTIC PREDESTINATION, AS WE have in the proper places delin-
eated it, is not only involved in endless difficulties and perplexities,
but in meeting the demands of a rational theodicy and of Scripture interpretation, it is an unnecessary hypothesis. The plan of the universe may
be rationally outlined; the text of Scripture can be naturally construed,
without owing it any obligations.

The Divine Plan, as embraced in God's predeterminations, is a
scheme strictly embracing only the Divine Actions. Supposing that in the
infinite eternal past, God is employed in selecting from all possible systems that which his wisdom best approves. The system he adopts is a system consisting, properly and directly, of his own future actions. Knowing
indeed by the absolute perfection of his own attribute of omniscience all
future possibilities, including all possible results from any supposed arrangements, God does, in full foreknowledge of all results in the case,
so plan all his own actions and courses as seems to him wisest and best.
Subsequently, his created free being will sin, for that sin the free being,
being fully able to avoid it, and bringing it unnecessarily into existence, is
alone responsible. He alone has intruded his rebellion into existence.

God neither predetermined, foreordained, willed, nor desired it.
God's predeterminations of his own future action, or courses of action,
are to be considered as so far contingent, as that their execution or coming into existence is conditioned upon the coming into existence of many
pre-supposed free actions of finite agents, which are able not to be put
forth. Yet, nevertheless, inasmuch as God's omniscience does truly and
fully foresee the free volition that will actually, with full power otherwise, be put forth, there is no proper danger that God will be deceived
in the perfect wisdom of his plans, or be frustrated in any of his actual
purposes.

Let us, as a theodicic illustration, suppose that a perfectly good and wise prince, absolute in authority, rules over as many tribes and nations as Persia's Xerxes; the large share of whom are hostile to each other, and desperately depraved. His plan is not to destroy, nor to interfere with their personal freedom, but so to arrange their relations to each other as that he may make them mutual checks upon each other's wickedness. The ambition of one may opportunely chastise the outrage of another; that those wrongs that will exist may be limited and overruled; and that even the crimes they commit may further his plans of reformation, gradual perfectability, and highest sum total of good.

If it is seen that a traitor will assassinate, the victim will be one whose death will be a public benefit. If brothers (as Joseph's) will envy their brother, let their victim thereby so conduct himself as that he shall be the saviour of great nations. If a proud prince will be wanton in his pride, so nerve him up, vitally and intellectually, as that his wantonness shall spread great truths through the tribes of the empire. If a warlike king will conquer, let the nation exposed to his invasions be one whose chastisement will be a lesson to the world. If a populous tribe is bent on devastating the earth, let their hoards so ravage as that future civilization shall spring from the desolations they make. So after long years the prince's scheme of development may work out its divine results.

If we may suppose that he was endued with a more than mortal foresight; if we may imagine that he had a plan, partly a priori, and partly based on foreseen deeds of his subjects we might then conceive that he could take all the passions, crimes, bold enterprises, and wild movements he foresaw men would exhibit, into his account, not as by him determined, but as cognized parts within his stupendous scheme of good.

WHOLE PLAN

He would so collocate men and things into a whole plan that their mutual play would work out the best results. And if his wisdom, as well as his power, is infinite, and his existence is eternal, then the entire scheme could be comprehended within his prescient glance in all its grandest and minutest parts, with all their causations, freedoms, and dependencies, and so comprehended that his predeterminations touch properly his own acts, leaving the free acts to the self-origination of free agents. And this may be, in the great whole, in spite of permitted wrong, the best possible system. We should then, in vision, behold all beings, however free, spontaneously, uncompulsorily, without command or decree, moving in harmony with his outlines of events. This is but the transcript of their free actions, and by their very iniquities and abominations, without any countenance from him or any excuse to themselves, working results they never dreamed, but which are in his plan.

Of this prince two sorts of language will be held. On, the one hand it will accurately and truthfully be said that he was a wise, a good, and a holy prince. He neither intended, nor necessitated, nor countenanced, nor purposed, nor decreed, nor ordained, nor instigated any wrong. He never foreordained the bad that comes to pass. No one ever sinned by any necessitative motive-force, or law of invariability. Each one had power for other volition. And so Scripture expresses itself when it describes the divine character or the comprehensive ethic of the divine government of the Lord. On the other hand it will be popularly and elliptically, though not with literal accuracy, said, that these brothers of Joseph were instruments in God's hands, to send their youngest to another land to be its saviour. It will be said that he sent his assassin to accomplish the beneficial death of that victim. It will be said that he armed this conqueror to chastise that nation, and that he poured those hordes over those plains in desolation. And so Scripture expresses itself when its standpoint is upon the plans of popular thought, and its purpose is merely to express the divine side of events. In literal truth, God neither ordered, did, nor approved any of those things. Yet as they were done under his administration, as they were cognized in his plans, as they worked out his results, so with a conventional, popular, conceptual truth, it will be said that he did the whole.

It might seem as if the very births and coming into existence of men involved human history in an inextricable interweaving of fatalism. Edwards has a passage (159) expatiating upon the immense number of physiological minutiae, requiring the whole train of antecedents that actually exist, which resulted in the birth "of the great conquerors of the world who, under God, have had the main hand in shaping the state of the world in after ages, such as Nebuchadnezzar, Cyrus, Alexander, Pompey, Julius Caesar," etc. Nay, what an infinite number of slight incidents have results in the birth of each one of us, and have, as it were, become solidly embodied in our persons; indicating that all those incidental antecedents, slight and slender as they seem, were as fixed as a most complex piece of adamantine machinery.

If, however, any man will consult his own consciousness, he will recognize that there is a Self within him, underlying all the facts of his history, in which he feels a deep, unchangeable, untransferable interest. He has an intransferable interest in his own joys and sorrow, well or ill-being, which he can conceive as extending through eternity. No alterations in his past or future history can change or diminish it. He can feel that there are points of time in which his whole history might have been revolutionized. His fortune, rank in life, place of residence, profession, matrimonial connections, and children, might all have been different. Yet that conscious interior Self, in which he feels that untransferable interest, would have been the same Self.

Still further, I can conceive that this Self might have had a different birth. I, this same conscious self-interested Ego, might have been born in Helvetia, in the time of Julius Caesar, of Gallic parents. My name, history, and entire stock of thoughts might have been different, and yet their subject might have been this same essential I. And so I can conceive that same Self as passing through thousands of reincarnations, as being born, living, dying, in a thousand different spheres, without any change in my underlying self-sameness, or any diminution of conscious interest in my own destinies.

If so, my essential Self lies deeper than my historical Self. Upon what slight chances of smiles and glances does marriage often depend? And yet the existence of your manly son or blooming daughter depended upon it? Not quite certainly so. That very son, in all that makes his essential Self interesting to himself, may have been born of other parents, even in another age and country, and with a totally different set of externalities. God can thus locate a human being at any point he pleases in human history without changing his essential self. Nor is our personal existence an accident of accidents, though it might seem.

1. God, in accordance with the laws of human descent, yet as wise Sovereign, bestows the individual personal human spirit upon each human body procreated. He furnishes, in what measure he pleases, the power and abundance respectively of intellectual, volitional and emotional nature. He, too, frames the body, furnishing its natural growth, its proportions, and its qualities of strength and beauty, or the reverse. He supplies, too, the vital power, the nervous vigor, and the animal exuberance, or their reverse.

2. He locates the individual in the system of men and things. In what country, parentage and family, rank, or time he pleases, he assigns us our existence.

3. He modifies our immediate being. Without touching our moral nature, at any rate for the worse, he may for the time being strengthen our powers and faculties, or weaken them; giving us extraordinary perspicacity, or eclipsing our intellects. He may suggest ideas not of unholy nature, but of a good, or of an unethical quality.

4. More or less resulting from these, arise juxtapositions and correlations, by which divine ends are most easily secured in the natural course of events. Without being a tempter, for instance, God may interpose before a man of raging passion the object whom he would have punished.

AMBITIOUS KING

Before a powerful and ambitious king, as Nebuchadnezzar,[1] to whom he has given birth in the royal family of Babylon, and placed upon its throne, God judges the guilty land of Israel. Voluntarily and unmoved of God, with full power of doing otherwise, the wicked king ravages the land as a beast of prey. The supposed end of God, the punishment of Israel, the monarch thus, without divine decree, temptation, influence, participation, or sanction, he accomplishes. In that work, though God's enemy, and guilty therein of crime and sin, he has become God's servant. God, nevertheless, needed not Nebuchadnezzar. He could have punished Israel by other hands; or by natural means as with earthquake, fire, disease, or storm.

At a certain time Jehovah would manifest his glory over the idols and the royalty of Egypt. He opens his series of plagues upon Pharaoh so powerfully that the proud heart of the monarch would have softened, not with penitence, but with fear. In order that the series of miraculous displays may be continued to their full number, God "hardens his heart," (Exod. iv, 21; vii, 3, 13, etc.) that is, strengthens its physical energies without touching his moral nature, or necessitating or tempting his will. And the proud king's own wicked will, resuming its courage, freely completes its wicked purpose.

---

1. In the following illustrations we take the Scripture instances adduced by Edwards, pp. 357–360.

God wills that his son should lay down his life to redeem lost men. There are thousands of methods, from heaven above, or from earth below, in which it can be accomplished. But God foreknows that at that period and juncture the worst of men are living and ready to betray and to crucify him. It was fitting that God should permit the world to show how wicked men could be, as well as how good is God. There is a traitor in the twelve who is ready and foreseen to be willing, to be the undecreed, unnecessitated betrayer. The Jews and Gentiles are both at Jerusalem, foreseen to be ready and willing to be the unobliged crucifiers. Jesus has but to take his position at that central point and bide his time. Freely, responsibly, without decree, participation, or sanction on the part of God, the traitor and the murderers accomplish the work. Thus God's end, that his Son should lay down his life, is accomplished. It is done by wicked men; yet neither are they to be thanked, or God to be implicated.

Thus, indeed, is God a wonderful King. Great in truth is Divine Sovereignty. Other monarchs have friends and servants to fulfill their orders; but for God the King, even enemies in their crimes run, without orders, connivance, or thanks, and with ready spontaneous subservience perform his purposes and win his battles.

And when men, or even Satan, thus subserve the accomplishment of God's end, Scripture does often give only the divine side of the transaction, and elliptically speaks as if the whole were done by God. That is, God, without causing the wicked act, or sharing its performance or guilt, accomplishes through it his holy purpose. In this sense, Scripture represents God as performing what the wicked instrumentally accomplish.

Thus may it be seen that the Calvinist version of predestination is wholly unrequired and useless in theology.

V

Christig Not Necessitated, but a Free Moral Agent

CHRIST WAS UNSURPASSABLY MERITORIOUS, yet Christ had no volitional power to sin. Necessity and just deserts are therefore intrinsically compatible. So Arminianism is false. Thus reasoned Edwards
through nearly twenty pages, on the distinct basis that the argument is
decisive of the whole question:

> I have been the longer in proof of this matter, it being the thing
> denied by some of the greatest Arminians—by Episcopius in par-
> ticular; and because I look upon it as a point clearly and absolutely
> determining the controversy between Calvinists and Arminians,
> concerning the necessity of such a freedom of Will as is insisted
> on by the latter, in order to the moral agency, virtue, command or
> prohibition, promise or threatening, reward or punishment, praise
> or dispraise, merit or demerit. (211)

Grant to Edwards the conclusiveness of his argument, and his claim
to have settled the compatibility of necessitation and deserts is undeniable. Yet, strange to say, a large class of Arminians, from a notion that
what they call "a liability to sin" includes some taint, or suspicion, of sin,
or corruption itself, grant all that Edwards argues, and so grant that necessitation of Will is no bar to merit or guilt. What need, then, of claiming
non-necessitation of Will in order to have deserts in any case?

The phrases "power to sin" and "liability to sin," as predicated of Jesus
or any other being, are of different import. The latter is not a true expression of our doctrine of Jesus. "Liability to sin," gives the impression of a
weakness justifying an expectation that the sin will probably take place,
and often implies proclivity to sin. Though free agents to those sins we
would hardly say that Aristides was liable to thieving, that Howard was
liable to commit murder, or that Washington was liable to be a despot.

The free, volitional power to sin, so far from being a defect, an impurity, an imperfection, implies and *is* a high quality; a condition to responsibility, to probation, to a high, well-deserving virtue or holiness. Not only may it be possessed by a being perfectly pure, but it must be primordially possessed by a being meritoriously pure. No being ever possessed the fullness and height of a moral nature without it. No moral being ever held command of the entirety of his moral nature, or over a lofty probationary moral career of destiny, without it. No finite creature ever attained the rewarding plaudit of the Sovereign of the universe without it. Effeminately to strip Jesus of the attributes of which this possibility is an implication, is not only to dehumanize him, but it is to snatch from him the conditions of his high achievements. It destroys the reward by nullifying the struggle. It makes his whole mission an automatic series of movements; a mere organic piece of a mechanical panorama.

Whether Jesus was "in a state of probation" is a question irrelevant to this point. The axiom that necessity is intrinsically incompatible with moral deserts is limited to no one sphere. It belongs to all actual and all possible being, whether in a probational state or not. Deserts, merit, guilt, responsibility, are in their own intrinsic nature, incompatible with volitional necessitation.

1. Christ was truly and perfectly human. He had a completely human body and human soul. All the physical and psychological sensibilities analysis finds in humanity existed in their completeness in his nature. Their superior purity consisted in their symmetrical proportions and their complete harmonious subjection to a free will that warded off the approaches of all stimulants to too intense an excitement, or to any irregular action, and held the whole being in blessed conformity to the moral law.

TEMPTATION WITHOUT SIN

How temptation without sin might take place may be illustrated by the case of the hungering Jesus. His rightful appetite existed, and food was the correlating rightful object by which it might be ordinarily gratified. The tempter presents the object contrary to the divine order and law. The mind's eye of Jesus fully recognizes the object, and fully understands its power to gratify and to satiate his demanding appetite. Thus far no sin on his part exists; for fully to understand intellectually, the desirableness of a thing is not to desire it. His sense of Moral right cognizes that between the object and the appetite, the divine Law interposes a veto. With that veto the Will coincidingly interposes, and shuts the object out from the mental desire or consent. It is the intellect alone that entertained the object, and only so far as fully to comprehend its correlations. Thus is temptation possible without sin.

2. He was a true and real free moral agent. In him, as in all other moral free agents, psychological analysis must find a Will able to choose either one of two, good and evil alternatives. This is the most striking attribute of all complete humanity. If he had a complete human soul, then he had a Will and a free Will. Without it in the nature the being is not a man. To separate it from Jesus is to dehumanize his nature. We might as well, and far better, with the ancient Docetæ, reduce his corporeity to a phantasm of a human body, as to reduce his soul below the conditions of a human free moral agent.

3. Without the power of volitional compliance, temptation is an unreality. Temptation to impossible act is impossible. It is preposterous to say that I am tempted to fly to the moon; or that I am tempted to make two and two to be five. But even for these I am able to make some abortive attempts at volition. I am able to be willing to do them. But in the case of Jesus, it is the very volition that is supposed to be out of his power. His so willing is supposed to be as impossible as my so flying. His willing is as impossible as my flying without a Will. Now in the very nature of things such a temptation is no temptation. Temptation is offered inducement to do something doable. The very supposition reduces the whole scene and history of the temptation to a phantasm and a figment.

4. If Christ were not a free agent, even between alternatives of good and evil, then he can be no example for human free agents. He is either exalted far above or sunk far below any exemplifying analogy. When he is proposed as an example of perfect virtue suffering temptation, the conclusive reply may be made, "Make it impossible for me to sin and I will be as holy as he." Nay, such a view of Christ sinks his virtue below the standard of genuinely tempted and truly resisting human virtue. If the beautiful sentiment of Fletcher is true, that "before the Lawgiver and Judge of all the earth the unnecessitated voluntary goodness of one angel or one man is more excellent than the necessary goodness of a world of creatures as unavoidably and passively virtuous as a diamond is unavoidably and passively bright," then does it irresistibly follow that the unnecessitated

virtue of one man is more excellent than the virtue of a whole world of necessitated Jesuses.

5. And this brings us to the final point. The fundamental Arminian maxim is: power to the contrary is prerequisite to all moral merit. It is applicable to all volitional agents whether "under probation" or not. And unless this fundamental axiom, lying at the basis of all just moral government, is to be upturned and totally abolished for all cases, then if we hold to the merits of Jesus we must hold to the free moral agency of Jesus. We shall otherwise be obliged to affirm the maxim that volitional necessity of nature is compatible with volitional responsibility. And that being granted, the statement of Edwards is incontrovertible that it "is a point clearly and absolutely determining the controversy between Calvinism and Arminianism."

The two general theses of Edwards's extended argument on this subject are, 1. It is impossible that the acts of the Will of the human soul of Christ should be otherwise than holy; and, 2. Christ in his holy behavior was a moral agent, subject to commands, meritorious and eminently praiseworthy.

In proof of the first thesis Edwards argues from God's promises to Christ, to uphold him, to give him an everlasting kingdom and priesthood; from God's promises to the Church, to the elect, that Christ should be a sure saviour, and from the surety of the salvation that Christ was to accomplish.[1]

All this needs here but a brief reply, which we will draw from the nature of God's foreknowledge and prophecy, and from the conditionality of God's promises.

1. We have shown previously that the prophecies of Scripture do not in any degree affect the necessity of any future event. If every future free act foreknown by God were written upon the skies, it would neither make nor prove it necessary. That record would prove not the necessity of the event, but the inexplicable character of its own origin.

2. Still less can be made from the promises of God founded upon God's foreknowledge; and which are, even when no condition is expressed, to a great degree conditional.

---

1. The texts are such as the following: Isa. xlii, 1-4; xlix, 7-9; 1, 5, 6; Psa. cx 4; ii, 7, 8; xiv, 3, 4; Jer. xxiii, 5, 6; xxxiii, 15; Isa. ix, 6, 7; xi, 1; liii, 13; Gen. xxii, 16, 17; Psa. lxxxix, 3, 4, etc.

The great Law of the conditionality of God's promises is expressed in various forms in the word of God, and is authorized to be ever inserted as tacitly implied when it is not expressed. Thus in Ezek. xxxiii, 13, we have the general principle of conditionality in regard to individuals: "When I shall say to the righteous that he shall surely live; if he trust to his own righteousness and commit iniquity, all his righteousnesses shall not be remembered; but for his iniquity that he hath committed, he shall die for it." The word "surely" here indicates the fact that the promise is made in the most unconditioned form; yet the principle nonetheless holds good that the condition is still implied. If the character of the promisee, in consideration of which the promise is made, becomes freely and voluntarily changed, the grounds of the promise disappear and its validity ceases. In the following context, verses 14-16, the same principle is applied in regard to the divine threatenings. No matter in how unconditioned a form the divine justice may be pledged, if the guilty character by which it was induced is changed by repentance and reformation, the force of the divine threatening ceases.

PRINCIPLE OF CONDITIONALITY

In Jeremiah xviii, 7–10 the same principle of conditionality is laid down in regard to God's apparently unconditioned promises and threats addressed to nations: "At what instant I shall speak concerning a nation and concerning a kingdom, to pluck up, and to pull down, and to destroy it; if that nation against whom I have pronounced, turn from their evil, I will repent of the evil that I thought to do unto them. And at what instant I shall speak concerning a nation, and concerning a kingdom, to build and to plant it; If it do evil in my sight, that it obey not my voice, then I will repent of the good wherewith I said I would benefit them." So in Jonah iii, 4, the threatening was, "Yet forty days and Nineveh shall be overthrown," without condition; yet the threatening was reversed by the repentance of the Ninevites. So also God promises entrance into Canaan unconditionally to the children of Israel in Exod. iii, 8, 17, and vi, 7, 8. Yet in Num. xiv, 30, 32, 34, he says, "Doubtless ye shall not come into the land, concerning which I sware (sic) to make you dwell therein," etc. "But as for you, your carcasses, they shall fall in this wilderness . . . and ye shall know my breach of promise."

In the above texts, the conditional promises in the unconditioned form affect the destinies of those to whom they are addressed, and not consequentially of someone else. The fulfillment of the promise is conditioned upon the faithfulness of the promisee, nor is the securing of that faithfulness any part of the promise.

But in 1 Sam. ii, 30, the unconditional promise of the priesthood to Eli and to his house forever is declared to be revoked in regard, not to himself alone, but, consequentially, to his posterity, on account of the unfaithfulness of Eli in not checking the wickedness of his two sons. "I said indeed that thy house, and the house of thy fathers, should walk before me for ever; but now the Lord saith, Be it far from me; for them that honor me I will honor, and they that despise me shall be lightly esteemed." The promise of the perpetual priesthood, though unconditioned in form, presupposed the faithfulness of the promisee. And the unfaithfulness of the head of the family produced the revocation of the promise, not only for himself, but for all his posterity forever.

From all this it follows that all the promises quoted by Edwards addressed to or made in behalf of the Messiah, however unconditioned in form, implied the condition on his part faithfully to discharge his transcendent trust; nor, be it marked, does the securing of that fulfillment, far less its necessitation, precluding the power or possibility of its non-fulfillment, form any part of the language or the essence of the promise. So far as Christ himself is, therefore, concerned, as the type of his people he stands upon the same foundation. The promises of God conditioned upon his perseverance of character, do not pledge or secure that perseverance, but hold their own fulfillment dependent upon it.

So far as the promises made on account of Christ to the Church or to the elect, are concerned, they stand parallel to the promises made to the posterity of Eli on account of their family head. Though unconditioned in form they lose their validity, consequentially, by the failure of their representative. The promises presuppose the faithfulness of the federal head; nor do they contain in their essence any securing of the actuality of that faithfulness. Far less do they imply any necessitation of his Will precluding the power of an apostate volition or an unfaithful career.

To the divine organic arrangement of the scheme of salvation, including "the eternal purpose and decree of God," "the salvation of all the saints who were saved from the beginning of the world to the death of Christ," and "the enlargement of his Church, the salvation of the Gentiles through him," etc., the principle elsewhere stated in regard to the theo-dicic predeterminations of God apply. God, in view of the future course free agents take and will with full power otherwise, predetermines his own plans and procedures. These procedures are so far contingent in their actual accomplishment as they are conditioned upon the real actuality of the free-agent's course in time; yet inasmuch as the divine foresight is clear and omniscient, the divine plans and procedures will never fail of accomplishment.

To many it seems a matter in which the fearful blends too much with the sublime, that interests so immense should be suspended upon a fiber so slight as the free human Will of the single man, Jesus. They seek a firmer security by changing the nature of that Will from freedom to necessity, and thus underlay a mechanical prop to the organic arrange-ment of God's kingdom. If they can only transform all the struggles and temptations and trials of Jesus to a showy automatic machinery, in which his nature is an unyielding substance that could no more give way under the hostile forces than a cube of solid steel could be annihilated by a hy-drostatic pressure, then all seems safe. But that is to change conceptually the nature of things and beings. It is the foolish result of a faithless and timid fancy.

NO UNCERTAINTY

The view we have given admits no uncertainty to the divine mind as to the accomplishment of the entire plan of salvation. For divine omni-science, according to its ordinary statement, embraces knowledge of not only all actual, but of all possible objects, events and beings, including under all possible conditions and suppositions. And in full view of all the possibilities of the case, the infinite wisdom and foreknowledge of God had selected for Messiah that Being he foresaw, would with perfect free Will, prefer God to Satan and in spite of all temptation, prove true to his redemptional office, and through every difficulty attain the summit of divine success and glory. Hence, while there was an intrinsic possibility in the thing, and an intrinsic alternative power of choice in the being, there was a full and perfect certainty upon which the Divine mind could rest with an infinite reliance, that the possible catastrophe of his failure would not take place.

That there was in the structure of Christ's Will no organic non-existence of power of alternative choice between good and evil, is proved by all those passages that specify the evil which, with effort, he avoided, and the motives for evil he meritoriously rejected. "Thou hast loved righteousness, and hated iniquity; therefore God, even thy God, hath anointed thee with the oil of gladness above thy fellows." Heb. i, 9. "The Lord God hath opened mine ear, and I was not rebellious, neither turned away back. I gave my back to the smiters, and my cheeks to them that lucked off the hair: I hid not my face from shame and spitting."[2] Isai. l, 5–6. If indeed, there was an organic impossibility in the constituted nature of Jesus to yield to these terrible assaults and pressures, what merit is in his resistance? It was simply a static balance of opposite forces, in which it was impossible that the major force should be outweighed.

But let the words of Christ himself settle the question. "Thinkest though that I cannot now pray to my Father, and he shall presently give me more than twelve legions of angels? But how, then, shall the Scriptures be fulfilled, that thus it must be?" Matt. xxvi, 53–54. Note there that it is in full view of the morally obligatory "must" that the Scriptures be fulfilled, in full view of the entire argument drawn from the mass of prophecy, decree, and divine plans, that our Saviour here avers his own complete intrinsic power as a free agent to avoid the endurance of the stupendous sufferings before him, and he completely negates the notion that he cannot do it. That is, neither prophecy, nor promise, nor foreknowledge, nor any supposed decree or predestination, neutralizes or negates his full power to will and to take a reverse course. The reverse course indeed, in the present case, presupposes the consent of his heavenly Father, and so presupposes no sin. But that fact no way affects the complete disproof from the passage of the notion that prophecy or promise do in any degree limit the freedom of the agent, or detract in the least from his intrinsic power for a reverse volitional course.

If prophecy that he should endure certain sufferings does not disprove his power to choose the avoidance of those sufferings, then prophecy that he shall pursue a straight path of rectitude does not disprove his power to choose the path of wrong. But this power to wrong is clearly implied in the text above quoted, which announces the reward of Jesus for rejecting the wrong—a reward, forsooth, for what he could not help!

---

2. If by probation is meant a state of endurance of trial upon which approbation and reward are dependent, then assuredly Jesus was in that state.

Surely every sensible Arminian must by this time see that all the positions, arguments, and evasions by which the free agency of Jesus is denied are necessitarian and Calvinistic; while all our arguments and replies are precisely the same, (and encounter the same logic) touching the specific case of Jesus, as Arminianism uses in regard to all other beings. That is, such an Arminian is a pro tempore Calvinist.

We may finally remark that, according to Edwards's own account of the matter, it is not correct "in strict propriety of speech" to say that there was any real impossibility in the failure of the plan of salvation, and the defeat and overthrow of God's decree. It is all a matter of mere moral necessity. Men say that a thing is in a man's power when a thing is at his election; and it was at the election of the man Jesus to sin, and defeat the Almighty. He had, according to Edwards's own theory, the same power that any man has to sin in those cases where they do not sin. Every man who does not sin, fails to sin by reason of the strongest motive, just as did Jesus; so that he, in this respect, was according to Necessitarianism just like any other man.

VI

Non-Necessitation of the Divine Will

THERE IS NO CONCEPTION from which the best elements of our nature so shrink as from the necessitarian conception of God. Motive, in the finite, is cause, and volition effect; the effectuation being as absolute as the existence of deity. The idea of self-determining power, that is, of Will's power to will other than fixed effect, is expelled from the universe.

All movement is but a being moved; all activity is but a passivity. All this finite metaphysical machinery, then being transferred to God, is simply rendered infinite.

God is thus an infinite substance, with no power but to be passively moved as external causation acts upon him. Necessity takes her standpoint outside and presses her causative forces on his being. Deity is a clay molded in the matrice of external causation, and hardened to solidity—an infinite adamantinized fossil enclosed in a tight casement of eternal fatalism.

Exterior circumscribing Causation is thus the God of God. It limits his power to one sole volition, and to one sole stereotyped set of volitions; and his volitions limit his power of actions. Omnipotence, then, is not power to do all things; it is only power for doing what is done; power for fulfilling the program of prescribing causation. Do you ask what God can do? Just what he does do and nothing else. Do you ask why God does all things?

There is in him no causal fountain of power for anything else. Do you ask why God does no more, no less? The actual is the exact measure and complete exhausting of his power. The whole process of things is the solely possible projectile from the divine nature as it is. All the causality there is in God goes forth into precisely all the effect to which it is equal. God and not-God are fixed correlatives; absolute counterparts of each other. Neither can exist without the other; neither can exist, in substance, form, act or position, other than it actually is.

Edwards bases his argument for the existence of necessitated meritoriousness in man upon its existence in God; and its existence in God he first bases upon Arminian concessions.

> Arminian writers . . . in general hold that there is no virtue or vice, reward or punishment, nothing to be commended or blamed, without this freedom. And yet Dr. Whitby . . . allows that God is without this freedom; and Arminians, so far as I have had opportunity to observe, generally acknowledge that God is necessarily holy, and his will necessarily determined to that which is good. So that putting these things together, the infinitely holy God, who always used to be esteemed by God's people as not only virtuous, but a Being in whom is all possible virtue, etc., this Being, according to this notion of Dr. Whitby and other Arminians, etc., is deserving of no commendation or praise. (195)

If the premise here is admitted, the consequences irresistibly follow. If from his physical substance, or from his necessary attributes or disposition, surrounding motives necessitatively cause the divine volitions to be right; if by dynamics as fixed as physical dynamics, the divine choice and action are absolutely limited to a certain unit, then the divine being is an infinite, excellent machine, good because he cannot help it; and because he cannot help it, without moral deserts.

It is not, however, so clear that Arminian writers really intend to grant that necessity of the divine Will. They have unwisely dallied with the nonsensical term "moral necessity," sometimes even admitting its nonsense.

Thus, Dr. Samuel Clark says, after attributing this quality to God, "moral necessity is distinguished from physical necessity just as all other figures of speech are from literal expressions: that is, 'tis in truth and philosophically speaking no necessity at all."[1] If, we reply, moral necessity is no necessity at all, then it is no moral necessity at all; that is, there is no moral necessity; and the term is nonsense. "And yet," adds Dr. Clark, "every one easily sees that the justice and goodness of an infinitely perfect Free Agent may as firmly and reasonably be relied on as the necessary effect of any necessary agent is known to be physically unavoidable."[2] Let

---

1. *The Works of Samuel Clarke* (London: Printed for J. and P. Knapton, 1738), 2:254.
2. Ibid.

our readers compare this with what we have said under the topics of uniformities of volition, and he will easily see that Dr. Clark here states about
correctly what we consider to be the true doctrine.

Rejecting the deceptive term "moral necessity," upon which Edwards
mostly builds his argument, we maintain that the rectitude of God's actions is what we may call perfectly probable and certain, practically reliable as any physical necessity, without admitting that the nexus is the
same or equally irreversible, and strictly admitting the power of contrary
choice.

We may add that Fletcher, while indulging the same unwise use of
the word "necessity," where there confessedly is no necessity, denies that
this necessity is "absolute." He hits the point very closely when he says,
"God's goodness consists in the perfect rectitude of his eternal Will," (his
eternal willing we would say) "and not in a want of power to do an act of
injustice."[3]

In Fletcher's phraseology the words "do an act" include the volitional
as well as the voluntary act.

DIVINE WILL

"If the divine Will," Edwards next argues, (331) "was not necessarily determined to that which in every case is wisest and best, it must be subject
to some degree of undesigning contingence, and so in the same degree
liable to evil." Such is the inveterate necessitarian conception. The divine
Will must be "necessarily determined" one way, or be "subject" and "liable" to some other way. It is a lifeless swivel, whirling under one causation or another.

And this necessity, Edwards continues, is no more degrading than
his "necessity" of "existence;" and so we suppose it is no more degrading,
or divesting of responsible attributes, for any agent to have a necessitated
Will than a necessitated existence. And so, according to Edwards, to suppose the divine volitions as necessary as the divine self-existence would
no way affect their meritoriousness. And the Younger Edwards explicitly
expresses what the Elder indicates, "The truth is, the divine volitions were
no more caused, whether by God himself or by any other cause, than the
divine existence was.

---

3. *Works of the Reverend John Fletcher*, 2: 197.

The divine volitions are the divine holiness uncreated and self-existent. And one attribute of God is not more caused or created than all his attributes, or than his existence." (1:321) So God's volitions are part of God's nature, as fixed as his self-existence!

And yet these same Edwardses every now and then have a lucid interval, in which they tell us that this necessity of theirs is nothing more than certainty! And their apologizing followers tell us that they taught "the highest kind of freedom," perfectly consistent with a power of diverse volition! It is very odious to attribute fatalism to them! We answer, their certainty is just the certainty of God's self-existence; their power of diverse volition is just the power of God's substance to be transmuted or substituted; and the attribution of these fixed qualities to responsible human volitions is called by a soft name when termed fatalism. And then deity himself is but an adamantine statue of a God, run in the mold of absolute Causation; excellent because he cannot help it; automatically excellent, but incapable of attaining a particle of moral deserts.

We, in opposition to all this, suppose the God of the Universe to be an infinitely free, excellent, meritorious Person. Infinity and Goodness are not inseparable ideas as attributable to a being. To prove the goodness of God to the naturalist has been a problem for the theologian. Manes had no difficulty in conceiving a bad deity, or in communicating the conception to others.

Zoroaster, as the latest research reveals, held that good and evil are opposite sides of deity. The Infinite of the Pantheist is all comprehending, of evil and of good alike. Nay, Calvinism itself has never yet been able to extricate itself from the charge of placing the intentional primordial authorship of evil in God. But we Arminians hold that God is freely good from eternity to eternity, just as a man is relatively good freely and alternatively for one hour. Infinite knowledge does not insure infinite goodness.

Infinite knowledge (which is a very different thing from infinite wisdom) is not an anterior cause of infinite goodness. But both Infinite Wisdom and Infinite Holiness consist in and result from God's volitions eternally, and absolutely perfectly, coinciding with, not the Wrong, but the Right.

God's infinite knowledge=omniscience is an eternal fixed necessary *be*-ing; God's wisdom and holiness are an eternal volitional becoming; an eternal free, alternative putting forth of choices for the Right. God's omniscience is self-existent; God's wisdom and holiness are self-made, or eternally and continuously being made. God is necessarily omnipotent and all-knowing through eternity; but God is truly wise and holy through all eternity, but no more necessarily than a man through a single hour. God is holy therefore not automatically but freely; not merely with infinite excellence, but with infinite meritoriousness.

God is holy in that he freely chooses to make his own happiness in eternal Right. Whether he could not make himself equally happy in Wrong is more than we can say. And, as we have previously said, it is the agent that often makes his motive. So between the infinite pleasure of infinite selfishness and evil and the infinite blessedness of infinite benevolence and god, God renders himself eternally holy by his eternal volition preferring good from the motive good, the same good being both motive and object, preferred for itself.

As therefore to God's omniscience there belongs an eternal necessary and excellent permanence, so to God's holiness there belongs an eternal free meritorious continuing.

It hence follows that the unchanging right choices of God do not come under any Law of Invariable Sequence, nor are they to be included as under any fixed Law of sequence whatever. Dr. Hitchcock [4] maintains that miracles are as truly under law as ordinary events, because God would by the law of his Will choose to interfere ever and always in the same circumstances.

Thus the law of causation upon natural events and upon the divine volitions is identical or equal. We reply that eternity bears to God the same relation as an hour bears to man; and it no more follows that God's volitions are bound by a fixed law from his willing eternally right, than it follows that man's volitions are by fixed law because he wills right through sixty times sixty seconds.

It is Dr. Day, former president of Yale College, if we rightly recollect, who argues that it is only from the doctrine of necessity that we can be sure of the unchangeable holiness of God. Truly such a position is very boldly putting the Eternal under necessitarian bonds for good behavior. We repose in perfect security, notwithstanding our freedomism, upon the

---

4. Edward Hitchcock, "The Law of Nature's Constancy Subordinate to the Higher Law of Change," 544–561.

unchanging integrity of many a merely human free agent, but much more upon the unchanging holiness of the God of ages.

A trust in God's unchangingness is as good as a trust in God's unchangeableness.

VII

Freedom Limits Not Omnipotence

SOUND PHILOSOPHERS OF ALL sects or parties are obliged to concede that the power of performing contradictions forms no part of the true idea of omnipotence. A contradiction unsays itself and becomes nothing. The contradictory act is equally self-canceling, and so no act at all. When we say God has potential to do all things, it is unnecessary in terms even to exclude contradictions; it is unnecessary to say that "God can do all things but cannot do any act which is no act at all." The exclusion of contradictions from divine power limits not omnipotence itself, but limits our thoughts to the true idea of omnipotence.

If contradictions can be accomplished by Omnipotence, then all reasoning is at an end. The logical law of non-contradiction is no longer valid, if it is reversible by power. We can bind no reasoning around a power that can dissolve all reasoning. The syllogism is no longer a necessary argument; and geometry is a pile of contingencies. Theology lies in ruins. If Omnipotence can perform all contradictions, then the self-existent can destroy itself and cause itself never to have existed. And after this state of self-annihilation, it may cause all events to happen without cause, being at the same time fully omnipotent and yet without existence. God can also on the same supposition govern the world with perfect wisdom and power, without any plan, purpose, decree, predestination or knowledge. And, finally, on the same supposition he can leave the creature free to choose either way in full defiance of his utmost power, without any derogation from his omnipotence or perfect sovereignty.

That a being should be left free to choose either of several ways, yet be previously secured by necessitative causation finite or infinite, to choose a certain one of those ways so there is no power of choosing otherwise than that one is a contradiction. It supposes that the same act is in the same sense at once possible and impossible. The power therefore to leave the Will free, and yet efficiently preordain, preform, or prenecessitate the volition being a contradiction, is not predicable even of a true omnipotence.

Necessitarians ordinarily argue that the supposition of an agent able to act either way by a power implanted within him is to suppose him placed away from the control of God. But the supposition does not imply God's non-possession of absolute power over the agent, but simply his self-imposed non-usage—upon principle and by rule—of certain power.

SELF-LIMITING LAWS

Such self-limiting laws—prescribed by God to himself—necessitarians will not deny to be necessary to the very existence of the kingdom of nature; and they do in fact give God his position as a Sovereign of nature. Such a divine law of non-use of power is still more necessary in the kingdom of living agents, and most of all in the realm of responsible agents. It is observable that the closer the divine self-restraint, and the larger the amount of powers in the agent left untouched, the more the created system rises in dignity, and the higher God appears as a Sovereign. Even in a system of living necessitated agents, as necessitarians must admit, God forbids himself to disturb the agent's uniform and perpetual acting according to strongest motive. And if this self-prescribed Law of non-interference and non-use places the being out of God's power, it is as rigidly and servilely done in God's binding himself not to touch the processes of necessitated agency as of free-agency.

The volitions of a Will necessitated by a highest motive are as truly and inviolably out of the divine power as the volitions of a free Will. A necessitated Will obeys the law of highest motive; and omnipotence itself cannot prevent it, in the case, without violating the law. Unless he violates his own law, God is obliged to attain a desired volition of the agent by somehow contriving to get the proper strongest motive before the agent. If this cannot be done, it is according to necessitarianism, wholly out of God's power. The Calvinistic Confession of Faith declares, "nor is the liberty or contingency of second causes taken away, but rather established." This cannot be true unless God, by fundamental law, abstains from taking it away, and leaves such causes to their own unviolated action; just as freedomists suppose God does with free agents. Necessitarianism, therefore, places the agent out of God's power, and diminishes his absolute sovereignty as much as is thought with Arminianism.

Against the Arminian doctrine, that there is an intrinsic contradiction between the necessitation and the responsibility of a volition, and that therefore it is impossible even for God to make it responsible, Calvinists contradictorily object. For they themselves equally hold that for a being not a moral agent to be held morally responsible is a contradiction, and so impossible even to divine power. The disagreement thus is not, as they often seem to fancy, about the existence of a contradiction between responsibility and the non-existence of moral agency, and the consequent impossibility for even Omnipotence to create such a responsibility. Here they agree with freedomists. The real difference is as to what constitutes moral agency, and what the terms of the contradiction are. Freedomists hold that alternative power is one of those terms, and necessitarians deny it.

We do not found the justification of God for the non-prevention of sin upon the absolute, universal impossibility, in any and every case, of God's attaining desirable free action on the part of the agent. In countless numbers of instances God foreknows that certain motives will be the motives freely and alternatively accepted by the agent. Yet it is not clear that in the best possible system Omnipotence could, consistently with universal unviolated free-agency, exclude all sin. And it is apparent, in myriads of instances, that the particular sin in the circumstances could not have been prevented without a change of circumstances, or a violation of free-agency. And this the necessitarian must also admit in his own system. In given circumstances the necessitated agent must obey the strongest motive; and God cannot prevent it but either by a change of circumstances, or a violation of the agent's laws of action.

In regard to the justification of the Divine non-prevention of sin we suppose three principles:

1. A system of free probationary agents is doubtless primordially better than a system of necessitated automatic agents, even though such free agency implies the possibility of sin.

2. In a probationary system the sin is not better than no sin, yet the non-prevention of sin is doubtless better than its prevention.

3. The present is doubtless the best possible system, in spite, not in consequence, of the actuality of sin.

VIII

Freedom Exalts Man and Dishonors God?

I T IS ONE OF the deep statements of Whichcote: "Liberum arbitrium, Free Will, which men so brag of, as it includes *posse male agere*, the ability to do evil, is an Imperfection; for such liberty or power is not in God. To do amiss is not Power, but Deficiency and Deformity; and infinite Power includes not in it a Possibility of evil."[1] It is a contrary statement, not so deep, of another writer, (in a foreign Quarterly Review) "Pelagianism, and Arminianism, and modern Morrisonianism pander to the pride of human Will; and to exalt man's Will would deny Will to God, negativing the decrees of God, and nullifying the Spirit's influence and special grace."

Neither of these conclusions, the deep one of the philosopher and the shallow one of the ranter, expresses the exact truth. It is not the power to do evil that is an imperfection; if it were, a statue would be in this respect superior to the first angels before they fell; but it is the evil exercise of that power which is the deficiency and the deformity. He who is right from incapacity is safely, but not nobly, nor meritoriously, right. It is the height of virtue to be in full possession of the mastery of both good and of evil, and yet to do good alone. Such a mastery and supremacy belong in the highest degree to God. For it is eternally that he possesses full power for choice of right or wrong; and it is eternally that he chooses solely right.

"To exalt man's will," which is the charge of the above ranter, is to exalt man in that respect in which he is in "the image of God," and in which to depreciate him below his measure is to dishonor his Original. But when we so exalt man's Will it is not merely to assert his dignity of nature, which in its place is a just procedure, but to show him responsible for his deeds, and to justify God in his judgments. It is indeed an exalted prerogative to be a responsible subject of the Government of God; and it

---

1. Whichcote, *Moral and Religious Aphorisms*, 4.

is but honoring that government to place in its full relief that faculty in which does mainly lie the qualification for that high citizenship. It is a foolish way, worthy the narrowness of a bigot, for the sake of humbling human pride to depreciate man's intellect and make him a brute, or to nullify his free agency and make him a block or a clock. The freedom of the Will in the moral agent does thus furnish the true condition for the moral government of God.

As a living being is superior to insensate matter, and human intelligence is superior to living animal being, so of human intelligence the highest is free moral being. So far as we know, the highest declarative glory of God consists in the existence of his retributive moral government. But the very existence of such a government requires of God the concession to his creature of a power which in its course of action he will neither annihilate nor violate. Thus he is leaving the capability, but not the necessity, of freedom to sin, which is judicable, or freedom to good deserts, which is rewardable, and of a free holiness, worship, honor, and glorification of God, which are the highest results of a moral kingdom.

FREEDOM OF MAN

Denying the freedom of man does not honor but degrades God's sovereignty, sinking him from the position of a Ruler of free subjects to a manipulator of mechanisms. It takes from him the possibility of justice by making him propel the act he is to punish. Nor is there any ascription of meanness to God. i.e. more mean than that which makes him attempt to inaugurate a glorious free probationary system, and yet to fail, purely from a penurious grudging of the necessary bestowment of power to constitute a true responsible agent, and from a fear that the possession of an alternative power of Will by the finite agent might disturb the stability of the throne of the Omnipotent. The former is a parsimony, and the latter a cowardice, which is discreditable to any man to ascribe to the God of the universe.

If the maintenance of freedom of the Will "exalts man's Will," and the denial of it degrades the dignity of man's Will, the same denial must degrade the dignity of the Divine Will. The assertion, therefore, of the necessitation of the divine Will, so strenuously maintained by Edwards and other necessitarians, does bring degradation and dishonor upon the divine Will. While, on the other hand, to maintain the freedom of the divine Will from any such causative determination of volitions is to maintain its dignity and honor.

Another argument against this view of divine sovereignty maintains that it is a supposition unworthy the divine dignity that any of his decrees or actions should be dependent upon the action or non-action of insignificant man. The assumption, we reply, that the action of God cannot be conditioned on the actions or other matters of a finite being (for it cannot be limited to the action, but must extend to every finite attribute of the creature), renders creation, preservation, government, retribution all alike impossible. In such case God cannot create a finite being, for the act of creation must be modified by, and conditioned upon the nature of the finite to be created. If he is to be one sort of a creature, one sort of creation must be performed; if another, another.

Preservation also must depend upon the actual existence, nature, and purpose of the creature to be preserved. Government requires laws that must depend upon the nature of the being or thing to be governed. No regard must be paid by God to prayer; nothing must take place in consequence of the prayers of the holiest finite being; for that would be making God's action dependent upon the action of a finite being, obliging him to wait until man performs before he can act. Nor can men be rewarded according to their works, blessed with heaven upon a life of faith and holiness, or cursed with hell on account of a life of wickedness. Such a doctrine shuts the Deity up in a dignified reserve from all the concerns of his creatures, making his sovereignty too exalted to be any sovereign at all. Nay, it deprives him of the power of producing any creatures, rendering a finite universe impossible.

Freedom is also held by necessitarians as attributing to man merit in exercising the act of faith and performing the conditions of salvation, so that heaven is attained not by grace, but by works. We reply,

1. By their own maxim of deserts necessitarians are as truly obliged to attribute merit to faith and works as freedomists. By that maxim it matters not how we come by our right volitions; whether by necessitation, causation, predestination, or creation, they are equally deserving of reward or condemnation. No matter, then, if our faith and works are foreordained, necessitated, created by the resistless influences of the Spirit, they are still volitions; are free with the highest degree of freedom conceivable, and are to be credited with all the merit, good deserts, and rewardableness that the loftiest Arminian can conceive. Thus, all the glory

that Calvinism claims to itself for overthrowing human merit is thus by itself overthrown. It teaches by its fundamental maxim of merit the meritoriousness of human faith, and works, and the attainment of salvation by our own good deserts.

2. Faith is excellent and well-deserving. It would be derogatory to God to suppose that he would not choose a good and excellent act as antecedent to our justification. As between good and bad, faith is good and not bad; it is ethically right and not wrong. Unbelief and infidelity are wrong; faith and obedience are right. The very reason why faith is a fitting condition for salvation, and a right initiation of a holy life, is that it is in itself a self-surrender and self-consecration to God and to all his goodness. Performed following a previous gracious aid, God's prevenient grace, it is an instrumental channel to salvation and an act that is pleasing to God. And yet,

3. Such is not the merit of our faith that we thereby intrinsically deserve justification; nor such the merit of our good works as that we thereby earn eternal life. Notwithstanding our faith, God, apart from his gracious promises, is under no obligation to forgive our past sins; nor do our works form any purchase of so great a gift as heaven and endless glory. Absolutely at the moment of an act of complete faith God needs us not, and he might justly drop us into non-existence. So that after all we are his workmanship, and all our salvation is from the free and abundant grace of God.

If man's act of accepting faith is not free and a choice, able to be withheld as to be put forth, possessing the freedom *from* as well as the freedom *to*, then there is the potential of divine government, but only an automatism. If man's will, in the given case, accepts divine grace, either by an intrinsic automatic spring of the Will, or by an omnipotent securing touch of the spring of the Will by the divine finger, then the very conditions of a free probationary system are destroyed. Men are the mechanically moving figures of a great panorama, and God himself is but a mechanical counterpart—both forming one stupendous reciprocal interactive automatism. Herein, Dr. Chalmers[2] assures us, lays the vital point of difference between Calvinism and Arminianism; and herein, we reply, lays the difference between a divine government and an automatism.

2. Thomas Chalmers, Book iv, Chap. viii, *Institutes of Theology: With Prelections on Hill's Lectures in Divinity and Four Addresses in the New College, Edinburgh* (Edinburgh: T. Constable, 1856)

IX

Responsibility of Impenitents and of Fallen Man

ARMINIANS GRANT, SAYS EDWARDS, that both impenitent sinners given over to their own hardness, and the whole race as fallen and without the atonement, are unable to keep God's law and yet are without excuse. If so, then Arminians accept the principle that necessitation is consistent with responsibility, and that commands are consistent with inability to obey.[1] We take the two, the cases of the impenitents, and of the fallen race, separately.

I. In regard to impenitents, we are led to the discussion of these Two Questions:

1. What is the influence of the self-superimposing of impenitence and non-recoverability upon the sinner's responsibility?

2. How far does the intensity of temptation excuse the sin?

For Question 1, from the Arminian admission of the responsible impenitence and guilty irrecoverability of the abandoned sinner, Edwards holds them to the universal admission that necessitation to sin is perfectly consistent with responsibility for sin. To which the Arminian replies, conclusively we think, with the broad maxim: The superimposing by the sinner's own free act, or course of action, of necessity upon himself to sin destroys the excuse from that necessity. The guilty beings given over by God are first freely, fully, and irrevocably given over by themselves. They have once for all made their own selection, have rejected God, renounced conscience, made evil their good, and divested themselves of all susceptibility to moral motive. Such a result, with all its irrevocability, was not

---

1. It should be noted by the reader that Edwards selects as instances of necessitated guilt by Arminian admission the cases of the Will of Christ, the Divine Will, the Obdurates, the Fallen Race, and the Damned in hell. The first he considers the most decisive. The argument, as well as our reply, in the last two cases being essentially the same, we add nothing further upon the last.

necessarily but freely chosen. Their very condition of necessitated guilt was not necessitated. That self-necessitation is an object of choice, and is freely chosen and so responsibly chosen; just as any other object is freely and responsibly chosen. The alternative to choose freedom to all good, or necessity to all evil, was before them, and they chose the latter. They are therefore responsible for that choice according to its nature, guilt, and magnitude.

Even the necessitarian admits this excuse from self-superimposing. Necessity of coaction, that is, necessity upon the body against the Will, says necessitarianism, does excuse; for if a man is imprisoned, he cannot be required to take a journey. But if he has locked himself in prison and flung the key from his window into the ocean beating against his prison wall, necessitarianism admits that he is not then excusable. If a parent ties his child to the bedpost he cannot require him to go to school; but if the child has tied himself even with a knot he cannot unloose, necessitarianism admits that the excuse is invalid.

Edwards has set the example of reasoning from the parallelism between this his so-called natural necessity to the moral and we follow precedent so authoritative. As the necessitarian argues that though natural necessity excuses, yet self-superimposing invalidates the excuse. So we have a right by parity to argue, that the volitional necessity excuses, yet the self-super-imposing of that necessity, where it did not before exist, invalidates the excuse, and leaves the agent responsible for his whole amount of self-necessitated sin and guilt.

If a man performing a dangerous journey in a dark night extinguishes his lantern, he cannot plead darkness as his excuse for the suicide wrought by falling down a precipice. No more can he who extinguishes the lamp of knowledge that preserves him from the precipice of woe plead ignorance. No more can he who eradicates from his own nature the powers by which to avoid motive to sin and work righteousness plead impotence.

We may suppose a free being born under conditions of free moral self-development to be self-wrought to a state of high perfection. So has he trained his own nature by dropping all evil indulgences, that all evil propensities are lost; and so has he formed his taste to good that none but motives of good can reach him. His habits are so perfected thereby that temptation ceases; he does right without effort, and ultimately even can no more do wrong than I can enjoy the central heat of a fiery furnace. The merit of virtue does not cease when its power is so perfect that its contest is over. Admitting the agent to be now necessarily right, his effortless virtue is none the less meritorious because it has become spontaneous.

The merit of his virtue does not cease as soon as he has perfected it. It has been earned as a great good; and considering his entirety of being as a unit, it has been and is a freely chosen good, and it bears the stamp of freedom and praiseworthy goodness through eternity. It is a settled point in orthodox eschatology that an eternity of good or ill may be responsibly chosen. Or if a being so self-developing freely chooses a permanent and eternal evil nature, by cherishing evil tastes and habits until his very substance has crystallized with sin, and the entire nature has so become correlative to wicked motive that it is susceptible of no motive for good, its badness is eternally guilty. A being created or born with both these alternatives accessible to his choice, with equivalent ability of will to choose either, is in full consistency with our doctrine, eternally rewardable for choosing the right, eternally responsible for choosing the wrong.

NECESSITATED INCLINATIONS

Responsibility for necessitated inclinations is one thing; responsibility for self-superimposed inclinations is another thing. Responsibility for necessitated inclinations induced by original, created, and permanent necessitation is one thing; and responsibility for necessitated inclinations, freely and unnecessitatedly taken upon himself by the individual, is another thing. Responsibility for inclination never in the power of the individual to change or exclude is one thing; responsibility for inclination alternatively cherished in the nature is another thing. Edwards, with a striking want of perspicacity, argues as if these two responsibilities are equal and one. The former responsibility is a nothing and an impossibility; the latter is a living reality.

Whitby, however, (perhaps to evade the irresponsibility resulting from necessity) maintains that the reformation of the sinner abandoned of God is not truly impossible but very difficult. Then, replies Edwards, if impossibility or necessity entirely excuses, difficulty proportionately excuses. From the amount of guilt apparent, strike the equivalent of the difficulty, and you have as remainder the amount of the guilt actual. Hence the conclusion, which would be necessitated from the Arminian principle, that volitional impossibility excuses is this: moral=volitional difficulty excuses as truly as natural=corporeal difficulty. But this conclusion, says Edwards, is notoriously false; for in truth it is an indubitable principle that while physical difficulty excuses, volitional does not; and from that indubitable principle it is to be inferred that volitional impossibility= necessity does not excuse.

If, Edwards further argues, volitional difficulty of avoiding sin from intensity of seductive influences excuses, then exposedness, predisposition, or liability to sin increases not the danger of guilt or condemnation. For the amount of liability=difficulty-of-avoidance cancels just its own amount in guilt; so that the case is no worse in result than if there were no exposedness, predisposition, liability, or difficulty at all.

2. We must then institute our second inquiry. How far does the intensity of temptation or the volitional difficulty of avoidance excuse sin?

Volitional incapacity, we maintain, excuses for a want of volition as much as bodily impotence excuses for want of performance of external act. Where the impotence is in either case total, and not self-superimposed, and so the necessity absolute, the excuse is complete, and the agent blameless. Where in either case the impotence is self-superimposed, and in the degree that it is self-superimposed, the self-superimposing cancels the excuse. And the volitional as well as corporeal overcoming great difficulties increases the merit of virtuous action. The overcoming of powerful motives in the way opposed to choosing right, is as true an increase of deserts as the overcoming of powerful physical obstacles opposed to the path of acting externally right.

Yielding to feeble motives is an act of stronger depravity than the yielding to stronger motives. To choose evil, not only for the weakest motives, but against the strongest motives, is the greatest depravity. On the other hand, to choose right for itself, and for no other motive than the rightness, is a pure virtue. So to choose in spite of strong motives is great good deserts; and the stronger the counter motives the greater the deserts. The highest virtue is that which is for virtue itself against the strongest motives for evil. Hence the high heroic virtue of the martyrs, and the sufferers for good in all ages. Herein lay the greatness of the piety of Enoch and Noah, who walked with God in the time of universal corruption. Hence the meritorious virtue of Jesus himself in the Temptation, rejecting the very highest motives for evil that time and earth can present. Hence the sublime virtue of Milton's Abdiel, "faithful among the faithless, faithful only he."

The authorities of the Bank of England one day received an anonymous note saying that the writer had access to their bullion room. Treating this as a hoax, they received some days after, a second note, offering to meet a committee from their body, at any hour they pleased, in said room. The offer being accepted, at the hour appointed, being midnight, the committee members were accordingly met by a man entering through the floor by removal of a plank. He was a laborer who had discovered the entrance while repairing the sewers beneath. How great was the temptation for so poor a man to make an unlawful fortune! The bank authorities rewarded his honesty with £800.

THEORY OF EDWARDS

But according to the theory of Edwards, contrary to common sense, he was no more meritorious than the millionaire who should decline a shilling unintentionally overpaid him by a brother banker. But if the greater the motives to evil overcome the greater is the virtue, then the greater the motive-difficulty to good, the less the guilt. That is, moral or volitional difficulty does excuse according to its magnitude just as truly as natural or corporeal.

And Edwards himself, when his argument requires it, readily and amply contradicts his own theory. An entire section of ten pages in another of his works, argues the greatness of human depravity from the greatness of the motive-force for good against which it sins.[2] The proposition heading that section is, "The native depravity of mankind appears in that there has been so little good effect of so manifold and great means used to promote virtue in the world." The opening sentence is, "The evidence of the native corruption of mankind appears much more glaring when it is considered that the world has been so generally, so constantly, and so exceedingly corrupt, notwithstanding the various great and continual means that have been used to restrain men from sin, and promote virtue and true religion among them."

These means consist of methods, advantages, warnings, punishments, etc., all "to restrain men from sin and induce them to virtue"; and all properly comprehended under the name of "motives divine and powerful," and for that reason enhancing the guilt of overcoming them. That

---

2. Jonathan Edwards, *The Great Doctrine of Original Sin Defended* (Wilmington: Printed and Sold by James Adams, 1771) Part III, sec. 8.

is, the greater the resistance of motive the greater the guilt. The less the motive the less the guilt. The greater the difficulty of goodness, therefore, the less the guilt, whether that difficulty is corporeal or volitional.

And at this point we may say that this position of Edwards overthrows all his claims of the consistency of necessity with guilt, responsibility, or deserts. If the volitional difficulty of good from counter motive-force extenuates guilt, then absolute impossibility destroys it. But according to necessitarianism, in all cases where the Will chooses evil, there is no power of contrary choice; that is, the contrary good choice was impossible, and therefore guiltless. There is no sin in the world, and a retributive divine government is an impossibility.

We go further; we say that in strictness, it is volitional difficulty alone and not the corporeal that excuses. Corporeal difficulty excuses only as it produces volitional difficulty. Strike out from consideration those external difficulties which render part of a complex action impossible. Let the case be where there is a difficulty to the performance of the entire action considered as one whole—not an impossibility of a part—and the external difficulty excuses only as it requires great determination, that is, great exertion of volition, to perform it. The command, as Edwards at large and justly shows, lays its contact upon the Will. What it requires is the volition. The corporeal act is only the external effect of the real energy of true volitional obedience or disobedience behind the exterior movement. Great exterior difficulty is a powerful counter motive to be volitionally overcome. If we succeed, proportionately great is our merit or good deserts; if we fail, some extenuation is caused of our guilt by the greatness of the counter motive-force, and in proportion to it.

So long, however, as volition is truly free, and so long as the only necessity is self-superimposed, that freedom used for sin is the basis of guilt. Motive, high or low, strong or weak, may only diminish or increase guilt, yet there will be guilt in the case, inexcusable and penal, so long as the Will is in the conditions we have in the proper place stated of volitional alterability.

The last point made by Edwards, that since guilt diminishes in proportion to power of temptation it follows that great exposure increases not the chances of guilt, has bearings worthy of consideration. Our view may be stated in the following terms: 1. Temptation, not absolutely necessitative in its power, does not excuse compliance, but sin and guilt remain. 2. It is not until the more extreme intensity of motive that it is doubtful whether the point of necessity is reached that the excusatory power of motive discloses itself. The ordinary motivation like the ordinary difficulty and physical right action seems unexcusing. 3. "Exposedness" is the condition in which temptations to sin, we will say of the ordinary motivation, are many and frequent. Its evil very much consists in the fact that the instances in which the motive might reasonably be resisted are multiplied.

GUILTS INEXCUSABLE

The guilts are therefore many and inexcusable. Yet there does in such condition arise a collective "difficulty," a cyclical necessity possessing some excusatory power. We may thence infer, what will be often relieving, in some degree, to a benevolent spirit contemplating some worldly scenes, that the true depth of guilt is often less, in apparently demoralized communities, than the superficial moral phenomena would seem to an unsparing judgment to indicate. How far the exclusion in such cases of truth, knowledge, moral motive, and the permanent presence of intense temptation and absolute necessitation, may lessen guilt, and so equalize the probational conditions of men, no human eye can gauge. This point will be discussed in a subsequent chapter.

II. In regard to the fallen human race, the charge of Edwards is, that Arminianism holds that though incapable of holiness and so necessitated to sin, the race is still responsible for sin. This thereby contradicts Arminians' own doctrine of the incompatibility of necessitation with guilt. He argues,

It is vain for Whitby to urge that the "Old Law" requiring Adamic perfection is abolished, and that a new and more merciful Law is introduced by Christ, requiring but "imperfect" obedience, and so inflicting no penalty for necessitated evil; for

1. There being, according to Arminianism, no guilt or sin for necessitated fallen man's not keeping the Old Law, Christ's death and even the new law is needless.

2. There can hereby be no responsibility for sin. Not by the "Old Law," for that is abolished; not by the new law, for that requires but imperfect obedience, and so allows sin to be irresponsible.

3. There can be no need for Christ to die to prevent the unjust penalty for our not keeping a law which we had not power to keep. To all which we reply:

1. The so-called "Old Law," being the standard of absolute right, can never be abolished, but must forever stand as the standard by which all responsible sinners are condemned, and to which all ultimate perfection must be equal.

2. By the atonement, man being re-elevated to the level of responsibility, (beneath which he had sunk by the fall), a new law, even the law of faith in Christ, is interposed, as a provisional standard of present acceptance. And man's present guilt for sin against the perfect Law being provided for by the atonement, aids and means are afforded for his final elevation to the complete standard of the perfect law.

3. By these means the absolute law is never abolished but remain, as: a) demanding atonement for sin responsibly committed by man after he is restored to his probationary state, when the law of faith is not by him so accepted as to afford justification; b) applying its own full standard of condemnation upon all sin not forgiven, through man's non-acceptance, by the law of faith; c) remaining as the standard of perfection to which the remedial system must finally restore man, who, by using offered gracious aid, accepts and complies with the gracious law of faith.

4. By these means man is never responsible for a law he cannot meet; Christ's death and the new law are demanded by his case; and all sin infringes both against the new law and the old.

Edwards's final argument (which has become a staple in Calvinistic theology) is that to furnish ability to keep the law is a matter of justice, not grace. This we have elsewhere amply answered.[3] We will simply reply here, that an item of justice in a system of grace, which is an item requisite to the existence of the system, is itself a grace. Taken alone, it may be but intrinsic justice; taken as a part of a gracious and glorious whole, to whose existence it is requisite, it is gracious. If a millionaire graciously takes an orphan boy, previously involved in ruin, into his service, and endows him with capital to be his commissioned agent, for the intentional end of bestowing on him the results in form of a munificent fortune, surely the first bestowing of the necessary capital (requisite though it be for the requiring

3. Daniel D. Whedon, "Arminian View of the Fall and Redemption." *Methodist Quarterly Review* 18, (October 1861) 661.

any service or results, and so an act of justice in view of the requirement) would be an act of great grace.

Others have smartly argued that Christ's atonement, as placing us on a new foundation of responsibility, becomes the cause of all our sin, so that we are in fact "damned by grace." No doubt, we reply those who abuse grace are "damned by grace." If either by the grace or gift of creation, of endowment with original powers, or of the redemptive atonement, we are raised to the level of responsibility, captious reasoners may attribute all the resultant sin, evil and damnation to the grace. And this attribution is just if they result by volitional or non-volitional necessity. But when the unnecessitated Will perverts the grace to evil and damnatory uses, as we have elsewhere said, it primordially originates the wrong; and the sin, wickedness, and damnability, as taking their primal start with that origination, cannot be traced back responsibly to the Grace.

X

The Free Appropriation of Our Depraved Nature

OUR POSITION IS THAT a hereditary depravity introduced into our nature, necessitating us to sin, however demoralizing it may be, is not totally responsible for our acts. The question then may arise: In what manner, and how far, may our natural depravity be by us personally so appropriated as that we can be held therefore accountable? The obvious answer is: That it is by our own free personal acceptance of it, and just so far as that acceptance extends. As, for what a man freely chooses to do, so for what he chooses to be, he is liable to a just account. To these views difficulties are objected; by none more ably than by Dr. Julius Müller,[1] whose views will be taken into consideration in our following remarks.

Dr. Müller asks: Could the volition that appropriates the guilt of our depravity be withheld? If so, why is it that guilt and sin are absolutely universal? And why is it that so momentous a volition, forming the crisis of our history, should be lost to our conscious memory? And how is it that, practically, in the blended impulses and volitions of our daily moral life, it is impossible to draw a clear distinction between our responsible and irresponsible sins, so that our conscience unhesitatingly passes a common condemnation upon the entire mass?

It is not necessary to our argument, we may respond, that we should be able to take a precise and infallible diagnosis of the moral history or moral status of our infancy and childhood, on which Scripture furnishes so little light, and of which our conscious memory retains so little trace. Assuming the gracious conditions of childhood, we know not what amount of conscious avoidable sin is requisite to banish the grace of that period and finish our young apostasy. Points of our existence, recorded as crises of our history in the registry of heaven, are not testified to our

1. Julius Muller, *The Doctrine of Sin* (Edinburgh: T. & T. Clark, 1852)

consciousness by any sensible warning or shock. Not always is the moment of adult regeneration, or of the abandonment to impenitence, or perhaps even the unpardonable sin, evidenced to the soul. But of the sin that appropriates the sin of our nature, our axiomatic principles require us to affirm that it is free and avoidable.

Yet back of that freedom we admit that there is a necessity that insures that, sooner or later, the free act of appropriation will be made. It is in this fact that the freedom and the universality of this fall are found to be reconciled. We have elsewhere noted that to average free agents, as probationary men are, the constant presence of a powerful temptation often insures that sooner or later the sin will be freely accepted.

Individually, the act is free; yet upon the collective rests the pressure of a sure necessity. So it is found in the doctrine of probabilities. Of a given cycle of throws of dice, each throw may or may not turn up a six; and yet such is the synthesis of causations in the great Cosmos, that within the cycle a six must turn up. These cycles of individually free volitions, continually occurring, and sometimes several simultaneously, become so innumerable that sooner or later the free responsible sins will be committed. And so a responsible depravity becomes individually and freely universal by necessity. What bearings this necessity, in spite of this freedom, may have upon our responsibility, may appear in the sequel.

COLLECTIVE NECESSITY

With regard to the effect of this collective necessity, in hearty accordance with our maxim, we maintain that, according to its quality and quantity, it is destructive of responsibility. The philosopher, who, like Kant, shall in effect say, I ought to do right with ideal perfectness through my whole life, therefore I can, lays no just basis of a responsibility. It could be replied with Baader[2], "The consciousness that I ought to act so or so compels me to acknowledge that I could so act if I would; but no less clear is the conviction that I do not will so to act, that I will to act otherwise. Now this perverse Will I am to repress by keeping it down with opposing Will, which is just as easy as—keeping in my breath or committing suicide."

We might still more strongly add by our view that the "I can" in its requisite extension is utterly destroyed by our collective necessity, and

2. Franz Xaver von Baader (1765–1841), was a German philosopher and theologian.

the basis of a just responsibility goes with it. And this remark of Baader's illustrates the utterly fantastic nature of that theory that bases responsibility upon a "moral ability" in the Will to enact a volition otherwise than the strongest motive, which it expressly admits no Will, finite or infinite, actual or possible, ever puts forth. Such a volition is infinitely more a phantasm than either the held breath or suicide. It is more like the act of drawing a pure geometrical figure with a charcoal. But even this ideal diagram is practicable and normal to a superior nature; whereas the ideal volition is unknown to any nature.

The blessed antithesis and compensation to this collective necessity to freely contract the guilt of original sin, is the free and perpetual availability of the Atonement. The aggregate necessity is hereby balanced by an aggregate freedom. The bane is primitively not removed, but the antidote is supplied. Free, individually in sinning and self-depravation, we are free, individually, in accepting justification and regeneration. It is thus that without losing its intrinsic character of stupendous grace, the atonement become a justice—a theodicy. It blends in with the terrible elements of our fallen state, and forms an average probational dispensation in which the divine Administrator appears not merely absolutely just, but practically equitable, and mercifully reasonable to our human reason.

The trial of our probation thereupon becomes—not the avoiding distributively with an ideal moral power every individual sin; that is, in keeping the law with an unfallen perfection, but—the alternative of our preferring the blessed means of escaping the power of sin and attaining an ultimate perfection, or a rejection of the offered remedial aid and persistence in our sin and ever deepening depravity. And thus we see that without the Redeemer no equitable system of probation for fallen man is a possibility. The Cross is the key to the mystery of our being.

But it is affirmed by Müller that, in the progress of our daily moral history, so does a man find necessary impulses and free volitions mingling together in the mass of his sin, that no distinction can be practically drawn. And conscience does in fact pronounce him guilty of the whole. In the practical act of repentance, we reply, it is not very necessary for a man to sort out his sins into impulse and volition, responsible and irresponsible. They are all his enemies, dangerous to his peace and safety, and he does well to get rid of them without waiting for a ceremonious analysis by the most summary process possible. He can afford to abjure them in the gross, and let God do the discriminating. Nevertheless, it is not true that conscience cognizes no difference; nor is it proved true by the fact that it is difficult, nay, often impossible, to pronounce infallibly of the guilt of many a single act. The reality of moral distinctions does not depend upon our skill in applying the principles to the actual case. My conscience does not recognize guilt for a primordial necessitation; and it does recognize guilt for a self-superimposed necessitation. It does not recognize guilt for a purely necessitated volition; and it does recognize guilt for a free alternative volition. Questions of the amount or nature of blame are every day occurring, in jurisprudence, in ethics, in our judgments of character, in which these discriminations are spontaneously made.

And when we look upon the body of sin within us, we find its varying nature requires a varying remedy. For our freely contracted guilt, there must be justification. For our freely contracted tendencies to sin, and to different classes of sins, there must be sanctification; and for that primitive and necessitative ingraining of depravity in our nature by which occasions and impulses and necessitations to sin exist, resulting in actual free responsible sins, we need the reorganization, the death and resurrection, the bodily reconstruction in the image of Christ.

Thus we see how by a free act, none the less individually free because universally committed, the guilt of our depravity is contracted. We see how that single free appropriative act, though a crisis, is not so momentous a transition as at first sight appears, and requires no shock to make it memorable. We see how the collective necessity of a universal depravity is balanced by the free availability of a universal atonement. God is hereby (and in no way without the atonement) justified in the equity of our probation.

The total inability of fallen man, apart from all provision, to keep the Law, arises from the fact that its holiness, as a normal course of conduct, is outside the conditions we have stated of possible volitional actions. The knowledge of the perfect way, in its rectitude and perpetuity, is as unrevealed to his moral perception as the view of a pure geometrical figure to the human eye. The feeling of love to God he is unable to beget in his own soul as is a sensualist to create in his heart a poetic sensibility. Even with a Savior, a Bible, a Church, and a blessed Spirit, the natural man, without an individual self-surrender to divine aid, cannot attain a final restoration to the divine image. Without these provisions, both gracious and just in their character, the elements of a righteous probational system have no existence. Without Christ the foundations of our present moral system could not be laid.

Our review of the Necessitarian argument is now closed. Our position throughout has been that the power of counter choice—being the indispensable condition to Responsibility—must be held to exist until an unanswerable argument has proved its non-existence. Our reader, who at this point coincides with us in thinking that none such has been found, may consider our whole work accomplished. The difficulties in the way of Responsibility are cleared by the completed defense of the reality of Freedom. Nevertheless, not only are some arguments worthy of statement, but there are some Necessitarian replies to that argument requiring answers that can best be made after the positive statement has been presented.

PART THIRD

The Positive Argument Stated

I

The Argument from Consciousness

S O VARYING ARE THE views of psychologists in regard to the nature of consciousness, or rather in regard to the meaning of the term, we find it convenient to adopt a nomenclature of our own, and speak of Consciousness, Self-consciousness, and Sub-consciousness.

I. *Consciousness.* At the threshold of this argument we are told that consciousness is a faculty that can take cognizance of mental operations alone, and knows nothing directly of powers. Thus the mind derives knowledge by logical inference from operations and can say nothing of an alternative power of Will. "For consciousness," says the Princeton Essayist, "is the mind's cognizance of its own operations; it never beholds naked, abstract faculties separate from their workings. It discerns them in and by these workings, and so becomes conscious of their existence and nature. This, and nothing else, is the office of consciousness. How, then, can it be cognizant of operations which do not exist?"

It is not claimed, we reply, that the consciousness is "cognizant of operations which do not exist," but of power for such non-existent operations. And if, as the writer admits, the mind becomes conscious, even indirectly, of the existence and nature of powers and so is truly said to be conscious of a power at all, the mind assuredly is conscious of power for operations, namely, volitions that do not exist. For before every volition it is about to make, and when it is as yet an "operation which does not exist," the mind is conscious of a power to operate it. Our volitions are all put forth in the light of a conscious previous power to put them forth. Otherwise they would not be put forth. And a conscious power for the act before the act is a conscious power for an action that does not exist.

Nor can it be truly said, as sometimes is said, that we can have no conscious sense of power for a volition left ultimately unperformed. That is, it cannot be shown that we have no conscious sense of power for volitions alternatively omitted. On the contrary, we naturally survey the alternatives of choice before us with a conscious sense that either is in our power, thus we have one power for either act. Our conscious sense is that previous to our determination the choices omitted were as truly in our power as the choice performed. Before that performance our conscious sense is that each and every choice is equally in our power, and that the choices omitted are not for non-possession of the power, but for not exerting it. So far, then, as consciousness decides, we possess amid choices an alternative power.

Let us suppose, then, several alternatives before the deliberating mind. The conscious feeling is that either object is in the power of the choice. A comparison of their relative qualities shows different recommendations in each object, appealing to different faculties of the mind. One quality appeals to the reason, a second to the moral sense, a third to the love of beauty, a fourth to the personal interest, a fifth to some one of the particular appetites. From the Will comes the determination between them and fixes the act. But suppose that on account of some one of these inducements the choice is made; the question is often put, "Could the agent have chosen otherwise?" And the reply often is: "No; not unless there was a motive otherwise." But we rejoin: There was a motive, nay, several motives otherwise, all before the attention, and co-existing in the mind. When the choice is made, it is of course made subsequently upon some one of the motives; and hence it is sometimes inferred therefrom that the relation of necessitative cause and effect existed between that motive and that volition.

HYPOTHESIS OF FREEDOM

But on the hypothesis of freedom as truly as upon that of necessity, there is a motive that lies in immediate previous order to the volition; there is a reason last occurring before the choice, in sequence to which the Will, terminating the comparative survey, makes the choice. But it is not for want of other motives that choice is made. The other motives co-exist in view of the Will. And the fact is, the Will, in and by choosing, brings the particular motive, on account of which it acts, into this order just prior to its choice. It does so by the very act of choosing subsequently to it and on account of it. By this view we see how the full conscious power of the Will over all and each of the motives is consistently and clearly verified.

But still further analysis perhaps will show that consciousness may take cognizance of the qualities of our mental operations, and that among these qualities necessity is cognized in the operations of the other faculties and non-necessity in those of the Will. If it is by consciousness that we know a volition from a perception, it must be because the qualities of each are cognized by consciousness. We can distinguish them only by their differences of quality. Nor are the true and final conclusions of all consciousness in regard to such qualities derived entirely from consciousness alone, or at least from consciousness unaided by experience derived from other faculties. When consciousness judges the number, intensity, or rapidity of the inward operations, she applies to those operations a measurement derived from other faculties. The very faculty of knowing the number is not consciousness, and yet the application of number shapes our conscious knowledge. And it is by a similar bringing from other faculties a discipline or a conception, that consciousness may judge the necessity of an operation. If consciousness, trained or supplied by other powers, can judge the intensity, why not the form and the fixedness of the form of a given operation? So consciousness judges that a sensation is necessitated. Power to pronounce an operation necessitated is also power to pronounce it non-necessitated.

Consciousness adjudges the difference, and so knows the difference; and knowing the difference, she must know *how* the operations are different. If consciousness knows that a faculty is necessitated in its operations, she may know that another faculty is not. So, certainly, consciousness does ascertain that sensation or intellection is necessitated. When we raise the question of the necessitation of an intellection, we introspect the intellection, examine its traits in comparison with the object, and judge. So, also when we raise the question of the necessitation or non-necessitation of a volition, we may introspect the volition in comparison with the motive, and pronounce upon its quality of necessary conforming to that motive.

We judge this quality just as we judge any other quality in an internal operation. And we may correct or confirm this conscious decision by a conscious comparison between the traits of intellection and volition, just as we consciously learn to distinguish at all those two mental operations by conscious comparison, by their traits from each other. We shall then see that a conscious sense of non-necessity is properly a consciousness of non-necessity, and that a consciousness of non-necessity is a consciousness that a different volition is a perfectly supposable thing in presence of the same motive presentations.

It is sometimes argued that if a watch were conscious it would suppose itself to tick freely. If in this illustration we reply, it is meant that a
conscious soul be added of which the watch frame is the body, then the
tick, being bodily, would correspond to the spontaneous motions of our
bodily frame, such as the beating of the heart. It would of course be felt
to be unfree. If it is meant that the watch frame itself becomes a spirit;
and its ticks become volitions, then it is no longer a watch but a spirit;
its volitions are no longer ticks, and they are not movable by mechanical
springs; and so the illustration vanishes. It disposes of all such illustrations to note that our perception of our own freedom depends upon the
perfection of our consciousness. As our consciousness is, we perceive that
our sensations and perceptions are unfree, but not our Will. Were our
consciousness more perfect we should doubtless perceive the difference
more clearly. But by a far less perfect consciousness the perception of the
difference would be obliterated. If a watch were therefore in any way conscious in sufficient perfection, it would be aware of freedom to the tick,
but not from.

If the doctrine of consciousness, maintained by Hamilton, is true,
then when we are conscious of a sense of power we are conscious of the
power itself for either volition. According to that philosopher we are not
only conscious of our knowing an object, but we are conscious of the
object we know. If I am conscious that I cognize the planet Mars, the
consciousness of the cognition of Mars is the consciousness of Mars as
cognized. There can be no consciousness of knowledge of an object that
is not consciousness of what the knowledge embraces. If so, there can be
no consciousness of a sense of a present power of alternative volition that
is not a consciousness of the power itself. We have therefore a conscious
power of free Will.

II. *Self-consciousness.* But besides the view of consciousness, as thus
limited by the definition of Reid, there is another presented by other philosophers, by which we might properly apply to the faculty the term Self-
consciousness, as being the direct intuition of self and its powers by the
conscious faculty. It seems indeed a circuitous route to the ascertaining of
our own existence, and of our self, to make it an inference deduced from
the premises furnished by consciousness. The obvious consequence would
seem to be that the existence of the self is less certain than the existence
of thought. Do I not in pronouncing *I*, and reflectively casting inward my
thought, consciously know myself? Do I not consciously know my being

and my powers? If so I may know by the same self-consciousness my Will, its attributes and efficiencies. I then understand this sense of power for an act not yet performed, and which is previous and conditional to the performance itself. I can then also understand that I may possess a consciousness of power for an act that I never shall put forth; and that I do not need first to perform the act and then discover by inference that I possess the power for its performance.

NATURE OF CHOICE

If next we look at the very nature of choice, it seems to be an act that intrinsically might be withheld or put forth. Necessity imparts to the very idea of volition a rigidity and hardness not belonging to it. The flexibility and lenience belonging to it disappear, and it receives a petrified, cubical, and mechanical quality unrecognized by consciousness. Hence also even necessitarians are usually dissatisfied with the unnatural character choice receives at their hands, and struggle to find something in it that their theory will allow to be called freedom. Between the view taken by the necessitarian as a philosopher and as a man there is a variance amounting to contradiction. Viewing the same thing at different moments, he is obliged to feel, and often to confess, that the results of his logic are irreconcilable with the perceptions of his natural consciousness.

III. *Sub-consciousness.* From beneath our moral natures come the utterances of perhaps a deeper and yet more articulate intellectual consciousness than our analysis has hitherto reached. Let us scrutinize its dictates.

The assumption that in the act of transgression I possessed full power for contrary action lies at the base of all moral self-condemnation, all true repentance, all remorse. How deep in our nature are these feelings? How terrible is remorse! No part of our intuitive nature so clearly attests its own authority as being the voice of God speaking, with a divine authority, within us. If any part of our being is infallible it is this. And its language is: "Woe is me, for I choose death when I might have chosen life. I did wrong though in the full possession of the power of doing right. I yielded to the baser motive when I had full power to have acted from the better and higher." In these affirmations of the moral nature we note four things:

1. They assume the axiom of responsibility that power underlies obligation; that a man cannot be morally condemned for non-performance of an act for which he has no power. In condemning himself for not doing

otherwise, he grounds the whole process on the assumption that he could have done, that is, willed, otherwise.

2. The power to do otherwise is assumed as existing in the self-same circumstances; that is, in the identical case. The affirmation is that the wrong volition was put forth with the full coexisting underlying power, otherwise. To affirm that he could have willed otherwise if other motives, or the same motives with different force, had reached him, is simply to affirm that he would have had power, not in the actual case, but in a case that did not exist. It would be to affirm that he had no power-otherwise at all.

3. It is assumed that the strength of motives did not exclude the power to will otherwise in the given case. The superior force of a given motive does not excuse therefore; it does not nullify the counter power. On the contrary, the very blame is for not rejecting the victorious motive. The very guilt is that the so-called strongest motive was obeyed. And so the very assumption is that there was power to reject the so-called strongest motive.

4. This power-otherwise is assumed as existing, not merely for the external act, but for the diverse volition. Edwards has clearly shown that obligation or command rests not so much upon the external muscle or limb, as upon the Will. God commands us to choose his service, to will the right alternative, and to determine to prosecute the path of holiness.

But the main point here is this. It is from the intellect, and not from itself, that the moral sense derives its assumption of power of otherwise willing in the self-same circumstances. It is an affirmation of the intellective consciousness. The moral sense assumes it because the intellect affirms it. Here, as in all cases, the moral sense pronounces its decisions upon the case as it is made up and presented by the intellect. The moral sense in effect says to the intellectual consciousness: "I pronounce a responsibility or blame for this volition, because you affirm that there is power for a different volition." To authorize the sentence the intellectual consciousness must respond: "The agent willed thus in full possession of the power of willing otherwise." That is, the responsibility is affirmed by the moral sense; the existence of the counter power is affirmed by the intellectual consciousness. The doctrine of the freedom of the human Will, therefore, is an axiom of the intellect affirmed by the common consciousness of all mankind. It is an inborn self-knowledge.

II

Argument from Possibility of Divine Command

NECESSITARIANS HAVE OBJECTED THAT the doctrine of volitional freedom is in statement and concept a contradiction, and therefore is a nothing in the world. To attribute it to the agent therefore is to attribute nothing; to deny it is to deny nothing.

This, we reply, may be legitimately affirmed when both sides are brought to agreement that the conception of freedom is a contradiction. But for the opponent of freedom to decide that it is so, and then draw the inference, is simply an assumption of the point in debate.

But if the assertion and conception of the sinner's power of doing otherwise than commit his actual deed of sin is contradictory, absurd, and a nothing, then so must be the obligation, the requirement, and the command. If to attribute the power and the act is to attribute a nothing, then so must the obligation upon the power and for the act be a nothing. Then so must the requirement and the command for the exertion of the power in the act be a nothing. And all penalties for non-exertion of the power must be penalty for nothing.

And all retributive government founded in requirement for such act, as well as all penalties for its non-performance, is founded on nothing; and such government has no status or possible rightful or real existence. From all of which, it follows that without a rational and real power of counter volition there can be no divine prohibition of actual sin, no just retribution for its commission, no divine government founded upon such retribution. That is, without the alterability of the Will, its self-determining power, its power for either of several volitions in the given case, a divine government is impossible. Necessitarianism cannot frame a Theodicy. The very possibility of divine command requires and demonstrates freedom.

In Part III, sect. iv of his book, Edwards undertakes to prove directly that necessitated volitions are proper subjects of command and prohibition, and that inability and requirement are consistent. He argues, 1. It is the Will in the exercise of volitions that is the proper object of command, rather than the external subsequent act, as we have elsewhere fully quoted. 2. When a generic volition, or predominant leading purpose, is put forth, all the volitions subordinate and conformed to that leading purpose are necessitated to obey it, any obligation or divine command to the contrary notwithstanding. 3. The aforesaid generic volition or predominating bias, which so necessitates the particular subordinate volitions, is also necessary. For "the inclination is unable to change itself," because "it is unable to incline to change itself." 4. And yet, though both the principal and the subordinate volitions are necessary, there being in the agent no volitional power to substitute or change them, most rightfully may divine command be imposed upon the Will (which is the point to be proved), requiring an opposite purpose, bias, or volition instead, whether principal or subordinate, to exist. For either such command, so requiring an opposite, is right, or, 5. The alternative consequence would logically follow (as even Arminians must admit), that no command could be imposed, but such as requires the existing volition, or one that will exist. But this alternative consequence would make command and volition always necessarily to coincide; the command must accord with the act; and then, consequently, obedience would be a necessity! And so the Arminian (who denies that "law and command are consistent with necessity") would "overthrow himself!!"

LINE OF REASONING

With this slender line of reasoning we may perhaps make short work. Arminians reject the necessity of both the general volition and its subordinates, and so have nothing to do wit the dilemma of alternatives deduced. Of the two horns of the dilemma we reject both, since if the volitions are necessary, we hold that neither counter command nor coinciding command would be suitable; for a necessitation is the suitable subject of no command at all. Quite ludicrous is the necessity into which Edwards makes us "overthrow" ourselves, namely a necessity of the divine command to coincide with our volitions, a necessity laid indeed upon the divine command. This imposes no limitations upon the freedom of the human Will, a necessity indeed too absurd for discussion.

We now deny that the generic volition is always necessary and unchangeable; and we deny that the subordinate is always necessitated to obey it. If we sustain this denial, the right of command against necessity is unsustained. Let us examine the argument.

It is maintained by Edwards that a volitional agent, while under the influence of a prevalent inclination, is necessitated thereto because he is unable to put forth a volition in a contrary direction, in the following terms:

> The Will in the time of that diverse or opposite leading act or inclination, and when actually under the influence of it, is not able to exert itself to the contrary, to make an alteration in order to a compliance. Then inclination is unable to change itself; and that for this plain reason, it is unable to incline to change itself. Present choice cannot at present choose to be otherwise; for that would be at present to choose something diverse from what is at present chosen. (232)

The first question here is: What is meant by inclinations? As we have in the proper place defined it, the term in its strict meaning applies to the feelings prior to, contemporaneous with, or subsequent to the volition. We are inclined to a thing, often, before we chose it. We choose it often in spite of a contrary inclination. After a volition has resolved the agent into a state of determination upon a course or object, one or more inclinations may be against. There may be various inclinations coexisting in the mind at the same moment; and during a very brief period the soul may fluctuate through a great variety of agitations, tendencies, biases, impulses, repugnances, and inclinations.

And none of these may reach the Will. There may not be a volition in the matter. The Will is not so properly said to be inclined, nor are its acts inclinations. The instantaneous act of Will is a volition; the permanent state of Will is purpose, resolution, determination, predetermination. By inclination as applied to Will nothing else can be meant than the determination or purpose.

Dismissing the criticism of terms, the argument of Edwards, if it has any meaning, must imply that while we entertain a volitional purpose we cannot change that purpose.

1. The statement may signify that the purpose is fully present to the mind or attention, and so present to the mind as to possess it entirely, excluding all counter thought, object, feeling, or motive. In this sense, and while this entire engrossment lasts, it is true that the mind cannot change the purpose; but this is irrelevant to the discussion. Where a counter course is excluded from mental knowledge or possible attention so as not to come as alternative before the mind, the agent cannot indeed choose it. This has been fully stated under the conditions of Will.

2. For a similar reason, if a purpose or determination is, after its first formation, deposited in the mind and memory, yet dismissed from the attention, it cannot while it and its subject are thus excluded from the mental view be reversed by the Will.

3. But when the determination is before the mind it may, even while it exists, submit to a change by the Will. Does the necessitarian really mean to say that a man cannot change his purpose, or reverse his determination, or break a resolution? Such a statement would be absurd. Now this change or reversal must take place while the purpose or determination yet exists; and the cessation of the existence of the purpose must in the order of nature be consequent upon the change. It is not true then that "the Will in the time of that diverse or opposite leading act or inclination" (or volitional purpose) cannot "change" that inclination or purpose.

The volition is often counter to the inclination, nay, even to the stronger and prevalent inclinations. The Will often acts in contradiction to the most intense passion, the strongest temptation, the deepest impression.[1]

1. With a crude philosophy the Princeton Essayist, like other necessitarians, assumes that the mind must be completely occupied with one "bias," which excludes all coexistent contrarieties. "Will any one pretend that it is conscious of a power to choose contrariwise, its ruling inclination of pleasure being and continuing to choose as it has chosen?" (254) What is meant by a ruling inclination's choosing, or a pleasure's choosing, we pretend not to say. But that the most intense feeling may coexist with a contrary volition, and may be overruled by it, is an ordinary fact of consciousness. What varieties of thought may coexist at the same instant in the mind, philosophers have too little realized. A man walks a narrow path, twirls his watch key, looks at a prospect, talks to a friend, and thinks of something else, all at the same moment. What volitions, perceptions, emotions, and abstractions, like so many little wheels in various simultaneous whirl, are that instant going on in his mind! Several distinct trains of volitions are going on together. Lord Brougham has a curious passage on the multitude of intellections occupying the mind of a public speaker at the moment. De Quincy gives the narrative of a lady who was drowned and recovered. At the drowning instant, "In a moment, in the twinkling of an eye, every act, every design of her past life lived again, arraying themselves, not in succession, but as parts of a coexistence. Her consciousness became omnipresent at one moment to every feature in the infinite review."

The opposite feeling and the volition often coexist in the mind at the same instant. We do what we intensely dislike; we decline what we intensely desire. We arrest our inclinations in full current by a strong counter effort of Will. Freedom thus exerts itself against the tide of necessity. In this meaning, therefore, the statements of Edwards are psychologically false.

"The Inclination," says Edwards, "cannot change itself." Very true. But the man himself can change his inclinations. He can incline himself a different way and to a different object. "Present choice cannot at present choose to be otherwise." Choice cannot indeed choose to be otherwise, for a choice cannot choose at all. But the being who at the present instant chooses one alternative, may at the next choose an opposite. An agent who is under one inclination or direction of Will, in the presence of different possibilities, is not under incapable of changing his choice. When the alternatives of choosing or retaining the purpose are before the attention, the purpose may be simply a motive for its own retention or prosecution, and the agent is able to decide the question by Will.

If, then, the generic volition and purpose is not itself necessary, and does not necessitate the volitions that subordinate themselves to it, if they in their acceptance or rejection of the generic volition are free, then the argument of Edwards, drawn from the fact that a command or obligation may be imposed requiring them to be substituted or withdrawn or not put forth, fails to prove that necessitated volitions are proper objects of counter command. Our original argument stands untouched, that freedom is necessary to the possibility of obligation, command, or divine Government. An obligatory command requiring an impossibility is itself impossible. The possibility of divine command requires freedom.

III

Distinction between Automatic Excellence
and Moral Deserts

A N AUTOMATON IS A machine, constructed sometimes in the human form, whose parts, by force of interior springs, are made to operate apparently like a human system, with self-motion. The movement of the parts is necessitatively caused to take place, in precise proportion and in the direction of the forces applied. When the whole is artistically framed we admire the beauty, the ingenuity, and perhaps the imitation—that is, the automatic excellence. But we attribute this to its action or its being the slightest intrinsic quality of moral merit or demerit.

The highest order of mechanical or automatic excellence is found in a watch. So numerous and nice are its parts, so exquisitely adjusted are its forces, and so beautiful is its aspect to the eye, that we gaze upon it with admiration. And then, in the pointing of its hand to the figure according to the true time, we behold one of the most wonderful adjustments of mechanism to the demands of mind. With but slight fancy we attribute to it the qualities of truth and reliability, or of falsehood and fickleness. We wish it gently handled according to its excellent nature. And yet, literally and coolly, we attribute only automatic excellence; and we are utterly unable to see in it the slightest intrinsic trace of moral merit or demerit. We are unable to see in it guilt or good deserts; we are, by the very nature of things, compelled to deny of it the possibility of penalty or reward.

Should the question be asked why, in a thing which is so noble and so pleasing to aesthetical sense, all moral merit must be denied, the answer might be, because it has no consciousness, and so cannot be made happy by reward or miserably by penalty. That this is an insufficient answer may be made evident by an additional supposition. Imagine the automaton endowed with sensibility in every particle of its substance, that it is consciously impressed by every contact and every force applied, and feels every movement it is made to undergo. Yet it is still an automaton, being moved solely in the proportion and in the direction of the forces applied. Its every operation is the exact mechanical measure of the causation. It is plain that its sensibility has not endowed it with the possibility of moral blame or merit, and for a very plain reason. It is seen not to be truly the author of its own actions. It moves only as it is moved. It acts only as its springs are touched. It has only the freedom to, not the freedom from.

ENTIRE BEING

There exists not in its entire being any power to move otherwise than as the fixed and constant result of the force received. Its operations are the necessitated effects of necessitative causation. It is guiltless, undeserving, irresponsible, because it can act no otherwise than it does act. Common sense demands not only sensibility but free self-control. We thence deduce the law, which is (apart from self-superimposing) universal and incontestable, that no act can be morally obligatory, responsible, or guilty—no agent can be morally obligated, rewardable, or punishable—unless there is in the agent adequate power for other acts than the act in question.

Rising from mechanical into animal existence, we recognize in the horse, for instance, every combination of both material and mental automatic excellence. Beauty of form, color, and motion, adjustment of parts for strength and speed, balance of forces there are, so as to fit him for his place in the economy of creation. And then in his mind there is just such a proportion of perceptive faculties and emotions as to produce that train of volitions and actions as will suit him to his intended uses. If, on the other hand, his dispositions are so badly proportioned as to produce irregular and refractory action, we apply severity or blandishment as we do the means to repair the watch, as adjustment. It is simply an alternative, which is not justice but an expedient. By applying the impulses of pain and fear, we alter the balance of forces and produce better modes and habits of action. We may thus so rearrange, that both mind and body may present again the model of automatic excellence. But being a simple automatic though mental organism, we have not yet found a particle of moral merit.

The beauty of appearance, the skill of the artist, the adaptation to the ends, the perfection of the working and the value of the results—these are the qualities of automatic excellence. When we find these in body or mind, we admire, love, and desire them. We appropriate the article to ourselves, confer upon it values and preferences. We make of the whole class pets, ornaments, and enjoyments. On the contrary, where the automatism of a thing or animal is defective, ugly, or offensive, we render it our disgust or hatred. We repel it from use, and are ready to abandon it to misery or destruction. But if we examine our feelings we shall find them purely non-ethical; we shall find ourselves absolutely unable to attribute to it the least element of moral merit or demerit. Its ugliness and its beauty, its precise action or mal-action, is not its own fault; it is entire automatic.

But is the animal Will or action automatic? Yes, as truly as the machine, if it is necessitated. Just as automatically an object strikes the retina, so automatically the perception rises. As automatically the perception, so automatically is the highest desire. As automatically the highest desire, so automatically is the volition. And as automatically the volition, so automatically is the action. So the whole round of impulses and effects are automatic because all are necessitated, and alike necessitated. The volition is here no less necessitated, and so no less automatic, then the perception or the desire.

But suppose that, with one term in this series of automatic mental states or operations, there is inserted a feeling, automatically rising, of right or wrong, of blame or moral approval. Suppose that after one automatic volition a consequent feeling of guilt or merit should emerge. The question then is: Would this entire automatic organism of intellect, however clear, of sensibility, however acute, of volition, however exact, and of moral feeling, however intense, constitute a moral being, truly capable of blamable and rewardable acts? Common sense can give only a negative answer. The feeling of blame or praise would be an arbitrary interpolation, false in its affirmations and absurd in its nature. It would be out of place. Should that feeling assume that the volitions of an organism possessing, in the given instance, no power for the production of any but that volition, were guilty or morally approvable, its assumption would be untrue.

In an automatic organism it can make no difference what the substance composing its series or system of parts, whether matter, electricity, or spirit; or whether the connection of its constituent elements or pieces is a current, emotion, ligature, or volition; provided the whole series transmits from part to part a fixed force, and a necessary action, landing in a solely possible result. We are as able to imagine what may with propriety be called a spiritual as a material machine. Of a machine nothing stronger can be said than that the causative action of one part upon the other secures the solely possible result. That can as truly be said of a mental organism as of a material organism; and as truly said of a resulting volition as of a resulting intellection or of a resulting mechanical material motion. Such a spiritual machine would be made of a conscious center and sensitive parts. Intellect, sensibility, and Will would be its constituents, just as weights, wheels, and hands are the constituents of a clock. And just as the gravitational force may pass from weights to wheels and from wheels to hands, and may bring the hand to a particular figure, so may the motive force pass from intellect to sensibility, and from sensibility to Will, and bring the Will to a given volition. The determination of the clock pointer may be no more fixed and necessitated than the determination of volition.

The causations may, in both cases, be as inevitable. If they are not equally mechanical, the difference is essentially verbal, consisting in the fact that the word *mechanical* is normally applied only to material organisms. But all that renders a mere mechanical action of a conscious machine incapable of moral responsibility exists in the case, namely, a necessitation previously fixing the given volitional action. Nor is there the slightest validity in the notion of some thinkers, who imagine that the very fact of its being a volition, and not some other thing or event, secures its responsibility. Ask them why a volition is responsible, and their only reply is: Because it is a volition. A volition, necessitatively affixed to the agent, is no more responsible than any other attribute, event, operation, or fact.

The human constitution is a compound of the spiritual machine and the bodily machine, cooperating in a sort of "pre-established harmony." The action of forces from the external world strikes through the corporeal frame inward to the spiritual organism, reaching its central power of action; and, from that central power, action comes forth through the corporeal frame upon the external world. If this process is simply action and fixed reaction, producing a solely possible result, then the whole process is, so far as responsibility is concerned, as non-ethical as any case of mechanical impulse and recoil.

The impulse of rays from the beautiful fruit strikes the retina of an eye, and the perception of the exact form and force by necessitation automatically rises. The impulse of perception necessitates the strongest desire automatically to arise. The moral emotion being automatically neutralized, the impulse of strongest desire strikes the Will, and automatically the volition springs forth, and from the volitional impulse comes the automatic action. The automatic corporeal action springs no more mechanically from the volition than the automatic volition from the automatic desire, and that from the automatic perception, and that from the ray of light, and that from the fruit. We admire or condemn the excellent, or defective automatism; but the mere arbitrary interpolation of an automatic moral emotion in the series calls not for the attribution by us of any moral merit or blame to the organism, or any part of its automatic action or substance.

DEMONSTRATE VOLITION

We thus demonstrate that if the volition is as necessitated as the emotion, the emotion as the perception, the perception as the receptivity of the retina, then the whole automatic chain forms a circle of automatic force as irresponsible as the streak of an electric circle. It is impossible for logic to show or common sense to see any more responsibility or moral merit or demerit in the necessitated volition than in the necessitated emotion, the necessitated perception, or the necessitated reception, or the necessitated receptivity of the retina, or the necessitated visual ray, or the necessitated fruit.

Nor can the universal common sense of mankind see that volition, emotion, perception, and sensorial retina, necessitatively subjected to automatic effect from automatic impulsions, are any more imputable with moral merit or demerit, praise or blame, reward or penalty, than a similar succession of material automatic parts, under exact and necessary physical forces. We can only find non-meritorious excellence. If this is true, then necessitated volition is non-responsible volition; and if none but necessitated volitions universally exist, moral responsibility has no existence in the universe. The "common sense of mankind" recognizes morality primarily in volition alone, and not in mere perception, because it recognizes in volition alone there is non-necessitation.

If we consider George Washington[1] as a living system of mental and bodily parts and forces so balanced; if clear perceptions and sagacious intellect were so proportioned with emotions of honor, patriotism, heroism, and self-sacrifice, as necessitatively to create that train of grand volitions by which he saved his country, then in body, intellect, and Will he was a most noble specimen of merely automatic excellence. We should admire him as a most perfect living and acting colossus. We would love him and wish him all happiness, just as we love and wish well to all noble automatism. But he is only fortunate; he is no more meritorious, morally, than Benedict Arnold. His was only a happier fate.

Washington was, as we view the matter, meritorious, because, being volitionally able to prefer to betray his country he saved it. He saved it amid temptations appealing to his apparent self-interest, his love of ease, and his fear of danger. He served his country after the Revolution by rejecting the motives that would lead him to a Napoleonic self-aggrandizement. The very magnanimity of his character consists in his choosing in accordance with right motives, in preference to powerful wrong ones possible to him and present before him. He could have yielded to the wrong; he chose to act by the right.

With regard to the human Will of our Savior, we concede that the automatism, if really existent, negates the merit. Were his a mere automatic Will, he would be a great mechanical figure in the grand panorama of redemption, striking as an automatic adjustment, but destitute of essential moral character. We hold, that from the infinity of all possible human souls Omniscience selected that one which, in the great crisis of the case, it foresaw would stand, though free to fall.

Still more appalling is the degradation of the divine Will to a mechanical automatism. A god like the evil omnipotence of the Persian god Manes, who from the eternal necessity of his own nature, has no adequate power for the production of a good volition, would be a being horribly evil, but not responsibly evil. A god automatically good, mechanically good, might be held excellent. But he would not be meritoriously excel-

---

1. "Is Washington entitled to no credit for giving freedom to his country, unless it can be proved that he was equally inclined to betray it?" Day, *An Inquiry Respecting the Self-Determining Power of the Will,* 116. The question is falsely put. We do not hold that it was necessary that he should be equally "inclined to betray it," but that he should be susceptible to the temptation and possessed of adequate power for the volition to betray it. Otherwise, we praise him for the non-performance of this contrary act.

lent. We should concede to him an infinite strength in only one way. He would be a cramped omnipotence, an almightiness not full-orbed, but mutilated and incapable—a blasphemous contradiction.

And so the moral merit of all beings, finite or infinite, arises from this, that in their proportion of power, space, and time, they, in the possession of the full and complete volitional power of doing wrong, do persistently and freely that which is right. A finite being does thus finitely, an infinite being infinitely.

If God were to create a being of perceptions, emotions, and volitions, all perfectly excellent and well adjusted, yet all necessary and automatic in their action, so that every volition, like the pointers of a perfectly true clock, should point exactly right, such a being would be innocent and lovely, and in that sense of lovely innocence it might be called holy. It could not be punishable. We should aesthetically admire it; we should sympathetically love it; we should wish it happy in a condition accordance to its nature. Yet we should nonetheless hold it incapable of moral responsibility, moral merit or demerit, moral good or evil deserts, moral reward or penalty. Nor could it, even by Omnipotence itself, be invested with a morally meritorious holiness. All its holiness would be simply a lovely and excellent automatic innocence or purity. The sum of all this is, that a necessitated holiness is no meritorious or morally deserving holiness.

SHOULD GOD CREATE

Again, should God create an automatic fiend; a being whose perceptions were, indeed, true, but whose emotions were purely and with a perfect intensity, yet automatically, malignant; and whose volitions were, with all their strength, automatically bad; we should hate such a being and wish it out of our way. We might still admire its vicious perfection. Yet, when we had indulged our abhorrence of it, and come to remember coolly its automatism, we should see that, though bad, it was unblamably bad. Its volitions, being necessitated, are as irresponsible as the springs of a gun lock.

Upon such a fiend, if the infliction of pain would set his volitions right, and make all his movements safe and beneficial, we should, for the common good, think expedient, to inflict it, simply as an alternative, just as we would insert a key and turn it round to set any other machinery right—simply as an alternative. Such infliction of pain could not be a punishment, in the sense of justice, or execution of a responsible crime. It would simply be an expedient, like a medicine or a mechanical adjustment, in which there can be no moral element.

We might, for the good of the world, wish such a being destroyed, not as a moral retribution to him, but for the common well being, and, if possible, painlessly. The sum of all which is, a necessitated depravity is no responsible or justly punishable depravity. As there is, therefore, what may be called a holiness without any meritoriousness or moral good deserts, so there is what may be called a depravity, or a sin, without any responsibility or morally penal deserts.

From all the above representations we derive the answer to the question concerning the possibility of a created holiness or a created unholiness. A created holiness would be necessitated and automatic. It might therefore be excellent, innocent, pure, and lovely; but it never could be meritorious, responsible, probationary, rewardable, or punishable. A created unholiness would be also automatic. It might be automatically excellent, innocent, yet unlovely, hateful, repulsive, perhaps destructive. Yet it is below the conditions of responsibility, deserts, probation, judgment, retribution. The being is evil, perhaps we may say morally evil; but not responsibly or guiltily evil.

If by morally evil we mean evil as compared with the standard of the moral law, the phrase would be correct. If by morally evil we mean evil so as that the penalty of the law is justly applicable, the phrase would be incorrect. There would be necessitated discomformity to the moral law; but the conditions of amenability to its penalty would not exist.

Thus man, as born after the fall, possesses, even before any volitional act of his own, a fallen nature. As compared with what, by the perfect law of God, he ought to be, he is wrong, evil, morally evil. Yet, as not being the author of his own condition, he is not responsible for his necessitatively received nature and moral state. His nature is no fault of his own until fully appropriated by the act of his own free will. That nature and state may doubtless be called sin, but only under a certain definition of the word. If all sin is anomie, (1 John iii, 4) nonconformity to the law, then there may be a sinful nature or state, as well as a sinful act. But where that nature or state is necessitatively received by the being, without his Will, or received only by the act of a necessitated Will, if sinful it is not responsibly sinful. It thence would follow that there may be disconformity to the law, unrighteousness, evil, moral evil, sin, sinfulness, all without responsibility, guilt, ill desert, just moral condemnality, or punishment.

The whole human race, viewed as fallen in Adam, and apart from redemption through Christ, is thus necessitatedly unholy. It is in discomformity with the ideal prescribed by the divine law. Judged by the standard of the moral law, it is evil; and, in the sense above defined, it is morally evil. But it is not responsibly evil. It cannot be retributively, and in the strict sense of the word, punished. Incapable it is, indeed, of the holiness and so of the happiness of heaven. It rests under the displacency of Heaven as not being holy in the sense of conformed to his law, which is but the transcript of his own character and the expression of his own divine feelings. What is to be done with it is a question for Divine Wisdom to solve.

POTENTIAL AND SEMINAL

It can come from a potential and seminal existence into actual existence only under the universal law of hereditary natural likeness to the lineal parent. The whole race is thus and then conceptually a generic unit, including the primordial parent and all his posterity. What would have been done with them without a savior is a question to which revelation furnishes no explicit answer. And yet there are grounds both from Scripture and reason for an obvious reply. The human race would never have been actually brought into existence under conditions of such misery. In other words, the redemption was the condition of the actual continuity of the race. Redemption underlies probationary existence. Grace is the basis of nature. And the reply is both a satisfactory and a beautiful theoretical solution of a theoretical difficulty.

If a being is, like Adam, created pure and disposed to right, yet as an agent freely able to choose right or wrong, his holiness, as created and before his free act, is pure and excellent. Yet it is not meritorious. It can claim no moral approbation or moral reward. His first meritorious and morally deserving personal holiness is derived from action. And that action must be volition put forth with full and adequate power of contrary action instead.

Again, if God should create or allow to be born a being of mixed character, (suppose it to be man), the automatic spring of whose volitions, under the touch of automatic motive forces, should be necessitatively sometimes in an injurious direction, and sometimes in a beneficial direction, such a being might be automatically excellent and perfect, but he would be below the conditions of probationary existence. His good or bad volitions being automatic, would be equally irresponsible and unmeriting of reward or penalty. Any ideas or notions implanted in his own nature of retributive approval or condemnation would be arbitrary and false.

Let us now suppose a being, such as man truly is, of a mixed character in another respect. Suppose him automatic in his perceptions, emotions, and desires, yet free and alterable in his volitions; capable of choosing either of diverse ways in a right direction or in a wrong one instead. He is now no longer in a pure automatic nature. He has mounted into the grade of a morally responsible being. He is henceforth capable of probation, responsibility, judgment, and retribution.

Again, let us suppose that this last being is able, by his free volitions, to modify his automatic propensities, namely his intellections, emotions, and desires, so as to make them better or worse than they naturally were. Either he neglects to restrain them from excess or wrong direction; or he directs, impels, develops, trains, and enlarges them for wrong; or he restrains and confines them to their proper degree and to a right direction. Even his automatic faculties would then derive a sort of secondary responsible character, at least for much if not all their so formed character; he would be volitionally and morally responsible. It is thus that a man's sensibilities, intellections, emotions, and beliefs become secondarily and consequentially responsible.

Again, a man may so train up into magnitude and force of will his automatic faculties as to render suppressed his freedom of volition for any good; and thus he is automatically evil. Such volitional automatism for evil being self-superimposed, is responsible, since where a man has freely annihilated his own power for good, he is responsible for the evil. Self-superimposed necessity is a responsible necessity. And from this view we can clearly understand how the sinner who has given up of God, or the sinner finally damned who sins and only sins, and that by a perpetual necessity, is responsible for his sins nonetheless. The holiness of the saints in Heaven is nonetheless rewardable because it has become necessary; they are rewardable, not only for their words during probation, but for their works of holiness, obedience, love, and praise before God in Heaven.

Finally, from all this we deduce three corollaries:

1. The necessitated volitional agent is with truth pronounced by freedomists to be an automatism, a machine. And the replies of Edwards and Day, that he is not a machine because he is a living intellectual, volitional being are without validity.

2. The imputation that necessitarianism is Fatalism is true and just. If all volitional agents are machines, still more confessedly so are all physical organisms and substances. All physical and all volitional machines thereby combine into one great interlocking machine. And this frames the Universe, including God himself, into one great clockwork. The limitless Whole thereby becomes an infinite eternal machine in which there is no conceivably more complete fatalism.

3. Just penalty can never be held as a mere preventive of future wrongs. Thus the Younger Edwards says: "It is inquired, Where is the consistence between God's laying a man under a moral necessity of sinning, and then punishing for that sin?—I answer: 1. How can God consistently make a man sick, and then apply medicines or any remedy toward his restoration? Punishment is inflicted to prevent either the subject of the punishment, or others from falling to the same practice." (1:444)

This explains punishment as method, not as a pure justice. So the English judge says to the condemned culprit: "You are not hanged for stealing a sheep; but you are hanged that sheep may not be stolen." The first clause of this piece of information excludes the consideration of intrinsic justice; the last states the ground of pure expediency. By intrinsic justice, as cognized by the moral intuition, there is a moral relation between responsible crime and deserts of penalty as essential, as eternal, as absolute as the relation between the circularity of a figure and the equality of its radii. But expediency is simply a contrivance in social mechanics. It is the mere principle of turning a peg to regulate the machine. Or, as Edwards here puts it, it is the physical remedy for a physical disease. If God manages his system upon this bleak principle, as the argument of Edwards obliges him to maintain, justice and true retribution have no existence in it. There is, then, under his hand an organism of great physical clockwork, but strictly speaking no moral government at all. Suffering inflicted to produce right action is expediency; suffering inflicted to meet the demands of intuitive right is justice. Both these may well meet in the same case; but they are not the same in essence.

IV

Created Moral Deserts Impossible

THE MAXIM LAID DOWN by Mr. Bledsoe[1] and used with great argumentative effect, that there can be no created virtue or viciousness, ought to read according to the doctrine of our last chapter, that there can be no created moral deserts, good or evil. So corrected, it would lose none of the argumentative efficiency with which his handling invests it. There can be a created conformity or discomformity to the divine law, but no created merit or demerit therein or therefore, or deserts of reward or penalty.

The righteous law, let us say, has a twofold office, namely, the judicatory or critical, and the retributive or penal. In its former character it is an ethical ideal by which is tested the active reality; it is the rule by which the ethical character of its subjects is measured. That subject, if automatic, if created and having moral status prior to free volitional action, is still tested by the law's ideal and equaled in measure by the perfect rule; but there the office of the law stops. The instant it should proceed to use its retributive function and inflict penalty; it would be by its own rectitude condemned. But the moment free volitional moral action commences, the result is accountability; and retributive righteousness or unrighteousness intrinsic to his personality and being.

It might be said, then, that if the agent is not free, the law has nothing to do with him, inasmuch as he lacks the qualification of a subject of the law. And we might grant that the law scarcely is his judge. It is only an instrument, as an ethical critique, to estimate the quality of the agent necessitated as good or bad without responsibility. Yet when the agent is placed, like Adam, at the historical commencement of a legal govern-

---

1. Albert T. Bledsoe, *A Theodicy: Or Vindication of the Divine Glory, as Manifested in the Constitution and Government of the Moral World* (New York: Carlton & Philips, 1854)

mental system, the law is installed already over him, and it is its office to pronounce, even if it pronounces that it has no jurisdiction, and that he cannot come into court. In such case the agent is necessarily placed in some relation to the law, and the law pronouncing must, as we conceive, pronounce him ethically but not retributively holy.

First we may suppose a being created in a world of chrysolite, where no external object is afforded temptation or possibility of wrong or sin, with a body of flexible chrysolite affording no propensity or power of corporeal sin, with a set of sensibilities so measured that there could be neither excess, deficiency, or irregularity of action. He would also have intellect from which all thought of wrong should be absolutely excluded. His world might offer to his free choice a thousand varying avenues of right and equally right action. He would be free for good alone. That good would properly be moral good. And as a being of precisely the opposite nature and condition might be conceived, free only to varieties of evil, so there would be the true contrast of a perfect moral goodness or badness. And as these beings are so created, there is a created goodness or badness prior to action; and both may be complete and perfect in their kind, yet neither retributively so.

Second, we may suppose a being, like Adam, created with a soul perfectly right. His preferential feelings prior to action accord with the divine law. His sensibilities are so under easy volitional control, his mind is so clear and pure, that all in its primitive undisturbed state is right. His Will is able to hold his whole being in subordination to the Moral Imperative. He is, in his grade of being, perfectly excellent; and his excellence is not mechanical merely or aesthetical, but ethical. It is a created moral excellence, perfect in its kind, yet wholly unmeritorious.

That the former of these two supposed holy beings by creation could not sin is doubtless clear; that the latter could sin may, by a little consideration seems equally clear. Though the prevolitional preferential feelings are accordant with the Law, the various desires and appetites have their specific objects. And those objects may be so presented as to excite the appetites above measure unless the Will either firmly excludes the influence of the object, or holds in check at the right measure the degree of desire. If, however, the Will allows the influence to enter by want of care, or allows the undue degree of desire to rise by consent, sin has begun. Thereby the feelings veer from their preference for the moral law, and another object is preferred. If after allowing the undue action of the prevolitional feeling, the Will proceeds to execute its dictates, then the sin appears in over act.

LOGIC OF EDWARDS

We will now notice the logic of Edwards upon this subject. The Socinian, Dr. John Taylor, denies the possibility of a created or necessary holiness. "A necessary holiness (says he) is no holiness. [Is *no moral desert*, he should have said.]. . . . Adam could not be originally created in righteousness and true holiness, because he must choose to be righteous before he could be righteous."[2]

To this statement of Taylor, Edwards replies thus: "If these things are so it will certainly follow that the first choosing to be righteous is no righteous choice; there is no righteousness or holiness in it, because no choosing to be righteous goes before it. For he plainly speaks of choosing to be righteous, as what must go before righteousness; and that which follows the choice, being the effect of the choice, cannot be righteousness or holiness; for an effect is a thing necessary and cannot prevent the influence or efficacy of its cause, and therefore is unavoidably dependent upon the cause, and he says a necessary holiness is no holiness." (278)

Here are two perfectly distinct arguments strung together, the first closing at the semicolon of the second sentence.

1. Taylor says that righteous character is consequent upon free choice.[3] Then, replies Edwards: The choice itself cannot be righteous; for you say that the righteousness is consequent, and so cannot exist until after the choice; the choice, being previous to, must be outside the righteousness. Grant it, we answer; but how does that show but that the free choice may produce—the thing that Taylor means—righteousness of character in the man, whether the choice is righteous or not? But we do not grant it. That righteousness of the man should be consequent upon the choice does not decide that the choice itself is not righteous. A man standing upon a straight line does not walk in the straight line until and just so far forth as he takes or has taken his first step in it; but that does not prove but that the first step is truly in the straight line. Consistently,

---

2. John Taylor, *The Scripture Doctrine of Original Sin* (Newcastle: Printed by J. Barker, 1845), 79.

3. For, of course, it is personal righteousness which Taylor affirms that "Adam could not originally be created in."

according to Taylor, man was created right, and his first right act freely accorded with God's law, and was therefore righteous; and his righteousness of personal character was the consequence of his right act.

2. Taylor also says that holiness cannot be created or necessitated, but must be the product of a free Will. But, replies Edwards, in his second argument above, if holiness is a product or effect of free Will, it must be necessary; for all effect is necessary. One of the most unmitigated quibbles on record! Taylor never thought of denying that holiness was intrinsically and so necessarily a quality of the free right act freely performed as all essential quality is necessary to its subject. He only denied that the right act of which this holiness was the inherent essential and necessary quality is itself necessary to the agent; and, not being so, then [meritorious] holiness is not a necessary quality to the agent. It was not created in him; he was not necessitated to acquire it. It was to Adam an unnecessitated righteousness, because it was a freely chosen righteousness.

But it is in his work on Original Sin (Part II, chap. I, sect. I) that Edwards endeavors to demonstrate at greatest length the reality of a created righteousness, meaning thereby created moral deserts. These arguments we will consider.

1. *Argument.* It accords with universal common sense that actions, in order to be good and right, must proceed from previous right principles or dispositions already existing in the soul. The truth is, "not that principles derive their goodness from actions, but that actions derive their goodness from the principles whence they proceed." Hence there must be principles, dispositions which are good and right and virtuous before action; and therefore choice, volition, doing, is not necessary to the existence of a virtue. There may therefore be a created righteousness, a necessitated virtue prior to action.

Answer. That there may be a created and necessitated righteousness before choice we admit; but the question is: Can there be a created meritoriousness, good deserts, or retributive righteousness before free choice? If that created righteousness or virtuous constitution prior to choice is such as to exclude all choice for wrong, but necessitates choosing according to the good principle, inclination, etc., previously existing, is there any imputable ethical merit? Or, if there be a created agent so totally evil, and so destitute of all possibility of good inclination, motive, or principle whatever, that choice according to them is out of the reach of the agent, then, though we admit that the agent would in such case be evil, and his actions evil, would he be ethically responsible for the evil? To all these questions common sense must reply in the negative. It may, then, be true that the choice must be for the good object, and from, or subsequent to a good motive or principle, or interior correlation for a good principle. Yet no accountable righteousness precedes the choice, but all accountability must follow choice.

PREVIOUS BAD PRINCIPLE

If there were no previous bad principle within reach, from which or subsequently upon which Adam could act, Adam would not be meritoriously righteous. If there had been no previous good principle, motive, or reason within Adam's reach, from which or subsequently upon which he could act, Adam would not be imputably wicked. We grant all that Edwards claims then; that there must be some previous good or bad motivation within reach, in accordance with which the action, in order to be good or bad, must be put forth. But that stands in no contradiction to the further truth that no merit or demerit accrues to the agent until the free volition has accorded with the previous motive, good or bad.

2. *Argument.* Passages are quotes from Hutcheson, sanctioned by Taylor, affirming that all actions morally good or evil flow from some good or evil affection, and that virtue or vice is either "some such affection or action consequent upon it." But righteous affection, previous to all action, must be necessary righteousness, prior to choice. Moreover, Taylor admits that love is the fulfilling of the law, and that this is that "goodness," or "principle of benevolence" that includes "all moral rectitude"; which, in fact, is resolvable into this principle. Consequently no volition prior to this principle can have any moral rectitude. An involuntary, non-volitional, and therefore necessary holiness, therefore, precedes all choice.

Answer. Love is, indeed, the fulfilling of the law, and all virtue is but a modification of love, as all material things are modifications of the same essential substance. But this love is not a mere inactive necessitated sentiment. So long as it is such it is "moral rectitude," indeed; but it is not moral deserts. It is excellence, virtue; but it is neither imputable nor rewardable. Imputable love, fulfilling the law, is not merely love experienced, but love voluntarily lived and exemplified in action. It is not merely love passive, but love active. It is love volitionally sanctioned, appropriated, and adopted as the controlling law of the energetic life, accepted as suffusing the active being. It requires therefore free volitional action before that love can attain the meritorious character requisite to a retributive probation. If that action is necessarily accordant, the imputability is still unattained. Or, on the other hand, if that action is necessarily discordant, if love in any of its forms of virtue cannot be in reach as a possible motive or prior principle of volition, there will be solely necessitated vicious action, but not responsible action. Necessitated love or hate, and therefore, necessitated virtue or vice, may precede free action, but not accountable virtue or vice.

3. *Argument.* It is affirmed by Dr. Taylor that it is the cause that is chargeable with the effect. But the same Dr. T. maintains that choice is the cause of righteousness as an effect. But the doctrine that choice effects righteousness stands in contradiction to Dr. T.'s doctrine that all moral rectitude is in the single principle of love, benevolence, or goodness.

Answer. The cause is chargeable with its effect; and the free causal agent is responsible for his act. The free choice is the antecedent of the chooser's accountable righteousness. The antecedent principle of benevolence, of right, or of reason, all being modifications of the principle of love, are simply initiating motions of volition, not single securings of it to any one choice. The free choice, according to the righteous initiating motion, produces an imputable righteousness in the agent.

V

The Maxim of Responsibility

IT IS SOMETIMES SAID that our doctrine of Will fundamentally decides our theology, or rather our theodicy. But in truth there is an underlying principle by which our doctrine of the Will itself is likely to be shaped and decided, namely, our fundamental Maxim of Obligation or Responsibility. If power to act must underlie and be commensurate with obligation to act, then there must be exemption from necessity to obey motive, however strongest, counter to obligation. But if our maxim is that no matter how we come by volition, disposition, state, nature, or what its cause, we are in any case responsible for its intrinsic good or evil, then freedom or non-freedom is morally an unimportant question. This maxim we now consider.

"A man is not to blame for what he cannot help," is the universal language of the moral sense and the common sense. If an act is positively done, without the power of not-doing, or not done for want of power of doing, there can be no guilt. For neither performance of what could not be avoided, nor for non-performance of what could not be done, can there be obligation, responsibility, guilt, blame, or just punishment. The wrong would be in the requirement, not in the non-compliance.

A command requiring an act requires the exertion of an existing power; and if the power does not exist, then there is the requirement for the exertion of a non-existence or nothing. To require the exertion of a nothing, is to require nothing; that is, the requirement is no requirement.

An act without power adequate to perform it is an event without a cause. To require such an act is to require a causeless effect. No matter what may be the agent or object of whom or which the requirement is made, whether he or it is mind or matter, intelligent or unintelligent, living or lifeless, to require of it a result for which there exists in it no adequate causality is to require a causeless effect. But to require a causeless effect is to require a nothing, and is therefore no requirement at all.

For the non-performance of this non-requirement just penalty is impossible. Pain can indeed be inflicted for nothing. A being of infinite power may inflict all the suffering a finite being is capable of enduring. He may inflict this pain in consequence of the imposition of a form of requirement that is not a requirement, and in consequence of the non-performance of an action that is no action. But such pain would be no just penalty, nor could the omnipotence of the author make it such. Such action or non-action is no basis for responsibility, for judicial sentence, or for a just retributive divine government.

The axiom that adequate power must underlie obligation is equally valid whether the required act is external or corporeal, or whether intellectual or volitional. It is equally true that an act for which there exists in the agent no adequate power is not morally required. This is true whether it is an unconscious effect of a lifeless cause, as the production of lightning from a solid cube of iron, or an external voluntary corporeal act, as to turn a planet out of its course with my hand, or an intellectual act, as to know the nature and number of the inhabitants of Saturn, or volitional act, as to put forth the volitions necessary to call all those inhabitants by their true names. And for just this reason, namely, that all these requirements are alike requirement of a causeless effect, and therefore no requirement at all.

We inaugurate, then, what we will call the axiom of freedom and responsibility, and hold it as valid as any axiom of geometry. Power must underlie obligation. There can be no full moral obligation to an act, volitional or non-volitional, for which there is not full and adequate power in the required agent. Otherwise, there can be no guilt or responsibility for act or volition, for avoidance of which there is not complete and adequate power; that is, for which there is no power adequate to counter an act or volition. If guilt, or responsibility, or obligation is a reality, then the power of counter choice is a reality. Responsibility, therefore, demonstrates free will.

The axiomatic character of these propositions is verified by the established tests of axioms. These tests are self-evidence, necessity, and universality. These propositions are self-evident, asserting their own truth to the mind that truly understands them, needing no proof but merely sufficient elucidation to render them perfectly understood. They are characterized by necessity, unable to be other than true, unable to be conceived to be untrue, not possible but to be pronounced true. They are universal, ever and everywhere true. And everywhere, and by all minds, assumed and acted upon as true.

It is not, however, claimed that all minds conceive them as formal and general propositions. Axioms are mentally and unconsciously subsumed by all minds, when the objects and occasions to which they belong arise; while few uncultivated minds form them into verbal propositions, and embrace them in that form. Dr. McCosh,[1] has illustrated, with great clearness and conclusiveness, the point, that while axiomatic propositions in their general and abstract form are educed late in the history of thought by the philosopher, they are occultly assumed and acted upon, whenever the particular occasion arises, by the rudest mind.

The law of the uniformity of nature's laws is still under philosophic discussion by the philosopher; but from time immemorial every boy has unhesitatingly assumed that the sun will rise tomorrow. The law that every event and finite object must have a cause is susceptible of still further elucidation by the schools. But every savage, though he never heard it announced, and is unable to think it separately, assumes it in every case demanding it. That the whole is the sum total of all its parts is assumed as a regulative principle of both judgment and action by those who have never isolated it in thought.

SHORTEST DISTANCE

That a straight line is the shortest distance between two points will strike a peasant as a new idea, although he has acted upon it ever since he could act intelligently. Nay, even the ass, who walks straight to the haystack assumes its truth as a regulative principle, though he is utterly unable to think it as a distinct proposition. It requires the highest metaphysics to analyze the latent and elementary, yet sure and valid, assumptions upon which the simplest intellects act. Without ascending into the principles of its own action, the common mind will instinctively observe the regulative laws for its own legitimate process. And thus the uneducated man may scarcely understand the proposition that power must underlie responsibility, and yet rare indeed will be the man who does not understand the

---

1. James McCosh, *The Intuitions of the Mind Inductively Investigated* (New York: Robert Carter and Brothers, 1860)

proposition, or feel any hesitation, in the suitable case, in using it: "I am not to blame for what I cannot and never could help."

Few intelligent though unschooled men would fail to indorse the proposition: "Neither anybody nor anything can be under obligation to produce an effect without a cause." And whether it were an external act, or an internal choice, we doubt if any man, not preoccupied with a theory or prepossessed by education, would hesitate to affirm: "Nobody can be under obligation to perform an act, or feel an inclination, or put forth a volition, for which he has not and never had the adequate power." This, therefore, is an axiomatic principle. It appears true by its own clear self-evidence. It insures assent by its own necessity; it is assumed in the proper individual instances by every man, and is, therefore, authenticated with the seal of infallible universality.

Our axiom laid down above needs but one elucidation. Where a free-agent willfully deprives himself of power to a given volition or act he does not thereby absolve himself from all obligation to that act. In this case, however, the wrong of all his actions arising from that self-deprivation may, perhaps, be viewed as so much aggravation of the guilt of his self-depriving act. Thereby the complete universality of our axiom remains, nor is it necessary formally to make the exception of self-superimposing.

A debtor may not willfully fling his money into the sea and then claim exemption from guilt for non-payment. A servant may not cut off his hands and then hold himself innocent for not laboring. A man may not destroy his own moral faculties by disuse, by abuse, by willful forfeiture, and then make his non-existence a bar to responsibility. Or if a man rejects or forfeits means and aids by which he might possess full power and capacity for doing right, or attaining to the perfect standard of the moral law, he can never claim exemption from responsibility. If a probationary being, who owes a measure of service to God, so abdicates his powers as to be unable to fulfill his task, then, as his alternative, he must do what he can do; meet the just penalty of his voluntary omission —voluntary because it was secured and chosen by his own free act.

When it is said that the divine Law of obligation cannot require an impossible act, it is assumed that the Law presupposes the essential and eternal natures of things to be as they are. Should a pure angel once sin, the guilt of that sin, like the historical fact of its commission, must intrinsically inhere to his being as long as his personality lasts. It might then be said, in a very metaphysical way, that the law nevertheless forever constantly requires that angel to be innocent, however impossible it be. Yet it could not, if the law presupposes the essential nature of things, be said that it requires such angel to cause that the past fact be never done, which is absurd and out of the question. No more can it be said that the Law requires the angel to make him innocent, for that includes the same absurdity. Both would be requirements of nothing, and so no requirements at all. What should be said is that the angel having once sinned, the law, prescribing no impossibilities, holds the being permanently and unchangeably guilty.

So if an angel, primordially endowed with the power of drawing a line of perfect rectitude through eternity, abdicates that power and diverges far below the straight line, the law holds it a settled point that the entire divergency is a fixed guilt, imputable on account of the original power of eternal rectitude. There is, then, an obligation to eternal rectitude because the power for eternal rectitude is imparted, and there is responsibility for the eternal deflection because of the primordial power of avoiding it. The Law, then does not hold itself as requiring the impossible or as condemning for the inevitable. Power still underlies obligation. The eternal rectitude is held as a unit for which there was power. So under this explanation we affirm that there is no proper exception to the maxim that power for right underlies obligation for tight and responsibility for wrong.

VI

Necessitarian Counter Maxim
of Responsibility Considered

T O THE CLAIM THAT free causation is necessary to responsibility for
an evil volitional act, Edwards opposes a broad proposition which he
esteems as thereto a contradictory position. The viciousness of an act of
Will lies not in its cause but in its own intrinsic nature.

We are not to look at the volitional cause, so as to ask whether or
not it is free, but to concentrate our view upon the act alone; and that,
whatever is the nature of the cause, free or not,[1] is by its own nature good
or bad. To Arminians, on the contrary, he attributes the doctrine that
the viciousness of "the dispositions or acts of the Will consists not in the
nature of these dispositions or acts, but wholly in the origin or cause of
them."

In disproof of this so-called Arminian maxim, Edwards tries his
hand at a second logical infinite series. If, argues he, the badness is not
in the act, but in its cause, then, for the same reason, it is not in its cause
but in the cause of its cause, and for the same reason in the next previous
cause; and so back in endless retrogression, it is ever to be chased but
never overtaken.[2] Whence he infers that the causation, whether alterna-

---

1. "How the disposition got there is not the question which the moral sense of man,
when he is unvitiated by a taste for speculation, takes any concern in. It is enough for the
moral sense that the disposition is there . . . Give to its view a wrong act originating in a
wrong intention, and it asks no more to make up its estimate of the criminality of what
has been offered to its notice."—Thomas Chalmers, *Lectures on the Epistle of Paul the
Apostle to the Romans* (New York: Robert Carter, 1843) Sec. 24.

2. But why cannot the evil lie in its cause and stop there? The enlightenment of the
moon lies not in itself, but in the sun. Is the sun therefore not self-luminous, but enlightened by some previous sources? A minor's wealth lies not in himself but in his father;
does it then run up through his whole pedigree?

322

tive or inalternative, has nothing to do with the ethic of the act. To this we reply,

I. Edwards wholly mistakes the issue between himself and the freedomist. The question is not: In what consists "the essence of the virtue and vice of dispositions of the heart and acts of the Will?" Nor has any Arminian ever said that the "vice of a vicious act of Will lies not in the nature of the act, but in the cause." The viciousness of the act of Will does lie in itself and nowhere else. The moral quality of the act does lie in its nature. A bad act is intrinsically bad. Wickedness is in itself wicked. Herein both sides agree. The question in fact concerns not the viciousness of the act, but the responsibility for the act.

EVIL OF AN ACT

To ask in what consists the evil of an act is one question; to ask what is the ground of responsibility in the agent for the evil is another question. It does not certainly follow that because an act is intrinsically evil or wrong, the author of the act is responsible or blameworthy. That evil is the nature or quality of the act itself; although the nature of every act is modified by the nature of the agent. But when it is the responsibility of the agent for his act which is concerned, to say that the nature or casual character of the agent does not come under view is a contradiction. Wherever the evil lies, the merit or demerit, the responsibility, self-evidently does lie in the cause, that is, the intentional agent.

II. Edwards fabricates for Arminians a quite absurd maxim, giving it a quite absurd form, and that apparently for a purpose; namely, in order to make it a basis for his reductio ad absurdum in the form of his infinite series. That "the vice of a vicious act lies not in the nature of the act," is to say (so far as it has any sense or meaning) that the essential quality of a thing does not inhere to the thing. What freedomists say is this: An act cannot be morally vicious unless the actor is a free moral agent. In order that a certain property should be in the effect, certain property or properties must be in the cause. Which is but saying that the quality of the effect is modified by the causality; that is, that the effect is produced by the cause.

Certainly no Edwardian can reject our maxim, or rather axiom, that a responsible viciousness in the act requires a moral agency in the actor. Then Edwards himself held or rejected just as truly as we the maxim that "the vice of a vicious act of Will lies not in the nature of the act, but in the cause." Edwards believed just as truly as we, that none but a moral agent could commit a moral offense. Where, then, lies our variance? Simply in this, that we hold an element of freedom in that moral agent, as requisite to his moral agency, which he denies. He believed that none but a non-alternative or necessitated moral agent could commit a guilty deed; we believe that none but a non-necessitated or free moral agent can incur such guilt.

III. It being settled that the guilt for the act lies in the cause, we affirm that the evil or wickedness of the act lies in the act. The moral evil of an act consists in this: that it is a disconformity to or transgression of the Law of God. As this disconformity or transgression lies in the act, so the evil, the viciousness, lies in the act. That viciousness does not, as Edwards says, arise from its "odiousness," but its odiousness arises from its viciousness; that is, from its variance from right and law, whereby it is most justly dreaded, avoided, and abhorred by all that is right and holy.

And now the question comes: What are the conditions by which the agent becomes responsible for the evil act? Edwards would say that he must be a rational moral being, that he must have been voluntary in the act, and have been free from external coercion. In all these answers, contradicting his own maxim, he admits that the grounds of the responsibility lie in the nature of the cause, namely, the agent. So far we agree, and now comes the difference. The responsibility accrues, we say, to the agent from: 1. the fact that the act is formally evil; 2. the fact that his intention was accordantly evil; 3. the fact that the act is performed with full volitional power of non-performance.

IV. But the real impact of Edwards's unshapely proposition is this: No matter what the causation that puts the volition in the mind, not only its intrinsic badness, but the consequent guilt of the agent is all the same. No matter how it got there, whether by freedom or necessity, by chance, by fate, by birth, by creation, or by divine implantation, the responsibility is unaffected. Now besides his infinite series, which we trust we have properly demolished, he adduces no argument, and his proposition stands unsustained.

If this necessitarian maxim be true, we submit to the reader whether the following inferences do not logically result:

1. It would be perfectly just for God to create an individual perfectly and necessarily bad, hold him responsible for that badness, and consign him therefore to an endless hell.

2. It would be perfectly just for God to create a race or a universe perfectly bad, and the next moment consign that race or universe to an endless hell for being what he created.

3. The doctrine of absolute reprobation is right. God may justly bring into existence a depraved race, pre-damned before it is born and ready for hell. And should he from that number arbitrarily and haphazardly select a few from the whole and omnipotently transform them into heirs of glory, it would be great mercy to them and no injustice to the rest.

4. The doctrine of infant damnation is just and right. God may bring a race into existence totally depraved and necessitated to evil, may give them a longer or shorter existence in evil, and as justly send them to hell three days old as thirty years.

5. All arguments in proof of divine rectitude or benevolence would be futile. Theists have studied the works and ways of God's providence to answer the cavil of skeptics, drawn from the sin and misery in the world, and demonstrate the righteousness of God. Why so? Were God to create a universe of as depraved beings as Omnipotence itself could furnish, and fill the universal space with the intensest hell to punish their wickedness, it would be all just and right. Nothing unjust, unrighteous, or inconsistency with benevolence would be done. It would still be a perfectly just divine government. And for it the brief theodicy would be: "No matter how these beings, this universe, became possessed of their wickedness, it is responsible and guilty; and it is right that the immensity should be a hell to punish them."

The man into whose moral sense the above maxim and its logical consequences easily fit is welcome to believe in the doctrines of necessity. Our calm and firm belief is, that as the universal common sense of mankind comes to a clear perception of the nature of these propositions and their connections, the whole will be repudiated and consigned to a perdition as final as that to which such facility they can consign the creatures of God.

V. Finally, Edwards flatly contradicts his own sense of his own maxim, that the viciousness of an act "consists not in the origin or cause." He does affirm, in words as clear as can be articulated, that the viciousness does depend upon the origin, the cause, and the causation. It consists in this: "A person's being or doing wrong, with his own will and plea-sure; containing these two things: 1. His doing wrong when he does as he pleases. 2. His pleasures being wrong. Or, in other words, perhaps more intelligibly expressing their notion, a person having his heart wrong, and doing wrong from his heart." (299)

Here are origins, causes, and causations plentifully marshaled as the things in which the viciousness consists. There must be "a person," and surely a "person" is a cause. There must be the "doing wrong" and that is a mode of causation. There must be "will and pleasure," "pleasure being wrong," "heart wrong," and these are so many origins. There must be "do-ing as he pleases," "doing wrong from his heart" and these again are modes of causation. And the requirement of the least of them all incurs the full force of Edwards's infinite series. If in any one or all these origins, causa-tions, and modes of causation, the viciousness lies, then it lies not in these causes, etc., but in the causes of these causes; and so on ad infinitum.

VII

Edwards's Direct Intuitional Proof
of Necessitated Responsibility

DWARDS ADDUCES HIS DIRECT argument that responsibility for necessitated volition "is agreeable to common sense and the natural
notions of mankind."

He first states, in words already quoted: "what the vulgar notion of
blameworthiness is." It is "a person's having his heart wrong and doing
wrong from the heart"; a notion, by the way, which, 1. Contradicts his
assertion that the origin or source of the volition has nothing to do with
blameworthiness; and, 2. Would render very difficult any explanation of
the sin of the first angels and of our first parents. But the "vulgar notion"
being thus, men act upon it without mounting into speculations as to the
freedom or non-freedom of the Will. "And that is the end of the matter."

I. Not quite the "end of the matter." We indeed grant that in these
conditions common sense does concede the responsibility of acts of
Will—but not of necessitated Will! Edwards here first professedly proves
necessitation upon Will, and then takes the intuitive human assumption
that Will is responsible (an assumption made under tacit subsumption
that Will is what it intrinsically is—free), in proof that Will, loaded with
necessity, is responsible. Herein the intuition subsuming that Will is free
is Arminian; and Edwards dexterously claps this Arminian subsumption
under his necessitarian overlay, so that we have: a necessitated volition is
responsible because intuitively a non-necessitated volition is.

II. A lurking consciousness of his sophism seems to have disturbed
Edwards's mind; and he thus forecloses the common sense of mankind
from any voice upon the subject:

> The common people do not ascend up in their reflections and
> abstractions to the metaphysical sources, relations, and depen-

dencies of things, in order to form their notions of faultiness or blameworthiness. They do not wait till they have decided by their refinings what first determines the Will; whether it be determined by something extrinsic or intrinsic; whether volition determines volition, or whether the understanding determines the Will; whether there be any such thing as metaphysicians mean by contingence (if they have any meaning); whether there be a sort of a strange, unaccountable sovereignty in the Will, in the exercise of which, by its own sovereign acts, it brings to pass all its own sovereign acts. They do not take any part of their notion of fault or blame from the resolution of any such questions. (300)

We reply, first, this is a fair surrender of any claim that the common sense affirms necessitation of Will. The common sense, according to Edwards, does not go up so far as that question. Necessity of Will is then no doctrine of common sense. But we claim that common sense does assume, as elsewhere explained, the freedom of the Will. The common mind is perpetually assuming axioms in the particular instances, of which it never separately thinks. It cannot isolate them in thought, nor frame them into language; but it instinctively and rightly assumes them as latent regulatives of its spontaneous and instantaneous natural judgments. "Common people," Edwards adds, "do suppose that it is the person's own act and deed." And, we add, they do subsume in their morally blaming that there was power of choice to do otherwise; not because they distinctly state that thought to themselves, but because it is naturally seen as a constituent of the notion of a free blamable act. When a proposition comes announcing that the choice was overlaid with a causative necessitation, securing its putting forth, and excluding from the agent in the case all adequate power for any other choice instead, a new, an unexpected, a foreign, and a very doubtful notion is introduced. It is felt that the judgment attributing blame was pronounced without inclusion of any such notion.

PROFOUND METAPHYSICS

It requires no more profound metaphysics for a man of common sense to perceive that necessitation destroys the responsibility of the volitional act than it does to perceive that compulsion destroys the responsibility of corporeal motion. Men decide the last without instruction from moral philosophers, and without any abstruse train of reasoning, by immediate moral intuition. Just as easily can they see with a glance of the moral instinct, that to fasten a man's volitions by necessitative causation, and then require a contrary volition from him, makes not a sinner of the man, but of the requirer.

III. Edwards adds, "The common people, in their notion of a faulty or praiseworthy deed or work done by anyone, do suppose that he does it in the exercise of liberty. But then their notion of liberty is only a person's having opportunity of doing as he pleases. They have no notion of liberty consisting in the Will's first acting, and so causing its own acts," etc. (301) Undoubtedly "the common people" have no such "notion" of "liberty" as Edwards's rigmarole attributes to "Arminians." But we apprehend that they would require the liberty or power to be located precisely in the faculty, organ, or part of the agent by which the required act is to be performed, and that the power be for just the act required.

If the act required is in the foot, "the common people" will require both liberty (that is, exemption from restriction) and power in the foot. If by the body, the liberty and the power will be required by "the common people" to exist in the body, and not in something else. If by the intellect, then in the intellect. If by the Will, then in the Will. If something is to be externally done, then the external must be at full liberty to perform. But when an obligation not to do, but to will, is laid upon the Will, common people will require something different from merely "the liberty" or "opportunity of doing"; even "of doing as he pleases." It will call for liberty and power in the Will, and for just the power, and just the amount and direction of the power and freedom adequate for the volition required. Even "common people" can see that obligation to act is an obligation to exert an existing power; and that the obligation to exert a power that does not exist, whether upon the body, intellect, or Will, is an obligation to nothing, and is no obligation at all.

IV. Edwards's next argument is this: If "moral necessity"—that is, necessitation of Will to particular volition—excuses, then approximation to such perfect necessitation proportionately excuses. His proof is this: For in "natural," that is, corporeal, necessitation such proportion exists; namely, the nearer a perfect corporeal necessitation, the nearer a perfect excuse; and the same rule must, by logical consequence, hold of force upon the Will. But, says Edwards, "the reverse of this is true"; that is, the degree of excuse for volitional or motive force is, in fact, not proportioned to the nearness to necessitation. And then he proceeds to prove this non-existence of volitional excuse proportioned to the necessitation in a decidedly adroit way; namely, by two successive changes of the question.

1. In place of necessitation upon the Will he substitutes "propensity" and "inclination" in the volitional agent; and the question then would become this: Would the excusableness of the volition be in proportion to the strength of the evil "inclinations" ? That is quite a new question. 2. In place of the Will or volition whose excusableness is the matter of question, he substitutes the moral character of the man or agent himself; and then the question, under the double slide, is this: Is a man excusable or commendable in proportion to the strength of his bad "inclinations?" And so finally it resolves into about this: Is a man the better the worse his propensities are? And of course to such a question Edwards obtains the ready negative. But unluckily it is not the question under discussion.

The question is not as to the view we take of the general moral character of the man as possessed of "inclinations"; nor as to the effect of his "inclinations" upon his volitions. The question is: What effect should the different increases of motive force and of approaches to necessitation produce upon the degree of responsibility for a volition? To which we reply, as we have previously more fully shown, that the power of temptation does often excuse proportionately to its strength, as much as the force of coaction on the external act. When an agent proves that there never existed in his created nature a ground of possibility that the tempting motive should be volitionally resisted, he is blameless. Approximations to this, not self-superimposed, do proportionately excuse. So Edwards's "reverse" must be absolutely reversed. The same law of excusableness, graduated by the degree of force, applies equally to motive force on Will and coactive force on body.

V. Finally, Edwards brings the substance of his distinction between "natural and moral ability" to the test of a full example. Suppose a prince has two rebels in separate prisons, to each of whom he offers pardon and restoration to favor, upon condition that he will come forward and make a full and voluntary submission. The former would accept the pardon, but bars and chains, alas! preclude him; and this is a case of physical necessitation or "natural inability." The latter has the same offer, but so powerfully do pride and hatred bar his heart, and his heart binds his Will, that by moral necessity he refuses. Now, Edwards argues, everyone can see that the two cases are very different; that the former case excuses, while the latter does not; that this latter necessitation, though producing what is called a "moral inability," creates no real "inability" since the latter rebel can submit "if he pleases," "though the vile temper of his heart is so fixed and rooted that it is impossible that it should please him."

SEE THE DIFFERENCE

We can indeed readily see the difference. The former of the two is a case of material, physical, or corporeal inability, but no more natural than a natural causative force upon the natural faculty of the Will would be. As being a force, precluding all adequate power from the required action, there is no responsibility. Were we allowed to conceive, however, that the free Will of the rebel was as opposed to the submission as the bars and chains were, those material obstacles would no longer be an excuse; his soul would be as responsible as if the body were free. This would be, indeed, a third case, combining the other two into one, but quite as illustrative as either.

In the latter case we will make two suppositions: It may have been a case of self-superimposed necessity; or it may have been a case of created, born, or objective and changeless necessity.

1. Supposing the man by nature volitionally free, he may have voluntarily and freely indulged, cultivated, and enlarged his malevolent feelings, and so have reduced, enfeebled, and destroyed his better feelings, that when the offer of pardon came he was at the moment so filled with excitement that all favorable motive was driven from his attention or thought. The alternative conditions of freedom did not exist, and he was volitionally unfree. Yet as he has freely superimposed this one-sided bondage and true inability upon himself, he cannot excuse this crime by previous crime. Nay, the man is responsible and guilty for his self-superimposed bad passions, with all their enormity and overwhelming power and consequences.

2. Suppose, however, this slave of passion to have been enslaved from the first moment of his existence. Suppose, as necessitarianism always claims, that he received at the first instant a completely necessitated being, state, and nature; suppose that, through every instant of his existence, his being, and state, and nature, and action have all been necessitated, so that his whole historic being, and state, and action, volitional and consequently corporeal, have been run in the absolute mould of fixing causation down to the present instant. Then we say that he can be no more responsible or guilty than a solid cube of granite, centrally imbedded in a primary

stratum, can be responsible for there lying in its adamantine hardness and fixedness through untold millions of geologic ages.

To Kant's formula, "I ought, therefore I can," (by which he asserted that power ever underlies obligation), Müller furnishes this supposed complete answer: "If to such an one it be said in the name of the practical reason, 'though oughtest to be holy in each moment of thy life; therefore henceforth, from this very moment, thou canst be so,' he would say, 'Truly I ought to be able, but I cannot.' "

In the solution of this problem, perhaps we may, from the principles we have laid down, find satisfaction under the three following suppositions: 1. The agent may have, by his own free adoption of his inability, superimposed it upon his own being. The case, then is clear; by our expositions, made in the proper place, his responsibility is rationally unquestionable. 2. He may have been overlaid with superimposed necessitation without fault of his own. His *ought*, then, is ideal; it involves neither obligation nor responsibility. 3. Nevertheless he may be placed probationarily under the law of that lofty ideal *ought* with a view to his restoration to its level, or a penalty for free, willful non-restoration. The ideal *ought* would then possess a critical, but not a retributive power. There may then be interposed by the divine Rector an intermediate law within the power of the agent; this intermediate law may serve as a standard of present acceptance, and as an upward sliding scale to the perfect law. That law stands as the gauge of the present irresponsible defectus, and as the standard of final elevation or measure of final condemnation. Here it will appear, in opposition to Müller's argument, that there is no retributive *ought* for which there is not the correspondent *can*.

VIII

Responsibility of Belief Demonstrates Freedom of Will

D<small>R. C</small><small>HALMERS, ONE OF</small> the most stringent necessitarians of our times, professedly solves the problem of the responsibility of a man for his belief.

The denial of that responsibility confessedly derives "all its plausibility from the imagination, that the belief is in no way dependent upon the Will. It is not morally incumbent upon man to see an object which is placed beyond the sphere of his vision, nor can either a rightful condemnation or a rightful vengeance be laid upon him because he has not perceived it. It must be within range of his seeing, and then the only question which needs to be resolved is, what the Will has to do with the seeing of it. Now to see is not properly an action of the Will, but to look is altogether so; and it is the dependence of this looking faculty on the Will which makes man responsible for what he sees or what he does not see, in reference to all those objects of sight that are placed within the territory of sensible vision."[1]

To relieve us from the irresponsibility of belief arising from the intrinsic necessity of belief apart from all volitional, Dr. Chalmers here calls in the aid of Will.

We institute then the grave inquiry: If a necessitated intellect cannot be guilty for its necessitated beliefs, how is it that a necessitated Will is guilty for its necessitated volitions? As the evidence seals the belief, so the motive seals the choice. As the emotive nature has no power of counter emotion, so the volitive nature has no power of counter volition. If then, one common necessity closes up all alike, why does not one common irresponsibility excuse all alike?

---

1. Chalmers, *On the Power, Wisdom, and Goodness of God*, 253.

A disbeliever in the responsibility of belief, aware of his necessitarianism, might thus have refuted Dr. C. upon his own ground. He further states. "The ground for my rejection of responsibility for belief is the acknowledged necessitated nature of belief. Show me that it is not necessitated and I am answered. But to show me that it is controlled by a Will equally necessitated, is no answer. If a necessitated faculty or operation can be responsible, then no solution of the responsibility of belief can be needed; if a necessitated faculty or operation cannot be responsible, then neither Will nor volition can be responsible. You must revolve through the whole circle of mental faculties and find necessity everywhere and responsibility nowhere."

According to Dr. Chalmers, belief without evidence is not a possible object of requirement, just because it is not in nature a possible performance. Divine Justice could not require a belief for which there was no power in the soul, any more than it could require a long and lofty strain of celestial music from the solid heart of the insensate rock. But then comes the question: If Justice cannot demand a belief, for which there is, in the instance, no adequate power in the intellect, how can it demand a volition for which there is, in the instance, no power in the Will?

If the counter evidence presented or the want of affirmative evidence renders it impossible and takes away the power to belief, certainly the presence of a counter motive or the absence of an affirmative renders impossible, and takes away the power to Will. Both may with equal propriety be called a moral inability. Of both may it be said with equal sense, or equal sophism, they are "not in strict propriety of speech," and all, to be called an "inability." But whatever the term by which they are designated, they are equally a non-existence of power to the thing required. They are in both cases a no-power, and both alike exclude the possibility of obligation or command under a righteous divine government.

To this whole argument Chalmers would have replied, with Edwards, that nevertheless it is an ultimate and axiomatic intuition of the moral sense, that obligation is affixed to Will and not to belief. The primary belief of the whole race finds blame in the wrong volition, however the volition is acquired, and finds it nowhere else. To this we again furnish the reply, and we call attention to it as perfectly conclusive, that the ultimate intuitions of the universal human soul do find blame and obligation primarily in the volition alone, but never in a necessitated Will or volition.

A Will, as the intuitions of men behold it, unnecessitated to one way but free to alterations, they do hold to be responsible; a Will, as necessitarianism overlays it with inevitable limitation to the forbidden act, they hold to be irresponsible. Men naturally hold Will responsible because they naturally see it free. They see its freedom as they see the other qualities which go to make the idea of Will, not with a power of analytically isolating this or any other one quality from the rest, but as blended and fused into the total unit.

Nor will the assumption that the "vulgar" mind does not enter so deeply into the matter as to be competent to take cognizance of necessitation laid upon Will for one moment avail. The "vulgar" mind—certainly the mind with which Dr. C. is reasoning—does cognize necessity when superimposed upon belief, and demands of the philosopher to explain how it can be responsible. If, then, common sense can see that a necessitation stops the responsibility of belief, it can also see that the same necessitation stops the responsibility of volition.

ADHERENTS OF EDWARDS

The necessitarian adherents of Edwards and the Chalmers express a permanent inability to understand what we mean by freedom of the Will. We may at this point reply: it is just that basis of responsibility, whatever it is, which exists in Will, but not in intellect.

In the matter of Regeneration we are told by necessitarian divines that the agent is the Holy Spirit, and that his operation therein in securing the consent of the Will is always effectual and irresistible. Yet we are told by their great standard divine, John Owen, that the Holy Spirit herein works upon our minds "according to their natures and natural operations." That is, the Holy Spirit secures the consent of the Will, in the natural and normal way, by presenting the necessitative strongest motive. This is the old mechanical freedom *to*, without freedom *from*. So Dr. Hodge quotes Stapfer[2] as saying that the Holy Spirit "so clearly carries truth into our minds, that they are unable not to assent, and presents so great motives to our Will that it is unable not to consent."[3]

2. Johann F. Stapfer (1718–1775) was a Protestant Swiss theologian whose writings were heavily influenced by Gottfried Liebniz and Christian Wolff.

3. "Veritatem tam clare mentibus ingerit, ut non possint non assentiri, et tanta motiva voluntati suggerit, ut non posit nolle." Charles Hodge, *Essays and Reviews* (New York: Garland Publishing, 1857) 11.

On the authority of Stapfer, Dr. Hodge asserts that this is the "true Calvinistic doctrine." That is, as the clear meaning is, the intellect and the Will are sealed up with an equal necessitation, the former by the evidence, the latter by the motive. Dr. Hodge, quoting another passage from Stapfer, interprets him as meaning that the Holy Spirit, "though producing conviction offers no more violence to the mind than a demonstration of a proposition in Geometry." It is thereby free not only in, but because of, its uninfringed, unqualified necessitation. He quotes Owen as saying of God's work upon our minds, wills, and affections, that "as it is certainly effectual, so it carries no more repugnancy to our faculties than a prevalent persuasion doth." That is, the Will is free, because it is unimpededly unnecessitated. So also he quotes Bates as saying of God's effectual operations, "we feel them in all our faculties congruously to their nature, enlightening their minds, exciting the conscience, turning the Will." From all which it follows that the intellect is as free in accepting a demonstration as the Will is free in obeying the motive. The freedom in both cases consists in the fact that there is no compulsion, coaction, or violence offered, but only securative causation resistlessly effectuating the work, excluding all power from the faculty of different action. Yet inasmuch as both faculties, intellect and Will, are caused to act, and do act, in a mode "congruous to their nature," both are perfectly free in the entire operation. They are free because they are necessary.

The venerable Westminster Confession of Faith contains these remarkable words: "God from all eternity did, by the most wise and holy counsel of his own Will, freely and unchangeably ordain whatsoever comes to pass. Yet so as thereby neither is God the author of sin, nor is violence offered to the Will of the creatures, nor is the liberty or contingency of second causes taken away, but rather established." (Chap. 3)

"God hath endued the Will of man with that natural liberty, that it is neither forced, nor by any absolute necessity of nature determined, to do good or evil." (Chap. 9) These terms sound so much like an assertion of the doctrine of volitional liberty as against necessity, as to deceive such men as John Wesley, Dugald Stewart, and Sir William Hamilton. "The theory of Jonathan Edwards," said Hamilton, "touching the bondage of the Will, is, on the Calvinistic standard of the Westminster Confession, not only heterodox but heretical."[4] And yet so many words conceal their ideas and

4. Sir William Hamilton, ed., *The Collected Works of Dugald Stewart* (Edinburgh: Thomas Constable and Co., 1859), 6:402n.

express their seeming reverse, that we may assert, on the highest Scotch Presbyterian authority, that these words actually deny the contradiction of philosophical necessity.[5]

When in the Confession it is denied that "violence is done to the Will of the creature," the meaning is that the Will is not violently prevented from choosing according to the highest motive, as an undisturbed intellect is not violently prevented from accepting the highest evidence, a demonstration. When it is said that the Will "is neither forced, nor by an absolute necessity of nature determined to good or evil," it is merely denied that any force or physical violence, compulsion or necessity, interrupts or deflects the free Will from obeying its law of necessitatively acting according to strongest motive.

VIOLENCE OR NECESSITY

There is no violence or necessity crossing the law of necessity. And when it is denied that the "contingency of second causes" is "taken away," the meaning is, that whereas some causes are complete and necessary in themselves, and other causes dependent on co-operation of additional conditions, and so are contingent, God's foreordination does not change the nature of these causes so but that the necessary is still necessary and the contingent is still contingent. All of this means that the responsible Will is free to be controlled by the absolute natural necessity of motive force; free to be necessitated, free because necessitated.

So John Owen says:

> Yet here observe we do not absolutely oppose free Will, as if it were *nomen inane*, a mere figment, when there is no such thing in the world, but only in that sense the Pelagians and Arminians do assert it. About words we will not contend. We grant man in the substance of his actions as much power, liberty, and freedom as a mere created nature is capable of.[6] We grant him to be free in his choice from all outward coaction, or inward natural necessity, to work according to election, and deliberation, spontaneous embracing what seemeth good to him. . . . Endued we are with such a liberty of Will as is free from all outward compulsion and

5. "Sir William Hamilton on Philosophical Necessity and the Westminster Confession" *British and Foreign Evangelical Review* 7 (January 1858) 199–252.

6. That is, "as much freedom as a mere created nature is capable of" in his estimation. That is, he grants just as much freedom as he grants.

inward necessity, having an elective faculty of applying itself unto that which seems good unto it, in which is a free choice, notwithstanding it is subservient to the decree of God.[7]

Similar also was the doctrine of Calvin:

If liberty is opposed to coaction, (or force) I confess, and constantly assert, that the Will is free, and I reckon him a heretic who thinks otherwise. If it is called free in this sense because it is not forced or violently drawn by an external movement, but is led on sua sponte, I have no objection to this. But because men in general, when they hear this epithet applied to the Will of man, understand it in a very different sense; for this reason I dislike it.[8]

According to these extracts freedom is an exemption from all interference with the law of unipotence or nonalternative necessitation. A freedom it is to be purely necessitated.

The non-freedom of this freedom will appear from a contemplation of the nature of the necessity of intellect, as appears, for instance, in the mental reception of a geometrical demonstration by intuition of the diagram shown, say, upon the blackboard. The figure, with its relations, is necessitatively what it is. The figure upon the sensorium, with the perceived relations is necessarily as the figure upon the blackboard. The perception must be as the figure upon the sensorium. But the volition in a given case being as necessitated as this perception, and the perception as necessitated as the mathematical figure, the logical result is that the volitions are as free and as necessitated as the nature and intrinsic geometric relations of a mathematical figure. The volition thereby is just as limited to be what it is as a circle is to be a circle. The entire totality of all volitions in all time and eternity, through all the earth and all the universe, are just as free as the inferential steps of a great mathematical demonstration, namely, to be just what they are and no otherwise.

No individual volition can be otherwise than it is, any more than any step of a conclusive demonstration can be otherwise than it is. No agent can will otherwise than he does will, any more than triangle can be a circle. No step of a demonstration can help being what it is, so no agent

7. John Owen, *A Display of Arminianism: Being a Discovery of the Old Pelagian Idol Free Will with the New Goddess Contingency* (London: I.L. for Philemon Stephens, 1643) 116, 179.

8. "Sir William Hamilton on Philosophical Necessity and the Westminster Confession" 224–225.

can help willing as he wills; and as the action is necessarily the result of the volition, so no agent can help doing what he does. Whether, therefore, he wills or does, if he is responsible at all, he is responsible for what he cannot help.

All this demonstrates our point. The freedom of the Will in volition and of the intellect in intellection is equal and the same. In spite of Dr. Chalmers, as the intellect cannot otherwise see, so the Will cannot otherwise look. For the object fixes the one and the motive fixes the other. The troubled inquirer about the responsibility of necessitated bad beliefs should be peremptorily told that a bad belief, however necessitated, is in itself responsible; for necessity is no bar to responsibility.

But in very truth we are responsible for our beliefs, because we can help our bad beliefs by our Wills. And we are under obligation to help our bad beliefs by our Wills because our Wills are not necessitated to leave our bad beliefs unchanged. Responsibility for belief therefore demonstrates the freedom of the Will.

IX

Coaction and Necessitation

COACTION OR COMPULSION IS a forceful causation acting upon the body, securing a given act, though against the Will. Necessitation is a forceful causation acting upon the Will securing a given volitional act, accordant with the Will because it makes the Will accord with itself. In the former case, the power of the body is nullified to perform any other than the given corporeal act. In the latter, the power of the soul is nullified to putting forth any other than the given volitional act.

In both cases the adequate power is excluded from the agent. In the former case, it is from the body to effectuate the act of the soul; in the latter case from the soul to effectuate the act of the body. In order for the final act in any case required, the conjoint power of both soul and body, of both Will and muscle, is necessary. The want of either excludes, and equally excludes, the act from the reach of the agent. If the power is, on account of strongest material obstacle, wanting in the muscle, no capacity of Will amounts to the adequate power for the required act. If the power is on account of strongest motive obstacle, wanting in the Will, no capability of muscle amounts to the adequate power for that demanded deed.

Whatever the required deed is, coaction by physical force or necessitation by motive influence places, and equally places, the act out of the power of the agent. The power of the agent, therefore, is equally at an end whether the obstacle is coaction or necessitation; whether it is by force of strongest material or of strongest motive. And if the required act is out of the agent's power, whether from coaction or necessitation, it is to him impossible. For this is the meaning of the word *impossible*, that for which there is no adequate power. And it is true that he cannot perform the required act; for that is the meaning of *cannot*; that for which an agent has not the requisite power.

Now power must underlie obligation. An act for which the agent has not the adequate power both volitional and physical, cannot be the subject of just obligation nor just command. Whether there is a want of power to act, through material obstacle, or a want of power to will, through motive obstacle, from that want of power arises the exclusion of all possible obligation to the act, and all divine requirements.

The necessitarian will put forward this case. Here is a man who ought to support his family by honest labor; but he is imprisoned and in chains. Does not that excuse him? Yes. Then "natural," that is, corporeal, inability discharges obligation. But suppose he is fully at liberty, but has no will, disposition, or inclination; does that excuse him? No. Then moral, that is, volitional, inability does not excuse. But, we reply, that "no" is given under assumption that the Will is non-necessitated and that necessitarianism is false. The true answer, then, to be substituted is this: "If necessitarianism is false, no; if necessitarianism is true, yes." No necessitarian has a right to utter that Arminian "no."

REVIEWING ROMANS

Dr. Chalmers, reviewing Romans v, 12–21, puts forth the case that "one may see a dagger projected from behind a curtain in the firm grasp of a human hand and directed with sure and deadly aim against the bosom of an unconscious sleeper, and seeing no more he would infer of the individual who held this mortal weapon that he was an assassin and that he deserved the death of an assassin."[1]

All this undoubtedly the spectator would assume without analysis and in the gross. It would be no moment to institute a grave philosophical inquiry in what that moral agency consisted, but all the elements included in responsible agency would instantly and intuitively be assumed. And one of these assumptions of the intuition would be, underlying the judgment of moral responsibility and deserts of divine penalty, that the volition for the act was performed in full power of willing or not willing the performance, and all attribution of moral responsibility would be at an end.

Dr. Chalmers next supposes that a lifting of the curtain discloses a person behind the supposed assassin grasping his hand and compelling him to infix the dagger into the bosom of the sleeper, who is in fact his

1. Thomas Chalmers, *Lectures on the Epistle of Paul the Apostle to the Romans*, 124.

bosom friend. Common sense of course affirms that the supposed assassin is no assassin, and is morally guiltless of the death of his friend. And upon what principle? Plainly upon the principle that where there is no adequate power of avoidance there can be no obligation to avoidance and no guilt for non-avoidance.

For instead of the material curtain suppose that the psychological curtain that covers the movements of mind were lifted up and it was seen that a controlling causation behind the man's Will propelled its springs and, excluding all contrary power, enforced the volition which, through the hand, drove the dagger into the sleeper's heart. What then would the moral judgment be? Why should physical chains, binding the arm, any more excuse an act than a ligature, stronger than the iron chain, fastening the Will, excuse the volition?

"An act against the Will," says Dr. Chalmers, "indicates no demerit on the part of him who performed it. But an act with the Will gives us the full impression of demerit. The philosopher may amuse himself with that ulterior query: What was it that originated the Will? But the peasant has no metaphysics and no speculation for entertaining such a topic. And yet he has just as fresh and just as enlightened a sense of a bad action, coming from a bad intention, as the most curious and contemplative inquirer."

If, we reply, the "peasant" has just as fresh and enlightened a sense of the demerit of a bad action coming from a bad intention as the philosopher himself, so he may have just as clear and quick a sense of the irresponsibility of a volition coming from a necessitated Will. He may be no more able to discuss one than the other. But he may have just as clear an intuition of one as of the other. While he will fully admit that "an act against the Will indicates no demerit," he will also assume that a volition of which there was no power of avoiding has no demerit, and affirm conversely that there ever is a power of avoiding the volition of which demerit can be affirmed.

X

Argument from God's Non-Authorship of Sin

THE ENTIRE ISSUE AS to God's relation to sin between the freedomist and the necessitarian is this:

The former maintains that while God foreknows that in a given course of the most wise divine conduct a free agent will, with full power to do otherwise, bring sin into existence, he, nevertheless, neither destroys the agent nor prevents his sin, but prosecutes his own course of most perfect wisdom to the best result. This may be called the theory of Non-Prevention.

The latter maintains that God, in view of the best possible results, to which the sin of the agent is an inseparable incident, necessitates the agent to sin, intentionally setting into efficient operation the train of causes by which his sinning is necessitatively secured. This is the theory of Necessitation.

The charge against the latter view is that by maintaining that God not merely non-prevents but necessitates sin, necessitarianism makes God to be "the author of sin." For to necessitate is not merely to permit, or not hinder or not prevent; it is to be the nonalternative securer and the intentional causer of sin. And to be the intentional causer of sin is to be the responsible author of sin.

I. In regard to Edwards, we may here note the very remarkable fact that, although his whole work aggressively maintains necessitation, yet when he comes to this point he defends only the theory of non-prevention! He seems to forget to which side he belongs, and quietly exculpates his opponents, the non-preventionists, from charging God with the authorship of sin. He makes two suppositions, as follows:

1. "If," says he, "by the author of sin be meant the sinner, the agent, the actor of sin, or the doer of a wicked thing;" (356) then—no matter what "then." For that is an imaginary "if." The real question is: Suppose by

"author" is meant necessitator of sin, the necessitator of all sin, the necessitator of the sinner to be the "sinner," "the actor," "the doer"; what then is the answer of Edwards? Nothing.

2. "But if," says he, "by the author of sin is meant the permitter, or not hinderer of sin, and at the same time a disposer of the state of events in such a manner . . . that sin, if it is permitted or not hindered, will most certainly and infallibly follow:" (356) then God is no author of sin. That is, the non-prevention theory—the theory of his opponents—does not make God the author of sin. This is a generous exculpation of us Arminians! But what does Edwards say in defense of his own theory, namely, of Necessitation? Nothing. He simply defends the position of his opponents, and leaves his own system defenseless and naked to its enemies. He has demonstrated Calvinism; he now defends only Arminianism.

It is not merely permission, not-hindering, non-annihilation, non-prevention, privative non-interference, nor the so arranging that sin, if not prevented, will take place, that Necessitarianism teaches. It teaches that God is the necessitative first cause, through a straight inevitable line of necessitating second causes, of the man's existence, and of his every act, and of his final damnation for that being and act. Necessitated to be what he is, to do what he does, of that necessitation God is the original necessitator who not only negatively precludes any different results from any possible existence, but positively necessitates that sole result to come into existence. That is, God necessitates his existence, his nature, his sin, and his damnation for that necessitated nature and sin. Man has no adequate ability for different existence, choice, act, or destiny.

In the question of responsibility for an intended effect, be it here noted, it makes no difference through how many intermediate necessary causes the causation has to pass from the first cause to the last effect. No matter how long the series of mediate necessitative causes, or how many the terms in the series, the first intentional causer is the responsible author of the final intended effect. If the necessary mediate causes are billions of billions, the intentional causer is as truly the responsible author of the effect at the far end as if it were an immediate voluntary act or a simple volition. The whole series is responsibly one act; the final effect *is* the one act. The right line of causation shoots through the whole series, and binds the first cause to a responsibility for the last effect.

Suppose a boy upon a high scaffold intentionally so arranges a number of standing bricks in a row, that when he pushes down the first,

Argument from God's Non-Authorship of Sin

that shall push down the second, and the second the third and so on, so that the last brick, according to his purpose, shall fall upon the head of a sleeping man, and fulfill his intention of murdering him. Would the act be less guilty or the boy less responsible than if he had crushed the man with a single brick, or assassinated him with a dagger, or willed him to an actual death by a volition? Or if the bricks were a small number, would the increase of them be a score, a hundred, or a thousand, diminish the responsibility?

MORAL EXCULPATION

It would be no moral exculpation of this boy to say that he merely "so disposed" the bricks that the murder, "if it be permitted or not hindered, will most certainly and infallibly follow." The statement would be false, for he did more than this. He necessitated and nonalternatively caused the brick to fall; and so he was author of the murder—the murderer. The causative force from his finger ran in a right line through all the bricks and murdered the man. The intention of the act ran through all the bricks and achieved the crime. He had excluded from each and every brick the adequate power or possibility for any other effect. Mere permission and necessitation are thus very different things in the question of responsible authorship.

Should the superintendent of an Atlantic telegraphic cable intentionally so manipulate as to transmit to another continent a malignant falsehood, the wickedness of the deed would not be diminished by the length of the cable. No matter through how many inches or particles of matter the lie has to pass, its guilt is as if the whole were done by nothing but a lying volition and a lying tongue. Every human act of overt sin passes through countless particles of matter. If a man is murderously shot, the action starting from the volition passes through the material particles of the brain, the nerves, the fingers, the gun, the trigger, the explosion, the bullet, and the victim's body. Yet through all the necessitative series, the intentional causer of the first movement is responsible author of the last effect.

It would be no excuse for the telegraph operator to say that he was only "the permitter, or not the hinderer of sin." (Edwards, 356), that is, of the lie; "and at the same time a disposer of the state of events, in such a manner, for wise, holy, and most excellent ends and purposes, that sin,

345

if it be permitted and not hindered, will most certainly and infallibly follow." To send the lie for "wise and holy ends," would be the true Jesuitical morality of "doing evil that good may come," or lying for the glory of God. To say that he was merely "the permitter or not hinderer" of the lie is itself a lie.

The first cause is the responsible cause of the last effect. If the first cause is a living being, he is not only the cause, but he is the causer. And if he intended that the last effect should exist, then he is the intentional causer that the last effect should exist. And if this first intentional causer is a supposed God, and the last effect is sin, the supposed God is the intentional causer of that sin. But surely the intentional causer of a thing is author of that thing. God then, according to necessitarianism, we charge, is the responsible author of sin.

And by the same doctrine it is further true that God is as truly the author of sin as if the sin were his own immediate intentional act. God is hereby the responsible author of the final effect as truly as if it were his own act, or his own simple volition. From the Will of God to the act of the sinner the line of causation through all the intermediates is a straight line. And to all the purposes of just responsibility it is a short line—a point.

II. Edwards next proceeds to the Scripture Argument. He adduces the cases of Pharaoh, of Joseph's brethren, of the king of Assyria, of Nebuchadnezzar, and of the crucifiers of Christ to prove—it is not very clear what. These passages, it is at present sufficient to say, have terms of causation that seem to ascribe the authorship of sin to God. These passages either prove God's necessitation of sin, or his mere permission or non-prevention. By Edwards's own argument they cannot mean the former; for he asserts there is nothing but mere permission. If there is nothing but mere permission, then they make nothing against Arminianism. He quotes but does not analyze them on this point, very much as if he meant, non-committally, to have a causation and a necessitation of sin, by the reader inferred, which he thought not best explicitly himself to express.

III. Edwards next defends a necessitating God from the responsibility for sin by the distinction between positive and privative causations. The sun by his direct ray is the positive cause, and, so to speak, the responsible author of day. But he is the author of night with her darkness, damps and monsters by privation, that is, simply by the withdrawal of his light, and so not the responsible author. So God is not the direct and positive, but only the private and so the irresponsible cause of sin.

But, we reply, necessity makes God the positive and not merely the negative cause of sin. God according to necessity positively sets all the first causes and materials in existence and action, just as the boy arranges the bricks and throws down the first, which throws down all to the last. The first start given secures the whole, excluding all but the given result. The line of causation from God's finger streaks through all second causes and secures the result. Sin is an act directly necessitated, and so not by privative but positive causation.

NECESSITY MAKES GOD

We reply, secondly, that necessity makes God positively cause the privative defectus, which demands the supply of remedy. The sun does not create the antecedents, causes, or circumstances that positively produce the defectus, night. God necessitatively creates all the previous positivities, all the conditions that necessitate the existence of the resultant privation. The very privative thereby becomes positive. Thereby a strict truth is found in Whitby's maxim, "Causa deficiens in rebus necessariis, ad causam per se efficientem reducenda est," i.e. "In things necessary the deficient cause must be reduced to the efficient." Where the defectus is the result of necessary causes, the withdrawal or withholding the reparative of the defectus, especially by the author of all the previous causalities, is equivalent to positive causation of the defectus and of all its necessary consequences. Privation is as positive a cause as impulsion: a caused darkness blinds as truly and as responsibly as light gives vision.

IV. But it is said further by Edwards, "Men do will sin as sin, and so are the authors and actors of it: . . . God does not will sin as sin, or for the sake of anything evil."(370) To this we reply:

1. More often than not it is but the most depraved among men and the devils who will "sin as sin," that is, for the sake of sinning. The great majority of sins men commit are committed not because they are sin, but for the sake of some "apparent greatest good" seen in the act or object, and in spite or disregard of their being sin. Sin is anomia, lawlessness, that is, disregard of law. That is, sin, as an act, is an act performed to gratify some particular propensity in spite or in disregard of the forbidding moral rule. Hence it is a transgression or overpassing of the boundary line of law and right. A deeper depravity may indeed develop itself in the form of sin as sin, and for the sake of sin. This would seem to be then element of the

devils, who hate God's law because it is his law, and trample upon it for their direct hatred of it. This direct and conscious sin against God stands liable to Edwards's famous argument to prove the infinite demerit of sin from its measurement as an offense against an Infinite Being.

2. But by Edwards's argument, God does will and necessitate "sin as sin." God necessitates sin as being what it is. Its sinfulness, its malignity, its blackness, its depravity of source in the dispositions, its atrocity of external act, all are necessitated by him. As the sinner wills it, so the necessitarian deity wills it. As the finite sins it so this Infinite sins it. God necessitates, wills, decrees, foreordains whatsoever comes to pass; the sinfulness of sin, sin as sin, comes to pass. God, therefore, necessitates, wills, decrees, foreordains the sinfulness of sin, sin as sin.

3. It is relevant to our argument, as will soon appear to add, that for the sin thus willed by God and necessitated upon the sinner, eternal death is affixed as a penalty by the same divine Ruler. But just penalty for an unavoidable act is impossible. It is as impossible even to omnipotence as a contradiction. It is a non-compliance with absolute conditions of justice. The double wrong is hereby ascribed to the Deity by necessity of securing the sinfulness of the sin and securing infliction that can never be just penalty.

V. But God "was willing to order things so evil should come to pass," Edwards adds, and necessitates it in the sinner, not for its own sake, "but for the sake of the great good that by his disposal shall be the consequence." (370) To this Edwards very justly anticipates the reply that, "All that these things amount to is that God may do evil that good may come." (372) If God may truly necessitate sin in the sinner, necessitate the sinfulness and guilt of that sin, and then necessitate an endless hell for the necessitated sin, all for some good and glorious end, then the maxim of the sons of Loyola, that the end sanctifies the means, is a fundamental maxim of the divine administration.

God is then admitted to be the Author of Sin, and he is justified in being the Author of Sin. The fact is granted and excused. In order to make a beneficial crime holy, the method is (as is well quoted by Professor Bledsoe from Pascal) "simply taking off their intention from the sin itself and fixing it on the advantage to be gained." Edwards makes the supposed divine necessitation of sin, guilt, and damnation all right and holy, by simply taking the divine intention from them and placing it on the good result to be obtained. If this is the divine morality, why not the human?

But is it possible that good can be imagined to result from such a course? Can any glorious result possibly be supposed to result from a divine necessitation of sin, a necessitation of guilt, an unjust necessitation of hell? Can the holiness of the universe be attained through such an unholiness? Can the blessedness of heaven be genuine at such a price? Can a holy being generously, wisely, holily accept heaven on such a condition? Can there be a heaven? But the thought is too awful to be traced to its ultimate bearings.

VI. But Edwards has his reply: "For God to dispose and permit evil, [he should say *cause, necessitate, predestinate,* and *will* sin,] in the manner that has been spoken of, is not to do evil that good may come, for it is not to do evil at all." (372) Certainly it is "to do evil" unless the goodness of the result changes the "do evil" and makes it good. But the doctrine that the "do evil" is made good by what "good may come," is the very pith and infamy of the Jesuit maxim. That maxim stands in opposition to the true doctrine that intrinsic evil cannot by any result be transmuted into good.

EDWARDS ARGUES

In his defense Edwards finally argues, that for God's supposed conduct herein to be evil "there must be one of three things belonging to it: either it must be a thing unfit and unsuitable in its own nature; or it must have a bad tendency; or it must proceed from an evil disposition, and be done for an evil end." He denies all three of the conducts he ascribes to God.

We affirm all three. We affirm them for the following reasons: *First.* The necessitating and willing wickedness, and causing it to be willed and done, is "unfit and unsuitable in its own nature." To so necessitate it that it cannot but be done, annihilating all adequate power to do right instead, is very "unfit and unsuitable in its own nature." To necessitate an eternal misery in hell, as the necessary consequences of necessitated sin, is horribly "unfit and unsuitable in its own nature." To do all this under the pretense of holiness, justice and righteousness, is, finally, "unfit and unsuitable in its own nature." And being thus intrinsically and essentially evil, "evil in its own nature," it is unchangeably "evil," and no ulterior ends can justify or transmute it into holiness and right. *Second.* It must have a bad tendency. For what were the intrinsic tendencies, imagine, of an unholy God over the universe? If a deity is guilty of falsehood and cruel wrong, who can rely on his pretenses, especially upon his pretenses that all this, forsooth, will be made to result for the best? But we turn from the horrible phantasm presented by this necessitarian theory to our view. *Third*. It must proceed from an evil disposition. For surely the very intention to commit intrinsic wickedness, that good may come, is "an evil disposition." But let us choose our view of these most wretched arguments. Where in all standard Protestant theology shall we find a chapter more replete with the logic of a sophist and the ethics of a Jesuit.

If God is holy, he cannot consistently with that character necessitate sin. But God is holy; sin is therefore unnecessitated. Holiness in God demonstrates freedom in man. If God is holy, man is free.

XI

Freedom the Condition of a Possible Theodicy

O F OUR VARIOUS ARGUMENTS as a whole, the summary conclusion is that necessitarianism attains but an automatism, and not a just divine retributive Government. It is incapable of framing a Theodicy. The necessary condition to the possible existence of a true Divine Government is the Volitional freedom, both of the infinite and the finite Person.

1. Necessity furnishes, as has been shown, but an automatic Deity. Of nothing is he capable but just what he does, volitionally and therefore extravolitionally. His effects are the intrinsic measure of the causation in his nature and being.

2. Man, being an automatic creature, is, as we have shown, no possible subject of command, of deserts, of blame or praise, of reward or penalty, and so not of Government. As God is infinite and man finite, so both combined are a composite single automatism.

3. A universal created system of volitions, automatically resultant from nonalternative particular causations, can constitute no just retributive system. Or if this organic system of volitions is not an intrinsically caused system; if without the impact of cause the action of all Wills, actual or possible, moved by an intrinsic spontaneity, by a law precisely coinciding with the Law of Causality, the Universe is still an Automatism. The one is an orrery (an apparatus for demonstrating the motions and phases of the planets) that moves by a force from without; the other is an orrery that moves in the same orbit by an intrinsic force, both by an equally necessitative Law. One is an automatism performing its actions from an external, the other from an internal impulse. But both do so with an equal fixedness by the same anterior and formulable programme, and to the same result.

Of no such constituents can even a Deity construct a Divine Government. For how can the Deity impose laws upon a system of beings whose actions are already fixed by the Law either of causation or of a spontaneity coinciding with causation? Either his law must coincide with those laws; and then those Laws are the law of his law, so that his law is no law at all, and he is rather ruled than Ruler. Or his Law must cross those laws, and thus most unjustly subject its subjects to conflicting jurisdictions, one of which they must obey, and yet be punished for disobedience to the other.

In order that God may be a just Sovereign, his law must be the expression of Rectitude; and his subjects must, uncircumscribed by laws of causation or invariability, be able to coincide with it. In order for him to be a just retributive Sovereign, prepared to administer reward or penalty, they must possess power to coincide or the reverse—a power uncontradicted alike by a universal Causation or an equally universal Spontaneity.

4. Retribution and automatism are incompatible in a moral system. Pain may be affixed as a result of bad action, and happiness as the result of good action. But if by necessitative law the action is as truly affixed to the agent as these results to the act, pain and happiness are consequences, but they are not ethically deserved reward and penalty. As expedients they may by their motives prevent evil action, as cause produces effect. But the whole operation and the whole system is then mechanical, not retributive.

5. The moral intuition of justice is either unsatisfied, or false and meaningless. Of all the above regulative expedients, by which pain is applied to the prevention of crime, the retributive sentiment knows nothing. What the moral sense demands and identifies is pure absolute justice; and if the system of the universe is automatic in distinction from alternative, such pure justice has no existence.

From all this, there results the conclusion that without free volition there can be no justice, no satisfying the moral sense, no retributive system, no moral Government, of which the creature can be the rightful subject, and no God, the righteous Administrator. The existence of a system, and the existence in the soul of man of a demand for a system combining these elements, demonstrates the reality of Volitional Freedom. If there is a true divine government, man is a non-necessitated moral agent.

THE END

Index of Names